5 : XII : 56

Kms, 1953

ENGLAND UNDER QUEEN ANNE

BLENHEIM

MAP I.

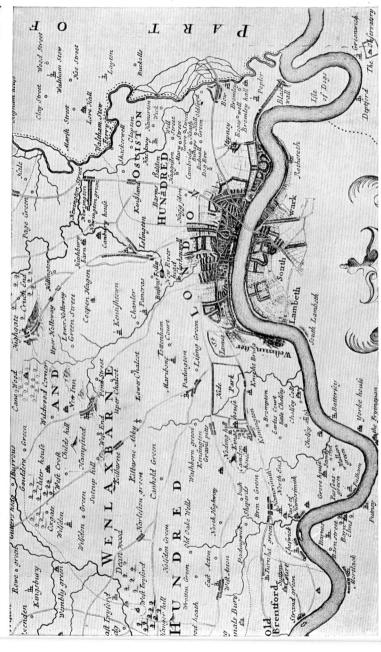

LONDON AND ITS ENVIRONS SHORTLY BEFORE QUEEN ANNE'S ACCESSION.
(From map in Gibson's edition of Camden's *Britannia*, 1695)

ENGLAND UNDER QUEEN ANNE

BLENHEIM

BY

GEORGE MACAULAY TREVELYAN, O.M.

REGIUS PROFESSOR OF MODERN HISTORY IN THE
UNIVERSITY OF CAMBRIDGE

*

WITH MAPS

LONGMANS, GREEN AND CO.

LONDON ◆ NEW YORK ◆ TORONTO

1932

LONGMANS, GREEN AND CO. LTD

39 PATERNOSTER ROW, LONDON, E.C.4
6 OLD COURT HOUSE STREET, CALCUTTA
53 NICOL ROAD, BOMBAY
36A MOUNT ROAD, MADRAS

LONGMANS, GREEN AND CO.

55 FIFTH AVENUE, NEW YORK
221 EAST 20TH STREET, CHICAGO
88 TREMONT STREET, BOSTON
128–132 UNIVERSITY AVENUE, TORONTO

BIBLIOGRAPHICAL NOTE

First Edition	- -	*September* 1930.
New Impression (three times)		*October* 1930.
New Impression	- -	*December* 1930.
New Impression	- -	*January* 1931.
New Impression	- -	*December* 1932.

PREFACE

I HOPE to complete the history of *England under Queen Anne*. But the present volume can be published and read by itself, for it has its own unity of movement and its own climax : all roads in it, foreign and domestic, lead to Blenheim. I do not, therefore, feel that any apology is due to readers for presenting them with this fragment of history, provided I can account to them for the omission of everything Scottish, everything Irish and most things Colonial. I have thought that each of these three subjects can be better treated *en bloc* at a later stage. There are, indeed, disadvantages in failing to record Scottish affairs for 1702–4 in their chronological order in this volume. The absence of the ' Scottish Plot ' and the Act of Security from the history even of the English Parliament in those years, is decidedly a blemish. But it is a choice of evils, and the disadvantage of breaking up the presentation of the Scottish scene and story seems to me the greater. The next volume will, among other things, deal at large with the whole matter of the passing of the Union and its causes, from start to finish. Ireland plays a very much smaller part than Scotland in Anne's reign, but I think the Irish scene also will be better described in a later volume.

In order that the general reader should not have his attention distracted by a heap of references, that mean little to him, at the foot of nearly every page, I have put the references together at the end of the volume.

For my part, I cannot abandon the older ideal of History that was once popular in England, that the same book should make its appeal both to the general reader and to the historical student. In these latter days there tends

to be division.   It is right there should be division in some
cases, but it is right that in other cases the older unity
should be attempted.

The materials, printed and unprinted, for the reign of
Queen Anne are of high interest and of great abundance.
The Historical MSS. Commission has done well for us all
in printing so many volumes of documents from private
collections not ordinarily available, wisely leaving the
treasures of the British Museum and Record Office for the
student to examine in the original MSS., as he so easily may.
The Venerable Archdeacon Coxe, who did much more for
historical study a hundred years ago than is realised in the
patronising notices of him in the *Dictionary of National
Biography* and elsewhere, among his other good deeds left
in the British Museum so many volumes of transcripts from
the Marlborough and Godolphin papers, that admission to
the Manuscript Room there is perhaps nearly as good as
admission to the original papers at Blenheim would have
been.   If, after the harvesting by Coxe and the gleaning by
the Historical MSS. Commission, the papers in Blenheim
have still any important secrets to reveal, we shall shortly
know, when the work of family piety, for which the world
is so eagerly waiting, sees the light.   Meanwhile, I thank
the Duke of Marlborough for his personal courtesy to me.
There are in the British Museum, besides these Coxe MSS.,
the transcripts of Sir J. Macintosh, the Hatton Finch, the
Ellis and the Stepney papers, the L'Hermitage transcripts
and numerous other collections to which reference will be
found in the lists below.   These, together with the diplomatic
and consular papers in the Record Office, furnish material
enough to occupy a whole regiment of historical students.

When the historian, inland-bred, deals with naval
matters, he is apt to be very much at sea.   I have had the
good fortune to be assisted in my navigation of the period
by the work of that great naval historian, Julian Corbett,
in the later chapters of his admirable *England in the
Mediterranean.*   I have also been helped by the kind
criticisms of my friend Admiral Sir Herbert Richmond,
though I do not wish to suggest that he is responsible for
what I have written.

As to the land war, Sir John Fortescue's first volume, and Frank Taylor's *Wars of Marlborough* constitute an unusually good starting point for the study of the voluminous contemporary records.

On the political side, some may think there is even more open to dispute. Certainly there are a hundred possible points of view. And yet I am struck by the amount of general agreement among competent modern historians as to the main outlines and issues of a reign in which party spirit was so hot. Those particular heats have burnt themselves out long ago. My debt to my friend, Mr. Keith Feiling and his *History of the Tory Party* will be clear to all scholars. If I have not produced a new and startling theory about the policies and personalities of the Whigs, the High Tories and the Moderate Tories, about the characters of Anne and Marlborough, I can only plead, to those to whom the plea may seem relevant, that any new and startling theory would have been wrong. Only those who have not followed recent historical writing will be surprised to find that I think Anne had a policy of her own, independent of her favourites.

If, indeed, the story of the great events and the great men of our Augustan age could be told in its truth and simplicity, as only the man of Athens could have told it, it would move like a five-act tragedy from start to finish, presenting in turn the overweening pride and the fall of Louis, then of Marlborough and of the Whigs, then of the Tories in their turn, while, through the crash of each successive crisis of war and politics, the fortune of England moves forward on the tide of destiny. And what men that little rustic England could breed ! A nation of five and a half millions that had Wren for its architect, Newton for its scientist, Locke for its philosopher, Bentley for its scholar, Pope for its poet, Addison for its essayist, Bolingbroke for its orator, Swift for its pamphleteer and Marlborough to win its battles, had the recipe for genius.

I should like to express my gratitude to Lord Dartmouth for kindly inviting me to see the complete MSS. of his distinguished ancestor, of which only a part was published by the Historical MSS. Commission. I am also indebted to the kindness of the authorities of Christ Church, of the Bodleian, of the Lambeth Library, and of the Rijks-archief at the Hague. I must thank for their kind help Colonel Goldney and several other officers of the garrison of Gibraltar, the Librarian and, above all, my friend the then Colonial Secretary, Major Hubert Young ; much that I discovered with their assistance will be of even more use in the next volume, when I come to the first defence of the Rock by the English.

NOTE ON METHODS OF DATING

Readers will note the difference between the New Style (N.S.) and Old Style (O.S.) of reckoning dates. Until 1752 the English at home always used the Old Style, after 1700 eleven days behind the New Style of Gregory XIII's Calendar, current in all continental countries except Russia. Our sailors, on service at sea and on coast operations like the taking of Gibraltar, generally used the Old Style familiar at home. Our soldiers in the Netherlands and Germany generally but not always used the New. Diplomats abroad most of them used the New, but some the Old. *I employ the O.S. for home affairs ; and for affairs outside England I put either Aug.* 13, *N.S., or Aug.* $\frac{2}{13}$.

Anne came to the throne on March 8, 1702—at least, so we say now. But our ancestors called it March 8, 1701. For, with them, the New Year began not on January 1, but on March 25. March 24, 1701, was followed after midnight by March 25, 1702. This is confusing to modern students of old documents, who are liable to get a year out in affairs occurring in January, February or early March, particularly in Parliamentary affairs, as the normal session was held in winter, astride of the two years. The Lords' and Commons' Journals of Anne's reign change from 1701 to 1702 only on March 25. All modern histories, including this book, begin the new year at January 1.

CONTENTS

CHAPTER VI

CHAPTER VII

CHAPTER VIII

CHAPTER IX

CHAPTER X

CHAPTER XI

CHAPTER XII

CHAPTER XIII

CHAPTER XIV

CHAPTER XV

APPENDIX TO CHAPTER XV

CHAPTER XVI

CHAPTER XVII

CONTENTS

ENGLAND UNDER QUEEN ANNE

CHAPTER I

England under Queen Anne. Defoe's picture of it. Forests and timber. Arable and pasture. Markets and organisation. The life of that day and our own compared. Wages. Poor Law. Yeomen. Freeholders and elections. Game laws and shooting. Lake District and Northumberland. Building and architecture.

THE story of the reign of Queen Anne is no parochial theme. It involves great issues, moves among brilliant societies, and reveals distant landscapes. Whoever writes of the England of that day must show Marlborough's many-coloured columns winding along the banks of Rhine, Danube and Maas ; English fleets heaving on Mediterranean and Biscayan waters, or coasting the West Indian islands and the misty Newfoundland shore ; Gibraltar's rock rising into azure above unwonted smoke and uproar ; envoys posting over land and ocean with Godolphin's gold and Marlborough's persuasive counsel to half the Courts of Europe from Lisbon to Moscow : nearer home, the fashionable arena of sedan chairs and glass coaches between St. James's Palace and the Parliament House, the battle ground of political and literary intrigue in the days of Swift, Addison and Pope—with Wren's dome in the distance still rising to its completion above the masts of the river, and beyond it the Tower, the workshop of Newton as Master of the Mint.

But all these fine doings had their roots amid homely scenes. Marlborough's war, like other wars,

> Moved by her two main nerves, iron and gold.

And those sinews of Britain's strength were forged in humbler surroundings than the world of patched cheeks and full-bottomed wigs. So too the game of politics played

B

by Sarah Churchill and Mrs. Masham, Bolingbroke and the Lords of the Junto, was set and decided by the needs and prejudices of common folk in manor house and village, in port and market town.   The island must first be surveyed if we would understand Westminster or St. James's, Blenheim or Utrecht.

When a survey is demanded of Queen Anne's island, of its everyday life far distant from the Mall and yet farther from the sound of war, our thoughts turn to Daniel Defoe, riding solitary on that very quest.   It was one of his tasks to traverse Britain on tours of observation ; in the evenings, at his journey's end, he wrote his report on local opinion to his employer, Robert Harley, a mystery-man like himself, and a lover of exact information secretly given.   On Sundays he would attend the Dissenters' Chapel, not unobservant of his fellow-worshippers and their business affairs.   For besides being a trader, he was a Noncon-formist, not indeed of the type laden with the proverbial conscience, for Defoe could be all things to all men, but a Puritan in his preference for solid work and homespun to fashionable display.   Like Cobbett who rode and wrote about England a hundred years after him, he was a realist and a man of the people, but he was not, like his successor, half blinded by rage against the powers that be. For the age of Anne was the prelude to a long era of content, and Defoe, more than Swift, was the typical man of his day. Defoe, the trader, hailed the advent of the era of business prosperity, as heartily as Cobbett, the disinherited yeoman, bewailed the rural past.   He first perfected the art of the reporter ; even his novels are imaginary ' reports ' of daily life, whether on a desert island or in a thieves' den.   So then, the account that this man gives of the England of Anne's reign is for the historian a treasure indeed.   For Defoe was one of the first who saw the old world through a pair of sharp modern eyes.   His report can be controlled and enlarged by great masses of other evidence, but it occupies the central point of our thought and vision.*

* He published it in the reign of George I, but the tours on which he based his observations were largely taken in the early and middle years of Anne.   The first edition of the *Tour through Great Britain* (1724–27) has been edited and re-published by Mr. Cole in 1927.

Now this picture of England, drawn by Defoe in much wealth of prosaic detail, leaves the impression of a healthy national life, in which town and country, agriculture, industry and commerce were harmonious parts of a single economic system. Much indeed of the administrative machinery of government, particularly of the ' poor decayed borough towns ' which Defoe despised, was antiquarian lumber too religiously preserved. As yet no cry was raised for Reform, because the principle of freedom then peculiar to England enabled individual enterprise to flourish, and new shoots to push up through the old jungle. The Bumbledom of that day could not suppress the economic initiative native to the island soil.

The England so ordered was prosperous and in the main contented even in time of war, partly indeed owing to good harvests and cheap food in the first half of Anne's reign. Industry, agriculture and commerce were all expanding their operations, and society was moving forward unconsciously towards the Industrial Revolution, which grew in the next hundred years out of the conditions described by Defoe. Overseas trade ; water-carriage up the rivers, particularly of coal ; sheep-farming and the cloth trade ; the national marketing of corn and agricultural products by wholesale dealers—on these things he lays stress, and it was these things that enabled the squires to pay the land-tax, the mainstay of the Marlborough wars. They grumbled but they paid, till the war was won, when they sent the Whigs about their business and made peace.

It is true that these rural squires over their October ale cursed the monied men and traders as economic parasites, war-profiteers, Dissenters, and would-be intruders into political life which was the proper sphere of the landed interest alone. But economically the activities of these undesirables doubled the rent of many a squire, as indeed he was partly aware.[1] And the Act of Toleration, though scarcely to be mentioned without a groan over degenerate times, gave riches as well as quiet to the countryside.

In the reign of Anne the old way of life for peasant and craftsman was still carried on, but under conditions peculiarly favourable. The enterprise of trader and middleman was finding new markets for the products of the peasant's and the craftsman's toil, and had already done much to relieve their mediæval poverty without as yet destroying their rustic simplicity of manners. Money made in trade was constantly put into land by improving landlords, who had won or enlarged their fortunes as mercantile investors. This interplay of the activity of town and country, not yet subversive of the old social order, gave to Queen Anne's England a fundamental harmony and strength, below the surface of the fierce distracting antagonisms of sect and faction.

While religion divided, trade united the nation, and trade was gaining in relative importance. The Bible had now a rival in the Ledger. The Puritan, sixty years back, had been Cromwell, sword in hand ; thirty years back, Bunyan, singing hymns in gaol ; but in Anne's reign the Puritan was to be found in the tradesman-journalist Defoe. The Quaker, too, had ceased to prophesy in public against steeple houses, and had become a thrifty dealer, studying to be quiet. For old sake's sake, Puritans and Quakers were still called ' fanatics ' in common parlance. But if there were ' fanatics ' at large, one of them surely was that ' Justice Bradgate ' who ' rode a horseback into the Meeting House ' at Lutterworth and told the preacher he lied.[2] Yet that zeal of the High Churchmen was perpetually being tempered by patriotic and economic considerations that worked strongly in the minds of the Moderate Tories, led by Harley, whose secret servant was this same Defoe. Here then was an island which, with luck and good leading, might in wartime display enough unity, wealth and vigour to bring to his knees the mighty Louis, the undisputed lord of nobles and poor peasants, who had got rid of his Nonconformists once for all by revoking the Edict of Nantes.

A bird's-eye view of England in Anglo-Saxon times would have revealed a shaggy wilderness of forest trees, brushwood, marsh and down, spreading from shore to shore, but slowly shrinking at ten thousand points where agricultural and pastoral clearings were gaining on the wild. Each clearing had its hamlet of wooden huts, and each hamlet was linked to the next by tracks meandering through the forest. The whole land was traversed by straight Roman roads gradually falling into disuse, and by rivers winding through undrained swamp and forest, their solitude sometimes broken by the transit of a war-galley or a laden barge, or by the rise of a town beside some notable ford.

Very different is the prospect viewed by the airman to-day. He looks down upon a chessboard of rectangular fields divided by hedges or stone-walls, and dotted with well-built farms, villages and fenced plantations of trees. But the green area is diminished by the creeping smoke-pall and the red and grey house-tops of industrial districts, already covering a substantial acreage of the island. The whole scene is overlaid by a network of busy railways and busier roads; but on river or canal little traffic appears save near the harbours of the sea.

Half way in character, though not half way in time, between these two very different scenes, lay the panorama of the England of Queen Anne. The bulk of the primæval forest had already disappeared. But the general aspect of the country, particularly south of Thames, was rich in woodland and coppice. The greater part of the acreage of the land south of the Pennines and east of the Welsh moorlands had already been reclaimed as arable or as pasture. It had not, however, as yet acquired the rectangular chessboard pattern, for the best agricultural lands of central England were still cultivated in open fields without hedges, while the enclosed lands that lay thickest to west and to south-east, were divided up into irregularly shaped orchards and intakes. Straight lines were not prominent in the landscape. The Roman roads had for the most part gone to grass long ago, or had been broken up by the plough. But the winding Saxon bridle tracks had become muddy roads and lanes, threaded all the year round by strings of packhorses and by solitary riders, and in summer time by waggons and coaches moving at a foot's pace. The rivers flowed through rich corn-fields and meadows from one prosperous market town to another, bearing on their waterways the heaviest traffic of the land. The industrial areas, except great London, were hardly as yet of a size to be distinguishable in the landscape, amid the gardens, trees and pleasure grounds that crowded close round every town of importance.   The industrial life of that day was scattered widely over the island ; it was absorbed as an integral part of the life of village and country town.   To a bird's-eye view England might have looked like a purely agricultural land, had not the bristling masts in every river-mouth and harbour told a tale of other activities than those of the peasant.

The disappearance of the primæval self-sowing forests of England exercised the minds of the subjects of Queen Anne.   Though there were many more trees then than now, men were more troubled by their decrease because they were less accustomed to trust to foreign supply for the first needs of life.   And timber was then required for several essential purposes where it has since been replaced by iron and by coal.   The Royal Navy and the mercantile marine were then built of wood ; iron was smelted by wood-charcoal * ; and the domestic hearth had to be kept alight by faggots, in those many regions in which neither peat nor coal could be delivered on account of the badness of the roads.

There had once been forests even in Cornwall, but when in the era of William and Anne the adventurous Miss Celia Fiennes extended her riding tour into that remote peninsula, she experienced in her own person the shortage of wood.   ' I was surprised,' she wrote, ' to find my supper boiling on a fire always supplied by a bush of furze, and that to be the only fuel to dress a joint of meat and broth.'   This was at Penzance, where the sea-borne supply of coal from the South Welsh mines had been cut off by French privateers hovering off the Land's End ; the more fortunate north coast of Cornwall, she tells us, still obtained coal from across the Bristol Channel even in time of war.†

* It is possible that the Darbys invented methods of smelting by coal and coke instead of wood and charcoal in the reign of Anne ; but it was long before it affected industry on the large scale.

† *Through England on a Side Saddle, The Diary of Celia Fiennes*, 1888, pp. 221–223.   This delightful and important record was composed on tours made partly in the reign of William III, partly in that of Anne.   Miss Fiennes was a lady of means and a Dissenter.   She was sister of the Third Viscount of Saye and Sele.   She travelled for pleasure and curiosity.

About the same date, Edmund Gibson, the antiquarian and future Bishop, in his edition of Camden's *Britannia*, commented on the words which the Elizabethan had written a hundred years before as to the Oxfordshire hills, ' clad with woods ' ; ' this is so much altered,' writes Gibson, ' by the late civil wars that few places except the Chiltern country can answer that character at present. For fuel is in those parts so scarce that 'tis commonly sold by weight, not only at Oxford, but other towns in the northern parts of the shire.'

The magnificent national inheritance of the royal forests had in Stuart times been alienated by royal favouritism and improvidence, or cut down by rebel greed. They were still incompetently administered, and ill-guarded from cattle and depredators. There remained indeed some sixty royal forests, but they were no longer able to supply a tenth part of the tale of oaks demanded in the Admiralty dockyards. The Forest of Dean in Gloucestershire, the New Forest and Alice Holt in Hampshire were the only royal forests of any great importance in this respect.

Most of the valuable timber of the island, for which the Admiralty had to compete in the open market with so many other demands, was now to be found in the chases, parks and woodlands of the nobility and gentry. These too had suffered from the soldiery in the Civil War, and still more from the Parliamentary fines on the estates of Cavaliers which had laid many a tall oak prematurely on the ground. But there was still a vast quantity of timber all over the island in private possession, fenced in as deer parks, or otherwise preserved alike for beauty and for profit. Forestry still had its proper place in the economy of an estate, and an attempt was usually made by landowners to cut trees at the right time and then to replant. An oak, it is true, would not ripen for a century or so, but men still believed that their great-grandchildren would inherit them. When Charles II came home, and the belief in the solidity of the upper class was restored with him, Evelyn's *Sylva* had taken its place on the bookshelves of the better-to-do gentry ; it was a work of propaganda, and preached to the governing class the national duty of planting and

caring for trees, especially after the depredations of the
late unhappy times.*   At the beginning of Anne's reign
both Evelyn and his book were still alive, and the old man
was giving his last advice to his grandson to 'restore the
name of Wotton' [Wood Town] by planting oaks, timber-
trees and copses, 'the only best and proper husbandry the
estate is capable of.'[3]

The eastern corner of the island south of Thames—
Kent, Surrey, Sussex and Hampshire—was the homeland
of oaks, growing on the stiff clay soil of the old Andreds-
weald.   It was therefore the chief source of supply for the
Admiralty dockyards.. But already there was talk of the
shortage of timber in that region.   The iron-forges were
moving to Shropshire and the Forest of Dean, although the
first railings set up round the statue of Queen Anne in front
of St. Paul's came from the old Sussex ironworks.

But the timber of England and Wales, though scanty
as compared to the wealth of remoter ages and the needs of
the actual time, was still very extensive as compared to the
present day.   When Anne came to the throne, it was
reckoned that, only ten miles north of Cheapside, there were
growing more than half a million fine oak and beech,
sheltering the deer of Enfield Chase.[4]   Throughout the
island, even the best cultivated districts were thickly
sprinkled with heaths, copses, dingles, hawthorn brakes
and natural groves, the haunt of the highwayman, the
gypsy and the whole tribe of Autolycus, bird-haunted
sanctuaries of old romance, destined to be enclosed and
ploughed up in the coming century and a half of agricultural progress.

The straits to which the Admiralty was put to obtain
oaks of requisite size for the dockyards of Plymouth,
Portsmouth, Chatham and Woolwich were not due to the
entire exhaustion of English timber in the aggregate, but
to the difficulty of tapping reserves in out-of-the-way
districts, particularly in the North, Midlands and West.
Even in Sussex, Defoe declared that it was impossible to

* 'Whether or not the *Sylva* actually caused the plantation of " millions of
timber trees," it is certain that the Restoration plantings matured in time to
carry the Navy through the wars of the later eighteenth century.'—*Albion*, p. 131.

find a market for much fine timber except in the neighbourhood of water-carriage. On a road close to Chatham
dockyard he saw a team of two-and-twenty oxen tugging at
a single oak.[5] The expense and difficulty were very great
of moving heavy trees of the battleship type over any considerable distance of the unmetalled roadways. The ironworks could move from Sussex to Shropshire in chase of the
vanishing forest, but the dockyards must remain on the
coasts opposite to Europe. For these reasons the Admiralty
was fain, partially and most unwillingly, to turn to Baltic
and American supply, which could be brought straight
from the felling-grounds by water.

The mercantile and fishing marine was already
accustomed to purchase most of its timber abroad. Moreover its lighter vessels could be built of English trees of the
smaller kind, which were of no use for the great battleships.
The timber of Berkshire was floated down the Thames from
Reading to London, where it was bought up to build the
merchant fleet.[6] Only the great East Indiamen, themselves veritable warships, seriously competed with the Royal
Navy for the best English oaks.

The demand for hemp, tar and timber, above all for
the tall, straight fir-tree masts that could not be grown in
England, had no inconsiderable place in our foreign and
colonial policy under Queen Anne. The southern shores
of the Baltic supplied us with oak and fir from the ports of
Danzig, Memel and Riga at the mouth of great navigable
rivers draining the forest-lands of Teuton and Slav. The
Swedish ports supplied masts and tar. It was therefore an
object of the first importance to our statesmen to keep open
the entrance to the Baltic for English trade, and to prevent
that inland sea from falling into the hands of any one power,
whether Denmark, Sweden or Russia. We sought the
balance of power in the Baltic hardly less assiduously than
we sought the balance of power in Western Europe. Nor
was it easy to keep the balance trimmed. In 1700 the
English fleet had protected Charles XII of Sweden from
a coalition of neighbour powers, who had sought to take
advantage of his youth. But throughout the reign of Anne
his fierce and incalculable temper caused anxiety, not only

by his repeated threats to attack Denmark and Austria, our allies against France, in his own private quarrel, but by his resentful attitude towards the English Navigation Acts, and his policy of economic reprisal whereby he refused to supply our Admiralty with tar except in Swedish ships and at the Swede's own price.

The diplomatic and economic tangle in the Baltic was indeed complicated by our stiff Navigation Act policy of restricting British commerce as far as possible to British ships, and by the slowness with which we relaxed it even to supply the needs of the naval war with France.   The Admiralty sought relief by a colonial policy of encouraging the importation of timber and naval stores from the North American Colonies.   Already in Anne's reign we were fetching masts and tar from the forests of New England. In 1704, under the stimulus of strained relations with the Swedish king, an Act was passed offering large bounties on the importation of naval stores from America, with a right of pre-emption for the Royal Navy.   The policy was not unsuccessful, though the Baltic remained the main source of our foreign supply.   The usual difficulties between British officials and American colonists arose when the broad-arrow was placed on trees of the primæval forest near coast or river-bank, to be reserved for purchase by the Admiralty ; the backwoodsmen of New England, as lawless and enterprising on land as her buccaneers and smugglers at sea, had little reverence for royal monopoly, and the marked trees disappeared by thousands from the unpatrollable wilderness.   Nevertheless, it can be safely asserted that in Anne's reign one of the chief reasons why the colonies were valued by the statesmen and coffee-house politicians of England was as a sure source of supply for the needs of the navy.[7]

Less than a hundred years after the accession of Queen Anne the people of England had acquired an invincible prejudice against eating any bread save wheat ; even for purposes of poor relief, under the ' Speenhamland system ' begun in 1795, wheat prices alone were used as the basis of calculation.   Yet in every century before the eighteenth, the bread of the great majority of our ancestors had been rye, barley, oats, or else one of these mixed with wheat ; in England, as in all the lands of northern Europe, pure wheat bread had been regarded as a luxury proper to the rich. It was only under the Georges that wheat became the staple diet. That defiance of the natural economy of our climate was achieved by means of large farming and the application of capital and capitalistic methods to the cultivation of the soil. If England had remained a land of small peasants, she would not, any more than Germany or Scandinavia, have grown any large proportion of wheat.

In the reign of Anne English agriculture had improved so far that already more wheat was grown than in mediæval times. Wheat was reckoned at thirty-eight per cent. of the bread of the whole population ; rye came next, barley and oats a good third and fourth. Prices were therefore quoted in terms of wheat and rye.

But wheat formed a much smaller proportion of the actual corn grown than of the bread baked, because enormous crops of barley were produced all over the island to make malt for ale. Cambridgeshire, for example, outside the grassy level of the drained fens, was ' almost wholly a corn country ' and, as Defoe observed, ' of that corn five parts in six is barley, which is generally sold at Ware and Royston and other great malting towns of Hertfordshire.' [8] Except in the cider counties of the West, ale had been unchallenged in former ages as the native drink of English men, women and children at every meal, and it was only beginning to feel the rivalry of strong spirits on the one hand and of tea and coffee on the other. It was still the drink of ladies. In 1705 Lady Carnarvon imputed the fact that Miss Coke was ' extremely fallen away and her voice weak and inward ' to ' her having had stale beer all this summer.' [9]

Not only did barley everywhere provide the staple drink, but in some districts it provided the staple food. The small farmers of the Welsh hills supplied themselves with an excellent barley bread. The peasantry of the northern counties consumed oats and rye in various forms ; and in Scotland, oats ' supported the people,' as Dr. Johnson was

still able to assert many years later.   In the central districts
of England, rye and barley divided honours with wheat,
and only in the drier climate of the south-east could wheat
be said to preponderate.

But already in the reign of Anne a great interchange of
agricultural products was going on between one district
and another, especially where river traffic was available.
Largely for this reason the deepening of rivers and the
making of locks was a movement specially characteristic of
the period, two generations before the era of Bridgewater's
artificial canals.*   The Thames all the way down from
Oxford, and its affluents the Wey, the Lea and the Medway,
were the scenes of an animated and crowded traffic—food,
drink and timber going down to London, and Tyneside
coal and overseas products going up-country in return.
Abingdon and Reading were each the emporium of a great
agricultural district, of which they dispatched the produce by
water to the capital.   The coasts of Sussex and Hampshire
sent their corn, Cheshire and other western counties sent
their cheese, by sea to London, running the gauntlet of the
French privateers from Dunkirk.   The roads were often
too soft for waggons, but in most weathers the sheep and
cattle, the geese and turkeys of the northern and midland
shires could be driven to the capital, grazing as they went.
Even before the Union, Scotland sent 30,000 head of cattle
a year into England ;   the strange speech of the Welsh
drovers was familiar on the roads near London ;   only the
Irish cattle-trade had been killed by an Act of the reign of
Charles II, a sacrifice to the jealousy of English breeders.

England and Wales already formed the most considerable area in Europe for internal free-trade, to which
Scotland was added in 1707.   ' 'Tis our great felicity in

---

* The *Statutes*, and the *Commons Journals* for Anne's reign, as well as local
histories, afford abundant evidence of this.   One case may be quoted for all :
in 1699 the inhabitants of Wisbech and neighbourhood (North Cambs.) petition
the House of Commons to have the River Lark made navigable, as the roads are
impracticable, and their district which itself produces only butter, cheese and oats,
is supplied with wheat, rye and malt from Suffolk (Watson's *History of Wisbech*,
1827, p. 385).   Among the rivers at this period deepened and supplied with proper
locks were the Bristol Avon, the Yorkshire Derwent, the Stour and the Cam ' from
Clayhithe Ferry to the Queen's Mill ' in Cambridge (*Statutes of the Realm*, VIII,
pp. 56–59, 172–178 ;   Barrett's *Bristol*, p. 697).

England,' wrote Defoe, 'that we are not yet come to a *gabelle* or tax upon corn, as in Italy, and many other countries.' The shrewd Venetian envoy, Mocenigo, at the end of his residence in our island, reported to his masters in 1706 that freedom from internal *douanes* was one reason why 'industry was further advanced in England than in any other part of the world.' London and every provincial city was an open market for provisions, with no toll taken at the gate. Favoured by this freedom, the corn-factors and middlemen of agriculture pervaded the whole island, buying up on speculation the farmers' crops as they grew in the field, or as they lay unthreshed in the barn ; penetrating to the most unlikely places, even to dangerous Highland straths, amid claymores and Jacobites, in search of cattle to be fattened in English parks ; everywhere forwarding the movement towards agricultural progress by opening new markets for the produce of remote estates and hamlets.[10]

Under this regime of enterprise and improvement England was sending corn overseas on a large scale. Since the Revolution the government had paid bounties on its export. In the middle of Anne's reign the employees of the Gloucestershire coal trade rose in revolt against the high price of corn, due to the scale on which the Bristol merchants shipped the local supply abroad. And even north of Trent, homely squires were calculating on sales abroad as an important item in their own and their tenants' fortunes.*

Nevertheless, this cheerful picture of agricultural and distributive activity must not delude us into imagining that England under Queen Anne was already the land of improved agriculture and reformed traffic that it became by the end of the century. The busy life of the rivers

---

* In July 1709 Robert Molesworth writes to his wife from Edlington, near Doncaster : 'If God sends good harvest weather, there will be a very great store of corn in the kingdom, and yet such are the wants abroad that it is likely to bear a very good price for several years to come. This must enrich our farmers.' And next year he writes : ' Corn must certainly rise in the price and that very suddenly, for the plague, which is got into the Baltic, will make soon both us and the Dutch to prohibit all trade there and then the Dutch must be furnished with corn from us.'[11]

was a measure of the badness of the roads.   The best
cornlands in England—the midlands, Lincoln and Norfolk
—were still for the most part unenclosed.   In those regions
the vast and hedgeless 'village field' was still being
cultivated on the mediæval methods of three-course agriculture, that would have won the approval of a Doomsday
commissioner, but were destined to shock the modern
intelligence of an Arthur Young.

The initiative of an improving landlord or farmer was
closely circumscribed on these 'village fields,' wherein the
scattered strips of individual owners had perforce to be cultivated on the plan laid down for the whole community.   The
Manorial Court might be in decay, but less formal village
meetings still regulated the commonfield agriculture, the
use of the town's plough, the rules of gleaning, the common
herd, and the pasturage on common and waste.   A country
town like Godmanchester still employed its bailiffs to
summon all the farmers to appear, according to old custom,
at the Court Hall, where they ' did agree that none should
sow barley in the commonfield before Friday, 21st March
(1700), and that day only headlands.' [12]

More initiative and therefore more progress was possible,
though by no means inevitable, on the enclosed portion of
a squire's demesne farm, and in the enclosed lands of
southern, western and northern England.   But the districts where enclosure was commonest were on the average
the less productive parts of the island, with the worst
climate.   It is true that Kentish hop-fields and west
country orchards and fruit-gardens must be reckoned among
the lands of early enclosure, but so must the intakes amid the
weatherbeaten moorlands of west and north.   Most of the
best cornlands of the midlands and East Anglia were still
unenclosed.[13]

Since many of the sheep and cattle were fed on heaths
and commons, and without the aid of roots or artificial
grasses, they were pitifully small and thin.   Their weight at
Smithfield market in 1710 was less than half that of ordinary
sheep and cattle in 1795.[14]   At the beginning of the century the difficulty of keeping beasts alive in winter was still
so great that, when they came off the summer grass, a very

large proportion had to be slaughtered and salted. When the price of salt rose in 1703 the House of Commons was petitioned, on the ground that it was 'a grievance to the poorer sort of people who mostly feed on salted provisions.'[15]

The days of Lord Townshend's turnip-fields and Coke of Norfolk's fat sheep and cattle were still in the future. But already the Wiltshire and Cotswold uplands, that bred sheep for the western wool-clothiers, were a wonder to behold. 'On the pleasant downs' within a six-mile radius of Dorchester, Defoe was informed that more than half a million sheep were feeding ; and he noted that on Salisbury Plain and the Dorset Downs the land was becoming so much enriched by the folding of sheep with pens in a new place every night, that the chalk lands thus manured, though hitherto fit for nothing but pasture, were rapidly coming under the plough.[16]

Ever since Tudor times, and more particularly since the Restoration, there had flowed from the press an ever broadening stream of books on improved methods of agriculture. The spirit of scientific enquiry emanating from the regions of the Royal Society into the walks of common life, was a constant stimulant but often a sore puzzle to the practical farmer. For the experts and modernizers were so seldom agreed. Jethro Tull, the great improver who introduced the drill and the horse-hoe into his own farming operations in the course of Anne's reign, was quite wrong on many other points, as subsequent controversies showed. But men were on the look out to adapt new methods as soon as they had proved themselves—especially where enclosed ground gave liberty for change.[17]

With the idea of agricultural improvement thus in the air, the movement for the enclosure of commons and heaths was not only practised, as it had been for centuries, but was preached by modern theorists as a duty to the commonwealth. When Anne came to the throne agricultural writers were denouncing the commons as 'seminaries of a lazy, thieving sort of people,' whose sheep were 'poor, tattered and poisoned with rot,' and whose heath-fed cattle were 'starved, todbellied runts, neither fit for the dairy nor the yoke.' Here already we have in full blast the famous controversy as to the social value of rights on the common, in which Cobbett a hundred years later was protagonist of the defeated commoners. On the merits of that dispute the historians of our own day are still divided. In Anne's reign there was not yet much enclosure done by Act of Parliament, but enclosure was going forward under the common law by agreement or otherwise.*

This old rural England, on the eve of the wholesale enclosures and the industrial revolution, is often presented to the mind's eye of posterity in one or other of two rival pictures. On the one hand we are asked to contemplate a land of independent and self-respecting peasants, most of them attached to the soil by small personal rights therein, contented with the country quiet and felicity which have been since destroyed, and celebrating their rural happiness in alehouse songs about 'Harvesthome,' which we have promoted to the drawing-room; and the same land, we are reminded, was also the land of craftsmen in village and market town, not divorced from rural pleasures because they pursued industry, using tools instead of watching machines, and therefore enjoying in their daily work the delight of the individual artist, for which a poor substitute is found in the feverish excitement of our modern amusements, organized *en masse* as a counterpoise to the dullness of mechanical and clerical toil. On the other hand we are shown the opposing picture: we are asked to remember the harsh backbreaking labour of the pre-mechanical ages, continued for thirteen or more hours in the day; child-labour instead of primary schools; disease and early death uncontrolled by medical science or hospital provision; and absence of cleanliness and comforts which we now regard

---

* In the summer when Marlborough was marching to Blenheim, a Yorkshire squire was writing to his wife:

' The law in England is (as I know now by experience) that every freeholder can enclose so much of his common as lies upon him (much more a lord of a considerable land), provided he leaves out as much common as is sufficient for those that have right, and disclaims any further title to put beasts on the rest of the common which he leaves out. This is the instance of Mr. Frettwell, of Hellaby, our neighbour, who carried it even against the Lord Castleton, who is lord of the manor, upon trial. And this is our case between us and Cunsborough.' [18]

as necessities ; neglectful and unimaginative harshness not only to criminals and debtors but too often to women, children and the poor at large ; and finally a population of little more than five and a half millions in England and Wales, less well fed than the present population of more than seven times that number.*

Confirmation of both these pictures emerges from a study of the period. But which picture contains the greater and more important body of truth it is hazardous to pronounce, partly because the dispute is about intangible values—we cannot put ourselves back into the minds of our ancestors, and if we could we should still be puzzled ; partly also because even where statistics would help, statistics are not to be had. It is true that, a dozen years before Queen Anne's accession, the able publicist Gregory King made a calculation from the hearth tax and other data of the probable numbers in various classes of the community. The figures he gave represent a shrewd guess, no more. They will indeed serve negatively as a check on the enthusiasm of the *laudator temporis acti*, by recalling the fact that, even before the great enclosures and the industrial revolution, the number of farmers and yeomen was relatively small, and the numbers of the agricultural pro-letariat large. By far the two largest classes in King's analysis of the nation are the ' cottagers and paupers ' and the ' labouring people and outservants.'[19] The former represent, we may suppose, those who attempted to be independent of wages and according to King made a very poor business of the attempt. Yet those who picked up a living off the common whereon they had squatted, or off the small field they owned behind their hovel, may have been happier than King knew, even if they were poorer than is realized by modern idealizers of the past. King's second large class, the ' labouring people and outservants,' are the wage-earners. But many of them had also some rights on the common, some garden or tiny holding which added to the interest and dignity of life, without entitling the owner to the proud rank of English yeoman. Even the servants of industry had many of them small gardens or

* See note p. 75, below, on statistics of population.

c

plots of land to till in their off hours, especially the woollen weavers in all parts of the island. On the stony heights around Halifax each clothworker had ' a cow or two ' in a field walled off on the steep hillside whereon his cottage stood.[20]

On the other hand there were very large numbers of employees both in agriculture and industry who had no rights in land and no means of subsistence but their wages.

The wages in agriculture and in industry were supposed to be regulated by schedules issued for each county by the Justices of the Peace, who also occasionally set a limit to the price at which certain goods might be sold. These schedules did not pretend to fix either wages or prices exactly, but only to set a maximum which was not to be surpassed. Variations were therefore permissible inside every county, as well as differences between one shire and the next. Moreover the maximum announced was very often transgressed in practice.*

Judging by negative evidence, we may conclude that concerted strikes and combinations to raise wages were not common. They could be punished under then existing laws, long before the celebrated Combination Acts of the younger Pitt. In 1706 the Leeds Quarter Sessions heavily fined six cloth drawers who had combined not to work except for three-halfpence an hour in place of the current penny an hour. The Elizabethan Statute of Artificers, that was still partially in force, penalized the leaving of work unfinished, as well as the giving or taking of wages above the maximum fixed by the Justices of the Peace. But the maximum was often exceeded when excess payment was to the interest of both employer and employed. If there was

* Wages differed from one estate to another ; in 1701 a Yorkshire squire wrote :

' The wages of a good husbandman in the parts about Barnsley and Wortley I find to be no more than £3 a year, and Sir Godfrey gives his keeper but £3 14s., and his bailiff £4, so that we are worse served for high wages. About Wortley all the husbandmen are up every morning with their beasts at three o'clock, and in our house they lie abed till near seven. But above all Warne's £20 vexes me.'

That year, we should remember, wheat stood as low as 34s. a quarter and other grain in proportion, and chickens could be bought in the West Riding at twopence apiece. [21]

little or no trade-unionism, there was much individual bargaining about wages.[22]

Even when the low prices are taken into account, some of the wages paid seem low by modern standards.* But they were high by comparison with the Europe of that day. The national characteristic of Englishmen, then as now, was not thrift but insistence on a high standard of life. Defoe, writing as an employer, declared that :

> Good husbandry is no English virtue. English labouring people eat and drink, especially the latter, three times as much in value as any sort of foreigners of the same dimensions in the world.

A Dutchman, he declared, lived well and provided for his family on a wage which meant misery to the improvident Englishman.   It is to be noted that in this pamphlet Defoe speaks of the English labourer as earning nine shillings a week, a rate greatly in advance of that of the Quarter Session schedules.   He declares that he himself ' offered nine shillings per week to strowling fellows at my door, and they have frequently told me to my face they could get more a begging, and I once met a lusty fellow in the stocks for making the experiment.'   Nor is this the only evidence that, in spite of the attempted control by Quarter Sessions, wages varied greatly from place to place.

Defoe's extortionate beggar is a type known in every age, and that period was not, upon the whole, propitious to him. Indeed many wanderers for work were more sinned against than sinning.   The monstrous Act of Settlement of the Poor, passed in 1662 in one of the lightest moods of Charles II's Cavalier Parliament, was still in operation unamended.   By this Act every parish in which a man settled could send him back to the parish of which he was native, for fear that if he stayed in his new abode he might at some future date become chargeable on the rates.   Nine-tenths of the people of England, all in fact who did not

---

* Truck payments were a common abuse.   The establishment of a sound currency in William III's reign had indeed set some limits to it.   But still farmers and bailiffs often ' compelled the poor labourers to take corn and other provisions instead of their hire, and that in such quantities that they cannot spend the same in their own families.' [23]

belong to a small class of landowners, were liable to be expelled from any parish save their own, with every circumstance of arrest and ignominy, however good their character and even if they had secured remunerative work. The panic fear of some parish authorities lest newcomers should some day fall on the rates, caused them to exercise this unjust power in quite unnecessary cases. The Act placed a check upon the fluidity of labour and was as much an outrage as the Press-gang itself on the boasted freedom of Englishmen. Yet it was seldom denounced until Adam Smith dealt with it in scathing terms. It is hard to ascertain the exact degree to which it operated, and Adam Smith appears to have exaggerated the harm done and the number of cases in which cruel wrong was inflicted. But at best it was a great evil ; it is the reverse side of that creditable effort of Tudor and Stuart England to provide for the maintenance of the poor through the local public authorities. That effort, on the whole, was not unsuccessful, and largely accounts for the peaceable character of English society.

In Anne's reign the parish provision for the poor chargeable on the rate was being very generally supplemented and softened by the establishment of Almshouses through private benefaction. The keelmen of the Tyneside coal trade contributed among themselves to build a hospital for their aged and sick members at a cost of £2000. But more usually almshouses and schemes for the employment of the workless were endowed by well-to-do men and women anxious to provide for their less fortunate neighbours. The age of Anne was very generous in foundations of this type, as well as in the establishment of Charity Schools.

But besides private beneficence, public policy, financed out of the local rates, was constantly establishing new workhouses and enlarging the ' parish stock ' of materials to give employment. When Anne came to the throne almost a quarter of the population was occasionally in receipt of parochial relief, and the poor rate stood at about £800,000 a year. It increased to a million a year before she died, but fell below £700,000 in the reign of George II, owing to better times and to the application of the workhouse test.

There was much to criticize in the English Poor Law, especially the Law of Settlement, but at least there was an effective system of public relief and therefore England was not shamed, at the end of the great struggle with France, by scenes such as Lady Mary Wortley Montagu noticed on her travels in 1718 :

> I think nothing so terrible as objects of misery, and all the country villages of France show nothing else.   While the post-horses are changed, the whole town comes out to beg, with such miserable starved faces, and thin tattered clothes, they need no other eloquence. This is all the French magnificence till you come to Fontainebleau.

Not only our parliamentary liberties but also, with all its faults, the English Poor Law stood between us and the social revolution towards which Louis XIV's famed system of despotism in Church and State was leading the French nation.[24]

The Yeoman was not a figure characteristic of mediæval society, which rested on the two bases of the serf and his lord.   But with the gradual emancipation of the villeins in the Fourteenth and Fifteenth Centuries, the yeoman had come to the front in the English scene.   He flourished under Tudor and Stuart, when the number of small land-owners and of large farmers was multiplied, in spite of some local destruction of peasant households by enclosure in early Tudor times.   The praise of the English yeoman in prose and verse is a favourite *motif* of our literature from the Fifteenth to the Eighteenth Century.

The reign of Anne was the culminating point of the fortunes of the English freehold yeomen, before their decline began, and it was no ill time for the still rising fortunes of the tenant farmers.*   The freehold yeomen were reckoned at about one-eighth of the population of the country, and the substantial tenant farmers at a little less ; it was believed that the freehold yeoman was on the average a richer man

* Until the later eighteenth century the word ' yeoman ' was used to include the substantial tenant farmer as well as the freehold cultivator.   In the most famous of all descriptions of the yeoman class, Hugh Latimer, preaching before Edward VI, states that his ' yeoman ' father farmed another man's land.

than the tenant farmer.*   A hundred years later the opposite was probably the case, in so far as the freehold yeoman
any longer existed.   For in the Georgian era of agricultural
improvements, the tenant farmer had the benefit of his
landlord's capital poured into his land, while the small freeholder had no financial resources save his own with which
to keep abreast of the times.   But Anne's reign was perhaps
a moment of no very marked economic difference between
the two types of yeoman.

The difference was political and social.   The freeholder
had a vote for Parliament and was often in a position to use
it as he liked.   The tenant farmer had no vote, and if he had,
he would have been obliged to cast it for his landlord.
Even the ideal landlord, Sir Roger de Coverley, was represented by Addison to an approving world as exercising over
his tenants an absolute, patriarchal sway.

But the independence of the freehold yeoman was
deeply cherished and stoutly maintained.   In the election
correspondence of country gentlemen we meet such expressions as ' The freeholders do not stick to say they will
show their liberty in voting.' [25]   The squire, who had
everyone else under his thumb, was for that reason often
disposed to buy out the freehold yeoman, and, as the century
went on, many freeholders were ready, on fair terms, to quit
the countryside, in which their old independence was
threatened by the increasing wealth of the large landlord
and his tenant farmers.

But in Anne's reign the 180,000 cultivating freeholders
enumerated by King, were still the class upon whose un-
forced and unpurchased support the structure of Church

* In 1688 Gregory King had calculated that there were over one million three
hundred thousand households in England and Wales, of which 160,000 (or 180,000)
were families of freehold cultivators with incomes ranging from £55 to £91 a year ;
while 150,000 families of tenant farmers enjoyed incomes averaging just over £42 a
year ; and that 15,000 gentry and squires had incomes ranging from £280 to £450,
without reckoning the titled folk and the larger landed proprietors.   In the reign
of Anne it is probable that the average income of the various classes was appreciably
larger.   For King's tables, see note 19 below.

It is exceedingly difficult to put these incomes into terms of present-day money.
How much has the value of money declined ?   On the one hand the price of wheat
stands not very far from the average of Anne's reign (see note 19 below).
On the other hand, many articles to-day cost five, ten, twenty or thirty times what
they cost then.

and State mainly rested, like the Ark on Ararat, in the staggering times that followed the great upheaval and backwash of the Revolution. The nicely adjusted balance of Whig and Tory interests was maintained or redressed at each successive election in the Queen's reign by the divided opinions of the ' forty-shilling freeholders,' most of them yeoman agriculturists. The ' forty-shilling freehold ' was the basis of the uniform Parliamentary franchise in every shire of England and Wales. On the other hand, in the towns privileged to return members, the varying and eccentric methods of election—sometimes by the Corporation, sometimes by a section of the inhabitants—rendered many ' rotten boroughs ' the political property of single grandees, or laid them open to a competition of influence and bribery. The freehold yeomen of the counties were therefore the class of voter with whom at election time genuine political considerations went farthest, and cajolery and intimidation least far ; just as, in a former generation, Cavalier and Roundhead had recruited their best cavalry from the same class by other means than drink-money.

But even more than politics, partridges caused squire and yeoman to look at one another askance. The squirarchical legislation of later Stuart Parliaments had excluded all freeholders of under a hundred pounds a year—that is to say the very great majority of the class—from killing game, even on their own land. Thus many poor families had been robbed of many good meals that were theirs by right ; and even those few yeomen whose wealth raised them above the reach of this remarkable law, were for that reason regarded with suspicion. The best that even the goodhearted Sir Roger can bring himself to say of the ' yeoman of about a hundred pounds a year,' ' who is just within the Game Act,' is that ' he would be a good neighbour if he did not destroy so many partridges '—that is to say upon his own land.[26]

For many generations to come, grave social consequences were to flow from the excessive eagerness of the country gentlemen about the preservation of game. Their anxieties on that score had grown with the adoption of the shot-gun. During the Stuart epoch shooting had gradually superseded hawking, with the result that birds were more rapidly destroyed, and the supply no longer seemed inexhaustible. In Anne's reign it was already not unusual to 'shoot flying.' But it was regarded as a difficult art, the more so as it was sometimes practised from horseback. But the 'perching' of pheasants by stalking and shooting them as they sat on the boughs, was still customary among gentlemen. Netting birds on the ground was a fashionable sport, often carried on over dogs who pointed the game in the long grass. It is written that Sir Roger 'in his youthful days had *taken* forty coveys of partridges in a season,' probably by this means. 'Liming' by twigs, snaring and trapping birds of all kinds, not only pheasants and wild duck but thrushes and field-fares, had still a prominent place in manuals of *The Gentleman's Recreation*. To lure wild duck into a decoy upon the water was a trade in the fens and a sport on the 'decoy-pond' of the manor house. But the shot-gun was clearly in the ascendant, and with it the tendency to confine sport more and more to the pursuit of certain 'game' birds. In that sacred category a place had recently been granted by Statute to grouse and blackcock : already the heather and bracken where they lurked were protected from being burnt except at certain times of the year, and the shepherd transgressing the law was liable to be whipped. Addison's Tory squire declared the Game Law to be the only good law passed since the Revolution.[27]

The squalor of the mediæval village had long been in retreat before the homely dignity and comfort of the rural middle class. In Anne's reign men were everywhere building or enlarging farmhouses, in stone, brick or half-timber according to the tradition or material of the district. The architectural results of rustic prosperity were most evident in those favoured regions where the cloth manufacture made a great demand for the local wool, as in the magnificent stone farms of the Cotswolds dating from the Fifteenth to the Seventeenth Century, or in the dwellings of the Cumbrian and Westmorland mountaineers whose fortunes had more recently risen with the Kendal cloth trade.[28]

Besides the fine old farmhouses familiar to the traveller in the Lake District to-day, there were then many cottages, since disappeared or derelict, wherein the poorer dalesmen brought up large and sturdy families. The children were kept at their mother's knee, spinning for the Kendal clothiers, until they were old enough to go up on to the fells to drive the sheep and to pile those great stone walls up the sides of the precipices which are the wonder of our less industrious age. It was only in the course of the Eighteenth Century that the beauty of Wordsworth's homeland attained the moment of rightful balance between nature and man. In previous centuries the valleys were ' choked, tangled, swampy and featureless ' ; in our day man is all too successfully regulating the face of nature with the machine. But in the reign of Anne the dales were just beginning to take on their brief perfection of rural loveliness, ordered but not disciplined, in contrast with the mountain magnificence above and around.

Nevertheless visitors were extremely rare in the Lake District, ' the wildest, most barren and frightful ' in England, as it appeared to Defoe and his contemporaries. The few strangers whom business or curiosity caused to ride up the steep stony tracks beyond Windermere and over Hardknot, complained of the bread of the Lake Valleys as ' exceedingly black, coarse and harsh,' and the houses as ' sad little huts ' of unmortared stone, more fit for cattle than for men. But already ' here and there there was a house plastered ' and sometimes the ' oat clap bread ' was cunningly baked and delicious. We may conclude from these travellers' impressions that the great improvement in the prosperity, the farm-building and the furniture of this happy region was by no means complete in the reign of Anne. But already the famous Windermere delicacy, ' the fish called charrs, came potted to London.'[29]

In the neighbouring county of Northumberland, recently so warlike and barbarous, the travellers along the coast and in the valley of the South Tyne, found ' plenty of good bread and beer ' as well as hens and geese, and famous

stocks of claret, no doubt on account of the neighbourhood
of Scotland where the gentry imported claret from France
in spite of the war.   When Anne came to the throne, there
was still a ' County Keeper ' for Northumberland, who
drew a salary of £500 in return for making good all cattle
stolen and not restored.   Although the wild moorlands
between Redesdale and the Roman Wall still had a bad
name, the County Keeper had the best of his bargain, and
' was able to inform travellers that the moss-trooping trade
is very much laid aside, and that a small sum will recompense
all the robberies that are yearly committed in the County.'
Peace with Scotland, the wealth of the Tyneside mines,
and the trade of Newcastle were factors already raising the
standard of life all along the border.[30]   But the more outlying rural districts of Northumberland were still very poor,
though more thickly inhabited than they afterwards became.
In many a ' township ' now consisting of a single prosperous
sheep farm, a cluster of half a dozen cottages of the crofter
type then maintained a hardy population of borderers,
unused to comfort, and tilling the moorland for a meagre
harvest of oats.

In the more southerly districts of England where
civilization was of older date, long peace was multiplying
the comforts of life.   Everywhere that perfectly beautiful
equilibrium between man and nature which marked the
Eighteenth-Century landscape, was in process of being
established.   While hedgerow and orchard were gaining
on the wild, the multiplication or improvement of cottages,
farm-buildings and Halls was going on, either in old
traditional styles, or in that dignified but simple manner
which we know as ' Queen Anne.'   That style, which seems
to us now native English, in its origin owed something
to Dutch influence.   Nor was the internal decoration
unworthy of the architecture : in 1710 a foreign traveller
noted that ' now in England tapestry is no longer in
fashion, but all is panelled at great cost.'   China-ware,
brought to Europe by the Dutch and English East India
Companies, was a passion with ladies, and we may conceive
the scheme of decoration in many Queen Anne mansions in
town and country, as blue and white jars in wainscoted

recesses, and tall grandfather clocks decorated with lacquered work from the East. Grinling Gibbons was still executing his marvels of woodwork. Mahogany was beginning to come in from the American Indies, and with it the lighter and finer furniture that we associate with Eighteenth Century taste. Already foreign art dealers were amazed by their opportunities over here, and ' fleeced the English rarely, selling for great sums what they imported for a trifle from France and Italy.' Foreign artists declared that the nobility and gentry over whom Anne reigned had secluded in their country Halls as many pictures by renowned Italian masters as were to be found in all the Palaces and museums of Rome itself.[31]

Vanbrugh's Blenheim House, with its magnificent conception and doubtful detail, is by no means characteristic of the architecture of Anne's reign. Usually a purer taste prevailed in the realm of ecclesiastical, academic and public buildings, while in ordinary domestic structures the note of the day was ' simple in elegance.' Wren was still alive and active over his London churches and his Hampton Court, and Gibbs was learning that skill which was soon to produce the Radcliffe at Oxford. Together they taught the succeeding generations to ' effect the fusion of classic grace with vernacular energy.' The rules of proportion which these great men laid down, filtering into the textbooks commonly used by local architects and builders, prepared for the Eighteenth Century a long and happy period of common English building in hamlet and country town. It was only when, after this school had decayed, and men attempted to restore the architecture of ancient Athens or of the Middle Ages in the Nineteenth Century, that the English tradition was lost, and was succeeded by a hideous anarchy of amateur fancies and exotic modes.[32]

Duke (Prince)

Squire (300# /yr)

CHAPTER II

The country gentlemen—variety of types. A squire's occupations and budget. Education and younger sons. The landed and the trading interests. Ladies. The marriage market. Gambling. Drinking. Smoking. Duelling. Hunting. Racing. Boxing. Out-of-doors life.

THE country gentlemen included many grades of wealth and of culture. At the top of the social hierarchy stood the Duke, who would in any other land have been styled a Prince, and whose manner of life outdid in magnificence the courts of allied monarchs drawing England's pay. At the lower end of the scale was the squire of £300 a year, speaking in the broadest provincial dialect, but distinguished from the yeomen, among whom he mingled almost on equal terms, by a small sporting establishment, by a coat of arms, and by the respect which all paid to him as a ' gentleman.' If once in his life he went to London on business, he was noticeable for his horse-hair periwig, his jockey belt and his old-fashioned coat without sleeves.[33] His library, traditionally at least, consisted of the Bible, Baker's Chronicle, Hudibras and Foxe's *Martyrs*, and, whether he read these works or not, his view on Puritans and Papists usually coincided with those expressed in the last two.

But in picturing to ourselves the culture of the country house of that time, we must not forget the grandees filling rural palaces with pictures from Italy, furniture from France, and editions of Italian, French or Latin authors which they not only collected but read—the men whom in the next reign Voltaire contrasted favourably with the French nobles as patrons of letters and science. There were philosopher Lords like young Shaftesbury ; scholar

statesmen like Somers and Montagu ; and the greatest of
all antiquarian collectors, Robert Harley, who, when too
much engaged as ' the nation's great support ' to hunt
books and manuscripts himself, still had his private agents
everywhere on the look out.*   The Lords of the Junto and
their followers and foes at Westminster and St. James's
prided themselves on being country gentlemen, whether
self-made or to the manner born, each with his country seat
to which the careworn statesman was ever anxious, at least
in theory, to return.   When a politician, a lawyer or a war-
profiteer had made his fortune at the public expense, he
put his money into land and founded a county family.   The
older families, who were mostly Tory, complained of the
parvenu families, who were mostly Whig, but the process
went on, and rural and urban society were to that extent
amalgamated.

The London season was over by the first week in June,
when people of fashion dispersed to their country homes or
adjourned to Bath.³⁴   A longer residence in town would
have ruined many families who had strained a point to
bring their daughters to the London marriage market, while
their neighbours were fain to be contented with a county
capital, or with the round of such rural visits as ladies could
accomplish in the coach in summer, and on the pillion
behind their brothers in the muddy lanes at Christmas.
The rival claims of town and country are thus celebrated in
a popular song of the period :

> Good bye to the Mall,
> The Park and Canal ; †
> St James's Square
> And flaunters there :
> The gaming house too
> Where high dice and low
> Are managed by all degrees.
> Adieu to the knight
> Was bubbled last night,

---

* Something of the organized method by which the great Harleian collection
was being built up during the busiest time of Harley's political engagements can
be seen in the *Harleian MSS. (B.M.)* 7526.

† St. James's Park and the long artificial water in it. The song is from
D'Urfey, *Pills to Purge Melancholy*, 1719, I, p. 5.

> That keeps a Blouze,
> And beats his spouse ;
> And now in great haste
> To pay what he's lost,
> Sends home to cut down his trees.
> And well fare the lad
> Improves every clod,
> That ne'er set his hand
> To Bill or to Bond
> Nor barters his flocks
> For wine or pox,
> To chouse him of half his days.
> But fishing and fowling
> And hunting and bowling
> His pastime is ever and ever.

The natural reply of ' the town ' was to harp on the reputation of the rustic gentry for too exclusive a devotion to drinking, hunting and shooting ; and this charge, so generally made, may well be credited, provided we remember that no description will cover the whole ground. Lady Mary Wortley Montagu, a brilliant blue-stocking, in a letter of which the dullest part is a quotation from Tasso, condemns the squires of a certain district of Sussex as ' insensible to other pleasures ' than the bottle and the chase. ' The poor female part of the family being seldom permitted a coach, their lords and masters having no occasion for such a machine, as their mornings are spent among the hounds, and their nights with as beastly companions—with what liquor they can get.'[35]   Yet in the same letter she regrets and praises the society of the squires of Northamptonshire. No less real, if more rare, than boorish Squire Western was the learned country gentleman, celebrated in Somerville's sententious lines :

> A rural squire, to crowds and courts unknown
> In his own cell retired, but not alone ;
> For round him view each Greek and Roman sage,
> Polite companions of his riper age. [36]

Nevertheless the impression left by turning over many hundreds of letters of the better-to-do gentry of the reign of Anne, is neither that of country scholar nor of country bumpkin. We read the actual thoughts of squires, anxious about their account books, their daughters' marriages and their sons' debts and professions : attending to their own estates, and to the county business on the bench of magistrates, as well as to their hounds and horses ; devoted to their gardens and their ponds a little more than to their books ; living, as we should expect, a wholesome and useful life, half public, half private, wholly leisured, natural and dignified. Many of the better-to-do gentry, as their letters and diaries show, were getting several thousands a year from their estates.[37]

The expenditure required of a country gentleman, rich or poor, was in one respect very small. It was not then considered obligatory that his sons should be sent at great cost to exclusively patrician schools. At the nearest local grammar school, the squire's children sat beside those sons of yeomen and shopkeepers who had been selected for a clerical career ; otherwise the young gentlemen were taught at home by a neighbouring parson, or in wealthier families by the private chaplain. Where a tutor was specially employed, he was often a Huguenot refugee, for the land was full of educated men of this type, welcomed by careful parents for their French, and doubly welcome in Whig families for their sufferings and their principles. Eton, Winchester and Westminster were indeed patronized by many but not by most of the aristocracy. And even at Westminster there could be found at the end of Anne's reign ' houses at which boys pay but £20 a year for boarding, and the schooling but five or six guineas.' It was only in the reign of George I that Harrow began to rise into the rank of the fashionable schools.[38]

It followed that, whereas a gentleman of moderate means in our day often thinks himself obliged to spend a sixth part of his income on the schooling of one boy, he could in those days be satisfied to spend a hundredth. Thus squire Molesworth, at a time when he was drawing a rental of just under £2000, paid £20 a year for each of his sons—including board, instruction, clothes and all charges. His heavy parental liabilities only began when the two lads left school, and the younger went into the army. Then indeed ' Dick must be furnished with a hundred pounds or he cannot stir a step. He has both horses, clothes and equipage to buy.' As ' he was not in the list of officers slain in the late glorious battle of Blenheim,' which would have been a sad economy, nor yet ' in any of the desperate attacks on Lille,' Dick continued for many years to be an increasing source of expenditure and pride to his Yorkshire home. The elder, Jack, had chosen diplomacy, a no less costly method of serving the State. In 1710 the father writes : ' I verily believe these two sons of ours have spent between them £10,000 within the last seven or eight years ' ; they and the daughters ' are all money-bound. It is well they have a good father's house to tarry in.' Five years later Dick's zeal for his regiment caused him to ' lay out £600 above what was allowed him, so well he loves the service.'[39]

Smaller squires paid equally little for their sons' schooling, and then prenticed them to cheaper trades than the army or diplomatic service. In the plays of Congreve and Farquhar the younger son of the manor may still expect to be ' bound prentice,' perhaps ' to a felt-maker in Shrewsbury ' ; and Steele declares that ' younger brothers are generally condemned to shops, colleges and inns of court.' * On these terms the gentry could afford to have large families, and although a great proportion of their children died young, they kept England supplied with a constant stream of high-spirited young men, who led her along the forward path at home and overseas. For the ' younger sons ' were willing, as the cadets of the continental nobility were not, to mingle in the common avocations of mankind and not to ' stand upon their gentry.' The fact that the younger son went out to make his fortune in the army or at the bar, in industry or in commerce, was one of the general causes favouring the Whigs and their

---

* In the *Gentleman's Magazine* for 1732, we read ' I remember (and am now near seventy-three) the younger sons of our best families were usually bound apprentices to eminent merchants. But now young master must be sent into the army as soon as he can strut tolerably well.' (*Gentleman's Magazine*, No. XXII, Vol. II, p. 1015.) See *Way of the World*, III, 15 ; *Trip to the Jubilee*, I, 1 ; *Tender Husband*, I, 1.

alliance with those interests, as against the desire of the High Tories to keep the landed gentry an exclusive as well as a dominant class. Dominant it remained for another century, but only on condition of opening its doors wide to newcomers, and fostering in a hundred different ways close alliance with interests other than agriculture, in scenes far remote from the manor house and the village church. The country gentlemen ruled Eighteenth-Century England, but they ruled it largely in the interest of commerce and empire.

It is indeed one of the curiosities of English life from the Fifteenth to the Nineteenth Century that, although the landed gentry looked down on the mercantile class as a lower order of society, many of the landed families had not only acquired their estates by money made in trade, but continued from generation to generation to invest in mercantile and financial adventures of every kind. The House of Russell, one of the main pillars of the Whig landed aristocracy, had risen and thriven not more by acquisition of monastic acres than by judicious investment in trading concerns throughout the Plantagenet, Tudor and Stuart periods. In the reigns of William and Anne, Sir William Blackett, the leading merchant and mineowner on Tyneside, sometimes member for Newcastle in the Whig interest, became also a landed proprietor in the heart of rural Northumberland, where he had bought the estate of the needy Jacobite, Sir John Fenwick. The Blacketts of the next generation became Tories under the influence of ' Osbaldistone ' rural society, but they remained mercantile as well as landed magnates, and put into agricultural improvement much of the wealth they acquired on Tyneside. These cases are typical of countless other instances. The close personal connection between the landed and trading interests gave stability and unity to the social fabric in England, which was lacking to the *ancien régime* in France, with its sharp distinction of interest between *noblesse* and *bourgeoisie*.

The common schooling of the upper and middle class was criticized, even in those days, for its too rigidly classical

D

curriculum. It was even declared by some that 'a girl which is educated at home with her mother is wiser at twelve than a boy at sixteen' who knows only Latin. Yet the second classical language was so ill taught at school and college that the excellent Latinists of Christ Church had not enough Greek to be aware that Bentley had proved them dunces over the *Letters of Phalaris*. It was only in the Nineteenth Century that the typical English scholar was equally at home with Aristophanes and with Horace.[40]

It would be a mistake to suppose that nothing was anywhere taught but classics ; there was considerable variety in the type of school patronized by gentlemen. Thus Robert Pitt, father of a mighty son, writes in 1704 to his own scarcely less formidable father, Governor Pitt of Madras:

> My two brothers are at Mr. Meure's Academy, near Soho Square, esteemed the best in England. They learn Latin, French and accounts, fencing, dancing and drawing. I think of settling them in Holland for their better education next summer : and should my wife's father-in-law, Lt. Gen. Stewart, accompany the Duke of Marlborough, of placing them under his care to see a campaign.[41]

Among the critics of our educational methods were the wise Locke and the good-natured Steele, who both urged that perpetual flogging was not the best method of imparting knowledge and maintaining discipline. Upper-class education was admitted on all hands to need reform, yet nothing was done to reform it. Swift, for all his hatred of the Scots, agreed for once with Burnet that the lairds gave their sons more sound book-learning than the wealthier and idler English.

Nevertheless, the Eighteenth Century, in spite of its educational defects, produced a larger proportion of remarkable and original men from among those who passed through its schools than our highly educated and over-regulated age is able to do. And in spite of cruel flogging by 'those licensed tyrants the schoolmasters,' and cruel bullying by the unlicensed tyranny of ill-disciplined school-fellows, there was also much happiness in boyhood, that still had leisure and still spent it in the free range of the countryside. Nor was severity universal : a young lord, newly arrived at Eton, writes home : ' I think Eaton very easy scholl. I am shure one cannot offend without they be meare rakes indeed.' [42]

Women's education was sadly to seek. Among the lower classes it was perhaps not much worse than men's, but the daughters of the well-to-do had admittedly less education than their brothers. It was before the days of ' ladies' academies,' and though there were ' boarding schools ' for girls, they were few and indifferent. Most ladies learnt from their mothers to read, write, sew and manage the household. We hear of no fair Grecians, like Lady Jane Grey and Queen Elizabeth in days of old. But a few ladies could read the Italian poets and were therefore held in some awe by their swains. And at least two women could meet Swift on terms of something like intellectual equality. Yet it was he who lamented ' that not one gentleman's daughter in a thousand should be brought to read her own natural tongue, or be judge of the easiest books that are written in it.' The want of education in the sex was discussed as an admitted fact, one side defending it as necessary in order to keep wives in due subjection, while the other side, led by the chief literary men of the day, ascribed the frivolity and the gambling habits of ladies of fashion to an upbringing which debarred them from more serious interests.

Nevertheless, country-house letters of the period show us wives and daughters writing as intelligent advisers of their menfolk. Such correspondents were something better than brainless playthings or household drudges. A whole class of the literature of the day, from the *Spectator* downwards, was written as much for ladies as for their fathers and brothers. And it was observed that the ladies took a part, often too eager, in the Whig and Tory feuds that divided town and country. As to rural pastimes, the prototype of Diana Vernon is to be found in Farquhar's Belinda, who tells her friend ' I can gallop all the morning after the hunting horn and all the evening after a fiddle.

In short I can do everything with my father but drink and shoot flying.' [43]

In the upper and middle classes, husbands were found for girls on the principle of frank barter. 'As to Cloky,' writes her father, squire Molesworth, 'we shall not have money enough to dispose of her here,' so she must be sent to Ireland to seek there a husband at a cheaper rate. Another squire, named Guise, who is in search of a wife for himself, writes, 'Lady Diana sent a very venerable person to view my estates, and was well satisfied with the report and I think did sincerely desire I might have her daughter.' But the daughter had other views, so Guise found consolation elsewhere :

> Being on the Bench at the quarter Session, a Justice of the Peace took me aside and asked me whether I would marry a woman worth twenty-thousand pounds. The lady I had seen but never spoke to, and upon the whole readily accepted his offer.

A Cornet of Horse writes with equal frankness :

> Not expecting anything this campaign I had taken thoughts another way, to try my fortune under Venus, and accordingly about a fortnight ago was (by some friends) proposed to a lady of very good fortune : but how I shall speed (farther than a favourable interview already) I can't tell.

Since almost everyone regarded it as a grave misfortune to remain single, women did not account it a universal grievance that their hands should often be disposed of by others. They were no doubt usually consulted as to their destiny, much or little according to character and circumstance. Swift, in writing 'to a very young lady on her marriage,' speaks of 'the person your father and mother have chosen for your husband,' and almost immediately adds, 'yours was a match of prudence and common good liking, without any mixture of the ridiculous passion' of romantic love. And this description would probably have covered a vast proportion of the 'arranged' marriages of the day. But since the 'ridiculous passion' sometimes asserted itself, runaway matches were common enough, like that of Lady Mary Wortley Montagu. Divorce was almost unknown. It was obtainable only through Church Courts, and then only if followed by a special Act of Parliament ; not more than six divorces were thus legalized during the twelve years of Queen Anne.[44]

Both sexes gambled freely, the fine ladies and gentlemen even more than the country squires. In London, Bath and Tunbridge Wells the gaming-table was the central point of interest, while in the manor house it was of less account than the stables and the kennel. The expenses of gambling and of sport, as well as a noble zeal for building and for laying out gardens and planting avenues, burdened estates with mortgages which proved a heavy clog on agricultural improvement and domestic happiness. Immense sums of money changed hands over cards and dice. As the pious Robert Nelson wrote to his young cousin, ' gaming hath brought footmen into coaches, and has made them walk on foot that before kept them.' Since politics were no less the rage than gambling, there were packs of political playing cards, Whig, Tory and patriotic—' Orange cards containing the happy Revolution in pictures,' Sacheverell cards, and ' Queen Anne cards,' recalling the military and naval glories of her reign. The Dissenters maintained a Puritan disapproval of gambling and even of card-playing as such. In 1711 the Assembly of the General Baptists passed a resolution :

That playing at cards and earnestly contending for the same in Christian families is unbecoming and unlawful for such as profess the Gospel of Christ and unfits them for Church Communion. [45]

Drunkenness was the acknowledged national vice of Englishmen of all classes, though women were seldom accused of it. A movement for total abstinence was out of the question in days before tea or coffee could be obtained in every home. But tracts in favour of temperate drinking were freely circulated by religious bodies and anxious patriots, setting forth with attractive detail the various and dreadful fates of drunkards, some killed attempting to ride home, others seized by a fit while blaspheming, all gone straight to Hell. Among the common folk, ale still reigned supreme ; but ale had a new rival worse than itself in the deadly attraction of bad spirits.   The acme of cheap spirit-drinking was not indeed reached till the reign of George II, in the days of Hogarth's ' gin-lane,' but things were already moving in that direction.

Meanwhile the upper class got drunk sometimes on ale and sometimes on wine.   It is hard to say whether the men of fashion or the rural gentry were the worst soakers.   But perhaps the outdoor exercise taken by the fox-hunting, sporting and farming squire made him better able to absorb his nightly quantum of October, than the gamester and politician of St. James's Square to escape the ill effects of endless Whig toasts in port and Tory toasts in French claret and champagne.   Magistrates often appeared on the bench heated with wine.   The leading physician in the capital, Dr. Radcliffe, whose highly rewarded skill and generous disposition stand commemorated in one of the noblest buildings of his old University, was once sent for at an unseasonable moment to attend the Princess Anne. He blurted out over the bottle that ' Her Highness's distemper was nothing but the vapours.'   This piece of truthfulness in wine, being reported at Court, had, his biographer tells us, the effect of permanently consigning the future queen and her family to other and less skilful hands—possibly with important consequences to the history of England.

Tobacco was still taken in long churchwarden pipes. A ' smoking parlour ' was set aside in some country houses. But Beau Nash forbade smoking in the public rooms at Bath, as disrespectful and unpleasant to ladies.   Among the common people of the south-western counties, men, women and even children smoked pipes of an evening. When in 1707 the Bill for the Security of the Church of England was passing through Parliament, Dr. Bull, the High Church Bishop of St. David's, being suspicious of the Whig proclivities of some of the Bench, kept watch ' sitting in the lobby of the House of Lords, all the while smoking his pipe.'   Swift describes how his brother parsons pull his character to pieces at their favourite resort at Truby's coffee-house,

And pausing o'er a pipe, with doubtful nod
Give hints that poets ne'er believe in God.

The taking of snuff became general in England during
the first year of Anne's reign, as a result of the immense
quantities thrown on to the London market after the capture
of Spanish ships loaded with snuff in the action of Vigo
Bay.[46]

The drinking and gambling habits of society, and the
fierceness of political faction, led to frequent duels of which
many ended ill. The survivor, if he could show there had
been fair play, was usually convicted of manslaughter and
imprisoned for a short term ; or haply ' pleaded his clergy,'
was ' touched with cold iron ' and so set free. It was the
privilege of all gentlemen, from a Duke downwards, to wear
swords and to murder one another by rule. As soon as
men were well drunk of an evening they were apt to quarrel,
and as soon as they quarrelled they were apt to draw their
swords in the room, and, if manslaughter was not committed
on the spot, to adjourn to the garden behind the house, and
fight it out that night with hot blood and unsteady hand.
If the company were not wearing swords, the quarrel might
be slept upon and forgotten in the sober morning. Fortunately the wearing of swords, though usual in London, was
not common in the depth of the country, among the
uncourtly but good-natured rural squires, whose bark was
often worse than their bite. And even at Bath, Beau Nash
employed his despotic power to compel the fashionable
world to lay aside their swords when they entered his
domain : in this he did as good service to the community
as in teaching the country bumpkins to discard their top
boots and coarse language at the evening assemblies and
dances. During his long supremacy as Master of the
Ceremonies, nearly covering the reigns of Anne and the
first two Georges, Nash did perhaps as much as any other
person even in the Eighteenth Century to civilize the
neglected manners of mankind.[47]

London and the county capitals were the commonest
scenes of such duels as Thackeray has immortalized in
Esmond. Even more often than Leicester Fields, the open

country behind Montagu House, the site of the present
British Museum, was selected by duellists as being at that
time on the edge of the new London. It was no unusual
thing for the town to be disturbed by such a double event
as the following :

> Ned Goodyear has killed Beau Feilding as is reported, and made
> his escape. The quarrel began at the Play House in Drury Lane.
> The same night a captain here did the like friendly office for young
> Fullwood, so that there will be two Warwickshire beaus the fewer.
> The captain is in Newgate. [48]

Fox-hunting, like so many other English institutions
under Queen Anne, was beginning to assume features
recognizably modern. In Tudor times the fox had been
dug out of its earth, bagged, and baited like a badger, or
had been massacred as vermin by the peasantry. For in
those days the stag was still the beast of the chase *par
excellence*. But the disorders of the Civil War had broken
open deer-parks and destroyed deer to such an extent that
at the Restoration the fox was perforce substituted in many
districts. In the first decades of the Eighteenth Century
there were no county or regional packs supported by public
subscription, but private gentlemen kept their own packs
and allowed their nearer neighbours to follow. The idea
that gentlemen should hunt ' the stag and the fox with their
own hounds and among their own woods,' was only
gradually yielding to the chase across the country at large,
irrespective of ownership. Already there were fox-hunting
songs, with the chorus :

> Will sometimes follow, will sometimes follow,
> Will sometimes follow the Fox's train.

The year after Queen Anne died, Addison poked fun
at the High Tory Squires under the title of ' foxhunters,'
taking that sport as the badge of all their tribe. But
scarcely less characteristic, though more old-fashioned, was
the chase of the hare, with a ' tunable chiding ' of hounds,
the gentlemen on horseback, and the common folk running,
headed by the huntsman with his pole.

Country pleasures were thus epitomized in a popular song of the time :

> The Country Squire loves running
>   A pack of well-mouth'd hounds ;
> Another fancies gunning
>   For wild ducks in his grounds :
>   This hunts, that fowls,
>   This hawks, that bowls,
> No greater pleasure wishing,
>   But Tom that tells what sport excels
> Gives all the praise to fishing.[49]

Ever since the Restoration, foreigners had admired the English bowling greens ' which are so even, that they bowl upon them as easily as on a great billiard table. And as this is the usual diversion of gentlemen in the country, they have thick rowling-stones to keep the green smooth.' In Anne's reign cricket was just beginning to take its place among village sports alongside of the far more ancient football. Kent was the county most renowned at the new game, and, ' among the Kentish men, the men of Dartford lay claim to the greatest excellence.'[50]

At cockfighting all classes yelled their bets round the little amphitheatre. If a foreigner should by chance come into these cockpits, we are told, ' he would certainly conclude the assembly to be all mad, by their continued outcries of Six to Four, Five to One, repeated with great earnestness, every Spectator taking part with his favourite cock, as if it were a party cause.' Horse-racing presented much the same spectacle in a more open arena. Race meetings were attended by spectators who were most of them on horseback. They were still regional or county gatherings. The only national meeting was at Newmarket. There indeed ' the vast company of horsemen on the plain at a match contains all mankind on equal footing from the Duke to the country peasant. Nobody wears swords, but are clothed suitable to the humour and design of the place for horse sports. Everybody strives to out-jockey (as the phrase is) one another.' The Queen, out of the secret service money, gave plates to be run for at Newmarket, and at Datchet near Windsor. Arab and Barb blood was being introduced by

Godolphin and other noble patrons of the sport—a change fraught with great future consequence to the character and appearance of horse-flesh in England.[51]

Sword-fighting was a coarse popular spectacle, not far removed from the gladiatorial shows of old Rome, save that the wounds inflicted on the platform at an English fair, though disabling, were not intended to be fatal. Hardly more alluring to our modern sensibilities is the notice issued in April 1702 'to all gentlemen, gamesters and others' of a fight between a 'bald-faced dog of Middlesex against a fallow dog of Cow Cross, being a general day of sport by all the old gamesters, and a great mad bull to be turned loose in the game-place with fireworks all over him and two or three cats tied to his tail and dogs after them.' Fighting of parties of men with sticks or fists, and 'women fighting in their shifts' were also popular spectacles. Foreigners waiting for the boat at Harwich saw with amazement two sailors, who had been promised a crown by 'two lords,' strip to their waists and fight with fists till their faces ran with blood, and 'whenever they wanted to give over the spectators tossed them a shilling to keep them to it. This is a common pastime of passengers.' The famous diplomat, Richard Hill, accustomed to less exuberant street scenes abroad, described his countrymen as 'a drunken Gothic nation that loves noise and bloody noses.'[52]

There was a good side to pugilism. The English common folk, below the rank of gentlemen-duellists who must return a stab for a blow, thought shame to revenge their injuries by murder. The quarrels of the common people were settled in England by the fist, not the knife. A story was current of an English sailor in a Chinese port, who, when rudely shoved out of the way at a Mandarin's train in the street, challenged the Mandarin and his officials to box ; the story ends with 'Jack' winning the amused favour of the Mandarin himself by knocking down his champion, a giant Tartar, in fair fight. Such already was the Englishman's idea of himself, and in particular of Jack ashore in foreign parts.[53]

When we try to imagine how the generality of our

ancestors disported themselves out-of-doors, we must remember that most of them lived widely scattered and in the country. For most men the village was the largest unit of their intercourse. A village cricket match, or hurly-burly at football, or races on the green were very different from the ' organized athletics ' of the modern arena. But most people took their ' exercise ' as a matter of course in doing their work, in tilling the soil, or in walking or riding to and from their daily task. Among the upper and middle class riding was the commonest act of the day.

The most usual ' sports ' that lay at many men's doors, were taking fish, and shooting and snaring birds of all kinds, particularly but not exclusively ' game.'* England was alive with game and with many birds now rare or extinct, from the Great Bustard of the Downs and the eagle of Westmorland and Wales down to many smaller friends that survived to be recorded by Bewick. Much of the land was strictly preserved and religiously shot by the owners, but great tracts were open to any man who could procure a net or gun or who was clever at setting a springe. In Anne's reign, and indeed for the rest of the century, as Gunning records, the fens and uncultivated lands round Cambridge were the common playground of the undergraduates, whence they returned with pheasants, partridges, duck, snipe, bitterns and ruffs, with none to say them nay. And in every part of the lovely island the uncared-for heaths, coppices and marshes, destined ere long to be drained, ploughed up or built over, were still the cover for abundance of wild life of every kind. The Englishman had only to move a few yards from his door and he was in contact with nature at its best ; and his love of field-sports led him to wander wide.

* See p. 24, above.

CHAPTER III

The parish clergy. Their status and influence. Queen Anne's Bounty.
High and Low Church. Toleration. Roman Catholics. Dissenters.
Belief in witches declining. Sceptics and anti-clericals. Nonjurors.
The religious and moral revival. Religious Societies and their work:
Charity schools; Reformation of manners; Propagation of the
Gospel.

In the Middle Ages, the economic and social position of the
village clergy had been identified with that of the peasants.
Parish priests took an active part in Wat Tyler's rising
against the proprietary classes, the wealthy monasteries and
the great princes of the Church. The Reformation not
only permitted the clergy to marry, and removed from them
a great weight of unpopularity by abolishing invidious
clerical privileges and powers, but also gradually raised the
social status of the parson. Before the end of the reign of
George III, Jane Austen depicted a society in which the
rural clergy are scarcely to be distinguished from squires in
education, in standing and in desirability as husbands for
young ladies—although even at that time there was a class
of poor parson of whom we hear nothing in those novels of
sheltered life.

In Anne's reign the village clergy stood midway between
the low social position they had occupied in the Middle
Ages and the high social position to which they attained
under the House of Hanover. Just because their status
was on the up-grade, it was equivocal and a subject of
frequent dispute.

As to his Priesthood [says one writer of the period], I see
nothing in that which can intitle him to more than the quality of an
ordinary Gentleman, for that, as I take it, the common courtesy of
England allows him, as well as an Attorny or Licenciat in Physick.

And being only a Gentleman by Profession, he is inferior to him who is a Gentleman by Birth.*

There were indeed many sons of squires in the priesthood. But most of the village clergy were themselves children of the parsonage, or else of the farmhouse. Yeomen with large families often sent one son to the local school to pick up Latin, and thence passed him through the University on the basis of semi-starvation. At Oxford the ' Servitours ' of this class sometimes slept four in a garret, pinched by poverty, and earning their keep by waiting on ' Gentlemen Commoners.' A Servitour's fortune was described in 1704 as consisting of ' the reversion of old shoes which Gentlemen Commoners leave off, two rags called shirts, a dog's-eared grammar and a piece of an *Ovid de Tristibus.*' Such was the rough educational ladder of old times, up which many remarkable men have climbed. The principle of equality among students, which became axiomatic in the Universities of the Nineteenth Century, was then impossible, for it must have excluded either the rich or the poor from Oxford and Cambridge.†

In an age when class distinctions were so universally accepted that not even philosophers called them in question,

---

* From a curious tract of 1700 entitled *Mrs. Abigail, or an account of a female skirmish between the wife of a country squire and the wife of a Doctor in Divinity.* It throws light on the question of the social position of the parsons and their wives.

† A brutal Hudibrastic poem of 1709, ' The Servitour,' describes the ' husbandman's ' son passing through the University on the way to a parsonage :

> ' For he conceived a mighty notion
> Of th'honour t'which he should attain
> By living among gentlemen ;
> Who ne'er before did any know
> Except his landlord 'twas or so.
> He struts, pulls off his cap to no man,
> And to conceal, betrays the ploughman.
> But checked for's insolent behaviour
> And fearing to be out of favour,
> His duty h'as so much regard of,
> He'll cap a master twenty yards off.'

See also C. E. Mallet, *History of Oxford*, III, pp. 66–67. Swift, in the *Education of Ladies*, writes, ' The sons of clergymen bred to learning with any success must, by reason of their parents' poverty be very inconsiderable, many of them being only admitted servitors in colleges, and consequently proving good for nothing.'

the position of such poverty-stricken aspirants to social advancement was equivocal, and left them an easy mark for the ill-natured satire which played so large a part in the politics and literature of the day. To make matters worse, the clerical profession was at that time over-stocked by rival candidates. Sycophancy towards patrons who had livings or private chaplaincies in their gift was only too common in the hungry host, jostling for their shares of an inadequate supply of loaves and fishes. Even the proud-souled Swift, though assuredly no sycophant, was notoriously preoccupied about his own promotion.

flattery

These characteristics of the clerical life of the day were commented upon alike by the friends and the critics of the Church. Addison, who was both at once, held up to censure the conduct of patrons who dismissed their chaplains from table before dessert, and forbade them to touch the jelly. But he represents Sir Roger de Coverley as bound by ties of equal friendship to the parson whom he has appointed to his parish, who 'understood a little backgammon,' and 'was a good scholar tho' he does not show it.' [54]

The private chaplain had, indeed, to suffer whatever indignities were put upon him, if he happened to fall in with inconsiderate employers. But the parson of a parish, once inducted, was a freeholder, and could with impunity defy both bishop and squire, unless he set out on the arduous pursuit of pluralities or of a better living in exchange. Such designs were pardonable when penury was at the door. Gregory King had estimated the average income of 10,000 clergy at £48 in the year of the Revolution ; and a return of the resources of the beneficed clergy of Lincolnshire in the reign of Anne does not lead one to suppose that much improvement had then taken place. Many even of the Rectories were valued at something between £30 and £60 a year. Some livings were not worth £10 a year, and many were so inconsiderable that no one could reside. Plurality, if sometimes an abuse, was more often a necessity, limited by the canonical rule that no one should hold two livings with cure of souls if they were more than thirty miles apart.[55]

Many parishes were tended only by curates. In the

diocese of Worcester a curate's salary was £24 a year, while the Bishop had fifty times as much. Some livings, indeed, were worth £200, like Epworth, the benefice of Samuel Wesley, the remarkable father of yet more famous sons ; and even Samuel Wesley was constantly in debt. In 1703 the Chancellor of Norwich Diocese writes :

> We have but one clergyman laid violent hands upon himself since I came here [two years before], but abundance have broke. Two who made a great show went off together out of this neighbourhood last week. [56]

Although the incomes enjoyed by the clergy represented a much greater purchasing power than the same money today, they were very small, especially when we remember that the parsonage so often contained a crowded nursery and school-room. Bishops' postbags were full of such letters as this—' I have six children all at my own charges, my wife is downlying, I owe £16 and know not how to pay 'em.' [57] The *Dictionary of National Biography* bears witness to many prominent men who were sons of the parsonage, answering to the ' children of the manse ' in Scotland. The duty of begetting and attempting to rear children left little over on which the parson himself could achieve a high and liberal culture in a remote village.

It was to remedy this state of things that Queen Anne instituted her famous Bounty. The ' first-fruits and tenths ' of benefices, originally exacted by the Pope, had, after the Reformation, been annexed by the Crown. Nominally, the incoming clergyman had to pay his whole first year's income and the tenth of every year's income ; but, in fact, the ' first-fruits and tenths,' like so many old English taxes, had become a fixed charge of a much less onerous character, estimated at about £16,000 a year for the whole country. The fund thus derived from the taxation of benefices had been used as a source of privy income by the Crown, not always in the most respectable manner. When Anne came to the throne, a thousand a year was being paid to a nobleman who had bought the interest in the fund enjoyed by Charles II's French mistress, the Duchess of Portsmouth. And a thousand a year was being paid to

Nell Gwynne's royal offspring, the Duke of St. Albans, who had become a Whig and a soldier of William. Burnet, the historian of the Reformation, whose researches had familiarized him with the history of the fund, first raised the question of its proper use. As Whig Bishop of Salisbury, the burly protagonist of Low Church offered a broad target for the abuse and ridicule of his clerical brethren. He repaid them in a manner worthy of a Christian, not only by constantly befriending the poorer clergy of his diocese with zeal exemplary in a bishop, but by urging upon his patron King William that the first-fruits and tenths ought to go to the relief of poor benefices. William's financial straits prevented him from acceding to Burnet's request, though he considered it favourably and though it was supported by Somers. But a few years later Queen Anne was persuaded to act a part worthy of her special love of the Church, at the instance partly of Burnet, partly of her ecclesiastical adviser, the prudent Sharp, the Tory Archbishop of York.

Accordingly, in February 1704 the announcement of Queen Anne's Bounty was made, and an Act of Parliament was passed that year to give it effect. She not only remitted all arrears of first-fruits and tenths to poor clergymen in debt to government on that head, but she made over the fund itself for the increase of inadequate stipends. Owing to bad debts and the existing charges on the fund, little could be paid to the clergy before she died. But by the early part of George II's reign the Governors of Queen Anne's Bounty were in a position to make frequent grants, which were invested to increase the value of poor benefices.[58]

It was also in the reign of Anne that a design was set on foot to circulate books among those provincial clergy who could not otherwise afford to study. The intention was excellent, and High and Low Churchmen worked side by side in this as in other similar movements of that factious but philanthropic age. Unfortunately the effort was made on too small a scale. In 1711 about forty-five towns in England were each receiving from this source a ' library ' of some forty religious books, representing the two prevailing schools of thought in the Church. But the library movement hardly touched the fringe of the rural parishes. In those days the bulky tomes in which learning was buried could not be had cheap, and it is not therefore surprising that the impoverished clergy were less accustomed to read Plato and the Fathers with their feet on the fender than their successors in the golden age of Queen Victoria.[59]

Swift's picture of the 'Country Parson,' wherein the author's natural acidity is tempered by his love of the Church of England, may stand for the portrait of the parish clergyman, if a single picture must serve :

> Parson, these things in thy possessing
> Are better than the bishop's blessing.
> A wife that makes conserves ; a steed
> That carries double when there's need ;
> October store and best Virginia,
> Tythe-pig and mortuary guinea ;
> *Gazettes* sent *gratis* down and franked,
> For which the patron's weekly thanked ;
> A large concordance bound long since ;
> Sermons to Charles the First, when Prince ;
> A chronicle of ancient standing ;
> A *Chrysostom* to smooth thy band in.
> *   *   *   *   *
>
> He that has these, may pass his life,
> Drink with the squire, and kiss his wife ;
> On Sundays preach, and eat his fill ;
> And fast on Fridays—if he will ;
> Toast Church and Queen, explain the news,
> Talk with churchwardens about pews ;
> Pray heartily for some new gift,
> And shake his head at doctor Swift.

Most of Swift's clerical brethren ' shook their heads ' at him over the bold imagery of his *Tale of a Tub*, and not at all in reproof of the ferocity of his onslaughts against Papists, Whigs and Dissenters, in which he hardly surpassed the warmth of the majority of the Lower House of Convocation. Zeal for the cause of the Church of England was then inflamed by two negative passions, anti-Popery and anti-Puritanism. Each was based on bitter experience of the past and consequent fear for the future. The fires of

Smithfield were the most living part of English historical tradition, popularized in Foxe's *Book of Martyrs*, the only book besides the Bible which was equally welcome in the home of the High Churchman and the Dissenter. And these feelings had been revived and strengthened by the recent action of James II in overthrowing the laws of the land in order to re-establish a Roman Catholic despotism in England, and by the renewal of an unprovoked, cruel and wholesale persecution of the Huguenots in France after they had for long years been good and loyal subjects. England was full of the French victims of contemporary Roman Catholic intolerance, and their case was not therefore likely to be forgotten. The supremacy of Louis XIV in Europe, which seemed almost established when Anne ascended the throne, would probably lead to the restoration in England of the Roman Catholic Pretender, whose cause the Grand Monarch had just espoused, standing by the death-bed of James II. In these circumstances, the Church of England, even the distinctively High Church section of it, showed no relenting towards Rome.

But if the events of that generation had renewed the fear of Rome, the events of fifty years back were responsible for an answering fear of Puritanism. The overthrow of the Church and the aristocracy, the beheading of the King, and the rigid rule of the Saints had left a negative impression almost as formidable and permanent as the memory of 'bloody Mary' and James II. The Cavalier and Anglican view of the Great Civil War held the field, even after the Revolution ; the Whigs scoffed at it in private but only occasionally dared to contradict it in public. Animosity against the quiet business men who attended Nonconformist chapels was fostered on the ground that they were one and all 'fanatics,' about to draw the sword and again destroy the Church ; such fears scarcely derived from close observation of contemporary facts, but were the result of historical memories, constantly kept alive in the parish pulpit, in Tory pamphlets, and in the talk of men. The Dissenters might seem humble and harmless burghers, but they were in alliance with the powerful and dangerous Whig lords, and unless they were kept low *'forty-one would come again.* Such was the belief. And the memory of Cromwell was scarcely more productive of bitter fears for the future than was the actual presence beyond the Cheviots of the Presbyterian Church of Scotland, established and intolerant.

The Low Churchmen, on the other hand, regarded the danger to the Church of England from Rome and France as real, and the danger from Dissent and Scotland as imaginary. The Bishops appointed by William since the Revolution, and the majority of the highly educated clergy of the capital, were Low Churchmen. When, therefore, Anne ascended the throne, the Upper House of Convocation was Low Church and the Lower House was High Church, and there was little love lost between them. Addison's Tory Fox-hunter remarks, ' There is scarce a Presbyterian in the whole county except the Bishop.' And the Whigs replied by taunting the High Church clergy with being themselves Presbyterians, since they were always defying the episcopal authority. The bitterness of invective in these contro-versies, as in most controversy in old times, is astonishing to modern students of long-forgotten pamphlets. Sacheverell, the leading High Church champion of the day, accuses the Low Churchmen as a body, including half the most highly respectable Bishops, of immoral lives and unmentionable vices, on no ground at all save his own party animus.* Such methods of debate caused less astonishment then than now. Yet even then such wrath among souls celestial helped to diminish the influence of the clergy, and to enhance that of ' scoffers and deists.'

The Low Church party desired friendship with the Dissenters in England and with the Protestant Churches abroad, in the common struggle against France and Rome. But the High Churchmen, though ready to maintain the contest for national independence, wished to do so without seeking the friendship of Dissenters and Scots at home or of Dutch and other allies abroad. And therefore Marlborough, though still a Tory in 1702, was to find by experience that the vast combinations of his European war policy could only be carried through by a breach with

* *Character of the Low Churchman,* 1702, pp. 17-18. This amazing piece of Billingsgate is repeated in the second edition, 1706, p. 11.

the High Church statesmen and an ever-increasing dependence first on the moderate Tories and finally on the Whigs.

Sacheverell himself thus defines the characteristics of the High Churchman :

> He is High for the divine right of Episcopacy, High for the uninterrupted Succession, High for the Liturgies against extemporary Prayers, High for the primitive Doctrine and Discipline of the Ancient Church. He much laments the destruction of the Episcopal Church in Scotland, and should be for addressing Her Majesty to restore it. He believes separation from the Church of England to be a damning Schism, and the Dissenters to be in a very dangerous state, notwithstanding the toleration. . . . He is so High as to observe the traditional customs as well as the written laws of the Church, and he always bowed very low before the Altar and at the name of Jesus.[60]

But there was no approach towards Rome, and no tendency to ritualistic innovation. Except among some Nonjurors like Robert Nelson, High Church Eucharistic doctrine and practice went little further than the attempt to make attendance at Communion weekly, an attempt in which many Low Churchmen joined with them in the work of the Religious Societies. The more usual custom in cities was for the clergy to celebrate monthly, and in rural parishes between three and seven times a year.[61]

In the dread of a return to Papal or to Puritan rule, the Church had the passions of common Englishmen on her side. All through the reign of Anne, and long afterwards, it was easy to raise a mob to burn either Catholic or Dissenting chapels. But these passions were, in the common Englishman, not the outcome of High Church doctrine but of anti-clerical instinct. The Church of England was liked because she did not attempt to interfere with life as Papist and Puritan in their different ways interfered. But when the High Churchman made clerical claims of his own over the laity, he at once aroused the same impatient temper as had destroyed successively the power of Rome, the power of Laud and the power of the Puritans. The history of England can never be understood unless we realize the presence of another force at work besides the rival religions, the unorganized but very real passion of anti-clericalism. This passion, at the service of the Church against Papist and Puritan, was at the service of the Whigs against the pretensions of the 'high-flying' clergy, when they clamoured for the suppression of unorthodox opinions and the reinforcement of Church discipline over the laity.

Antagonism to the Church no longer took the form of a militant Puritanism demanding 'a godly thorough Reformation,' as in the days of Pym and Cromwell ; the Dissenters would have been only too thankful to be sure of the undisturbed enjoyment of the Toleration Act and of the schools they had founded to educate their own children, without again provoking persecution by another attempt to capture the Establishment. The anti-Church feeling that gave most vigour to the Whig party in the days of Somers and Wharton was of a different order from Cromwell's. It was the nascent latitudinarianism of the new century, a feeling against 'priestcraft' in all its forms which already appeared in not a few pamphlets and in common talk. Two centuries of rival religious persecutions, Catholic and Protestant, Puritan and Anglican, ending in the anti-Roman revolution of 1688, had aroused in England a movement of resistance to clerical claims of all sorts, destined to pass in a more virulent form to the Continent, when the bankruptcy of Louis XIV's persecuting policy had become fully apparent over there. The day of Voltaire was yet to come, but in England under William and Anne the attitude of open disrespect for the clergy already alarmed the High Church party, especially in connection with the 'Socinian' and 'Deistic' philosophy of the 'Freethinkers.' * The cry was raised for fresh laws to keep Dissenters in due subordination, and for State action against impiety and abuse of the clergy. Clerical writers complained that the word 'parson' was used in many companies as a word of contempt, and that young lawyers called them 'black locusts.' Bishop Trelawny wrote in 1703 that ' in Westminster Hall, Atheism, Socinianism and perfect detestation

* The word ' freethinker ' came in at this time. 'Atheist is an old-fashioned word, I'm a Freethinker, child.' Addison, *The Drummer*, Act 1.

of the principles and government of the Universities is allowed and justified.'

Yet it may be questioned whether the Universities were not themselves at the bottom of the trouble. Collins, Toland and the professed deists made the noise, but did not carry the weight ; more profoundly and ultimately influential was the system of exact reasoning conducted by such giants as Barrow, Newton, Locke and Bentley, and the work of the Royal Society, in place of the mere learning and oratory of the academic world before the Restoration. These greater men sometimes descended into the field against the ' Deists,' but they were themselves laying the foundations of the larger reasonableness and latitudinarianism of the Eighteenth Century.

The avowedly anti-clerical writers, while showering abuse on ' priestcraft,' were careful to confine their philosophic arguments within bounds. They eschewed the ' atheism ' of which they were accused, but claimed that reason must be the arbiter of all doctrines ; and while they tended by implication to efface the supernatural, they retained the divine element in religion. There was nothing of Bradlaugh in Toland, Collins and young Lord Shaftesbury under Anne, or in Bolingbroke and Pope in the following reigns. They suffered therefore nothing worse than a certain measure of social obloquy and a shower of enraged pamphlets, and even these penalties were only dealt out to those of them who were both Whigs and commoners.[62]

For, in spite of the outcries of the Lower House of Convocation, times were not propitious in England for persecution. The Church was rent by her own political divisions, and her official representatives belonged to the party that favoured toleration. And most Englishmen, though they derived their political opinions chiefly from their dislike of other people's religions, were heartily tired of persecution in practice. The harsh enforcement of the Clarendon Code in the reign of Charles II had made life uncomfortable for everyone, and had admittedly been very bad for business. Moreover in 1702 a united front for the war against France was desired on patriotic grounds by many strong High Churchmen, like the famous Tory pamphleteer Davenant, and Queen Anne herself.   The Whig aristocracy protected the free expression of opinion, whether Puritan or Deistic.   The Puritans were only too glad to make common cause with the Rationalists, to render Toleration secure.   Some of the Tory leaders, like St. John, the future Bolingbroke, were as pronounced freethinkers as Collins himself, and were moreover libertines desirous of anything rather than the revival of the authority of the Church Courts over morals.   The poems of Ned Ward, the popular Tory poet, though full of hearty abuse of Papists and Dissenters, are also full of ribaldry, libertinage and something very like scoffing at religion.   The High Church clergy, who for a short while believed that the accession of Anne meant a return to the age of Laud, raised a cry for the revival of a compulsory penance and the ' primitive discipline of the Church,' but such pretensions, though actively enforced by the clerical democracy of Scotland, were in England a long-lost cause.*

The Press, too, had entirely escaped from ecclesiastical control.   The censorship had never been renewed since its lapse in 1695 ; anyone therefore could print what he liked,

* E.g. *The Church of England's Wish for the Restoring of Primitive Discipline,* 1703.
    It is remarkable that in 1705 the Chancellor of Worcester Diocese pronounced sentence in the Bishop's Court on a Baronet for incontinency, condemning him to appear in a white sheet in the cathedral during service on a stated day.   Whether the sentence was carried out does not appear.   Diary *Francis Evans,* p. xvii.   Such discipline, common in Scotland, was very rare in England in Anne's reign.   In answer to the Bishop's question, ' Have any public penances been performed since my last visitation ? ' almost every parson in Bucks replied, ' None,' except in a case which was to defend a woman's character from slander, not to punish immorality. In Lincolnshire there were some half dozen penances done for the whole county. But in some rural districts the authority of the Church Courts over sin died rather more slowly.   In country parishes of Oxfordshire the Churchwardens still occasionally fulfilled their increasingly unpopular duty of ' presenting ' neighbours for incontinence or the ' fame ' of it, before the Church Courts.   Public penance was in such case generally ordered, but seldom enforced ; it was occasionally commuted for money, more often neglected.   Occasionally persons were excommunicated for this, or for refusing to pay Church rates or other dues.   But excommunication in Anne's reign meant nothing more than exclusion from the rites of the Church which the sinner probably and the Dissenter certainly had no wish in the world to attend.   In the Isle of Man penance was done in Church in a white sheet as late as the reign of William IV (see A. G. Bradley, *Our Centenarian Grandfather,* pp. 162–163).   *Wake MSS., Misc.* 5 and 11, *Epist.* 5 ; *Lambeth MSS.* 1115 ;   S. A. Peyton's *Oxfordshire Peculiars* (1928, Oxf. Record Soc.), pp. lxx–lxxv and *passim.*

subject to such proceedings as might afterwards be taken against him in Parliament or in a court of law for sedition, libel or blasphemy. The Toleration Act, though strictly limited in scope by its text, had in practice been extended to persons outside its actual provisions, like Unitarians and Papists, and had created an atmosphere antipathetic to the persecution even of highly unpopular opinion. England had moved far since the days of Elizabeth, when Unitarians had been burnt at the stake.

The Roman Catholic body benefited by this change of atmosphere. During a war with France on behalf of the Protestant Succession, English Roman Catholics, who could scarcely fail to be Jacobites at heart, might have been expected to suffer something analogous to the cruelties inflicted on the French Huguenots. But nothing of the sort occurred. Roman services, so long as they were conducted with some degree of privacy, were not interfered with at all. At St. Winifred's shrine there was a continual come and go of pilgrims, catered for by a whole regiment of priests in thin disguise, which the Protestants of the neighbourhood understood and respected. In every county in England, Roman Catholic nobles or gentlemen kept priests whose presence was neither obtruded on public notice nor enquired into by the authorities. They ministered to small congregations centring round the manor house. The Whig Duke of Devonshire, who had suffered under James II and was ' a steady opposer of Popery and the French power,' lived on excellent terms with the Roman Catholic gentlemen in the neighbourhood of Chatsworth, ' and remembered his Master King William saying that he came over to defend the Protestants and not to persecute the Papists.'
    In the Eighteenth Century, Roman Catholicism was an aristocratic but unfashionable faith. It declined because it dared make no public propaganda in face of the laws and in face of a hostile public opinion. It was weakest in the towns, except in so far as the immigration of Irish poor into certain slum districts was beginning. The Roman Catholics were strong only in Lancashire, and there alone were they accused of making open propaganda. They

made a certain show also among the landowners in North-umberland, Durham, Yorkshire and the English counties of the Welsh border. In Wales itself they were negligible. And in the typical midland and southern shires they were few and far between. Enquiries frequently made throughout the reign were answered in parish after parish by the parson's assurance that there was ' No Papist,' and occasionally by the addendum ' Nor, God be thanked, no Dissenter.' [63]

To judge of the treatment of Roman Catholics merely by reading the Statute Book would lead to error. For in England the only part of the harsh laws against them which was actually enforced was the laws excluding them, as the Protestant Dissenters also were excluded, from civil office, and a further law which subjected Roman Catholics to pay double land tax. ' Only these two laws are put in practice,' wrote Cardinal Paolucci's secret agent in the year 1710. ' As regards the exercise of their religion they enjoy it entirely free.' Such was the Roman Catholic official account of the position in England under Anne. But the same agent made a very different report as to the treatment of his co-religionists in Ireland.*

The Protestant Dissenters, other than the Unitarians, had obtained, under the provisions of the Toleration Act of 1689, the privilege of public worship in their own Meeting Houses. Except for occasional attacks by incendiary mobs in time of political excitement, this open public worship was everywhere enjoyed throughout the reign of Anne by the congregations of licensed Dissenting ministers. But unlicensed preachers were still liable, like Daniel

---

* *P.R.O. Transcripts*, 9, *Rome*, 101. The report (which is in Italian) adds : ' There is no person of distinction who cannot if he so desires keep a chaplain, whether in town or in his country seat, without the government making any enquiry.' Like many foreign reports of the day, it calls the Tories ' Anglicani ' and the Whigs ' Presbiteriani.' *H.M.C. Portland*, iv. pp. 86–87, gives typical instances of the non-enforcement of the laws purporting to prevent Papists from owning arms and good horses and travelling freely about England. Even at the crisis of the war (1704) they rode what they liked, where they liked, armed as they liked. But after the rising of the Catholic squires of Northumberland in 1715, priests and their congregations were persecuted for awhile in the Northern Counties, see *E.H.R.*, July 1929.

Skingle at Hitchin, to be haled into the Spiritual Court and forced to desist and to ask pardon. Few country villages had a Meeting House, but few market towns were without one or more.

The three principal Nonconformist bodies were Baptist, Presbyterian and Quaker. It is uncertain which was the most numerous in the country as a whole. The Quakers had begun to decline in numbers and propagandist zeal, after the revivalist ardours of George Fox and his immediate disciples, which had swept over the common people of England in the days of Cromwell and of the second Charles. Toleration had not caused them to increase. But there were still, even in remote hamlets, many more Quakers than in later times. Denunciations of Quaker blasphemy and misbelief were still an important part of Church literature. In some towns the wealthy and educated Dissenters were beginning that drift towards Unitarianism which became a marked feature of English as distinct from Scottish Presbyterianism.

According to Davenant, Nonconformity in Anne's reign was strong among seafaring men, among "lower trades-men and artificers, manufacturers and day labourers." In some rural districts, like Bucks and Devon, the Dissenters were much stronger than in others. All over the country they were stronger in the market towns than in the villages, in the cities stronger still, and in London they were strongest of all.[64] In 1711 a House of Commons Committee reported that English Dissenters and French Huguenots together made up a fifth of the half-million inhabitants of the London suburbs, exclusive of the City, and that they had built themselves 88 chapels;[65] the remaining 400,000 potential Churchmen of the suburbs had only 28 parish churches among them. At the end of William's reign a Lord Mayor of London had been so indiscreet as to attend his Nonconformist Meeting House with the official insignia of the City. This had aroused a storm of indignation and a cry of 'Church in Danger,' to which the accession of a Tory Queen gave fresh encouragement. The violence of the language commonly used in attacks on Dissenters is the violence common in the mouth of dominant parties ; the replies of the Puritans were of a milder strain, very different from the intolerant tone of the days of their prosperity fifty years back.[66]

In some districts, however, the relations of Churchmen and Dissenters were more kindly than the controversial literature of the time might lead one to suppose. In the Yorkshire dales, where Nonconformity was strong, there was much good feeling; and in some parishes, even in the south, there were religious folk who attended both Church and Chapel.[67]

In one respect the progress of science and scepticism had already won an important battle for humanity. The persecution of supposed witches had reached its height under the Puritan Commonwealth. It had since been declining, most rapidly among the educated class. The reign of Anne saw the real end of witch trials. Judges and country magistrates refused to convict old women of compacts with the Devil, on the evidence of their neighbours' prejudiced imaginings, or even of their own frantic confessions. This marked a great advance of common kindliness and good sense over primæval cruelty and superstition. It was a victory of reason imposed by an educated aristocracy on a rural population that still retained its old belief in witches, but was in no position to assert it against the will of its ' betters.'

The decline in convictions for witchcraft was also one sign among many others that the scientific laws of evidence were better understood by bench and bar. Courts of Justice were beginning to weigh the value of testimony, and to trust less to the oath of informers and prejudiced or ignorant persons than in the days of Titus Oates and all previous ages, when every oath was an oath and weighed so much in the judicial balance.

In 1702 a rascal named Richard Hathaway was convicted at the Surrey Assizes for falsely accusing an old woman as a witch on the evidence of pins which he spat out of his mouth and declared that she had placed in his belly. In 1712 took place the last case of a conviction for witchcraft in England. In that famous case, the jury, indeed, found Jane Wenham guilty of witchcraft, but the judge, Sir John Powell, who had lightly remarked when she was accused of flying that there was no law against flying, respited her and she obtained a pardon.   Her case attracted general attention and became the subject of a warfare of pamphlets.   Some Church clergy took the field against the accused and attacked the judge, but the majority of the upper class could not feel sure that, because some sheep had died in fits, the farmers were necessarily right in saying that Jane had bewitched them.   Others pointed out that, even if several cats had been seen going about the village each with Jane Wenham's face, the Devil might have been malicious enough to manage the affair without her connivance.   Some bold spirits avowed their disbelief in the possibility of any such phenomena, Scripture texts notwithstanding.   These were the minority.   But witch-trials in England were drawing to an end.   In 1736 the law punishing witchcraft by death was repealed.[68]

Similarly the upper class in this more sceptical generation were beginning to be annoyed when they were compelled, by the fears of their servants, to shut up half the rooms in an old manor house as ' haunted.'   Stage comedies about sham ghosts indicated, not indeed entire materialism, but a new readiness to look supernatural stories in the mouth.   The atmosphere of the capital was peculiarly inimical to old rustic romance.

I have known many a country lady come to London [says a character in Addison's *Drummer*], with frightful stories of the hall-house being haunted, of fairies, spirits and witches ; that by the time she had seen a comedy, played at an Assembly, and ambled in a Ball or two, has been so little afraid of bugbears, that she has ventured home in a chair at all hours of the night.[69]

But only a small proportion of the villagers of either sex ever visited town.   Most people remained all their lives under the influence of Pan and his magic.   The mental food of English children was just such cottage fire-side tales of ' the hall-house being haunted, of fairies, spirits and witches,' perhaps only half believed but pleasantly shuddered at. Now that the witch could be pointed out but no longer hanged or ducked, such earth-born legendary lore was no unwholesome fare.   The fairies still danced in the woods, though when the wayfarer came round the bush they had always vanished.   Books in the village were few.   The ordinary farmer and cottager saw no printed matter of any kind except Bible, Prayer Book and

> The ballads pasted on the wall,
> Of Joan of France and English Moll,
> Fair Rosamund, and Robin Hood,
> And the Little Children in the Wood.

And therefore, even at the end of the ' Century of reason ' and of artificial poetry among the governing class, the faculty of wonder was not dead in the English people. Wordsworth attributed the growth of imagination in his own mind partly to the fairy tales and ballads of the rustic North that he heard in childhood, in contrast to the rationalism of the Nineteenth Century schoolroom.[70]

No city-made newspapers or magazines stamped a uniform mentality on the nation.   At the beginning of Anne's reign villagers seldom saw a printed newspaper, but depended for their news on gossip or on the ' news-letters ' written to the squire by his correspondents in town. Partly for this reason it was easy for gentry and clergy to mould the political opinions of the village.

In this isolation from the world at large, each shire, each hamlet had its own traditions, interests and character. Except for some unusual event like the Battle of Blenheim or the trial of Dr. Sacheverell, country folk had little to think or talk about except their own affairs.   Their shrewd rustic comment on things they knew and understood was expressed in the pithy dialect of their own countryside. For gossip and sensation they were satisfied with the daily human drama of their own village, with its poaching affrays and smuggling adventures, its feuds and loves and suicides, its quarrels of miller and innkeeper, of parson and squire.

In his dislike of Papists, Dissenters and Deists, of Whig Bishops and Dutch allies, Swift was at one with his high-flying brethren, and has become their mouth-piece for

all time.   But, as an Irish Protestant, he was not wholly
typical of the English High Churchman.   He was more of
a Williamite, and continued to the end more whole-heartedly
hostile to the Pretender than many of his English Tory
allies ; it is not in the writings of Swift that we must seek
the uneasy and hesitating attitude of the average High
Churchman towards the questions of non-resistance, divine
hereditary right, the Revolution and the Hanoverian
Succession.

In defence of the Church of England against the direct
assault of James II, the High Church laity had taken as
leading a part in the Revolution of 1688 as any other
section of the community.*   In the following year, the
Toleration Act had been granted with their full and free
consent, in payment for the Dissenters' support of the
Church against James.   In 1701 the Tories in Parliament
had taken the lead in passing the Act of Settlement, fixing
the reversion of the Crown after Anne's death on the House
of Hanover, to the exclusion of James II's Catholic son.
Nevertheless, many High Churchmen still found it hard to
accept the consequences of their own successful act of
rebellion.   They feared the growth of Dissent under the
Toleration Act.   They could not stomach being called
rebels and resisters of the Divine Right of Kings, for they
had themselves made non-resistance and Divine Hereditary
Right the shibboleth of good Churchmanship under
Charles II.   The inhuman doctrine that non-resistance was
the subject's duty under every royal provocation had indeed
broken down in practice, but it had not yet expired in
theory.   Because they were men, the Tories had resisted
James ; because they were men, they afterwards tried to
deny their own inconsistency, to explain away their own
action and to avoid its logical results.   In Anne's reign
some Tory writers refused to admit that their beloved
Queen reigned ' on a Revolution foot.'   But they hardly

* According to Swift, the Revolution was ' wholly brought about by Church
of England hands,' against the Dissenters (*Examiner*, No. 37).   This is a partisan
travesty of the facts, but it is no more untrue than the opposite assertion, that
the Revolution was the work of the ' Whig aristocracy ' against the Tories !   It is
impossible to say whether Whigs or Tories, Churchmen or Dissenters were foremost in the rebellion that brought William of Orange from Torbay to London.

knew what to say about her exiled brother, who would certainly be King if the Revolution had not happened. Many Tories continued to salve their consciences by regarding the Pretender's birth as doubtful, while the Whigs had no longer any use for the warming-pan and rejoiced to think that an Act of Parliament could exclude a Prince otherwise legitimate.[71] So anxious were the Tories to avoid the plain fact that they had been rebels in 1688, that they often argued that there had been no ' resistance ' in the Revolution itself ! *

The divided and uneasy attitude of many Churchmen towards the Revolution and towards the Dynastic question which the Revolution had created, was the source of fundamental weakness in the Tory party, otherwise the strongest in the State. These difficulties were greatly increased by the action of the Nonjurors, or consistently Jacobite clergy. Five out of the Seven Bishops whom James had prosecuted in the famous trial, refused to take the oaths to William, on the ground that Parliament could not change the divine right of hereditary succession. One of them, Lake of Chichester, declared on his death-bed that the ' religion of the Church of England taught me the doctrine of Non-resistance and Passive Obedience, which I took to be the distinguishing character of the Church of England.'[72] The nonjuring Bishops were followed in their refusal to take the oaths by about four hundred other clergy. They were all, in due course of law, extruded from their sees and benefices. The deprivation of Bishops by Act of Parliament they regarded as of no effect, and therefore formed themselves into a small rival Church of England, strong beyond its numbers in piety and learning, though hardly in common sense. They treated the great body of their clerical brethren as schismatics, and even had a form of absolution for admitting a ' penitent ' from the false Church of England to their own more select communion.[73]

The sees of the Nonjuror Bishops, including Canterbury vacated by Sancroft, were filled up in William's reign by

---

* *The Best Answer*, by a student at The temple, 1708, p. 8. In regard to the High Church and Tory attitude I refer the reader particularly to Mr. Keith Feiling's *History of the Tory Party, 1640–1714.*

Low Churchmen, or as we should now call them Broad Churchmen—the only unhesitating clerical supporters of the new regime. The appointment of men of this school of thought was a necessity to the State struggling for life against domestic and foreign foes, but it was naturally resented by the High Church party, which included the majority of the parish priests. The continuance of the Nonjuror Schism throughout the reign of Anne deprived the High Church clergy of the leadership of many of the ablest, most sincere and learned members of their party. As party-leader Sacheverell was a poor substitute for Sancroft and Ken, especially as Sacheverell by his own showing ought to have been a Nonjuror. Meanwhile the Bench was crowded with able and learned Low Church Bishops like Tenison and Burnet, as the official fathers of the Church. A High Church party is more formidable when led by its Bishops, as in the days of the two Kings Charles, than when led against its Bishops, like Convocation in the reigns of William and Anne.

The immortal part of the Nonjurors' protest, which had far-reaching effects on Anglican thought at the time of the Oxford movement, was their insistence on the spiritual independence of the Church of England as a self-contained body, not a mere appanage of the State. The removal of the Nonjuring Bishops by the State for political reasons they regarded as a proof that the Church was in chains. But their claim for ecclesiastical independence was couched in a form which would have meant clerical domination in England. The Nonjurors did not claim the separation of the Church from the State, but the submission of the State to the Church : because the Church had once believed in the Divine Hereditary Right of Kings, England, they claimed, was for all time to be an absolute monarchy, subject to a Roman Catholic Prince : even in politics the will of the people of England was to be overruled by the clergy. The Nonjurors claimed self-government for the Church, meaning the clergy alone ; for the laity had at that date no voice in the government of the Church of England, except in so far as they were represented by the supremacy of the Crown in Parliament : therefore an established

Church uncontrolled by the State would have meant an uncontrolled clergy, dictating to the laity alike on matters spiritual and political.

The deprived Jacobite clergy stood on the flank of the body which they had left, stirring the uneasy consciences of the beneficed High Churchmen. The latter had no wish to be mere time-servers like the Vicar of Bray. But they heard themselves called so by indignant Nonjurors on one side and by the irreverent multitude on the other.[74] The death of James II, followed shortly by the accession of his Anglican daughter Anne in place of William, eased the situation a little for the High Church conscience, and even brought back a few Nonjurors to the national fold. But, partly owing to the stricter terms of a new oath abjuring the Pretender,* the relief was but partial. The end of the Queen's reign was to see the Church of England and therewith the Tory party split from top to bottom on the dynastic question, when the time for nuances and reserves drew to an end, and the actual choice became imminent between Restoration of the House of Stuart or Accession of the House of Hanover.

When the highest questions of Church and State were thus inseparable, the boundary between religion and politics could neither be defined nor observed. It was a common saying, doubtless greatly exaggerated, that more was heard in the parish pulpit of Charles the Martyr than of Jesus Christ. Nevertheless the reigns of William and Anne were a period of purely religious activity and revival, which left a permanent mark on the life of the country, and sowed the seed of great developments in the future. An age to which we owe the Charity Schools and the Society for Promoting Christian Knowledge was not wholly absorbed in the rancorous political feuds of High and Low Church. In some of these better activities, members of the two Church parties co-operated with each other and with the Dissenters, and were greatly helped by Robert Nelson, the lay Nonjuror, a man in whom the instinct to lend a hand to

* See p. 159, below.

F

every good cause worked more powerfully than the exclusive and scholastic spirit of his sect.

The religious revival had its origin in the brief and stormy reign of James II.   That King, having watched the conduct of English public men throughout the reign of his brother Charles, had drawn the conclusion that there was no religious conviction or moral feeling in England sufficient to resist the force of royal displeasure and royal favour, if steadily exercised, to make men change their religion.   The challenge was an insult to the nation, perhaps not wholly undeserved.   But it aroused a memorable response.   It was not the treachery or intrigue of individuals that drove James from the throne, but the moral rally of a whole people.   The Tory pamphleteer Davenant, in the early years of Anne, thus recalled how those times had stirred men's souls :

> The measures King James the Second took to change the religion of the country, roused up fresh zeal in the minds of all sorts of men ; they embraced more straitly what they were in fear to lose. Courtiers did thrust themselves into the presence to quit their offices, rather than be brought to do what might prejudice the Church of England.   Nor had the licentious ways of living in fleets and armies shaken our seamen and soldiers in their principles.   They all stood firm.   The clergy showed themselves prepared to die with their flocks and managed the controversial parts of Divinity with primitive courage and admirable learning.   The Churches were everywhere crowded, and the prospect of persecution, though peradventure at some distance, begot devotion.[75]

The symptoms of this moral and religious revival did not wholly subside with the crisis that gave it birth.   In the first instance it gave an immense impetus to the work of the already existing Religious Societies inside the Church of England.   These Societies were groups of ' serious young men,' who came together, usually under the influence of some active clergyman, to strengthen each other in religious life and practice.   The original idea of John Wesley, many years later, was merely to form such ' societies ' within the Church as those which that zealous Churchman his father had helped and defended in the reigns of William and Anne. The first object of these groups was to promote a religious life in individuals and families, to encourage church attendance, family prayers and Bible study. But more public activities soon grew out of the impulse thus given. Of these activities some were carried on in rivalry to the Dissenters, others with their co-operation.[76]

The Dissenters, who were excluded from both the Universities by law, and from many schools either by law or by custom, had started all over the country a number of excellent schools and academies of their own, covering the whole field of primary, secondary and higher education. These caused much jealousy, and at the end of Anne's reign the High Churchmen at last succeeded in passing the Schism Act to suppress them—an act of persecution quickly repealed under George I. But the Church also reacted to the challenge of the Nonconformist schools in a more generous fashion. In the reign of Anne, Charity Schools were founded by hundreds all over England, to educate the children of the poor in reading, writing, moral discipline, and the principles of the Church of England. They were much needed, for the State did nothing for the education of the poor, and the ordinary parish had no sort of endowed school, though in many villages 'dames' and other unofficial persons taught rustics their letters in return for fees; here and there an endowed Grammar School gave secondary education to the middle class.[77]

The able men at the head of the Charity School movement introduced the principle of democratic co-operation into the field of educational endowment. They did not depend merely on the support of a few wealthy founders. The policy at headquarters was to excite the local interest of a parish in the setting up of a school. Small shopkeepers and artisans were induced to subscribe and to collect subscriptions, and were taught to take a personal interest in the success, and a personal part in the control of the school for which they helped yearly to pay. The principle of 'joint stock enterprise' was being applied to many sides of life in that era, among others to the cause of philanthropy and education. By the end of Anne's reign there were 5000 or more boys and girls attending the new Charity Schools in the London area, and some 20,000 in the rest of England. The movement was already being taken up in Scotland by the General Assembly. Essential parts of the scheme were to clothe the children decently while at school, and to apprentice them to good trades afterwards. In 1708 a 'poor boy' could be clothed at nine shillings and twopence, and a 'poor girl' at ten shillings and threepence in one of the London schools.[78]

Another characteristic organization of this period was 'The Society for the Reformation of Manners.' In its open ranks Churchmen and Dissenters co-operated against the licence of the age. Scores of thousands of tracts were issued against drunkenness, swearing, public indecency and Sunday trading. We know not what success attended the *Kind cautions against swearing* distributed among the hackney coachmen of London, and the similar *Kind cautions to watermen* distributed among the West Country bargees. More effective, perhaps, were the innumerable prosecutions instituted. Magistrates were shamed into enforcing laws which had become obsolete. These activities aroused furious opposition. Some of the High Churchmen, like Sacheverell, clamoured for the 'ancient discipline of the Church' to suppress vice, immorality, heresy and schism, instead of this new-fangled Society for the Reformation of Manners in which laymen and even Dissenters were allowed to take a part. Some prudent Bishops like Sharp, and Judges like Holt, feared that organized delation would lead to ill-feeling, corruption and blackmail. Many magistrates positively refused to receive the evidence of the philanthropic informers. The mob in some places was dangerous, and at least one active member of the Society was murdered outright.

Nevertheless there were tens of thousands of successful prosecutions. It was said that no one but a person of quality could safely swear in a public place. There was, indeed, a strong body of opinion that supported these proceedings. Many quiet citizens had found the magistrates, ever since the Restoration, scandalously lax in restraining drunkards from annoying the sober, in protecting women from insult, and in preserving any show of decency

and order.   Nor was Sunday trading really desired by the
bulk of the community.   The Mayor of Deal, a courageous
and energetic man, undertook single-handed a crusade
against the behaviour of the town, carried most of his points
and was re-elected Mayor in 1708.   It is indeed probable
that many of the prosecutions, especially for swearing and
for travelling on Sunday, were vexatious, and the time
came under the Georges when the Society was doing as
much harm as good, and could disappear.   But its activities
in the reign of Anne helped to make the streets and taverns
less unpleasant for decent people, to reduce drunkenness
and to secure Sunday as a day of rest from business and
labour.

The more gloomy side of the English Sunday struck
a German visitor in 1710:

> In the afternoon to St. James's Park, to see the crowds.   No
> other diversion is allowed on Sunday, which is nowhere more strictly
> kept ; not only is all play forbidden, and public-houses closed, but
> few even of the boats and hackney coaches may ply.   Our hostess
> would not even allow the strangers to play the *viol di Gamba* or the
> flute, lest she should be punished.

He added, rather sourly, that Sunday observance was
the only visible sign that the English were Christians
at all.[79]

But the most important and lasting impression of the
religious revival was made by the Society for Promoting
Christian Knowledge, and its offshoot, the Society for
the Propagation of the Gospel in Foreign Parts.   The
self-same men were the supporters of both, above all the
indefatigable Dr. Thomas Bray.   The same spirit as afterwards characterized the societies that abolished the Slave
Trade and Slavery, inspired these voluntary societies of
evangelists, lay and clerical, High and Low Church, Nonjuror and Nonconformist.   The last years of William's
reign and the first of Anne's saw them fully at work.   The
diffusion of Bibles and of other religious literature was their
chief object.   They were therefore great advocates of
the Charity Schools where the poor could be taught to
read them; the two movements went side by side.   The
Society's publications were welcomed by Marlborough in

the army, and by Benbow and Rooke in the fleet. Cheap Bibles and Prayer Books were furnished in the country districts. And a supply of Bibles and other books to America was begun on a large scale, and to the rest of the world on a scale, modest indeed as compared to the gigantic work of the Society in later years, but ever growing with the growing power and wealth of England oversea. These activities betokened an instinctive movement of the English religious world to get away, on one side at least, from the denominational and political feuds in which it was entangled, into a field of broader vision, where zeal might produce something better than hate.

In the reign of Anne, as also long before and long after, religious differences were the motive force behind political passions. It is doubly impossible, therefore, for the English historian to ignore religion, if he would explain other phenomena. But he must not be tempted to forget that there was more in the religious sense of the nation than the feuds out of which, incidentally, our political liberties in large part arose. The religious life of many quiet parishes and humble families moved on its way, little concerned with partisanship of High and Low Church; English religion was, in the main, a free and healthy function of that old-world life, nicely guiding itself between superstition and fanaticism on the one side and material barbarism on the other.

The movement towards philanthropy instead of persecution, as an outlet for religious enthusiasm, was one of the characteristic fruits of the Revolution, as also was the improvement in public justice, both political and criminal. Because the Revolution Settlement was not a party victory, but an agreed compromise between Whig and Tory, Church and Dissent, it made humanity, moderation and co-operation the main current of affairs in the Eighteenth Century. The stabilizing and securing of these gains, in the face of violent counsels urging a return to former methods, was not yet certain when Anne came to the throne; but she herself and her chosen servant, Marlborough, stood, with certain reserves, for the new system of moderation at home, and were prepared to defend it in arms against assault from abroad.   By proclaiming the Pretender a few months before Anne's accession, Louis XIV had for the time rallied the whole nation to the Revolution Settlement.   The Tories had resented his action no less fiercely than the Whigs.   Above all, the great City of London was behind the new system and ready to defend it against King Louis with purse and person.   In London, more easily than elsewhere, Churchmen and Dissenters cooperated in philanthropic or patriotic causes, and religious toleration was regarded as essential to the life of a great trading community.   Such a trading community London was already, and the whole of England was on the way to become.

CHAPTER IV

London. Her trade and population. Her political and financial power.
Her relations to the Revolution governments. The Tower. Westminster. London's self-government and privileges. The City. The
river and environs. St. James's. Coffee Houses. Plays and music.
Literature. Newspapers. Posts and roads. Mining. Apprenticeship
and child labour. Cloth trade. Industry under rural conditions.
Decay of municipal life. The Justices of the Peace. State of the prisons.

Two miles away from the Parliament at Westminster
and the Queen's Court at St. James's lay the centre of
the greatest City in the world, less under the jurisdiction
of Court and Parliament than any other portion of English
soil. London was governed by her own freely elected
magistrates; policed, in so far as she was policed at all,
by her own constables; guarded by her own militia;
and rendered formidable to the neighbouring seat of
government by the largest and least manageable mob in
the island. With only a tenth part of her present population, and much less than a tenth of her present area,
London had more than her present relative importance.
She surpassed her nearest English rivals, Bristol and
Norwich, at least fifteen times in number of inhabitants.
Her merchants and her markets controlled the larger business
operations of the towns and villages of England, 'sucking
the vitals of trade to herself.' It was the peculiar boast
of the men of Bristol that they alone kept their trade
independent of London, bringing American goods to their
own port and disposing of them in the west through their
own carriers and agents. Everywhere else the strings
of trade were pulled from the capital. 'Norwich buys
Exeter serges, Exeter buys Norwich stuffs, all at London.'[80]
Every county joined in the great national business of sup-

plying London with food, coal or raw material.   In return she sent to every county the finished goods of her own luxury trades, and the distant products of her foreign merchandise.   To the port of London belonged practically all the East India trade of the country, most of the European, Mediterranean and African, and much of the American.

The lower strata of the population of the capital, the dockers and unskilled casual labour of a great mart and port, lived under the most filthy conditions of overcrowding, without sanitation, police or doctors, and far beyond the range of philanthropy, education and religion. Such was their state both in the City proper and in the liberties beyond, when the new century and the new reign began.   The death-rate among them was appalling, and was still going up because they were learning to drink spirits instead of ale.   The privileged sanctuary of outlaws in ' Alsatia,' so outrageous to the dignity of the neighbouring lawyers at the Temple, had indeed been abolished a few years before, but the fraternity of thieves, highwaymen and harlots had only been scattered thence to spread themselves more thickly over the whole metropolitan area.   Their secret organizer, the great Jonathan Wild, flourished under Anne, ostensibly as a zealous magistrate, really as a receiver of stolen goods on an immense scale.   Some of his methods of preserving discipline among his subordinates are ascribed to Peachum in the opening scene of the *Beggar's Opera*, which was written immediately after Wild's belated exposure, trial and execution in 1725.   His life's story argues an inefficiency on the part of magistrates and constables that only began to be remedied in the middle of the century, when the famous brothers Fielding set up their office in Bow Street.

Even honest workmen in the ranks of unskilled labour in London were totally without education : Jonathan Brown, a leading personality among the bargemen, confessed to Calamy, the dissenting preacher, that he and his companions ' had never so much as heard who or what Christ was,' [81] though they could easily be set on by their

betters to burn Meeting Houses or Popish Chapels according to the religious requirements of the hour.   It was to
combat this state of things that the Charity Schools were
being founded by public subscription, and that in 1711
Parliament voted the taxpayers' money to build fifty new
churches in the suburbs for several hundred thousand
persons unprovided for by the Established Church ; the
Dissenters, whom the Committee reckoned at 100,000 in
that district, already had their own chapels.*   Similarly, it
was to remedy the material wants of this neglected mass of
humanity that under the first two Georges hospitals were
founded by private benevolence, and medical assistance was
provided.   The material and medical advance in conditions
of London life under the Georges so lowered the death-rate,
that the population went up with startling rapidity in the
period of the early Industrial Revolution.   We may imagine
then what the life of the London poor was like in Hogarth's
boyhood.[82]

But London was above all a city of contrasts.   The port
and mart where the goods of England and the world were
exchanged, required not only the muscular efforts of unskilled labour, but a supervising army of foremen, clerks,
shopkeepers and middlemen of every variety.   Moreover,
London was not only a mart ; she was also the seat of manufactures, of finishing processes and luxury trades, employing
the most skilled workmen in the island.   Many thousands
of Huguenot silk manufacturers had recently settled in
Spitalfields, and other skilled trades previously conducted
in France were now practised in Longacre and Soho by
refugees who were rapidly becoming Englishmen and were
already voting Whig.[83]   The finest native craftsmanship
was also concentrated in London.   In the best shops of the
City the apprentices were sons of country gentlemen, likely
to die richer than their elder brothers, and dressing in full-
bottomed wigs when off duty.[84]   Greater London was the
centre of English literary and intellectual life, and of fashion,
law and government.   For all these reasons the capital contained, alongside of the most brutal ignorance, an immense
and varied stock of skill and intellect.   London wits were

* See p. 58, above ;   *H. of C. Journals*, April 6, 1711.

sharpened, not only by the processes of national and world commerce, but by daily contact with the lawyers and politicians of Westminster, and with the noblemen and persons of fashion of St. James's.   During the season, the leaders of Society lived in private mansions or in boarding houses west of Temple Bar, and were as much Londoners as the annually returning swallow is English.

Such a city, containing more than a tenth of the population of England * and a good half of its trained thinking power, placed beside the seat of government at Westminster in juxtaposition so close as to form a single metropolis, could not fail to exercise a decisive influence on the course of English history in the days when the difficulties of travel still isolated Court and Parliament from the other towns and shires of the land.   At no time, indeed, did London seek to govern England as Rome had governed Italy or as Athens sought to govern Greece.   She accepted the government of England by the Monarchy or by Parliament, so long as the rulers of the land remained at Westminster outside her gates, leaving her ancient municipal liberties undisturbed, and so long as they conducted the religious and foreign affairs of the country in the main in accordance with principles that were popular in London.   The Kings and Queens whom she favoured—Henry VIII, Elizabeth, William III and Anne—left behind them political structures that survived.   Those who quarrelled with her built for the day—Mary Tudor, the two Charleses and Jameses, and the Protector—though Oliver and the Second Charles each owed his rise to power largely to her support.

In Tudor times, the action of London enabled a strong national Monarchy to be erected on the ruins of ecclesiastical and feudal privilege.   In the following century the quarrel of London with that Monarchy resulted in the transfer of political power to Parliament.   The seat of English

---

* It has been estimated from the registers of baptisms that in 1700, when England and Wales contained rather more than five and a half million inhabitants, the Metropolitan Area contained 674,350. Of these the ' City ' proper contained about 200,000 (Mrs. George, *London Life*, etc., pp. 24–25, 329–330).   On the figures of population for England and Wales, see Talbot-Griffith, *Royal Statistical Society Journal*, 1929, Vol. XCII, Pt. II, pp. 256–263.

government lay just outside the gates of the City, as London's hostage : when Charles I at Westminster attempted to arrest the Five Members, over whom London threw her shield, he was forced to fly from his palace, and he never returned save as a captive. In the Civil War the wealth, brains and sea-power of the City proved more than a match for the Crown.

The Restoration of the Monarchy upon terms in 1660 was the joyous, voluntary act of London, tired of the rule of saints and soldiers. But Charles II and his brother quarrelled with her again, and leagued with France against her liberties. Taking advantage of Whig and Tory divisions in the City, the royal brothers seized her Charters, and made her for awhile the slave of arbitrary power. James lived to pay the price. On the rumour that William of Orange was about to sail, the Lord Chancellor Jeffreys humbly brought back the old Charters to Guild Hall, too late to save himself and his master. When the crown was offered to William and Mary on terms stricter than the terms of Charles II's restoration, London endorsed the deed, without any of those hesitations and regrets that moved some of the other elements in the body politic.

Thenceforth the City was the surest bulwark of the new regime. And in return the Revolution Settlement offered complete security to the restored privileges of London, and to the high place claimed by London in the counsels of the State. The City might have only four members in Parliament, but after the Revolution she exercised an influence like that of a separate estate of the Realm. That influence, unknown to the law of the constitution, was resented by the Tory squires, who held that political power should be monopolized by the landholders. But the governments of the Revolution, whether Whig or Tory, had to fight for their life with France, and only the City could supply the sinews of war. The establishment of the Bank and the National Debt in William's reign forged new links between the Ministers and the Merchants, and emphasized the political and financial meaning of the new constitution.

To these things also Anne was heir. Whether she called herself Whig or Tory, High Church or Low, she must accept the alliance with London because she was heir to the Revolution, and needed defence against Louis XIV and his client, her brother on whose throne she sat.   And the men of London, on their part, required in 1702 that their trade with the Mediterranean and America should be saved from the open attack of the new Franco-Spanish power.   The capital would never again suffer the government to assume towards France the dependent attitude of Charles and James II.   And so, by a series of linked inexorable facts of public life, no less than by her private attachment to Sarah Churchill, Anne was bound to choose Marlborough and Godolphin as her confidential advisers rather than her kinsman Rochester and the more high-flying Tories, who did not see things at home and abroad as the City saw them.   In the November after Anne had ascended the throne, a foreigner noted :

> In the evening there was an illumination in the City, in memory of King William's coming.   [And next day] a Pope of straw with the Devil behind him, are set on a cart : they go from house to house begging contributions for a great bonfire, into which they cast Pope and Devil.[85]

With London in this mood, there might be a Tory Queen and a Tory Parliament, but none the less let Louis and the Pretender beware.   Seven years later, when Louis had been brought low and London mobs began to cheer for Sacheverell and to burn Meeting Houses instead of Popes, the deferred High Church holiday could safely take place.*

The Tower of London, which was to have overawed the citizens, had been built by William the Conqueror on the side of the City away from Westminster.   Partly for that reason, it had not overawed them long.   In Stuart times it could not, in its isolated position, serve to protect Westminster and Whitehall from the insults of the London mob. In Anne's reign the Tower still served as the great Arsenal whence cannon and gunpowder were shipped to the wars

* Ned Ward, in his Tory poem *Vulgus Britannicus,* celebrating the burning of Meeting Houses by the Sacheverell mob in 1709, distinctly and repeatedly states that this London mob had previously been Whiggish (*e.g.,* at pp. 43–47 of the ed. of 1710).

oversea, and as the Mint presided over by Newton himself
as Master.   Its outer walls enclosed a network of streets
inhabited by the officers of these two establishments.   On
occasion it was still a State prison.   But already it had its
lighter side, as the Zoo and Museum of the Capital.
Visitors were taken to see the Crown Jewels, and the newly
finished Armoury where a line of English Kings sat mounted
in battle array.   The stock of lions and other wild beasts
had been maintained ever since the days when the Tower
had been a favourite residence of mediæval kings ; it was
finely replenished by presents to Queen Anne from the
monarchs of North African ' Barbary,' with whom the
English merchants traded, and with whom the captors of
Gibraltar made treaties of alliance against France and Spain.[86]

Between the Tower and Temple Bar stretched the
length of the City proper ; its meagre breadth extended
northwards from the river only as far as the ' bars ' of
Smithfield, Holborn and Whitechapel.*   But the march
of bricks and mortar had burst the municipal bounds,
chiefly in a westerly direction, attracted towards the seat of
national government at Westminster.   At the Strand began
the jurisdiction of that City.   But the municipal privileges
of Westminster were no rival to those of London.   Neither
London nor the Court nor Parliament had ever wished to
have to deal with a Lord Mayor of Westminster.   So
Westminster was never permitted to enjoy self-government,
or to acquire a corporate sense.   It was ruled by twelve
burgesses appointed for life by the High Steward, and even
their powers were being rapidly superseded by those of the
Justices of the Peace and of the Vestries of the different
parishes.   It is true that the parliamentary franchise in
Westminster was democratic, and in the days when most
boroughs had a narrow franchise, the election of a member
of Parliament for Westminster caused unusual political
excitement long before the time of Charles Fox, as when
General Stanhope stood in 1710 in the Whig interest and
was defeated after a fierce contest and a hot canvass.   But
Westminster's local government was a mere bureaucracy,

---

* These ' bar ' boundaries were, of course, more extensive than the original
City bounded by the wall and gates, *e.g.* Temple Bar was farther west than Ludgate.

so far as it was anything better than an anarchy of rival jurisdictions.

On the other hand, the City of London enjoyed complete self-government in an unusually democratic form. At that time very few boroughs in England were so free of the element of oligarchy, unless it were Ipswich and Norwich. In London as many as 12,000 ratepaying householders voted in their respective Wards to elect the 26 Aldermen and 200 Common Councillors. These ratepayers at the Wards were almost identical with the Liverymen of the 89 Gilds and Companies : in their double capacity they controlled by their votes the complicated mediæval machinery of London self-government.

The electorate of shopkeepers chose men of their own class to represent them on the Common Council, rather than the great merchant princes known in the world of high finance and politics. The City magnates were more often chosen as Aldermen. Common pride in the privileges and power of London, and jealous care for her independence, prevented a serious breach between the great men of the Exchange and the shopkeeping democracy. But there was sometimes friction, and in the course of Anne's reign a tendency became apparent for the democratic Common Council to be Tory, and for the Mayor, Aldermen and wealthy City magnates to be Whig.

The jurisdiction of London's elected magistrates was not confined to the area of their own City. Their power stopped short of Westminster, but they clipped it in on every side. They possessed the Shrievalty of Middlesex and the Bailiwick of Southwark. They administered and taxed the port of London. The Lord Mayor was Conservator of the river from Gravesend and Tilbury up to a point just above Staines Bridge—a course of over sixty miles. London levied coal duties in a radius of twelve miles, and enforced her monopoly of markets in a radius of seven.[87]

The City proper was the most densely populated acreage in England. It was not, as now, abandoned to ' cats and caretakers ' at nightfall ; the merchant prince and the shopkeeper slept, each with his family, over his place of business—servants and prentices above in the garrets, and porters and messengers packed away anywhere in cellarage and warehouse.   Old Jewry and Basinghall Street, in particular, were reputed to contain the homes of some of the richest men in England.   But the nobility of the realm had already deserted their ancestral palaces in the crowded City, whence gardens were vanishing apace : ' the great ' resided, during the season, round Covent Garden, Piccadilly, Bloomsbury, or St. James's Square, or in some other section of Westminster.   And the rich merchants, who still inhabited their beloved City for reasons alike of business and of sentiment, had also their country houses and villas among the woods, fields and pleasant villages within a twenty-mile radius of London.   In their suburban and riverside retreats—in Hampstead, West Ham, Walthamstow, and below Epsom Downs, already a great pleasure resort, and especially along the green shores of the Thames from Chelsea upwards— there was perhaps as much good eating and drinking done by Londoners as in the City itself.   The poorer sort walked out for a holiday in the country to less distant places like Dulwich.[88]

In London the river was the most crowded of the highways.   Passengers in boats were perpetually threading the heavy commercial traffic, to the accompaniment of volleys of traditional abuse exchanged between boatmen and bargees.   On the north bank, between London Bridge and the Parliament Stairs were at least thirty landing places, where boats waited by the steps to carry people along or across the river.   Statesmen and parsons going over to Lambeth, or prentices and budding barristers on lighter errands to Cupid's Garden hard by, one and all crossed by boat.   There were ferries with platforms to take a coach and horses.   For until Westminster Bridge was built in 1738, London Bridge was the only road over the river.   The street that stood upon it had been rebuilt in a more modern style since the ravages of the Great Fire, but the projection of its ancient piers still hindered and endangered traffic. To ' shoot the bridge ' was still an adventure ; it was said that London Bridge was made for wise men to go over and fools to go under.

The big shipping, therefore, came no higher than the Bridge. Below it, a forest of masts covered the Pool of London, with which no scene in the world save Amsterdam could compare. The fairway was the more crowded because scarcely any of the great docks had then been dug out, except those at Deptford, and the single dock at Blackwall used for the vessels of the East India Company.[89]

To pass from the City to Westminster by land, Fleet Ditch had first to be crossed. It was spanned by the bridges of Fleet Street and Holborn ; below them, glided barges laden with coal, where to-day the solid traffic of Farringdon Street moves at a scarcely more rapid pace. But the headwaters of the Fleet River, rising amid the hills of Hampstead and Highgate, flowed through the green fields of St. Pancras and Clerkenwell.

A few years before the Queen's accession, the learned Edmund Gibson had appended to his edition of Camden's *Britannia* a list of more than a hundred ' rare plants growing wild in Middlesex,' which botanists may read with envy to-day. The *Osmunda regalis* fern still grew on Hampstead Heath, for popular ignorance of bird and plant life still gave the less common species a chance to flourish, and the collector had not yet plundered England.

Amid the hayfields on Thames bank stood Chelsea Hospital in solitary grandeur, inhabited by four hundred red-coated pensioners of Sedgemoor, Landen and the Boyne, discussing the weekly news of Marlborough's doings with the professional earnestness of Corporal Trim.   A little way off lay the village of Chelsea, where a few persons of fashion had taken the fancy to build themselves retreats, as far removed from the turmoil of London and Westminster as Kensington Palace itself.[90]

Since coal was burnt on almost every London hearth, the air was so infected that a foreign scholar complained ' whenever I examine London books I make my ruffles as black as coal.'   On days when the north-east wind carried the smoke-cloud, even Chelsea became dangerous to the asthmatic, as the philosopher Earl of Shaftesbury had reason

to complain.[91]   There is no wonder that King William had
lived at Hampton Court when he could, and at Kensington
when he must.   Westminster would have been death to
him.   Anne, on her accession, could safely move the royal
residence from country to town, from Kensington to St.
James's Palace.   But that was all the satisfaction she would
give to her loving subjects ; not only was she often at Bath
and yet more often at Windsor, but, even when she came to
town, the doors of St. James's were open only to her
Ministers and her female favourites, and to those whom
Ministers or favourites introduced by the front stairs
or the back.   Throughout her reign she was an invalid.
What asthma was to William, gout or dropsy was to Anne.
To be jolted in a coach to Westminster to open Parliament,
or to St. Paul's to give public thanks for some famous
victory, was a penance that she could only occasionally
consent to endure.

Queen Anne therefore kept Court as little as her predecessor.   Metaphorically as well as literally, the Whitehall
of the Merry Monarch lay in ruins, never to rise again.
Except the Banqueting House of tragic memory, the whole
Palace had been burnt in 1698, and its roofless walls still
cumbered the river bank.   Buckingham House was still the
residence of a subject.   The fashionable world parading in
chairs and six-horse coaches in the Mall, or sauntering in
the more private garden immediately below the windows of
St. James's Palace, had to be content with remembering
that they were near the invisible Queen.   It was more to
the point that in the other direction the Houses of Parliament were but a few minutes' walk away from the centre
of fashion.

As in the reign of Charles II, the Coffee House was still
the centre of social life.   It afforded a much needed relaxa-
tion of the severe drinking habits of the time, for alcohol
was not to be had on the premises.   A list of some of the
Coffee Houses in Queen Anne's reign runs to nearly five
hundred names.   Every respectable Londoner had his
favourite house, where his friends or clients could seek him
at known hours.

'Remember, John,
'If any ask, to th' Coffee House I'm gone,'

says the citizen to his apprentice as he leaves the shop.

Then at Lloyd's Coffee House he never fails
To read the letters and attend the sales.*

The *beau monde* assembled at White's Chocolate House in St. James's Street, where, as Harley bitterly complained to Swift, young noblemen were fleeced and corrupted by fashionable gamblers and profligates. Tories went to the Cocoa Tree Chocolate House, Whigs to St. James's Coffee House. Will's, near Covent Garden, was the resort of poets, critics and their patrons ; Truby's served the clergy, and the Grecian the world of scholarship ; nor were there lacking houses for Dissenters, for Quakers, for Papists and for Jacobites. The 'universal liberty of speech of the English nation' uttered amid clouds of tobacco smoke, with equal vehemence whether against the Government and the Church, or against their enemies, had long been the wonder of foreigners ; it was the quintessence of Coffee House life.

The Coffee House filled the place now occupied by the Club, but in a more cheap and informal manner, and with a greater admission of strangers. In days when men stood much on their rank, it had a levelling influence : at the Coffee House 'you will see blue ribbons and stars sitting familiarly with private gentlemen as if they had left their quality and degrees of distance at home.' But that was not all. In days before telegrams and effective journalism, news could be most easily obtained at the Coffee House. The Windsor, at Charing Cross, advertised itself as supplying the 'best chocolate at twelve pence the quart and the translation of the *Harlem Courant* soon after the post is come

* In Ned Ward's *Wealthy Shopkeeper* (1706) his day is thus apportioned : rise at 5 ; counting-house till 8 ; then breakfast on toast and Cheshire cheese ; in his shop for two hours ; then a neighbouring coffee house for news ; shop again, till dinner at home (over the shop) at 12 on a 'thundering joint' ; 1 o'clock on Change ; 3 Lloyd's Coffee House for business ; shop again for an hour ; then another coffee house (not Lloyd's) for recreation, followed by 'sack shop' to drink with acquaintances, till home for 'a light supper' and so to bed 'before Bow Bell rings nine.'

in.' Not only was news sought for its political, military and general interest, but for the strictly business purposes of commerce as at Lloyd's. Edward Lloyd, whose surname instantly rises to men's lips when they speak of shipping to-day, was, when he walked the earth, nothing more nor less than a Coffee House keeper in Lombard Street in Queen Anne's reign. To his house merchants came for the latest information, and for the personal intercourse and advice necessary for all transactions. Newspapers had then no commercial column and no details of shipping. The spoken word did many things that print does to-day, and for merchants the word was spoken at Lloyd's. Before Anne's reign ended Lloyd had set up a pulpit for auctions and for reading out the news.[92]

At six o'clock the theatres began to fill. A patriotic Briton has thus described the scene :

The pit contains the gentlemen on benches ; and on the first story of boxes sit all the ladies of quality ; in the second, the citizens' wives and daughters ; and in the third, the common people and footmen ; so that between the acts you are as much diverted by viewing the beauties of the audience, as while they act with the subject of the play ; and the whole is illuminated to the greatest advantage. Whereas abroad, the stage only being illuminated, and the lodge or boxes close, you lose the pleasure of seeing the company. And indeed the English have reason in this, for no nation in the world can show such an assembly of shining beauties as here.[93]

The footmen aloft in ' Olympus,' had been originally admitted there free to form a *claque*, and had conspired to treat this concession as their inalienable privilege ; they had become the tyrants of the house, a plague to managers and to the politer part of the audience, interrupting the most affecting passages in the play with savage clamour.[94]

But on the whole the London theatres catered for people who were cultured or desired to be thought so. The drama had not yet been divorced from literature to marry commerce, and was still conducted on a repertory basis. Shakespeare was gaining rather than losing ground, though in versions disastrously mangled. The genius of Betterton and Mrs. Bracegirdle in the early years of Anne, and the critiques of the *Spectator* in the latter part of the reign were preparing the way for the apotheosis of the national poet in the era of Garrick and Johnson.   Actors' reputations were made in *Hamlet* and *Othello*, as they seldom are to-day.

Sometimes, indeed, the ladies of the audience were insensible even to the charms of Betterton acting Shakespeare. In 1709 a susceptible Irish baronet complains ' that they can talk of indifferent things while the tenderest passions of their whole frame are called for.   Whereas I own freely had not Desdemona been very ugly I had certainly pulled out my handkerchief.   There will be another trial of them this night at *Hamlet*.'

Betterton's power was matched by his restraint.   Instead of ranting as Hamlet, at the entry of the ghost, ' he opened with a pause of mute amazement ; rising slowly to a solemn, trembling voice, he made the ghost equally terrible to the Spectator as to himself.'   In Brutus quarrelling with Cassius, ' his spirit flew only to his eye ; his steady look alone supplied that terror which he disdained an intemperance in his voice should rise to.'   But his greatest part was Othello.[95]

But most of the plays acted belonged to the contemporary comedy of manners ; its best writers, Congreve, Vanbrugh and Farquhar are still, after more than two centuries, familiar to ' the town,' or at least to the suburbs. In their own day, the attack launched on the immorality of the stage by Jeremy Collier, the Nonjuror, was a theme of discussion constantly renewed throughout the reign of Anne.   Collier's first blast had been blown in 1698, but the argument was carried on for years by other clergymen —' venomed priests ' as they were called in Vanbrugh's Prologues.   The clerical critics were able to draw on a formidable armoury of undesirable passages quoted from the dramas of the day.[96]   The assault, though exaggerated and in part misdirected, was neither unprovoked nor ineffectual.   Colley Cibber, actor-manager and dramatist, confessed that :

the calling our dramatic writers to a strict account had a very wholesome effect.   They were now a great deal more upon their guard ; indecencies were no longer wit ; and by degrees the fair sex came again to fill the boxes on the first day of a new comedy without fear or censure.[97]

Colley Cibber's own play, *The Careless Husband*, which appeared in 1704, turns on the reclamation of an erring husband by the virtues of his wife. Cibber, who was very far from being the dullard that Pope afterwards made him out, had perceived shortly after the accession of Anne that the moment had come for a play with a moral ending, but still enlivened by dialogue and situation not too refined : with the help of the rising star of Nance Oldfield, *The Careless Husband* became the theatrical success of the winter that followed Blenheim. The dramas of Anne's reign were, on the average, less heartless than those of the preceding decades. The comedies of Addison, Steele and Mrs. Centlivre gave a kindlier and less cynical view of men and women than the abler work of Congreve, who never wrote a play after 1700. Indeed, by the end of the Queen's reign sentimentalism was a fault of the modern playwrights, both comic and tragic. The tragedies of Rowe, like the essays and plays of Addison, were addressed to ' the fair sex ' that now mingled with the male part of the audience without fear of being put to the blush. And increasingly the tone of the theatre was set by the middle classes rather than by the Court. The stage therefore became more respectable and more sentimental than in the period of the Restoration Comedy.

One peculiarity of the stage at this time was that nearly all the dramatists were Whigs, and that consequently the army, during the Marlborough wars, was represented in a sympathetic light, instead of being pursued with the rancour which Tory writers like Swift so often showed in speaking of a redcoat.[98] Congreve, Addison, Rowe, Mrs. Centlivre and Colley Cibber were Whigs, and Farquhar, Vanbrugh and Steele were not only Whigs but soldiers. But the politics of the audience was by no means entirely Whig. Indeed, during the period of Marlborough's greatest unpopularity with the Tories, at the close of the war which he had won for England, the management thought fit to interpolate in the middle of the deceased Farquhar's

Recruiting Officer a chorus of soldiers in uniform, to sing a scurrilous song against Marlborough's avarice, ending every verse with the chorus :

> But Marlborough not a penny.

One of the Duke's daughters who was present ' blushed scarlet,' but the play was interrupted for a quarter of an hour by the frenzied cheering of the Tory ladies and gentlemen.[99]

In music, the age of Anne saw the invasion and conquest of England by the Italian Opera, under the able leadership of Nicolini and his band of eunuchs. There was a short struggle, in which native musical tradition attempted to hold its own. Steele, in the Epilogue to his *Tender Husband*, exhorted the audience,

> No more th' Italian squalling tribe admit,
> In tongues unknown ; 'tis Popery in wit,

while Addison's other friend Tickell denounced it as,

> Nonsense well tuned and sweet stupidity.

But the ladies loved to see ' Nicolini strangle a lion with great gallantry,' and the Italian opera took hold. It became the vogue to depreciate Purcell and old English songs and music, once held to be the best in Europe. Nothing is more striking than the inability of the English to stand by their native traditions in art ; the following of French fashions in so many things had prepared the way for this musical surrender to the Italians. By the end of the reign Addison had sadly to admit : ' The foreign tone and manner which are expected in everything now performed among us, has put music itself to a stand.' It was not till the following reign that the ingenious Mr. Gay created in the comic or ballad Opera a refuge for English humour and English musical genius, where they survived in a state of semi-obscurity, with the help of Dibdin, till the advent of Gilbert and Sullivan.[100]

The reading public was still so small that authors could not live by their sales alone. It is true that Defoe, Addison and Swift were creating forms of literature and journalism that greatly enlarged the area influenced by the pen. But patronage was still necessary for authors to subsist, and it could be courted in a variety of ways : the aspirant might present copies, or dedicate editions of his works to ' a person of quality,' who might reward him with a bag of guineas, or haply with a living or with a post in public or private service ; or else he might write political poems, pamphlets and Reviews for the Whig or Tory parties, to earn similar rewards from the party leaders.

Of the personal relationship of author and patron, the following example will serve, though here too an element of the political can perhaps be detected : a certain Joseph Harris writes to Thomas Coke, M.P. : [101]

> Some time since I presented to your honour a book which I writ on my Lord Duke of Marlborough ; and last summer I presented another book to you, called Luzzara, being an encomium on Prince Eugene of Savoy.   As yet I have never had any return for either of those presents to your honour, wherefore now, by reason I am very ill and lame of rheumatism, I humbly make bold to address myself to your honour either for small charity, or for return of the books that I may present them to some other persons of quality.   I have nothing but what I get by translating out of Latin, Greek and Spanish to maintain my wife and four children.

There speaks the authentic, unhappy voice of Grub Street. There were many more servants of the Muse living like poor Harris than like Secretary Addison, Dean Swift or Sir Richard Steele.

In his life of Matthew Prior, Dr. Johnson remarks : Throughout the reigns of William and Anne no prosperous event passed undignified by poetry.' The flood of such patriotic verses, dedicated to all the statesmen and generals in the country, has sunk, as floods sink, into the ground in deserved oblivion, all save Addison's *Campaign* that still adds lustre to Blenheim.   But the prose of Whig and Tory polemics contained a larger proportion of stuff destined to endure : Swift and Addison, as journalists, spoke to their day but they have been overheard by the ages.   The importance of the pamphlet and of the political Review, and the price that political leaders were ready to pay the writers thereof, naturally resulted from government by Parliament and by public opinion.   It was for this reason that Voltaire

in his youth found that literary men were much more highly
esteemed in England than in his own despotically governed
country.   Political power could not be exercised in England
unless a wide public had first been persuaded.   As there
was then no reporting of speeches or publication of parliamentary debates, and very few political meetings of any
kind, literary men had to be employed to say to the people
what the political leaders wished to have said.   Men with
this gift occupied, therefore, a very high place in the society
of Queen Anne's reign, while their brother poets were
starving in garrets.

The rich rewards of political literature were one of the
causes why men of letters, though they still wrote verse as
well as prose, were turning away even in their verse from
poetry and imagination to the prosaic and journalistic spirit
of the clear, rational Eighteenth Century.   Milton, indeed,
had written political pamphlets, but their best passages
had retained the quality of great poetry rather than of
skilled pamphleteering.   This cannot be said of any writer
in the age of Anne.

The Censorship had been removed in 1695 and a vested
interest in free literature had consequently sprung up.
When it was proposed to restore the censorship in 1703 ' to
restrain the licentiousness of the press,' the workmen
printers of London petitioned the House of Commons that
they would be thrown out of work in great numbers if the
Bill became law.[102]   This national industry born of freedom
was settled almost entirely in the Capital.   London sent to
the farthest ends of the land the outpourings of her seventy
printing and publishing houses.

In the days of the Popish Plot and the Revolution, it
had been customary to satisfy the thirst for news by ' news-
letters ' in manuscript sent down from the capital to correspondents in the provinces.   But when Anne ascended the
throne, written communications were beginning to be
replaced by the printing of a dozen London newspapers.
The newspaper usually consisted of a single sheet of two
printed sides, sometimes folded into four pages ; it appeared
two or three times in the week, and contained the main

items of home and foreign intelligence, set down without comment. The last half page was devoted to advertisements of such items as patent medicines, sales of houses, meetings for ' the noble and heroic sport of cockfighting,' or the vent of Portugal wine by Messrs. Brook and Hellier. Some papers gave a Tory twist to their news, like the *Postboy*, or a Whig twist like the *Postman*. But the news was much the same in all, and there was no leading article.

There was, however, another type of periodical, like the Whig *Observator* and Defoe's *Review* in the early years of the Queen's reign, giving little news but commenting at length upon news reported elsewhere. A few years later this new method of journalism reached its perfection in the *Spectators* and *Examiners* of Steele, Addison and Swift.

By the end of the reign, a few of the largest provincial capitals had started newspapers of their own, upon the London model. Such was the *Newcastle Courant* begun in 1711. The first serious check to the rapid and healthy growth of journalism that signalized the reign of Anne was the effective measure taken to muzzle the press by Bolingbroke, when in 1712 he put a heavy duty on newspapers and their advertisements.[103]

Some counties had no printing presses at all, and the greatest provincial capitals seldom had more than one or two apiece. All England looked to London as the original source of news, opinions and arguments of every colour in politics, religion, literature and fashion—and to London, Oxford and Cambridge for works of learning. The printer was generally a publisher, and the publisher was generally a bookseller, who sold the books he printed. The London booksellers were most of them attached either to the Whig or Tory cause, and some of them to the Jacobite.*

London was the focus not only of literature, journalism

---

* Nichols's *Lit. Anecdotes* (1812), I, pp. 289–312. The printer and publisher in Newcastle-upon-Tyne put the following advertisement into his paper, the *Newcastle Courant*, in 1711: ' This is to give notice to all Gentlemen and lovers of learning who are willing to publish any book in the Northern parts, that John White, printer, living in the Close in Newcastle-upon-Tine, is furnished with great variety of letters and presses and will be ready to print the same upon reasonable terms.'

and public news, but even of private correspondence. The General Post Office with a staff of forty sorters, was established in Lombard Street, and nearly all letters in England sent by the public post had to pass through it : the first ' cross posts,' going straight between two important towns without touching London, were only set up a few years before Anne came to the throne. But in the rural parts letters were sent by private messengers to a much greater extent then than now. The London area already enjoyed a penny post, under the management of the Lombard Street Office, with delivery every few hours.[104]

The time which it took for the Post Office to deliver letters in the country, like the pace of all traffic by land, varied greatly according to the wet or dry condition of the roads. The postboys reckoned to accomplish the journey from London to Edinburgh in six days on the average. But in the storms of winter, postboy, horse and mailbag were apt to disappear in crossing a flooded valley : the horse may well have been a greater loss than the letters, of which there was sometimes only one for all Scotland in the mail from London. On a fine summer day, a good coach-and-four could accomplish the fifty-three miles from London to Cambridge between five in the morning and eight at night, a record easily broken in modern times by undergraduates on foot. Only the very best coaches had springs, and the cumbrous machines were seldom moved at a trot, except on the not infrequent appearance of a horseman of suspicious aspect. Highwaymen lurked in security in the unfelled thickets and unenclosed heaths, and were in league with many keepers of inns, like Boniface in the *Beaux' Stratagem*. In Scotland, indeed, the highwayman was unknown ; he would have wearied of waiting for the rare passengers, and would have been little richer after their plunder than before. But in England no one began a journey wholly free from the fear of such encounters.

A more common sight upon the roads than the coach was the yet slower ' hooded waggon,' with passengers and luggage inside, and the carrier walking at the head of his eight horses. And more usual than any form of wheeled vehicle was the string of laden pack-horses, sometimes as many as fifty in a single file, following a leader with a bell round its neck.[105]

During the war with France, the most usual route to the Continent lay through Harwich and Rotterdam. Travellers in an ordinary coach took two days between London and Harwich, and they were often held up a week at the port, waiting for weather in which to cross, with ' nothing to do, poor fare and a terribly long bill ' at the inn. The crossing itself might take another week, or might be accomplished in twenty-four hours if the breeze held and the French privateers from Dunkirk were avoided.

Even on the Great North Road, delays and perils were much increased in winter or foul weather. When in January 1709 the antiquarian Thoresby was leaving Huntingdon for London, the guide refused to proceed southward after a night of snow and flood. The party, however, rode on without him, causing the good folks of Royston to run out of their houses to gaze at such venturous travellers. They made thirty miles that day and slept at Puckeridge. Next day they reached London, but not before Thoresby's horse had plunged belly deep into the water by the roadside at Enfield, ' by the breaking of the ice.'

Such in winter was the Great North Road itself, in its best section. North of Grantham it consisted only of a narrow stone causeway with soft ground on both sides. On such a highway wheeled traffic could scarcely pass in wet weather ; and even horsemen, when shoved off the causeway by the pack-horse trains, sometimes had difficulty in getting back out of the morass into the middle of the road. Many highways were of this ' causeway ' type. Village roads were mere mud tracks or broad green lanes. It was well, perhaps, that so many roads were unenclosed for the greater part of their length, for passengers were therefore able to ride or walk off the morass of the road itself through the neighbouring heaths or corn-fields. Farmers complained, but the law upheld the rights of the distressed traveller in this matter. In enclosed counties like Kent, two horsemen could scarcely squeeze past one another at many points on the main road between London and Canterbury, and a coach entirely blocked the way between the hedges. The

Weald of Sussex, described as ' a sink fourteen miles broad,' was so ill drained that the roads between the North and South Downs were deep in mud till the middle of a dry summer.   One picture by Defoe stays in the mind :

Going to a Church in a country village not far from Lewis I saw an ancient lady, and a lady of very good quality I assure you, drawn to Church in her coach with six oxen ; nor was it done in frolic or humour, but mere necessity, the way being so stiff and deep, that no horses could go in it.[106]

The badness of the roads was due to the want of any adequate administrative machinery for their reconstruction or repair.   Every parish through which a road passed was legally bound to maintain it by six days a year of unpaid labour given by the farmers, under no supervision save one of themselves chosen as surveyor.   The unfairness of laying the burden of repair not on the users of the great roads, but on the parishes through which they happened to pass, was equalled by the folly of expecting farmers, who had no interest in the matter, to act gratuitously as skilled makers of highways.   The result was that few hard roads had been made since the Romans left the island.   In the Middle Ages, when there was little commerce, this had mattered but little.   Under the later Stuarts, when commerce was large and rapidly increasing, it mattered much ; it was beginning to be felt as a national disgrace.   The new system of turnpikes to make the users of the road pay for its upkeep was therefore enforced in a few of the worst sections by Acts of Parliament.   When Anne came to the throne the usual machinery of local Justices of the Peace was employed to manage the turnpikes, but towards the end of the reign special bodies of Turnpike Trustees were sometimes established by Statute.   It was not, however, till the House of Hanover had been some time on the throne that anything approaching a general reform was effected by this means.[107]

Under such conditions, sea and river traffic, however slow, held a great advantage over road traffic, especially for heavy goods.   Fish could be sent up from Lyme Regis to

London by relays of fast trotting horses ; but coal came there by sea. Even so, while it cost but five shillings per chaldron at the Tyneside pit's mouth, it cost thirty shillings in London, and anything up to fifty shillings in the towns of the Upper Thames. This was partly because sea-borne coal was taxed, both to pay for the rebuilding of St. Paul's and to pay for the French war. Coal was cheaper in those towns of Yorkshire, Lancashire and the west Midlands to which it could be floated from the pit's mouth on rivers like the Calder or Severn. For coal carried on inland rivers was not taxed, like the coal carried by sea, neither was it exposed to the attacks of the Dunkirk privateers, nor harassed by the consequent restrictions of an inadequate convoy system supplied by the Royal Navy between Tyne and Thames.[108]

Whitehaven was springing into importance by exporting Cumbrian coal to Ireland. Bristol shipping exported coal from South Wales. In three-quarters of the counties of England where it is raised to-day, coal was being raised in Anne's reign. The ownership of mines and an interest in their working was not deemed beneath the dignity of the greatest noblemen of the land, for in England, unlike most countries of Europe, all minerals except gold and silver have been treated as the property of the owner of the soil. Among the aristocratic coal owners of that time was Lord Dartmouth, to whom belonged many of the Staffordshire mines near his country house at Sandwell. He had a rival in a country gentleman named Wilkins, who was said to have 'engrossed the coalworks of Leicestershire to himself.'

It was then usual to leave pillars of coal to support the roof of the mine, rather than to use timber props. Shafts were sunk to a depth of 400 feet and more, and in Lancashire the science of the engineers had devised in the year 1712 a machine for pumping water out of the mine which has been described as 'the first genuine steam-engine.' On Tyneside, wooden rails were used to run the trucks down to the river for loading the keels ; twenty thousand horses were employed in the transport of coal in the environs of Newcastle alone. Since the larger mines were deeper below the surface than in the Middle Ages, explosions due to fire-damp were already frequent, as at Gateshead in 1705 and at Chester-le-Street in 1708, when a hundred miners perished ' besides great damage to many houses and persons for several miles round.   One man was blown quite out of the mouth of the shaft, which is fifty fathom, and found at a prodigious distance from the place.'   Two years later another explosion at Bensham, in the same North Durham district, killed eighty more.   But the amount of surface mining was still considerable ; in the west there were many scores of small workings, each conducted by two or three colliers, and sometimes by a single man.[109]

The miners of all kinds and the quarrymen of every county form an important exception to the statement that in old England the method of industry was domestic. Other exceptions there were, but they are harder to specify and define.   Many workshops had premises so large, and contained so many apprentices and paid journeymen, that they may be reckoned as standing half-way between the domestic and the factory system.   The normal basis of industry still was apprenticeship, the only legal doorway to a trade whether for boys or girls.   The apprentice system was often abused by cruel masters and mistresses, and pauper apprentices were at least as badly treated as children in the worst days of the subsequent factory system.   There were no inspectors and no checks on ill usage.   On the other hand, the apprentice was part of his master's ' family,' and the average man does not like to see unhappy faces at his own board and in his own household.   Moreover, apprenticeship was invaluable for the discipline and skilled training that it provided during that important ' after-school age ' so much neglected in our own day.   It largely compensated for the deficiency of school education.   Apprenticeship was the old English school of craftsmanship and of character.*

* Already in Anne's reign there were complaints that apprenticeship was not made as universally obligatory as the laws dictated.   In 1702 the Corporation of Kendal petitioned for a new and stricter law, because ' although there are laws against persons setting up any trade without having received seven years' apprenticeship, when such persons come to be prosecuted they meet with such favour that very few have been punished of late.'   *H.M.C. Bagot*, R. 10, pt. iv., p. 336.

Before they were old enough to be apprenticed, small children were sometimes set to work in their parents' cottages at an age full as early as the factory children of later times. Especially was spinning for the cloth industry conducted in this fashion : Defoe noticed with approval at Colchester and in the Taunton clothing region, that ' there was not a child in the town or in the villages round it of above five years old, but, if it was not neglected by its parents and untaught, could earn its bread.' Again in the clothing dales of the West Riding he found ' hardly anything above four years old but its hands were sufficient for its support.' Poor little things ! But at least, whenever their parents let them go to play, they had fields near at hand, instead of the boundless wilderness of slums.[110]

Spinning was done chiefly in country cottages by women and children, and weaving chiefly in towns and urban districts by men. Both processes, though conducted under domestic conditions, required capitalist organization and supervision, either by employers, or by middlemen who bought the goods manufactured by the cottager. The methods by which the cloth trade was organized differed in the many different regions of England where it flourished.[111]

While the coal trade of Anne's reign interests us especially because of its future, the cloth trade was the typical industry of the time. Two-fifths of English exports consisted of cloth woven in England. Many of our domestic laws and many measures of our economic and foreign policy were aimed at the great national object of promoting the manufacture of cloth and pushing its sale at home and abroad. It was felt that here lay our real advantage over Dutch rivals in the carrying trade of the world, for we had this great staple manufacture with which to load our outgoing ships, whereas they had little to export except herrings, and acted mainly as carriers between other nations.

The cloth industry was encouraged by various legislative devices. Even the dead were compelled to be buried in good English cloth :

' Odious ! in woollen ! 'twould a saint provoke '—
Were the last words that poor Narcissa spoke.*

* Pope, *Moral Essays*, I.

Severe laws were passed and partially enforced against exporting raw wool abroad to help foreign manufacturers. But 'owling,' or running of English raw wool to France, went on all through the war, from Romney Marsh in Kent, the favourite haunt of smugglers and Jacobites, or from Sussex and the Lincolnshire marshes, with many a skirmish between smugglers and dragoons. Much English wool was exported to the Continent from Scotland, with the connivance of the Scottish Government prior to the Union. Irish wool was smuggled to France on an even greater scale, and with more moral justification, because the English Parliament had in 1699 prohibited the export of Irish cloth, by one of the most iniquitous and short-sighted laws ever passed by Parliament in obedience to English trade jealousy, in utter disregard even of the 'Protestant interest' in the neighbouring island.[112]

The desire to keep open the great markets of the world for English cloth was a chief incentive to taking up arms in 1702 against the Franco-Spanish Power, which was at that moment, at the command of Louis XIV, proceeding to close Spain, the Netherlands, South America and the Mediterranean to our goods. The taking and keeping of Gibraltar in 1704 was symptomatic of more than military and naval ambition : a free entrance to the Mediterranean and Turkish trades was vital to the cloth industry. Not only were great quantities of our cloth sold in those parts, but our merchants brought back from Spain and Southern Italy oil used here in the manufacture of cloth. Spanish merino wool was worked up in England and sold back as cloth to Spain herself, whose native industry was in the last stages of decline. Of late years the fine quality and great quantity of English-grown wool had been yet further increased by means of 'clover and other grass seeds' to feed the sheep. Our American Colonies were valued largely as markets for our cloth. In Russia, too, a great demand for it was growing up in the new century.[113]

Only in the Far East it was impossible to sell the heavy English cloth, and this was the most damaging argument which the East India Company had to meet in pleading its cause before Parliament. But the tea and silk it brought

to England sufficed to condone the high economic crimes of
failing to sell English cloth and daring to export bullion to
buy cloth substitutes.   In vain the merchants of the rival
Turkey Company pleaded that ' if silk be brought from
India where it is bought cheap with bullion, it will ruin our
trade with Turkey, whither we send cloth for their silk.'
The demands of fashion and luxury outweighed the argu-
ments of clothiers, Turkey merchants and orthodox econo-
mists.   ' Our stately fops admire themselves better in an
Indian dressing gown than in one made at Spitalfields.'
The ladies, besides, were all drinking ' tay.'   So the Indian
Trade was permitted to flourish, and in spite of that the
Cloth Trade flourished as well.[114]

Though the cloth trade was organized in the cities, the
cloth was spun and woven for the most part in market
towns and hamlets, in farms and cottages.   Nor was the
cloth manufacture exceptional in being thus seated amid
rural surroundings.   Industry was less urban than in
Plantagenet times.   Only a small part of the manufacturing
activity of the country was any longer conducted within city
walls or subjected to municipal control.   It is true that many
towns, especially London and certain other seaports, were
much larger than of old, because commerce had increased,
and commerce must needs be concentrated in cities.   But
many other towns had decayed or stood still, because manufacture had ceased to be municipal and had become national.
The master workman, in choosing where to set up his workshop, was at more pains to plant himself outside the area of
pettifogging borough regulations, than to seek safety within
the walls of a city as in the rough society of the Middle
Ages.   The villages and open market towns were now
sufficiently civilized and secure to become the homes of
highly elaborated craftsmanship.

The return of industry to urban areas came later, with
the advent of modern machinery and the modern factory
system.   But from Elizabeth to George III, the bulk of the
industrial population lived under rural conditions of life.
The typical Englishman was a villager, but a villager
accustomed to meet men of various crafts, occupations and

classes—by no means a mere rustic boor, ignorant of all save the plough handle. Ploughing and agricultural operations constitute indeed a highly skilled trade ; but it was not only ploughmen, but all sorts and conditions of men who made up the society of the villages and small market towns during the Stuart and early Hanoverian reigns. Partly for this reason, the English of those times made famous colonists, handy men able to adapt themselves to new conditions, and to meet sudden and various demands on their ingenuity and skill, more easily than the ignorant serf of the feudal age, or the over-specialized miner, city workman and clerk of to-day.

Partly because industry had thus broken the bounds of municipal control, the municipal life of the boroughs was already in Anne's reign suffering from senile decay. The corporate spirit of the burghers was so enfeebled that they could project no new forms to give it a fresh lease of life. They were content to watch the mediæval institutions of their City or Borough degenerate into antiquarian lumber, until at length the Municipal Reform Bill of 1835 swept it away and began a new era in town government on the basis of modern democracy.

Except in London and a few other towns, municipal government was oligarchical in one form or another. In some towns the oligarchy was of immemorial date ; in others the burgher rights of the Freemen were still in process of disappearing. If English trade had still, as in the Middle Ages, depended on efficient control by City Gilds and magistrates, the needs of commerce and industry would assuredly have caused a demand for Municipal Reform long before the era of Bentham. But in Anne's reign, so long as industry was unfettered, and so long as the individual enjoyed political, religious and economic liberty as those terms were then understood, inefficient and corrupt municipal government was not very deeply resented.

There was infinite variety among the governments of the numerous English Boroughs. Hardly two of them were quite the same. One very common form of local government was that exercised by Justices of the Peace for the Borough, who were either identical with the Municipal

Officers or were appointed by them.   On these urban
Justices of the Peace were conferred, within the area of
the Borough, much the same powers as those enjoyed
throughout the county as a whole by the Justices of the
Peace nominated by the Crown.[115]   In this way, though
there was no uniformity, there was a general similarity
between the type of government in town and in country.
This contributed to the peaceful character of English life in
the Eighteenth Century.   If there had been a self-assertive
or democratic spirit in municipal life, it must have come into
collision with the land-owning aristocracy that ruled the
island.   But as things were, the towns, with the notable
exception of London, were nearly always ready to fall into
line administratively and politically, obedient to the *mot
d'ordre* for the country at large.   As often as not, the citizens
were willing to see the members of Parliament who were
supposed to represent them at Westminster nominated by
the landed grandees of the neighbourhood, who more and
more asserted their ownership of ' rotten boroughs.'   The
other side to this system of mutual accommodation was the
respect paid by the ruling squirarchy to the real or supposed
interests of trade.   The squires usurped the Borough mem-
bership at Westminster, but they used their power there to
wage wars and make laws and treaties in the interest of
English industry and commerce.

   In the rural districts there was even less local self-
government than in the towns.   It is true that the rural
elections for Parliament were less farcical than the elections
for rotten boroughs.   But for purposes of local government
there were no rural elections at all.   Until the County
Council Act of 1888 the English countryside was judged,
administered, and rated by Justices of the Peace appointed
by the Crown from among the local gentry.   In Anne's
reign the power of these magistrates was becoming yearly
more independent and more extensive.   Since the Revolution, the Crown was more than ever afraid to interfere with
the proceedings of local magistrates whom it appointed.
Early in Anne's reign, Defoe reported to Harley how in
a dozen counties the High Tory justices were openly inciting

the people against the Moderate Tory War Ministry. They did not seem to fear dismissal by the Crown merely because they were opposing its policy. On the other hand there were many politicians who held the view that the rural magistracy should go in and out with the Ministry, that when there was a Tory Ministry all Whig Justices should be dismissed, or *vice versa*. In this matter there was no settled theory or practice. The Queen and some of her Ministers were for the moderate course in this as in other matters, while high-flying Tories and zealous Whigs clamoured for a system of ' spoils for the victors,' and the extrusion of all magistrates of the wrong party. Few disputes in the reign caused more bitterness, and few indeed were of greater importance than this unsettled question.*

The power of the Justices of the Peace was constantly on the increase, as it had been for centuries past. In the absence of a paid bureaucracy like that which served the French Monarch, most new functions of government had to be placed on the shoulders of the Justices of the Peace. The limit of the ability and goodwill of these amateurs in government was the limit of royal power in England, as James II had learnt to his cost. Except the magistrate's own clerk, there was no trained service on which the central government could rely to carry out its orders in the country-side. But the members of the Parliament at Westminster trusted the Justices of the Peace just because they were squires like themselves. Parliament, indeed, might be called the grand national Quarter Sessions. And so Statute after Statute thrust new duties upon the amateur magistrates. For example, in 1702 an Act gave to the Justices assembled in Quarter Sessions the power of assessing every town or parish for the upkeep of bridges, at a rate not exceeding threepence in the pound.[116] Police work, petty justice, the poor law, and every function of local government depended upon the same magistrates. Without a staff of specialists through whom to work, the Justices of the Peace were not, judged by our later standards, equal to the proper perform-ance of all their tasks. English freedom and the old

* See pp. 206–208, below.

English dislike of taxes and officialdom were not conducive to perfectly efficient administration.

Nothing better illustrates the inadequacy of the governmental machine than the state of the prisons. Because Quarter Sessions would have found difficulty, financial and other, in maintaining the gaols as public institutions with a staff of public officers paid out of the rates, therefore the prisons were farmed out to gaolers of the type of Lucy Locket's father. This system prevailed both in London and the provinces. The prisoners were absolutely at the mercy of these sharks, who had paid the authorities high prices for the post of gaoler and recouped themselves by practising extortion on the victims committed to their charge. The prisoner, on arrival, was struck in irons, which were only removed on payment. If he could not or would not pay ' the garnish money,' at Newgate, he was removed to the cell known as ' Tangier,' and there he was ' stript, beaten and abused in a very violent manner.' The poorer prisoners, and above all the debtors, suffered the worst ; and innocent men or discharged debtors often remained in prison for years after they might otherwise have been free, solely because they had no means of paying the prison fees which they had incurred. Men and women were often kept without bedding, and almost without food, till they died of ill-usage or found friends to pay their ' garnish.' In 1711 Mary Pitt, in the Gatehouse prison, was ' thrown down a pair of stairs because she had not money to pay for a bed,' and was ' put where she was almost poisoned ' by the stink of a corpse fifteen days old.*

Such enormities were, it is to be feared, as old as public justice itself, but they were beginning at long last to attract the indignation of philanthropists. In the reign of Anne reports were made and enquiries held into the conduct of gaolers, at least in London. But, as is well known, it was only at the other end of the century that Howard obtained the first effective measures of reform.[117]

* On the other hand, those prisoners who could pay well were, on the same principle, permitted to purchase extraordinary privileges, including that of absenting themselves under surety from the Fleet or King's Bench Prisons ' in a hackney coach privately,' or ' publicly with what they call a day-rule.' Macky, *Travels*, II, pp. 1-3, 234.

Such was the England of Queen Anne—a land of many faults and abuses, sadly wanting in the efficiency of its public organization, but not markedly inferior in that respect to other countries of the time, and superior to them in freedom and in the vigour and initiative of her individual citizens.   The war that occupied the reign was destined to render England for the first time the acknowledged head of European civilization on its political side, in place of the France of the Grand Monarch; it was owing to this change in the distribution of power that free institutions and the spirit that must accompany their exercise began to take a leading place in the thought and aspiration of mankind.

CHAPTER V

William, the Whigs and the Tories, from the Revolution to the Act of
Settlement. 1689–1701.

In the reign of Anne the struggle for power at home and
abroad revolves round the person of Marlborough. But in
the preceding reign there had been no dominant figure
among the subjects of the land : except for the King himself,
it had been a contest rather of parties than of persons.
King William, the Whig Party and the Tory Party are the
three forces whose mutual attraction and repulsion governed
the uneasy movements of the English body politic. We
may picture William as a coachman, without whip and with
rotten reins, trying to impel two high-mettled steeds, shy
of one another and of their driver, along a difficult road,
without a spill.

It was at once the weakness and the security of the
Dutch King in dealing with his English subjects, that he
cared as little for the domestic feuds that were their meat
and drink, as Gallio for the points of the Jewish law.
The one aim and passion of his public life of thirty years
was to curb the power of the French monarchy in
Europe.

When he had first stepped to the front of the world's
stage at the age of twenty-two, a young Prince far more
severe and taciturn than his kindly ancestor whom men
had accidentally called ' the Silent,' events were taking place
which marked out for him his task in life. In 1672 the
French armies, aided by England as their ally at sea,
occupied as insolent conquerors four of the Seven United
Provinces. Louis XIV declared the territories which he
had over-run to be annexed to his Crown. The Province

of Holland itself was only saved by the dilatory movements of the French Generals, that just gave time for the Dutch to cut the dykes and drown the approaches to Amsterdam and the Hague.

The terror and humiliation of that year permanently altered the outlook of Holland. Not only the policy of William during the rest of his life, but the policy of the Dutch statesmen who succeeded him in the period of the Marlborough Wars, have their origin in the events of 1672. William owed to those bitter memories half his power as Stadtholder at home, and half his influence in Europe : he stood before the world as the most formidable foe of Louis, whose ambition had become an object of dread to all.

After two years the French were extruded from the soil of the Republic, but Holland did not recover her old sense of security. In the time of the De Witts she had relied too exclusively on her navy : but now, reverting to the earlier tradition of Prince Maurice, she again sought the added protection of a large and well-disciplined army, recruited from every Protestant country in Europe. It crippled her finances and her prosperity, but she had no choice. The Dutch army, destined to play a great part in the wars of Marlborough, was very different in numbers and in quality from the regiments which had so signally failed to protect the territory of the Republic against the first onrush of Louis in 1672.

Henceforth, too, the United Provinces were protected by a system of alliance with foreign powers, in the formation of which young William showed his peculiar skill. France had become a manifest danger to the petty Princedoms of Germany and Italy, to the vast inanimate bulk of the Spanish monarchy, sprawling over two hemispheres like a dead leviathan, and even to the Hapsburg Holy Roman Emperors at Vienna. Every State of Europe, Catholic or Protestant, that still aspired to independence, saw in William the leader who could save them from the hegemony of France.

Louis threatened Austria, Spain and the Pope with vassalage, and thus forced those Catholic Powers into alliance with William ; but he threatened Protestantism with extirpation. He was extirpating it in France with the

dragonnades and the Revocation of the Edict of Nantes.
1685   The conquest of Holland or of any other State by
the French armies would, ere long, be followed by
like measures against Protestants in the conquered territory.
To Protestants, therefore, war against Louis was a war for
their religion, though fought with the help of Catholic allies.
The common literature of the reigns of William and Anne
shows that the struggle was so regarded in England.

While the object of William's life was to curb the power
of France, he saw that success could only be achieved if
England could be brought to play an active part in the
struggle.   For that reason, and not for the *beaux yeux* of the
English, or for the glittering bauble of a crown, he had
decided to run the enormous risk of invading our island in
November 1688.   Louis' fleets and armies lay on his flank,
and he had nothing on which to depend except the momentary union of all sections of English opinion against James.
The venture had, by a series of chances so wonderful that
men regarded them as providential, resulted in a bloodless
revolution.   England did not plunge into a fresh civil war
in consequence of William's invasion, as Louis had contemptuously reckoned when he permitted him to sail
undisturbed by the French armaments.   Contrary to the
precedents of former Stuart reigns, the two rival factions
agreed on a policy, chose William and Mary as King and
Queen, and entered as a united nation into the war against
France.   William had achieved the object for which he had
come over.   He had brought England into line against
Louis.

The glory of the ' glorious Revolution ' did not consist
in the triumph of a party but in the reconciliation of parties.
There was, indeed, little glory in the mere expulsion of one
foolish mortal from an island where he had made himself
universally detested, but there was glory in the lasting
treaty of mutual toleration that followed the regifuge, in the
Revolution Settlement that staunched the blood-feud of
Anglican and Puritan, Roundhead and Cavalier, and
launched Britain afresh on her career of domestic unity and
freedom, European influence and trans-oceanic expansion.
Throughout the reign of William England still staggered

from the shock of the political earthquake of the Revolution, but she kept her feet.   Only in the following reign was revealed all that the Revolution Settlement had done to give her strength.

As King of England, no less than as Stadtholder, William was guided in his conduct by his antagonism to the French power.   Since this was England's interest, he cannot be said to have deflected her course to suit his private ends.   He set her head straight once again, because her true course happened also to be his and Europe's.

Fear of Louis was no peculiar doctrine of the Whigs. The Tory Danby and the Trimmer Halifax had seen years before that it was the true policy of our country to oppose French predominance.   But the faction fight of Whigs and Tories over the Exclusion Bill, and the Roman Catholicism of Charles and James II had postponed the entry of England into the European arena.   During the years when English kings and statesmen were the pensionaries of Louis, his power on the Continent had grown so great that in 1689 all Englishmen could see the danger from France as clearly as Danby had seen it in 1674.   Neither Whigs nor Tories opposed King William when he employed the resources of the island in the maritime and continental struggle.   From the Revolution to the Peace of Ryswick, Parliament willingly voted the war supplies.

1689–1697

The reasons why England, in the reigns of William and Anne, felt constrained to take part in the wars against Louis are the same reasons that have periodically guided her action in great European crises from the reign of Elizabeth to the reign of George V : commercial and colonial rivalry, exacerbated in earlier times by the exclusive character of the commercial and colonial policy of each nation ; the need to secure the safety of our small island by preventing the predominance of any one State on the Continent—the policy known as the Balance of Power ; and the imperative demand on behalf of our maritime security that the Low Countries should not fall into the hands of a great military and naval Empire.   These were the reasons why England fought Philip II, Napoleon and

Kaiser Wilhelm. They were also the reasons why she fought Louis XIV. But there was an additional motive compelling England to fight France in the reigns of William and Anne. Louis in 1689 and again in 1701 adopted the exiled Roman Catholic branch of the House of Stuart and attempted to restore it by force of arms to the English throne. Therefore both Whigs and Tories had to fight to defend the Revolution Settlement, the Protestant or Anglican establishment, and the political independence of the nation. The fortunes of the Roman Catholic Stuarts were identified with the fortune of the French arms. Whether the chance of a Jacobite restoration was increased or diminished by being thus put to the hazard of battle, it is not easy to say. At least it made it certain that so long as the wars of William or Anne continued, nothing except French victory would restore the exiled line. The English would never in time of war send to the enemy's Court for their King.

William treated the Whig and Tory Parties merely as two indifferent instruments necessary to his task of bridling France. He regarded them with impartiality tinged with contempt. He disliked their factiousness, their furious quarrels over trifles and old memories that meant nothing to him and impeded their union in the common cause.

He began his reign with some suspicion of the Whigs for their anti-monarchical views. He thought they were more republican than they were, and he could not at once forget that they had, under the leadership of Shaftesbury, set aside the claims of his wife and himself to the throne, in order to place thereon the bastard Monmouth as the instrument of their faction. The Tory Danby had, in Charles II's reign, been the most active friend of the reversionary claim of the House of Orange to the English throne. It was not the Whigs but Danby who had, under great difficulties, negotiated the marriage of William with James's daughter Mary, precisely in order to strengthen that claim, and to bind England and Holland together against France.

William therefore began with no prejudice against

the Tories, nor was he opposed to their principles in domestic politics. They were Royalists and he had no objection to Royalism, for he was a Prince with a will and a policy of his own, brought up as the head of the anti-Republican Party in Holland. What he disliked in the Tories was their High Church principles. He was both a Calvinist and a Latitudinarian, and though his Latitudinarianism softened the rigour of his Calvinism, the two combined to put him out of sympathy with the High Church standpoint. He was not deeply concerned with the religious aspect of High Church zeal, but he dreaded its political and European consequences. High Church doctrine despised a parliamentary title to the Crown. High Church hostility to English Nonconformists divided the nation while at war, and High Church hostility to foreign Protestants stood in the way of a hearty alliance with Calvinist Holland. These tendencies, which troubled William, were destined to give no less trouble to his successor, who, though a High Churchwoman herself, was head of the fighting alliance against France.

Whigs and Tories had both taken their full share in the armed risings of November and December 1688, which drove James from England. But in the Convention Parliament of January 1689 it was the Whig majority that placed William on the throne on equal terms with Mary. The Tory minority in the Convention had striven to give him a place inferior to his wife's, as Regent or King Consort only, though charged with the administration. The Tories in 1689 had not resisted his claim to the throne from any personal objection to him, but to save their own faces as apostles of the doctrine of divine hereditary right. When the Whigs had outvoted them, they finally acquiesced in the Whig proposal to place William and Mary on the throne side by side, with equal titles, derived not from strict hereditary right, but from the vote of Parliament.

The Whigs looked for a rich reward for their support on this momentous occasion. They expected William to act as King of the Whigs, as Charles II in his later years had acted as King of the Tories. William preferred the rôle of King of England. He began by choosing a mixed

Whig and Tory Ministry, even while there was a clear Whig majority in the Lower House ; and when, in 1690, that Whig majority tried to take retrospective vengeance on their Tory enemies, and held up the Act of Indemnity instead of getting on with the war, William dissolved Parliament and aided the Tories to obtain a majority at the General Election. This strictly constitutional *coup d'état* gave internal peace to the land, and won for William several years of Tory loyalty and gratitude.   The Tory majority in the new Parliament supported him through the most dangerous crisis of the reign—the Boyne campaign and the reconquest of Ireland.

1690–
1692

But as time went on, and the centre of interest was shifted to the war on the Continent, the relations between William and the Tories began to cool.   Queen Mary's death in 1694 snapped a personal link between the party and the Crown.   The Tories loved the House of Stuart —provided its members were Anglican.   Mary and Anne, the Anglican daughters of the Romanist James, enjoyed the full measure of Tory loyalty which their father had once possessed but had sacrificed on the altar of religious fanaticism.   Mary, indeed, had no use for loyalty to herself if it were not extended to her husband.   But Anne was always on bad terms with William, whom she and her friend, Sarah Churchill, familiarly spoke of as ' Mr. Caliban.'   After Mary died in 1694, Tory loyalty and Tory hopes for the future were concentrated on Anne.

And so, for the last eight years of William's now solitary reign, the Tories looked forward with growing impatience to the day when Anne should ascend the throne.   She was everything they could wish.   She was the daughter of King James and yet a devout Anglican.   Mary indeed had been both these, but Anne was something more which Mary had never been—a High Churchwoman, and therefore a Tory.   Under her, it was confidently believed, there would be no more Whigs appointed as Bishops, or as Ministers of State, or as Justices of the Peace ; and with the help of the Crown at election time there would, it was hoped, never again be a Whig majority in the House of Commons. These party hopes for the golden age under Queen Anne would have been realized to a greater extent than they actually were, had it not been for cross-currents arising out of the renewal of the war with France.

The increasing alienation of the Tories from William was only one cause of the trouble between the King and his Parliaments in the years that followed the peace of Ryswick. The attitude of many even of the Whigs was lukewarm or hostile. It is true indeed that the Whig Ministers were becoming increasingly devoted to William. The two ablest of the Whig Junto, the Chancellor Somers and the great financier Charles Montagu, as the King's confidential servants in time of war and national peril, had been admitted to see the inner side of that nature, so repellent in the chill mask presented to the world, but so wise and constant in the crises of great affairs. And after peace had come in 1697, the Whig Ministers were flattered and to some extent misled by a tendency on William's part to prefer them to their Tory rivals and to keep them in office after they had lost their popularity.

But there were many independent Whig members who, after the return of peace, no longer felt bound to support Ministers or to gratify the King. The old tradition of their Party before the Revolution, that they should act as a ' Country Party,' opposed to the Court, was still strong on the Whig benches. And it was still thought to be the business of the House of Commons, without distinction of party, to oppose the Executive. The private member still regarded himself as sent by his constituents to keep a watch on the King's Ministers—' placemen ' as they were opprobriously called—to curb their schemes of private avarice and to thwart their plots against the liberties of the land. The honest private member, whether he called himself Tory or Whig, was often zealous in this duty—until he got a place or a pension himself.

For these reasons many Whigs united with the great body of the Tories on the floor of the House to vex the Whig Ministers and to over-ride the King on the questions of a standing army in time of peace, Irish grants and Dutch Guards.

1698-1700 (margin)

1698-1700 (margin)

It is clear that Whig party discipline was less strict in William's reign than in Anne's, when the Lords of the Junto established an absolute sway over the parliamentary movements of their followers. In 1698 many Whig members thought of Somers and Montagu, not as Whig Ministers, but only as the King's Ministers, and therefore as fair game. The implications of party government were not yet fully understood even by party men.

But while, for the first three years after the peace, William and his Ministers were badly supported by the Whigs as a whole, they bore the full weight of Tory displeasure. The increasing animosity of the Tories against William was due to many causes. His appointment of Low Church Bishops aroused as much political as religious indignation. The death of Mary had emphasized both the non-hereditary and the Dutch character of the occupation of the throne, both repugnant to Tory feelings. The end of the war with France made it possible for patriotic politicians to oppose the King's government. The Tories were incensed at the lavish grants of English Crown lands and the still more lavish grants of forfeited Irish lands, to William's Dutch friends, such as Bentinck, first Earl of Portland. Bentinck, a faithful but an ill-tempered and disagreeable man, did great injury to his master by his bad manners to the English and by his greed in accepting scandalously munificent gifts. The Parliament of 1698–1700, of which the majority was composed of Tories and anti-ministerial Whigs, forced William to accept an Act cancelling the Irish grants wholesale ; right in principle, it was a violent and unjust measure in detail, and the Commons forced it through the House of Lords by the device of 'tacking' it to a money Bill—a device of doubtful constitutional propriety of which more was to be heard in the reign of Anne. The Commons also compelled the King to send home his Dutch Guards. William, accustomed to command the polyglot army in the service of the United Provinces, had failed to understand the resentment of the English against the presence of foreign troops in their island.

These measures were popular in the country and were

supported by many Whigs. But the Tories took the lead in them and reaped popularity for expressing the national feeling against the Dutch. The Whigs stood as the champions of national feeling against France, the Tories against Holland. This difference, not perceptible prior to the reign of William, remained a constant feature of politics under his successor.

But by far the most serious measure taken by this somewhat irresponsible Parliament had been the reduction of the

1698 army to a peace footing of 7000 men, besides the garrison of 12,000 needed to keep Ireland down. In this also many Whigs joined the Tories, for the dread of a standing army, though strongest in the Tory ranks, was by no means confined to them. Louis, meanwhile, kept 180,000 men on foot. The consequent disparity in the military force of France and England that existed during the negotiations that ensued over the Spanish Succession, certainly reduced the chances of a peaceful solution, for Louis had the impression that he could do what he liked in Europe so far as England was concerned ; while the Spaniards in casting about to preserve the unity of their Empire, supposed that Louis was all-powerful and William impotent.

The worst part of the King's troubles with Parliament between 1698 and 1700 had been due to the transitional character of the English constitution in that epoch. The Royal Ministers had, at the Revolution, become once for all responsible to Parliament and dependent on the support of the House of Commons for effective action either at home or abroad. After the Revolution, a Ministry at loggerheads with the Commons could no longer play the tyrant. It was merely reduced to impotence, like a sailing-ship without the wind. It followed that Ministers would have in future to be chosen from the same party as the majority of the House of Commons. But that logical necessity was not at once recognized either by the King, or by the Commons, or by any of the leading statesmen who had made the Revolution. Only slow experience led men to this conclusion, and much of the bitterest experience was undergone in the closing years of King William.

Under the system to which William succeeded, the loyalty of Ministers was due, not to each other, not to the Commons, not to a party, not to a Prime Minister, but solely to the King. The King's will alone gave to the Ministerial counsels the unity which is to-day secured by party ties and by the influence of the Prime Minister. All through his reign William had worked with Ministries partly Whig and partly Tory. The two sides had been fairly even in his first Ministry, although there was a large Whig majority in the Convention Parliament. During the Tory Parliament that followed in 1690, the Ministry had the same mixed character ; by the end of the war in 1697 it was principally Whig, and so was the Parliament elected in 1695. But after the Peace of Ryswick, the Tories and independent Whigs out-numbered the Ministerialists in the House of Commons elected in 1698. The King would have been well advised if he had at once altered the character of his Cabinet in a Tory direction. His conduct in pre-serving a Ministry predominantly Whig to meet a House of Commons predominantly Tory was not regarded as uncon-stitutional ; but it edged the acrimony of the Commons' attack on the standing army, the Dutch Guards and the Irish grants. If, after the election of 1698, William had at once done what he finally did in 1700, if he had dismissed Somers and Montagu not because he had ceased to trust them himself but because they were distrusted by the House of Commons, even so the Dutch Guards might have been sent home and the Irish grants overhauled, but with far less bitterness and rudeness to the King ; and certainly the army would not have been cut down to a figure so perilously low as 7000 men, if there had been Ministers who had the confidence of the House to plead with it against such folly.

William scrupulously adhered to the law and custom of the constitution as it had been fixed by the Bill of Rights at the Revolution. He cannot be blamed because he did not at once perceive that Parliamentary Ministries were a neces-sary corollary of the Revolution Settlement. His English advisers foresaw the future development of the constitution of their own country as little as their foreign King. Somers and Montagu clung to office in 1699 like limpets to a rock,

till they were pulled off by the personal attacks of the House
of Commons.

At length in 1700 the King had learnt the lesson of
experience.   He took a number of leading Tories into the
Ministry in place of the Lords of the Whig Junto.   Above
all he entered into an understanding with Robert Harley,
the moderate Tory and skilled parliamentary manager.
From that moment affairs in England began to mend and
the moment was none too soon, for the French troops were
on the point of occupying the territories of the Spanish
Empire.   By Harley's help as Speaker in 1701, the Tory
House of Commons was induced to take the two great steps
which govern the domestic and foreign history of Queen
Anne's reign.   In 1701 the Tories passed the Act of Settlement, fixing the Crown on the Protestant House of Hanover
after Anne's death, and in the same year the Tories, step by
step, authorized the European alliances and undertakings
made by William for a renewal of the war with France.
Neither of these great decisions were as agreeable to the
party feelings of the Tories as to the party feelings of the
Whigs, but on both issues the Tories of 1701 did what the
interests of the country required.

The closing chapters of Macaulay's *History* give an
illuminating account of the quarrels of William with his
later Parliaments.   But Macaulay died before he had completed these chapters.   The consecutive part of his narrative
ends with April 1700.   After that we have only two frag-
ments : one deals with the death of James II in September
1701, the Proclamation of the Pretender by Louis and the
English General Elections that followed : in the other, the
historian, himself dying, describes the death of William.   He
did not live to write an account either of the Act of Settlement of 1701, or of the gradual acceptance of the war policy
by the Tory Party in the same year.   These measures
were taken by the Tory Ministry and House of Commons
during the very months when they were, with the utmost
partisan acrimony, impeaching the fallen Whig Ministers.
For this reason Macaulay's *History*, because it was left
incomplete owing to his death, conveys an impression
too unfavourable to the patriotism and good sense that

was found side by side with the bitter partisanship of the Parliament of 1701.   A distinguished historian of our own day has filled up this important gap in the annals of our country.   In Mr. Keith Feiling's *History of the Tory Party* justice is done to the part played by Harley in bringing the Tory Party into line with the national interest, both as regards the necessity for the War of the Spanish Succession, and the necessity for an Act to settle the reversion of the Crown on the House of Hanover.

To set out clearly the circumstances under which the Tories reconciled themselves to a renewal of the war will require a separate chapter.   But the Act of Settlement needs less explanation.   In July 1700 Princess Anne's only surviving child, the little Duke of Gloucester, died.   With him died the hopes of England, and in particular the hopes of the Tories, for a line of native Princes bred in the Anglican faith, and directly descended from James II.   The Duke of Gloucester's succession would have been welcomed by the Tories almost more than by the Whigs, and the Jacobites would therefore have had scant chance of success in opposing it.   Indeed it might have eliminated Jacobitism as a force in English affairs.   His death rendered the dynastic future again uncertain.   For the Acts of Parliament passed at the Revolution, though they debarred any Papist from reigning in England, had not fixed the succession on any persons more distant than the children of Anne and of William. It was now regarded as almost certain that William and Anne would both die childless, and as probable that they would both die soon.   At any moment, perhaps in time of war with France, the country might be faced by a dynastic crisis ; a disputed succession might lead to a civil war or even to a restoration of the Roman Catholic Stuarts.   It was necessary at once to fix the succession by Act of Parliament on some race of Protestant heirs.

The House of Savoy was the most nearly related to the Stuarts, but it was Roman Catholic.   At one time indeed the proposal had been made that a son of Victor Amadeus, Duke of Savoy, might be brought to England and educated as an Anglican and as heir to the throne.   The young

Savoyard was great-grandson of Charles I.* The Duke, who was no religious zealot, had welcomed this plan for his son's promotion. But towards the close of the late war he had made one of his crafty periodic changes of side, deserting the Allies to join Louis for a while. Therefore in 1700 Victor Amadeus and his family were out of favour with William and the English.

The House of Hanover was not only a Protestant House, but was stout on the side of the Allies against France. The Dowager Electress Sophia was the grand-daughter of James I of England, for she was daughter of Elizabeth of Bohemia and the Palatine, the Protestant heroine and victim of the Thirty Years' War. Sophia was fixed upon in the mind of William and many of his sub-jects as the most suitable person to succeed Anne on the English throne. The proposal to fix the succession upon her and her children had been made in 1689, but had been left in abeyance for another decade. She was a woman of much more than ordinary character and intellect, and her friend, the philosopher statesman Leibnitz, was well able to recommend her cause without appearing to press it. She herself either felt or affected an indifference to the glittering prize. She described herself as an old woman, past ambition, and her children as strangers to England. Her son, the reigning Elector, afterwards George I, was indeed more particularly a German Prince than his vivacious and internationally-minded mother. Sophia stated to William's emissaries the obvious objections to the promotion of her House to the English throne, and expressed personal sympathy for James II's son whom she refused to regard as supposititious. Historians are not agreed how far her resistance was serious. She held out for some time, but at length, under the influence of Leibnitz, and of William, who came to visit her and press England's suit, she con-sented in the early weeks of 1701 to become parliamentary candidate for the throne, on behalf of herself and her children after her.[118]

It was reported, and it is not impossible, that William had an additonal motive to get the succession settled ere he

* See p. 121, below.

died, in his suspicions of Anne's ultimate intentions with regard to her half-brother at St. Germains. It is said that William at this time received a warning from the English Ambassador in Paris to the effect that Anne was in correspondence with her father James, that she had asked his permission to accept the Crown on William's death for her own lifetime, on the understanding that she should use her endeavours to pass the succession on to her brother as James III. James II has left to posterity a fragment which appears to record that his daughter approached him with some such proposal and that he spurned it. But we have neither the text of Anne's letter to her father, nor its date. No one knows what was really passing in her mind after the death of her last child. But, in any case, the very distressing position in which Fate had placed her in relation to her father's family rendered it doubly desirable to secure the Protestant succession by Act of Parliament before her death began to draw near. She was obviously not a suitable person to burden with the task of naming her own heir.[119]

The House of Commons in 1701 was so constituted that the Act of Settlement could not have passed without the goodwill of the Tories. But the Tories were never less Jacobite than in 1701, just as they were never more Jacobite than in 1714. At the end of William's reign they were looking forward eagerly to Anne's accession ; they regarded the Jacobites as bloody traitors involved in the recent assassination plot ; and they had as yet no reason to regard the Hanoverian heir as their enemy. At the end of Anne's reign all this had changed. Many Tories were then living on intimate terms with Jacobites, and the party had by that time quarrelled with the future King George. The difference between the High Tory attitude to Hanover at the two dates can be seen in the attitude of Henry St. John, the most brilliant of the younger Tories in 1701, the future Bolingbroke of 1714. A few weeks after the Act of Settlement became law, he wrote to his friend, Sir William Trumbull,

I might venture to go to Hanover, where I should propose serving my country by being near those that are like to wear the crown of England, and laying the foundation of a future fortune to myself.[120]

If this hopeful plan had been carried out, it might have made a great difference to the history of England, or at least to the history of St. John.

In this mood the Tory Party of 1701, maugre all theories of divine right and hereditary succession, listened to the request of William, and settled the reversion of the Crown on Sophia and her children after her, being Protestants. By virtue of this Act of Settlement, George I succeeded without challenge in 1714. In that year the Tories found, to the chagrin of some, including Bolingbroke, that they had tied their own hands thirteen years before.

But the form of the Act of Settlement was not so much to William's taste as the substance. The offer of the Crown to the foreign House of Hanover was conditioned by eight provisions limiting the Sovereign's freedom of action, and some of these provisions implied a criticism of William's own methods as a foreign king. Since the Revolution the Tories had ceased to be a Court Party and were at least as eager as the Whigs to limit the powers of the Crown, when it could not be worn by a Stuart and a devotee of the Anglican Church, such as Anne. In abandoning the divine hereditary right of succession, the Tories also ceased to defend the prerogative rights of the Crown.

APPENDIX TO CHAPTER V

THE ACT OF SETTLEMENT, 1701.

ON March 3, 1701, the House of Commons passed this resolution :

That for the preserving the peace and happiness of this Kingdom, and the security of the Protestant Religion, by law established, it is absolutely necessary a further declaration be made of the Limitation and Succession of the Crown in the Protestant line, after his Majesty [W. III] and the Princess [Anne] and the heirs of their body respectively. And that further provision be *first* made for the security of the rights and liberties of the people.

In pursuance of this resolution, in particular of the last sentence, the following eight provisions were passed *before the motion settling the throne on the House of Hanover was moved.* These eight resolutions were embodied in the Act of Settlement, *to come into force when the House of Hanover should succeed.* In fact clauses IV and VI never came into force, *because they were altered in* 1705, and so the Parliamentary Cabinet system was not prevented by law from developing under the House of Hanover.

I. That whoever shall hereafter come to the possession of the Crown, shall join in communion with the Church of England, as by law established.

II. That, in case the Crown and Imperial dignity of this Realm shall hereafter come to any person not being a native of this Kingdom of England, this nation shall be not obliged to engage in any war for the defence of any dominions or territories, which do not belong to the Crown of England, without the consent of Parliament.

III. That no person, who shall hereafter come to the possession of the Crown, shall go out of the dominions of England, Scotland or Ireland, without consent of Parliament.

IV. That, from and after the time that the further limitation by this Act shall take effect [viz. *after the succession of a monarch of the House of Hanover*], all matters and things relating to the well government of this Kingdom, which are properly cognizable in the Privy Council, by the laws and customs of this Realm, shall be transacted there, and all resolutions taken thereupon shall be signed by such of the Privy Council, as shall advise and consent to the same. [*Never operative, because repealed in* 1705.]

V. That, after the limitation shall take effect, no person born out of the Kingdom of England, Scotland or Ireland, or the dominions thereunto belonging, although he be naturalized or made a denizen (except such as are born of English parents) shall be capable to be of the Privy Council, or a Member of either House of Parliament, or to enjoy any office or place of trust, either civil or military, or to have any grant of lands, tenements, or hereditaments from the Crown to himself, or to any others in trust for him.

VI. That no person who has an office or place of profit under the King, or receives a pension from the Crown, shall be capable of serving as a Member of the House of Commons. [*Never operative, because altered in* 1705 *so as to allow of re-election of a member after he has received a ' place of profit under the Crown.' If it had come into force in its original form the Parliamentary Cabinet system, as we know it, could never have grown up. Ministers could have sat in the Lords, but not in the Commons.*]

VII. That, after the limitation shall take effect, Judges' Commissions shall be made *quamdiu se bene gesserint*, and their salaries ascertained and established. But, upon the address of both Houses of Parliament, it may be lawful to remove them.

VIII. That no pardon under the Great Seal of England be pleadable to an impeachment by the Commons in Parliament.

THE RIVAL CLAIMANTS TO THE THRONE

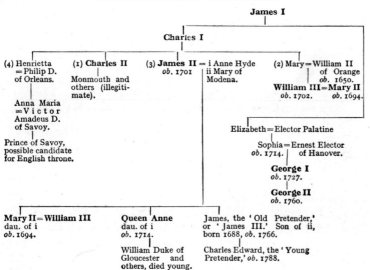

CHAPTER VI

The Spanish Empire and the problem of the Spanish Succession. The
Partition Treaties. The acceptance of Charles II's will. The subsequent errors of Louis. The drift to war and the party struggle.
The Netherlands and the Dutch Barrier seized by France. The *Asiento*
for a French Company. Effects on English opinion, Whig and Tory.

At the close of the Seventeenth Century, Spain was the
sick man of Europe. The Spanish Empire, without
national or economic unity, was saved from disruption
rather by the atrophy of its parts than by any principle of
sound administration from the centre or of self-government
in the Provinces. Famous marriages and wars of old had
brought together an incongruous collection of lands and
peoples, with nothing in common save that all were mis-
governed from Madrid.

There was indeed the link of language between Spain
and her half-breed colonies in America. The 'Spanish
Indies,' as they were called, included Florida, Mexico, the
Isthmus of Panama, Cuba and other islands, and all South
America except the Guianas and Portuguese Brazil. The
Philippines in the Pacific and the Canaries off the coast of
Africa belonged to Spain. In Europe the keys of the
Mediterranean and of the English Channel were, potentially
at least, in her keeping. For in the hands of an energetic
power, Milan, Sicily, Naples, Sardinia and the Balearic
Islands, in addition to the *terra firma* of Spain, could render
their sovereign master of all the States of Italy and all the
waters of the Mediterranean.* On the Northern seaboard,
the Spanish Netherlands, roughly corresponding to modern
Belgium and Luxemburg, formed the buffer State protecting
Holland from France ; and if once France had Holland,
it would be strange if she failed to acquire the naval control

* *See Map X at end of book for the Spanish dominions in Europe.*

of the English Channel. Therefore, in the wars of William III, when Spain adhered to the Alliance against France, the Netherlands had been defended by the armies of England and Holland, since the Spaniards themselves could no longer make any serious military effort outside the Iberian Peninsula.

'The Maritime Powers,' in other words the Dutch and English peoples who throve by traffic at sea, had indeed an interest as great as that of any people in the world in the future disposal of the King of Spain's heritage. For if his Empire as a whole fell under French domination, English commerce and manufacture and the Dutch carrying trade would be fatally injured. Of recent years the Spaniards, incapable of conducting either industry or commerce for themselves, had allowed English and Dutch merchants, thinly disguised under Spanish names, to carry on the trade between the mother country and her American colonies through the port of Cadiz ; cloth which had been woven in England, even if it had been grown on the backs of Spanish merino sheep, was imported on a vast scale into Spain herself, her American colonies, and her possessions in Italy and the Netherlands.[121] But if once French influence became supreme at Madrid all this would come to an end. Dutch and English merchants would be excluded in favour of their French rivals in every one of these great markets. The Mediterranean would be closed to their ships. And in addition to economic ruin, the national independence of England, based on her control of the narrow seas, would be seriously threatened by the French in the Netherlands ; while Holland would be exposed to the armies of Louis gathered on her very frontiers along the Scheldt and the Maas.

Such fears were not visionary. When Anne came to the throne every province of the Spanish Empire was occupied either by the armies of Louis or by Spanish garrisons acting as his allies. If these newly sketched frontiers of French influence could be made good as a permanent fact, based on accepted Treaties and guaranteed by the law of nations, the independence of every State of Europe, not excluding England, would remain at the mercy of the Grand Monarch. It is true that the fleets and armies of

Spain no longer weighed in the balance of power as at the time of the Armada, or even of the Thirty Years' War. There was little use in warships that could never put to sea, or in regiments that could never take the field. But great use could be made of the harbours, fortresses, territories and populations belonging to Spain in both hemispheres. In November 1700 all these at a stroke of the pen were placed at the disposal of France. Vast provinces and unnumbered millions of men, who had figured as allies of William III in the war that ended in 1697, were four years later arrayed on the opposite side.

Why did the Spanish Empire thus cease to be the antagonist of Louis and become in effect his property for the purposes of the new war ? It is necessary to give some answer to this question before attempting to unravel the wars and policies of Queen Anne and her servant Marlborough.

The Spanish Empire from 1665 to 1700 belonged to the imbecile invalid, King Charles II. The conditions under which this most exalted and most miserable of mankind dragged out his existence have been described in the last chapters of Macaulay's *History*.* By an irony of fate, cruel alike to Charles and to Europe, his grotesque sufferings were prolonged year after year, contrary to all expectation. He lingered till November 1700, and died at the precise moment when nothing short of a World War could decide the question of his inheritance.

If Charles II had died before the Peace of Ryswick in 1697, while Spain was still at war with France, the Spanish Empire would have passed either to the Austrian or the Bavarian candidate, and France would have been powerless to interfere. That was one reason why Louis had been eager to conclude a general peace, because, so long as France

* The account of the Spanish Succession question from 1697 to 1700 in Macaulay's *History of England* is no less picturesque and more reliable than his account of it in the youthful essay on the *War of Succession in Spain*. That essay, as he himself has recorded in a letter most kindly given to me by Dr. Temperley, was written for the *Edinburgh* ' very hastily, with very little assistance from books, during the tumult of a contested election at Leeds ' (1832). Given these remarkable conditions of authorship, the result, though not an historical authority, is an historical *tour de force* certainly never equalled by any other parliamentary candidate !

was in a state of war against Spain and Europe, the French claims on the Spanish inheritance would go by default.

1697   When, therefore, peace was restored at Ryswick, the minds of European statesmen were at once directed to solve the problem of the Spanish Succession before the death of Charles II should actually take place.

The three most important candidates were three young Princes—the French Bourbon, Philip; the Austrian Hapsburg, Charles; and the Bavarian, Joseph Ferdinand. Both Louis XIV and the Emperor Leopold of Austria were sons-in-law of Philip IV of Spain and also grandsons of Philip III. Following the natural order, the eldest son of Louis XIV would succeed Charles II. But at the marriages of Louis XIII and Louis XIV respectively to the two Infantas, the French claim to the Spanish throne, resulting from those marriages, had been solemnly and officially renounced by the parties concerned. Next came the claim of the House of Bavaria ; there also renunciations had been made, but privately and not in a manner affecting the law of Spain. But the Emperor Leopold, in view of these renunciations, claimed the whole inheritance for the House of Austria, though he was ready to renounce it for himself and his eldest son, the future Emperor Joseph, in favour of Charles, the cadet of the family.*

* TABLE OF THE SPANISH SUCCESSION

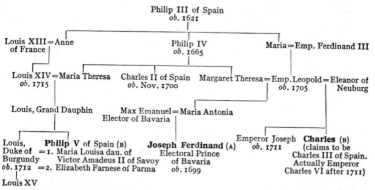

Philip III of Spain
ob. 1621

Louis XIII=Anne of France

Philip IV
ob. 1665

Maria=Emp. Ferdinand III

Louis XIV=Maria Theresa
ob. 1715

Charles II of Spain
ob. Nov. 1700

Margaret Theresa=Emp. Leopold=Eleanor of
ob. 1705   Neuburg

Louis, Grand Dauphin

Max Emanuel=Maria Antonia
Elector of Bavaria

Emperor Joseph
ob. 1711

Charles (B)
(claims to be Charles III of Spain. Actually Emperor Charles VI after 1711)

Louis, Duke of Burgundy
ob. 1712

Philip V of Spain (B)
=1. Maria Louisa dau. of Victor Amadeus II of Savoy
=2. Elizabeth Farnese of Parma

Joseph Ferdinand (A)
Electoral Prince of Bavaria
ob. 1699

Louis XV

(A) Recognised heir of Charles II and chief beneficiary of the First Treaty of Partition till his death in 1699.

(B) Rival claimants of Spain after Charles II, the elder brother of each resigning his pretensions.

As regards the character of the renunciations made, see *History*, January 1928, Sir Richard Lodge's article.

No one outside Vienna expected Louis to consent to the annexation of the whole Spanish Empire by any member of the House of Austria. Nor would Austria, or any State of Europe that aspired to independence tolerate a French Prince as Lord of Spain, the Spanish Indies, Italy and the Netherlands. In such a case, compromise was a necessity to the life of Europe. Partition alone could have averted war ; and after twelve years of war Partition was accepted by the tired combatants at Utrecht.

Of the three claimants, the young Bavarian was by far the most popular among European statesmen interested in the balance of power. For under him the Spanish Empire would remain independent of both Austria and France. The neighbours of the Spanish Empire—Holland, England and the German and Italian States—had nothing to fear from a Bavarian ruler of the whole inheritance. France could endure him better than an Austrian Prince and Austria could endure him better than a French Prince. Nov. Therefore, Charles II by his first will made Joseph 1698 Ferdinand heir to his whole Empire, to counteract the designs of Partition that were hatching beyond the Pyrenees.

Nevertheless some Partition was inevitable. For though most of the States of Europe would have accepted the Bavarian as sole heir, neither Austria nor France would have consented to forego their respective claims without compensation. That was the reason why William and Louis had made the First Partition Treaty, between Oct. France, England and Holland, to save the peace 1698 of Europe. By this Treaty most of the Spanish Empire went to the young Bavarian, but important consolation prizes were assigned to France and to Austria. In particular, Milan was to go to the Austrian Charles, while Naples and Sicily were to be detached from the Spanish and added to the French Crown.

William and Louis were making honest and praiseworthy efforts to avert another European War. It might have been thought that if France, England and Holland were agreed to keep the peace by supporting some plan of Partition, peace would be kept. But peace and Partition had two constant enemies—the obstinacy of Austria and the obstinacy of Spain herself.

The Emperor Leopold of Austria continued to claim the whole Spanish inheritance for his younger son, Charles. The intransigent attitude of Vienna was a major cause of the War of the Spanish Succession.

Equally fatal was the refusal of the Court and the people of Spain to consent to any diminution whatsoever of the world-wide territories that they themselves were admittedly unable to defend. The Spaniards, noble and simple, were indifferent to the question who should succeed to the Empire—French, Bavarian or Austrian—provided the whole inheritance in Europe and America passed unimpaired. How the safety and interests of the rest of Europe were affected, whether peace was preserved or not, was of no account to Castilian pride. But no province, no fortress must be given away, even to avert Armageddon.

During the fifteen years of diplomacy and war that intervened between these first abortive Partition Treaties and the final Partition at Utrecht, it may be doubted whether any single statesman of France, Spain, Austria, England or Holland ever gave a disinterested thought to the wishes or interests of the Italians, Flemings, Walloons and American half-breeds, whose future was the subject of these high disputes. Such ideas were not then current. European diplomats, busy with the mosaic work of adjusting States and boundaries, were not then called upon to make the rules of their art conform to the embarrassing demands of nationality or self-determination. The subjects of the Spanish Empire were merely counters for bargaining, make-weights in the balance of power. Nor, with the exception of the inhabitants of Spain herself, did the populations in question show any effective resentment at being so regarded.

If Charles II had died in the last months of 1698 there might have been no War of the Spanish Succession at all, and almost certainly no general war involving the Maritime Powers. By the will of Charles II, the Bavarian Prince would have been his successor. He would have been accepted as such in America, Spain and the Netherlands ; Austria, having no sea-power, could not have asserted her claims in any of those regions.   And the Spaniards would have been equally unable to do more than protest at the compensations in Italy awarded to France and Austria by the First Partition Treaty.   A war in Italy between French and Austrian armies was the worst breach of the peace likely to have occurred if Charles II had died before the Electoral Prince.

Unfortunately it was not the long-moribund King of Spain but the Bavarian boy who died in February 1699. At this brute stroke of chance the elaborate edifice of peace so carefully constructed by William and Louis crashed to the ground.   Unwilling even then to despair of peace, the two veteran antagonists took up again their task of goodwill, and produced the Second Partition Treaty.   Louis dreaded a renewal of war on a grand scale for his impoverished country and went a great distance along the road of concession to avoid it.   In 1699 he was as moderate and prudent as two years later he was arrogant and impolitic. He actually consented in his Second Partition Treaty with William that the Austrian candidate should become King of Spain and the Indies, and ruler of the Spanish Netherlands.   France was to be compensated by Naples and Sicily, as in the former treaty, and in addition by Milan ; but she was to give Milan to the Duke of Lorraine in exchange for his province, already practically in French possession.*

It seems wonderful that Louis should have consented to such terms, which may be regarded as a masterpiece of William's diplomatic skill.   Yet those who stood most to benefit by the arrangement were the reverse of grateful. Leopold of Austria had the incredible folly to refuse his support to a treaty which would have given to his younger son three-quarters of the Spanish Empire with the consent

---

* By a curiously bad slip in a generally accurate work, the *Cambridge History of British Foreign Policy*, I, p. 42, says that Charles was to get only Spain itself, and that the Netherlands, the Spanish colonies, the two Sicilies and the Milanese were to go to France.   If William had made such an agreement, he would have been traitor to England, to Europe and to his own life's work.

f France.   He preferred to fight for the whole without
chance of success.

The English people were no better pleased than the
Emperor.   Overlooking the larger fact that William had
induced Louis to forego claims which would be far more
perilous to England and to the world, they fixed on the single
point that Naples and Sicily were to be added to the French
crown.   On the danger of this arrangement Tory squires
and Whig merchants and cloth manufacturers were
agreed.   William's subjects were persuaded that France in
possession of Naples and Sicily could close the Mediterranean to the ships of rival powers.   It was assumed that
England's Turkey and Levant trade could not run the
gauntlet of French naval bases in Sicily and southern Italy.
William, on the other hand, was sure that with a friendly
monarch in Spain, the English fleet could hold its own in
the Mediterranean in time of war and cut the sea communications between France and Naples, while the Austrian
armies in Italy could dispute the land route.   Naples and
Sicily, so far from adding to the strength of France, would
in fact be hostages for her good behaviour.   Such, at least,
was William's view, and he was not in the habit of giving
way points to Louis.

England's great naval historian, Julian Corbett, has
singled out William as the first statesman after Cromwell
to grasp the full importance to our country of a naval
position in the Mediterranean, and to lay plans of diplomatic and naval strategy in accordance with that idea.   The
war plans that Marlborough afterwards carried out against
Gibraltar and Port Mahon and attempted against Cadiz
and Toulon, he had inherited from William.   In the course
of the negotiations with Louis leading up to the Partition
Treaties, William had claimed Port Mahon and Gibraltar
or Ceuta for England, as guarantees for her naval position in
the Mediterranean in the event of Spain being allotted to
a French prince—a suggestion identical with the actual outcome at Utrecht after a dozen years of world war.   In
particular, William had fixed his prophetic eye on Port
Mahon as the base most suited to England's needs.   It was
neither from too great love of France nor from neglect of

K

English maritime interests in the Mediterranean that William had been ready to concede Sicily and Naples to France as the price of peace.[122]

But whatever be thought of the substance of the Partition Treaties, the manner of their making was open to grave objection from the point of view of English constitutional practice. William had negotiated the Treaties without the knowledge of his English Ministers and had presented them with the *fait accompli*. And Parliament had been kept in the dark all the time.

These proceedings had not been illegal, but the Tories did good service when they put a mark upon them as unconstitutional. Such methods might have passed muster before the Revolution, but were out of keeping with the new relation established between Crown and Parliament. The Impeachment of Somers for his acquiescent part in the affair was useful in stopping such action by future sovereigns. It is true that the attack on the Whig Chancellor was pursued with the vindictiveness then usual in party warfare, and that much irrelevant matter was added to the charges brought against him by the Commons. The Lords protected Somers, and the Impeachment was eventually dropped, after a quarrel about procedure between the two Houses of Parliament.

William learnt his lesson. He saw that he must consult both his Ministers and his Parliament in grave decisions of English foreign policy. And, therefore, in the year 1701, when the crisis of the Spanish Succession came to a head in a new and terrible form after the death of Charles II, he was careful to carry his Tory Ministers and his Tory House of Commons with him in every important step that he took abroad, in every treaty or commitment by which he bound England. For that reason he was eminently successful in the last act of his life, the creation, with Marlborough's help, of the Grand Alliance of 1701 to fight the coming War of the Spanish Succession. He had striven in vain to render war unnecessary, and been roundly abused for his pains in England and in Europe. But when the disaster which he had tried to avert became inevitable, his diplomatic preparations for the struggle obtained the country's consent and securely laid the foundations of the edifice of Queen Anne's glory.

The obstinacy of the Emperor Leopold of Austria in failing to sign the Second Partition Treaty and accept the lion's share it awarded to his son Charles, was partly due to mere procrastination and inability to take a decision, characteristic of the statesmanship of Vienna ; but it was partly due to the belief that Charles II's strong-minded German wife would assert herself as usual, and bully him into leaving the whole inheritance to the Austrian candidate. In building thus on the influence of the German Queen, the Emperor forgot that the able representatives of France at Madrid, especially the Ambassador Harcourt, had since the peace four years back gained much ground, against the German party, with the Court and people of Spain ; and he forgot, moreover, that Louis, if defied, could march his troops into Spain, where there were no native armies capable of resistance.

The Spanish grandees had a more lively sense of the real situation of their country than Leopold in distant Vienna. They shivered at the thought that the unprotected passes of the Pyrenees alone lay between them and Louis' redoubtable legions. They heard that William had quarrelled with his Parliament and that his army had been disbanded ; such, they reflected, was always the way in England, a country of heretical madmen, not to be relied on. They knew that Austria, having no fleet, could send no troops to protect Spain from French invasion and maintain the authority of the Austrian Charles in America or the Netherlands. Yet they were determined that there should be no partition. Only one course, then, was open now that the Bavarian prince was dead—to proclaim Louis' grandson as Philip V, and call on his grandfather to defend the whole Spanish inheritance against all comers. Since France was in a position to defend the Spanish Empire and Austria was not, the French candidate must be preferred.

For these reasons, Cardinal Porto Carrero and the Spanish grandees, supported by the mob of Madrid, drove the German Queen and her party from the bedside of the dying King and overawed his feeble mind with solicitations that assumed the character of commands, while the whole enginery of superstitious terrorism was applied for the same purpose by practised hands.   Thus overmastered, Charles II abandoned his life-long enmity to the House of Bourbon and his life-long attachment to the other branch of the Hapsburgs.   He signed his last Will and Testament in favour of Louis' grandson, Philip, and promptly died in November 1700, bequeathing to the world this apple of discord.

The famous Will of Charles II represented neither the result of French intrigues through the Ambassador Harcourt, nor the personal whim of the imbecile testator.   It represented the proud, blind determination of the Spaniards of Castile to keep every inch of the Empire which they called their own.   For that they were prepared to set all the nations of the world fighting.   The strongest fighter, France, they had bought to do battle for their cause by naming a French prince as their King.   But they had no special love for France, except as the hired champion of their imperial unity.   Charles II, therefore, had, at Porto Carrero's dictation, made it a condition of his dying bequest to the French prince that, if Louis would not sanction the acceptance by Philip of the whole Empire, the whole was to go to the Austrian Charles.

What would Louis do ?   All the world waited to hear. He was, indeed, placed by the dead man's offer in an awkward, though a proud position.   He had just signed a new Partition Treaty with William allotting Spain and the Indies to Austria.   And now the whole Empire was offered to his grandson if he would throw over the Partition Treaty.   He was a grand gentleman ; could he condescend to break his word just plighted to another King ?   No doubt if he could enforce the Partition Treaty, he was bound in honour to uphold it and so give Europe peace.   But, in fact, he could not enforce it, and his refusal to accept Charles II's Will would not give Europe peace.   For Austria had not accepted the Partition Treaty, though its terms were so favourable to her candidate.   If, therefore,

Louis now refused the whole Spanish inheritance for his grandson, Philip, Leopold was free to accept it for his son, Charles.

Torcy, the wise French minister, thus stated the case in his memoirs :

If the King refused to accept the Will, this same Deed transferred the entire succession to the Archduke Charles. The same courier that had been despatched into France would proceed to Vienna : and the Spanish nation would, without any hesitation, acknowledge the Emperor's second son for King. The House of Austria would re-unite, betwixt the father and the son, the ancient power of Charles V, a power formerly so fatal to France. . . . The King, by rejecting the Will had no other course left than entirely to resign the Spanish Succession, or to wage war in order to conquer that part which the Treaty of Partition had assigned to France.

The prospect of such a war was not inviting to Louis. The best part of the territories assigned to France by the Partition Treaty lay in Italy where Austrian armies could most easily come. And it was far from certain that England and Holland would support Louis in arms : for he would be fighting to annex Sicily and Naples and certain Tuscan ports to the French Crown in accordance with the Partition Treaties—the very arrangement which had aroused the strongest commercial and national jealousy in England. In the Christmas of 1700, the Tories were loudly declaring that it was better that the whole Spanish inheritance should go to the Bourbon Philip, on the condition that the Crowns of France and Spain should never rest on the same head, rather than that Naples and Sicily should be annexed to France. Many of the Dutch were at that moment of the same opinion.

Therefore, neither England nor Holland was likely to give warlike sanction to William's Treaty of Partition. If Louis rejected the Will, and went to war with Spain and Austria for his portion under the Treaty, he would get no help on the thorny road of honour. But if he chose the primrose path and accepted the Will, he would have Spain on his side ; her territories, fortresses and harbours would everywhere be open to his troops and fleets in time of war, while it was most doubtful whether England and Holland would dispute Philip's accession. Austria, of course, would declare war, but without the help of the Maritime Powers she could not transport her armies to America, Sicily, the Low Countries or Spain. The war would be confined to Italy under circumstances peculiarly favourable to France.

All these arguments considered, it is difficult to blame Louis for accepting Charles II's Will on behalf of his grandson. What else could he be expected to do in the face of the obstinacy of Austria and Spain, and the unreliability of England and Holland? In November 1700, Louis decided to accept the Will, and sent his grandson to Madrid to reign there as Philip V.

Up to this moment Louis had acted with great moderation in the matter of the Spanish inheritance. For several years he had seemed above all else anxious to avoid the renewal of war with the Maritime Powers in the then economic condition of France. That was a policy worthy of a great King, if only he had continued it to the end. But now that, as the Spanish Ambassador declared in the enthusiasm of the moment, there were no more Pyrenees, the brilliancy of the new prospect turned every head in the French Court. Louis was again the Sun King, *nec pluribus impar* ; William was beaten in the game of their life-long rivalry. The Grand Monarch and the upstart Dutch Princeling were back in their relative positions of thirty years before.

Such was the voice of the French Court, raised in a pæan of joy and adulation. In an air so infectious as Versailles no wonder Louis was again attacked by one of his recurrent fits of arrogance. In a few months he fatally compromised the position of moral advantage which he had held when he first accepted the Will ; he united and armed his enemies against him, and roused England and Holland from acquiescence in the Will, to a grim determination to fight by the side of Austria for a fair Partition of the Spanish inheritance.

The great war was made inevitable, not by the acceptance of the Will, but by the interpretation which Louis put upon it in the following months by seizing the Dutch

Barrier, by showing that he regarded the Spanish Netherlands as French territory, by excluding the English merchants from the American trade, and by treating the
Spanish Empire as a prize for French commercial exploita-
tion and a field of manœuvre for French armies.   By these
measures he converted the English Tories to the need of
war, before ever he crowned the edifice of pride and folly
by proclaiming the Pretender as King of England.

Against these errors, which were to prove so fatal
to France, Louis received fair and full warning.   His
Ambassador in England was Marshal Tallard, whose name
was ere long to be associated with the most memorable
episode in the fulfilment of the premonitions he now made
to his master.   In December 1700 Tallard wrote to Louis
that the English people hated the Partition Treaty and that
it was dead ; he declared that the English positively preferred the Will to the Treaty.   But, he added, they do so
under the belief that they are to be given security for their
trade in the Spanish Empire, and that Flanders will be
governed independently of all French influence.   The
English people, he said, want peace, but only if security
be given.*

William meanwhile confessed to Heinsius that neither
England nor Holland would fight, that the Will was
accepted by public opinion in both countries.   For the
moment he was powerless, and had the sense to know it.
His strength was to sit still, and say nothing to alienate
any further his irritable and suspicious subjects, until Louis
should have done his work for him, and persuaded English
Tories and Dutch burgomasters that they must fight or be
slaves.

Optimism and pacifism reigned at the festal boards of
Englishmen in the Christmas of 1700.   But with the New
Year these sentiments received a series of rude shocks.

* St. Simon represents Tallard as a figure of fun, sulking absurdly because the
Partition Treaties which he had negotiated were thrown over in favour of the
Will. But there is no sign of this mood in his despatches. In December 1700
he accepts the new situation frankly and on that basis gives his master excellent
advice, which if taken would have saved France from disaster. *P.R.O. Tr.* 3.
France, 186, ff. 270–280 and *passim*.

In the first weeks of February the French armies poured
into the Spanish Netherlands and occupied all the fortresses,
including Nieuport and Ostend opposite the English coast.
This unexpected news, Tallard reported, had greatly disturbed opinion, and unfavourably affected the results of the
General Election then taking place.   Though the ' Wigts '
had not a majority in the new House, they were more
numerous than Tallard had hoped, and even the
Tories were turning hostile to France.   Already in
February he noticed that the popularity of Lord
Rochester and the friends of France was declining.   His
foreigner's account of the General Election is remarkable :
at the previous election, he writes, the constituencies had
chosen solid country gentlemen to maintain their liberties
and keep down taxation ; but this time more than forty-
three merchants have been chosen, by favour of the Court
and by profuse expenditure of their own money—men not
subject to the land-tax who will, therefore, vote for war more
easily.   The ' Wigts,' he says, are the Presbyterians, the
Tories are the Anglicans ; there is also a third party
attached to Marlborough.   Opinion is running hard
against France.   The best he can do is to tell the English
that Louis will withdraw the French troops from the
Spanish Empire, as soon as Spain is able to defend her own
provinces—a date suspiciously like the Greek Kalends.
Meanwhile the Ambassador begs his master for more and
more *louis d'or* with which to bribe the Duke of Hamilton
and the seamen at Chatham, and so stir up revolts and
revolutions.   But the time had gone by when such proceedings could turn Britain from her course ; they only
provoked angry denunciations in the House of Lords,
where the Whigs declared that France was at her old game
of corrupting the nation with gold.[123]

The occupation of the Milanese by French troops was
reasonable on the ground that the Austrian armies were
pouring over the Alps to dispute Philip V's Italian possessions in the name of the Archduke Charles.   But in the
Netherlands there was no such excuse.   No Austrian
troops could reach Flanders.   The Maritime Powers were

Feb.
1701

not disputing Philip's claims there, or indeed anywhere else. The Elector of Bavaria, who had for some years past been acting as Governor of the Netherlands for Spain, had proclaimed Philip without encountering any opposition. If he had been merely loyal to Spain, he had no need of French troops. But in fact he was in league with France. The Spanish Netherlands were administered in his name by Bedmar as his lieutenant governor, who took his orders not from Madrid but from Versailles.

It is clear from Louis's own correspondence that the French armies were sent into the Netherlands not to protect them for Spain but to annex them for France. Before the end of the year he began to broach at Madrid a proposal for the partition of the Netherlands between himself and the Elector of Bavaria. He was met at first by the assurance of his Ambassador that he dared not even mention it to Philip, lest his subjects should get wind of the scheme. It was precisely to avoid partition that the Spaniards had handed themselves over to Philip, and already it had come to this ![124]

But Louis did not confine himself to occupying the Spanish fortresses in the Netherlands. He seized the Dutch Barrier guaranteed by international treaty. Ever since the French invasion of thirty years back, Dutch policy had been directed first and foremost to prevent a repetition of that catastrophe. Not only was a large and effective army now kept up by the United Provinces, not only were European alliances formed, but the Dutch had obtained Treaty Rights to occupy with their own troops a number of fortresses in Spanish territory, stretching in a broken line from Luxemburg to the sea. The inefficiency of Spanish garrisons and armies fully justified this precaution. But the precaution was not enough, for the Dutch garrisons were widely separated from each other and were left under Spanish command.

Such was the Dutch Barrier in 1701. It was weak militarily, and it was not rendered self-subsistent by the political and commercial privileges which Holland claimed for the Barrier restored after the recovery of the Netherlands by Marlborough. In 1701 the Spaniards felt no objection to the presence of the Dutch garrisons, and it was not the Court of Madrid that demanded their extrusion. It was the high-handed act of Louis himself in pursuance of a purely French policy.*

The betrayal of the Dutch Barrier fortresses to the French troops was arranged between Marshal Boufflers and the Elector of Bavaria, who, though Spanish Governor, had now passed over entirely into the interest of France. At his orders the French were admitted into the fortresses. They disarmed the Dutch garrisons, who hardly knew whether it was their duty to resist. They were kept as prisoners of war for some weeks, till the States General formally acknowledged Philip as King of Spain. Then they were contemptuously permitted to go home.

Holland and her six sister Provinces had hoped to find safety by a timid approval of Charles II's Will. They awoke to find their Barrier gone, the roads and fortresses of the Netherlands choked with French armies, their own frontier open every moment to attack. It was 1672 come again—almost but not quite. For this time the Republic had on foot a well-disciplined army of 45,000 men, which was at once ordered to be raised to 80,000. England was very differently prepared for the crisis ; the Parliament of 1698 had cut down her army to 7000. Had it not been for the more adequate Dutch force, Louis might have marched unimpeded to the Hague and forestalled the formation of the Grand Alliance against him, before England had time to rouse herself to action and re-equip her disbanded regiments. This immense initial service was recalled by the Dutch in later years, when Swift and the Tories complained that they left the burden of the war increasingly on England.[125]

Both Louis and William temporized in the summer of 1701. Though the outlying Dutch Barrier had been

---

* *P.R.O. Spain*, S.P. 94, 75. Aglionby writes from Madrid, May 4, 1701, that the Spaniards ' never had any apprehensions of the Dutch remaining in their towns in Flanders and it is not they but France who has driven them out and will never give the fortresses back to Spain.'

The first Dutch Barrier, thus destroyed in 1701, consisted of Luxemburg, Namur, Charleroi, Mons, Ath, Oudenarde and Nieuport. *See Map VIII at end of volume.*

seized, the territory of the United Provinces was not invaded. And William for his part still walked warily. He was negotiating the great European alliances that were to wage war on the new Franco-Spanish Empire. Such a combination was not to be made at a week's notice but step by step, and for each new step of diplomacy abroad he had to win the consent of his agitated English Parliament, where the whole mass of opinion was in confusion, faced by the unexpected aggression of the French King.

The news that the French had occupied Belgium came as a thunderclap to the English. It had much the same effect as the news of the German occupation of the same country two centuries later ; with equal certainty it led England into the war, though at the slower pace of all happenings in that more leisurely epoch. Another piece of news that quickly followed was scarcely less disagreeable to the islanders. Louis compelled the Spaniards to make over to a French Company the coveted ' *Asiento* ' or ' Contract,' for supplying Spanish America with African slaves, and the Company's monopoly was enforced by the ships of the French Royal Navy policing the American waters. The Government of Spain ostensibly forbade other nations to trade with her colonies at all, but the slave-trade permitted under the *Asiento* carried with it an amount of half recognized smuggling of other goods. ' The French ships,' it was presently reported, ' go frequently to all the Spanish ports in the West Indies under pretence of carrying niggers according to their agreement, and at the same time introduce their and other nations' commodities and return with the proceeds to France, which the Spaniards resent, but can't yet help it.' This *Asiento* contract and its opportunities for smuggling on a larger scale was one of the most coveted things that England won for herself in the war and pocketed at the Peace of Utrecht.[126]

The American trade was not the only one in peril. ' The vent of English cloth,' always a first object in the eyes of the nation and its public men, was likely to be shut out from three of its largest European markets by the entry of the French troops into the Netherlands and Italy, and by the subjection of the Spanish peninsula to French influence. Aglionby, an able English diplomat who arrived in Madrid in February, wrote home that the French Ambassador Harcourt was 'holding councils in his own house,' where Porto Carrero and the grandees of Spain came to pay him 'the lowest submission.' 'This country,' wrote the Englishman in April 1701, 'is nothing but an instrument in the hand of France.' What prospect, then, was there for the continuance of English trade in any part of the Spanish Empire, or indeed in any part of the Mediterranean, which was becoming a French Lake? 'There is not,' Aglionby reported in June, 'a port between London and Leghorn where we can shelter ourselves in case of war and so refresh. Leghorn itself is but precarious now, so that the Turkey trade is quite out of doors.' Aglionby's reports from Madrid were borne out by his Dutch colleague Schonenberg. In June, Portugal made an alliance 1701 with France and Spain. In October, English and Dutch merchants in Spanish ports were being forced by the authorities to sell their goods at half price. Every month that passed, the hatred for England and Holland grew greater at the Spanish Court and the dependence on France more abject.[127]   The meaning of Charles II's Will, as interpreted by Louis, was becoming clear to all Englishmen. Our country must either fight the French or abandon to her rivals commercial prosperity and naval power.

Such were the reasons why the House of Commons elected in February 1701 sanctioned the successive steps by which William in that year prepared England and Europe for war, or at least for a demonstration of warlike power which should bring Louis to reason. As early as February 1701 20th the Commons asked the King to enter into negotiations with the United Provinces and 'other potentates,' and promised to support the Treaty of 1677 by which England was bound to defend Holland with 10,000 men if she were attacked. Such was our immediate response to the French invasion of the Netherlands. From that first resolution of the newly elected Tory Parliament sprang the whole movement that led on to Blenheim, Ramillies and Utrecht. It came as a disagreeable surprise to the Courts

at Paris and Madrid.   Harcourt confessed to the Spaniards
that he had not looked for it, ' but the English are the most
unsteady people, easy to be blown to violent resolutions.' [128]

After that first step things marched more slowly for
a while.   The Tories were in the majority in the Commons
and they hoped for peace, if it could be kept with safety
and honour.   They trusted that Louis would yet see reason
if they showed a stiff front to his aggressions.   Their
leading pamphleteer, Charles Davenant, was engaged in
the double process of heaping abuse of the most libellous
character on the Whigs as corruptionists, and preaching
a *via media* abroad, based not on surrender to France, but
on an honourable agreement.   The French *chargé d'affaires*,
Poussin, whom Tallard left behind him in England in
April, was in close touch with Davenant, persuading him
to alter passages in his pamphlets too unfavourable to
France, promising that Louis would be reasonable, urging
him to trounce the Whigs.   Though Davenant attacked
the Whig clamour for war, he himself wrote : ' What
Englishman can bear to see Flanders in French hands ?
And what mischiefs to our trade may not be expected from
their being in a manner masters of Spain and Italy ? '   But
if Davenant supposed that anything short of defeat in the
field would induce Louis to withdraw the French armies
from the Netherlands and to give English merchants access
to the Spanish markets, he had allowed Poussin and his own
wishes to get the better of his often excellent judgment.[129]

The Whig opposition, on the other hand, was beating
up the country for a war.   As Louis's arrogant proceedings
over commerce became known, the war spirit in London
and the Home Counties swelled high.   The Whigs strove
to fill their own sails with the rising blast.   They attacked
the Tories as pensioners of France, as disloyal to the good
King, as men who had disarmed the nation in the face
of the enemy.   The famous ' Kentish Petition,' drawn
up by the Grand Jury and freeholders at Maidstone quarter
sessions, was presented to the House of Commons on
May 8th.   It ' humbly implored the Honourable
House to have regard to the voice of the people,
that our religion and safety may be effectually provided

May
1701

for, that your loyal addresses may be turned into bills of supply and that his most sacred Majesty may be enabled powerfully to assist his allies before it is too late.' The Kentish Petition and others modelled upon it were indeed part of an organized Whig propaganda, but they were also genuine expressions of the changing temper of the country.

The Tories were stung to fury by the accusation of want of patriotism. In revenge, they pressed the impeachment of Somers with redoubled zeal. They raised the cry that the Constitution was being destroyed by democratic attempts to overawe the independence of Parliament, and the five gentlemen who had presented the Kentish Petition were imprisoned for the remainder of the session by order of the Commons. Yet Poussin had to report to France that the petitions organized by the Whigs in London and the provinces had had a most unfortunate effect on opinion, and that when the King asked for troops to be sent to defend Holland in case of attack, the Commons had granted it.[130]

In the summer, Parliament was chiefly engaged in passing the Act of Settlement.* The fury of domestic faction and the imminence of foreign war only served to hasten its passage. In September the European crisis came to a head with the signature of the Treaty of Grand Alliance at the Hague and the proclamation of the Pretender at Versailles.

1701

* See p. 119, above.

CHAPTER VII

Marlborough at the Mauritshuis. The Grand Alliance and the war aims of the Allies. Proclamation of the Pretender by Louis. Whigs and Tories in William's last Parliament. Louis invades the Bishoprics. The eve of war. The death of William.

THE Grand Alliance between England, Holland and Austria represented the result of months of anxious work by William and Marlborough, in adjusting the very different views of the Emperor and the Maritime Powers. In this delicate task Marlborough served his apprenticeship in great international affairs, under the master whom he was destined to succeed as the leader of the European league against France.

Early in the reign, Marlborough had headed the party of the Princess Anne and of the Tory malcontents against William ; and he had been deep in abstruse Jacobite plots, with what precise motive no one then knew and no one now knows. Since the death of Mary had made Anne the immediate heir to the throne, the relations of the Marlboroughs to the King had somewhat improved. And William, to whom personal resentments were nothing when the common cause was at stake, had fixed on Marlborough to carry on the work to which he himself was becoming unequal and which he must soon relinquish altogether. It was a policy at once magnanimous and subtle to admit his late enemy to his innermost counsels for the salvation of Europe ; to send abroad the Englishman who had a few years before posed as the leader of the anti-Dutch party, to work as the colleague of Heinsius at the Hague ; to give Marlborough a near view of Europe as the field of his future ambition, and so to engage his interests and affections in the conduct of the great struggle with France. When once he had seen the real aspect of continental affairs from inside, his strategic genius would never permit him to adopt the comfortable belief held by so many of his fellow Tories, that naval operations against Spanish Colonies and treasure-ships were the chief part of all that England need do to bridle the ambition of Louis.   William desired that, before he himself left the scene, Marlborough should be personally committed to the common cause of Europe. Anne could be trusted to follow his lead.   The future Queen had long been accustomed to take the sage advice offered her by the husband of Sarah Churchill.

With these ends in view, William in the first days of July took Marlborough with him from Harwich to the Hague, as English plenipotentiary and Commander-in-Chief of the forces that Parliament had agreed to send for the defence of Holland.   Already the first of English subjects, Marlborough was treated like a Prince and lodged in the Mauritshuis.   A finer work of art has never been shown there.   The statesmen of Europe were received at the top of the staircase by a glorious living portrait of a Milord, every inch a soldier and a courtier ; said indeed to be fifty years of age but in the prime of manly beauty, with a complexion like a girl's ; talking charmingly in bad French ; seeming to understand all and sympathize with everyone.*

July 1701

It was a most engaging picture, whatever passions or schemes were hid behind the canvas.   Those the future might reveal—or haply never reveal.   But though the Dutch could not pluck out the heart of his mystery, contact with him gave them fresh confidence.   The terrible position in Europe and on their own frontier seemed somehow lightened by the presence in the Mauritshuis of this courteous, dignified man, giving the sense of immense reserves of power.   It cheered the Allies hardly less than the news that the great Prince Eugene with his Austrians had broken out of the Alpine passes by a masterpiece of

---

* Even after Ramillies, when he was nearer sixty than fifty, a Dutch Deputy, who knew him well, noticed his beauty ' de blanc et de rouge qui puisse braver le plus beau sexe ' ; also his bad but charming French.   See van Goslinga's *Mémoires*, ed. 1857, pp. 42–43.

strategy, and begun the war in the plain of the Po to advantage, while Holland and England still negotiated. There was something in Austrian unreasonableness after all ! Perhaps Louis was not invincible. Milord's smile said as much.

Above all Marlborough won the confidence of Heinsius, the Grand Pensionary of Holland. It was as well they should be friends, for they two would have to carry on William's diplomatic task when he was gone ; and they would have to conspire together to keep their two jealous countries on a common course, when the Stadtholder King no longer united the governments, when the Tories ruled in England and the burgher oligarchy raised its head in Holland.

In those summer months spent by Marlborough in the Hague beside the still waters of the Vyver, he acquired his consummate knowledge of the element in which his life's work must thenceforward move. He mastered the details of the political and military map of Europe. He learned to deal at close quarters with the slow, reliable selfishness of Vienna ; the greed and jealousy of some German Princes, the greed and public spirit of others ; the bourgeois tremors of Dutch deputies and generals ; the raw barbarian pride of Charles of Sweden. On each of these he learned to play as on an instrument : all could be used to make or mar the harmony of the Alliance. They must be attuned to one another and to the island prejudices of the squires in the Parliament at home.

The first difficult adjustment of these factors, the common work of William, Marlborough and Heinsius, took shape in the Treaty of Grand Alliance. It was signed by Austria, England and the United Provinces—Marlborough alone signing for England.

Sept. 7 (N.S.) 1701

The three principals bound themselves to exact certain terms from France and Spain, by negotiation if possible, or if that failed by war. Other Princes were to be invited to join the League as accessories.

With great difficulty Leopold of Austria had been persuaded that his Allies could not be bound to win the whole Spanish inheritance for his son Charles. In 1701 neither

England nor Holland was ready to fight on those terms, though they changed their minds two years later. The original Treaty of Alliance accepted the rule of Philip V over Spain and the Spanish Indies, on condition that the crowns of France and Spain should never under any circumstances be united, a point on which Louis had offered no satisfaction to Europe. But in return for acknowledging Philip at Madrid, the Allies bound themselves to obtain for the House of Austria ' a just and reasonable satisfaction ' in the shape of Milan, Naples, Sicily, the Spanish Mediterranean islands, and finally the Netherlands.

The Allies, in fact, engaged to fight for a 'Partition' of the Spanish Empire, such as was afterwards effected at Utrecht. Many years later Bolingbroke, when accused of treachery to the allied cause for having made peace on those terms, justly defended himself by referring to the Treaty of Grand Alliance :

The object of this war, which King William meditated, and Queen Anne waged, was a Partition, by which a Prince of the House of Bourbon, already acknowledged by us and the Dutch as King of Spain, was to be left on the throne of that dismembered monarchy. The wisdom of those counsels saw that the peace of Europe might be restored and secured on this foot and the liberties of Europe would be in no danger.[131]

The Treaty of Grand Alliance did not, however, assign the Netherlands unconditionally to Austria. For in that quarter Holland considered that her own most vital interest lay. By Clause Five the Allies bound themselves to recover the Spanish Netherlands ' with the intention that they should serve as a dyke, rampart and barrier to separate and keep off France from the United Provinces.' What precisely these words might mean the future would reveal. The bear had better be killed first, before the hunters fell out over dividing the skin. Five years later, when the victory of Ramillies had driven the French from the Low Countries, the difference between the Austrian and the Dutch interpretation of Clause Five became only too apparent. The Austrians then claimed full, immediate sovereignty of the reconquered lands, while Holland claimed practical sovereignty till the war was over, and afterwards a perpetual barrier of fortresses much stronger and more independent than the Barrier which Boufflers had so easily swept away in the February of 1701. The vagueness of definition on this point in the Treaty of Grand Alliance was due not to bad draftsmanship but to the diplomatic necessity of postponing an irreconcilable dispute.[132]

The special trading interests of England and Holland were secured by a clause guaranteeing to them the same commercial privileges in the territories remaining to Philip V as those which they had enjoyed under Charles II ; the same clause expressly barred the French from becoming possessed of the Spanish Indies, or even from sending any vessels there to trade ' directly or indirectly under any pretext whatever.' England's general interests were otherwise sufficiently safeguarded by the provisions under which the Spanish holdings in the Netherlands, Italy and the Mediterranean islands passed under Austrian rule : Austria could be no object of jealousy to England, for she was an inland power with no fleet and no naval ambition.

At Marlborough's instance, a clause was added authorizing England to seize and hold for herself at the peace any parts of the Spanish Indies that she coveted. Such colonial expeditions he knew to be the ideal of the coming war cherished by many of his Tory colleagues, though in his own mind European operations by land and sea held a prior place. The same privilege of territorial plunder in South America was, *pro forma*, conceded to the Dutch, who were even less likely to exercise it.

In the weeks following the signature of the initial Treaty of Alliance, Marlborough showed admirable prudence and firmness : he resisted the entreaties of Heinsius and the wishes of William that he would pledge England to provide a specific number of troops, to balance similar undertakings by Austria and Holland. ' Before God I will die rather than do so fatal a thing,' wrote Marlborough to Godolphin, in language unusually impassioned from his pen : the numbers must be left to the free vote of Parliament, or that jealous assembly would throw everything overboard. And to Secretary Hedges he wrote :

Oct.
1701

If the King should be prevailed upon to settle this by his own authority we shall never see a quiet day more in England and consequently not only ruin ourselves but also the liberties of Europe. For if the King and Parliament begin with a dispute France will give what laws they please.

The impeachment of Somers for the affair of the Partition Treaties had served as warning ; English diplomatic procedure was being duly adjusted to a parliamentary system of government.[133]

Marlborough in fact proved to be no mere apprentice, learning the diplomatic trade from William. Still less was he a mere instrument of the King's foreign policy, like Portland or Somers. In these negotiations that laid the basis of the Alliance so well, Marlborough asserted his own personality and the rights of the English Ministry and nation, yet in a manner that gave no offence to his master. He so prepared the Treaties of Alliance that they would be acceptable to Parliament. Marlborough would not have been England's greatest leader in war if he had not understood the necessary relation between her war effort and her civil constitution. In that understanding he was not surpassed by Chatham himself. Long absences abroad, great victories in the field, the flattery of all Europe never made that cool head forget that he must answer for all he did to the Commons of England.

Marlborough also took the lead in negotiating a Treaty that pacified Charles XII of Sweden. He persuaded that prickly but Protestant monarch, in return for English gold, to dissociate his interest from Louis and leave his late enemy the King of Denmark free to hire out Danish troops to fight on the Western front for the Allies. It was not the last time that Marlborough would be the means of dissuading the fiery Swede from falling on the rear of the Alliance.[134]

That winter, Treaties were rapidly made with the King of Prussia, the Bishop of Münster, the House of Hanover, and other German Princes, by which each covenanted to send prescribed numbers of cavalry and infantry, usually in return for specified payments by England and Holland. Already the Maritime Powers were the paymasters of the Alliance. These subsidiary Treaties grew in a thick cluster

round the original Treaty of Grand Alliance between the
three principals. The international army that Marlborough
was to lead in the spring was signed and sealed for, on the
faith of the English and Dutch exchequers. For all this
the English Parliament readily consented to stand sponsor,
partly owing to the prudence of Marlborough, but still more
owing to the crowning imprudence of Louis.

The Treaty of Grand Alliance had been signed on
September the Seventh, though it was not yet ratified, and
was kept a secret for some weeks.* Louis was still ignorant
of its contents, though informed as to the general attitude
and intentions of the Allies, when on September the
Sept. 13 Thirteenth he stood by the deathbed of James II and
(N.S.) promised to acknowledge his son as James III. A
1701 few days later the young man was, on his father's
death, proclaimed in France as the new King of England.

By this act Louis proclaimed himself above all law
save his own will; he broke the Treaty of Ryswick, by which
he had acknowledged William as King and had pledged
his word of honour not to countenance any attempt to
disturb the English Government ; and he flouted the Act
of Settlement, which Parliament had passed only three
months back, for the precise purpose of cutting off from
future hopes of succession the Prince whose claims he now
championed before the world.

No defence of his conduct is to be found in the sophis-
tical pleading of Torcy. That able Minister of France,
anxious to minimize the anger of England, argued in his
best diplomatic style that the proclamation of the Pretender
was a pure formality and meant no more than the English
King's retention of the antique title of King of France. No
one in Europe believed that, least of all Torcy himself. In
the very month when Louis publicly proclaimed James III,
he was conspiring in secret with his ally, the new Pope
Clement XI, to bring about a Jacobite restoration on
William's death. Hard cash was sent to Paris by the Pope,
to be used by the French Government to bribe the Scots
Parliament through the agency of the Duke of Hamilton.

* The Treaty of Grand Alliance was disclosed to Louis on November 10 by
the Swedish Minister. *Klopp*, IX, pp. 397, 410.

Torcy himself, even while he was assuring Europe that the proclamation of the Pretender was a mere form, was assuring Cardinal Gualterio, the Papal Nuncio at Paris, that if there were a war an armed attempt to restore James would be made, and that even if there were no war the young man would be helped by France to mount the English throne the moment William was dead.[135]

If Torcy opposed and deplored his master's hasty and emotional act in proclaiming James III, it was not because he disapproved attempts to overset the Protestant succession in England, for he was even then plotting such an attempt himself. He only thought it unwise to stir the warlike ardour of the English people by letting them know the truth. They would have been yet more angry if they had known the whole truth, and had realized that the Pope himself was conspiring with Louis to restore the Roman Catholic line in England.

Torcy's disclaimer of any real intention was therefore not made in good faith, and need deceive no one. The real defence of Louis' action, from his own point of view, is very different. He had determined not to make any of those large concessions which the Allies were bound to demand of him as the price of peace. Therefore, though he still hoped for peace on his own terms, he was fully prepared for a renewal of war, under conditions that seemed to ensure victory. Everything surely had been changed in his favour since the last European struggle. The Netherlands and the whole Empire of Spain were now at his disposal ; the new Pope was his ally ; the Elector of Bavaria would raise his standard on the banks of the Danube. William he knew to be dying,[136] and he had been advised that on his death the Republican and pro-French party would revive in Holland and overthrow Heinsius ;[137] as to England, he believed that, even if he failed to effect the restoration of James III, the Tories would come in with Queen Anne, and either keep peace or wage half-hearted war. When William was gone, what other Prince or general could give unity to the military operations of the Allies, if any such were undertaken ?

It never occurred to Louis that these calculations would

be overset by the English nobleman whom William had recently taken the odd fancy to push forward at the Hague. As yet the name of Marlborough had no terrors in the French ear. The secrets of his double disloyalty in the past were better known at St. Germains and in the French Chancellery than in London ; while his military successes over English peasants at Sedgemoor and Irish bogtrotters at Cork, however remarkable in fact, had made little noise among professional soldiers abroad.

Louis, therefore, though he still hoped for peace, did not fear war, and he did not fear the English. Why then should he not indulge his personal sentiments of pride and generosity, and promise the dying James to place his son on the throne at the earliest opportunity ? The gesture would win the applause of the chivalrous French people. And it would restore to him in case of war the confidence and co-operation of the Jacobites of England and Scotland, who considered that the King of France had betrayed them at Ryswick.

But all that Louis gained with the Jacobites he much more than lost with the rest of the nation. The proclamation of the Popish Pretender by France gave to the coming war a dynastic and religious character in the eyes of the English, without distinction of party. It was the High Tory Chief, Sir Edward Seymour, who moved in the House of Commons that a clause be added to the Treaty of Grand Alliance, binding the Allies not to sheathe the sword till Louis had acknowledged the Protestant Succession in England. In April 1702 this clause was accordingly added to the Treaty ; Holland and Catholic Austria thereby undertook to fight for the Protestant Succession as the price of England's continued support of their own claims. Austria had no feeling for the Stuarts who were the catspaws of France. The English dynastic question took a leading place in the war aims of the Allies ; and the somewhat shadowy Hanoverian Succession, hovering aloof in space and in time, came nearer to English hearts when English soldiers fought for it at Blenheim and Ramillies.[138]

The proclamation of the Pretender was not indeed the

reason why England joined in the War of the Spanish Succession.   Her participation had become certain a week earlier when Marlborough had set his name on her behalf to the Treaty of Grand Alliance.   Though the Tory Ministry and Parliament were ignorant for some time of the precise terms of the Treaty, they had given their previous sanction to the formation of an Alliance to obtain security and compensation from Louis and Philip.   They would, in any case, have gone to war in support of the Treaty.

But it is by no means certain that, without the spur of Louis's final insult, England would have made the great military and financial effort necessary to achieve victory. Many of the Tories who accepted the war as unavoidable, were still, like Rochester and Jersey, unwilling that England should fight ' as a principal ' in Flanders and Germany.   They still disliked their Dutch allies, the four-shilling land-tax, and the regular army of which they had hoped to see the last at the disbandment of 1698.   They wanted to attack the Spanish Colonies and to do as little as possible on the Continent.   But the rage produced in England by Louis's insult governed affairs in the last months of William's life, and after his death enabled Marlborough to commit Queen Anne to the policy of a great Continental war in the summer of 1702.   His success in that first campaign rendered it impossible for his High Tory colleagues to withdraw England from an enterprise so happily begun.*

The French recognition of James III was not the only

* A song popular in English alehouses at the beginning of 1702 shows the feeling against Louis and the rising interest in the continental war, then confined to Eugene's campaign in Italy :

> In the Ryswick Charte remember
> He great William lawful names ;
> But grown doating last September,
> Loudly sounds, loudly sounds another James ;
> Routs our trade too,
> And would invade too,
> Could turn the Oglio into Seine,
> Which our boys in Italy
> All resolve shall never be.
> Drink, drink, drink we then
> A flowing glass to Prince Eugene.

D'Urfey, *Pills*, II, p. 226.

provocation endured by England in September 1701. In that same month Louis prohibited the importation of all British manufactured articles into France.[139] The dynastic outrage and the economic injury combined set all England aflame. The Tories were reconciled to war ; but the temper of the nation made the electoral opportunity of the Whigs. For a year past they had been denouncing the Tories as Francophils and Jacobites. Here, they were now able to say, is the outcome of the Tories' tenderness for France and their slowness in declaring war. Louis flouts us because he no longer fears us. Let us have men to conduct the war who intend to win it and will vote the necessary measures. In the winter of 1701–1702 the nation, though united for the coming struggle abroad, was torn by the rage of faction at home.[140]

What course would William take ? Portland, Somers and other ex-Whig Ministers, still threatened with impeachment by the existing House of Commons, saw the road back to safety and power opening before them. They besought William to hold another General Election at once. Now was the moment to get a Whig Parliament and a Whig Ministry as the necessary prelude to a vigorous conduct of the war. Such was their advice to the King, and their reasoning was supported by the counsel of the mystery-man of English politics, Robert Spencer, second Earl of Sunderland. Once James II's pseudo-Papist tool and then his betrayer, Sunderland now acted behind the scenes as William's occasional confidant, for he was skilled in the cool prognostication of storms of State, though he had wrecked himself by sailing too near the wind in the greatest tempest of all.[141]

William yielded to their persuasions so far as to dissolve Parliament, though it was not ten months old. He cared little about the Whigs, but he saw that a House elected in the present state of public feeling, whether Whig or Tory, would be pledged to prosecute the war with vigour. But he still walked warily. He would not change the Tory Ministry before the Dissolution ; and, therefore, the influence of the Crown and Government, always an important make-weight in

Nov. 1701

elections, was not thrown decisively on the side of the Whig candidates.

When the new House met in January 1702, parties were evenly balanced ; the Whigs had improved their position, though less than they had hoped except in the London area.* But the Assembly as a whole was strong for war. The 'Poussineers,' as Davenant and the friends of the late French Minister were called, had been rejected by the constituencies.

William's conduct in dissolving the old Parliament was justified by its European results. For although some months after Anne's accession the new one was succeeded by another Tory Parliament, it sat long enough in both reigns to initiate the Continental war by sea and land according to the ideas of William and Marlborough, to the exclusion of the half-hearted policy of Rochester and the High Tories. And that first step gave the direction to the whole course of the war.

But it was inevitable that the Tories were bitterly aggrieved at the dissolution. As a party they never forgave William. It was his last act in relation to them, and it coloured their picture of him in memory. After his death they forgot how he had helped them against the Whigs in the Christmastide of 1689–1690, and remembered only the Christmas of 1701. The feelings of the average Tory towards William and the Whigs at the moment of the November dissolution are expressed in a private letter of Henry St. John : [142]

The King is desirous to meet a Parliament of good Englishmen and Protestants, in order to which he dissolves us, and thus we are sent to the country with labels affixed to our backs. The Dutch . . . were resolved not to enter into a war but upon the foot of the last . . . and so have raised these wretches [the Whigs] once more to oppress our unhappy country. If in the next Parliament people continue thus mad and the majority of the House be modern Whigs (as from the

* Vernon wrote to Shrewsbury, 'I wish the people all over England would choose with the same spirit they have done in Westminster, London and Southwark, where they have shown great aversion to Jacobitism and a French faction. . . . The lists of the new choice contain many of the old members and some of the hottest, only Hammond and Davenant happen to be dropt.' B.M. Add. MSS. (Coxe) 9090, f. 118.

ill temper of the nation we have some reason to fear it) why then *actum est*, at least we are on the very brink of destruction. But if the contrary should happen, then . . . the child unborn may rue the hunting of this day, to use an expression out of the noble ballad of Chivey Chase, and these fellows while they have been endeavouring the ruin of their country, may have worked out their own.'

Fortunately in the newly elected Chamber the balance of the two angry parties was so even that neither could oppress the other. Parliament met in January, strong for war, prepared to send large English armies to the Continent and a great English fleet into the Mediterranean. The High Tory policy of fighting the land war through subsidies alone was abandoned in face of the demand of the constituencies for more vigorous measures. But while a large majority of both Houses was united on foreign and military policy, in domestic affairs Whig and Tory still raged against one another as though no enemy were at the gate.

1702

The close balance of parties in Parliament was reflected in the Ministry : Godolphin, the finest of Tory adminis-trators and financiers, resigned, greatly to the chagrin of Marlborough, his friend and kinsman by marriage. But William still adhered to the principle of keeping both parties in his service. Somers and the Whig Junto were not brought back to power. But the mixed Ministry, like the Parliament, was united on a vigorous conduct of the war.

It was, indeed, time for England to show that she meant business. Before Christmas all hope that peace could be kept in the following spring had been abandoned by both sides, and armies were taking up their positions accordingly. Louis, whose forces preponderated in the Low Countries and Lower Rhine, brought off a great blow there late in November. To forestall the Allies, he extended the area of his invasion of the Netherlands by sending the French armies to occupy the whole Bishopric of Liège and some important Rhine fortresses in the Bishopric of Cologne, including Bonn. In so doing he isolated the outlying Dutch possession of Maastricht, occu-pied the valley of the Maas up to the borders of Dutch

Nov.
1701

Brabant, and threatened an invasion in the Spring of the United Provinces from bases on the Rhine and the Maas, the route of 1672. The chain of his armies and fortresses ran from Bonn and Kaiserswerth to the sea.*

He had invaded the two Bishoprics in the strength of his new alliance with the Elector Bishop, Joseph Clement, whose brother was Max Emanuel, Elector of Bavaria and Governor of the Netherlands. These two brothers of the House of Wittelsbach between them gave the keys of all the Netherlands and of the Upper Danube to Louis. The Chapter of Cologne, as often before, took the opposite side to its Bishop, and called in Allied troops to garrison other towns in the Electorate.[143]

Such was the situation of Europe when William met his last Parliament. The King's Speech, ably drafted by Somers, called the nation to arms to defend its safety and honour, and asked the Gentlemen of the House of Commons to show by their votes of supply ' that they shall never be losers who trust to a Parliamentary security.' The news of the enthusiastic reception of this speech by the two Houses put fresh heart into hesitating princes abroad, and speeded their preparation for war against France. Now for the first time the Treaty of Grand Alliance, signed four months back, came into the full vigour of active life when ratified with the consent of the English Parliament. ' You will easily guess,' wrote Stepney, our Minister at Vienna, ' what a favourite I am grown since his Majesty's Speech has reached us and the noble resolutions of the Commons.' The statesmen of the Hague, long accustomed to read the fortunes of their country in the debates at Westminster, declared in February that no House of Commons had ever done better business in less time.[144]

Jan. 1702

The number of soldiers to be supplied by England, which Marlborough had so wisely refused to fix on his own responsibility in October, was freely voted by the new House of Commons at the splendid figure of 40,000 †— 18,000 to be British and the remainder foreigners in English pay. And 40,000 English seamen were to man the fleet. Thrown on to the streets without provision after

---

* See *Map VIII at end of volume*.   † See pp. 147-148 above and **Ap. A.** below.

the Peace of Ryswick, many of the sailors had taken to piracy and the soldiers to marauding on the highway ; they now returned from these and other more honest employments to knock the raw recruits into shape.   In the early months of 1702 the naval press-gang was let loose on the merchant ships and the seaboard towns ; and William's veteran army, destined to see better fortune as Marlborough's, was hastily called back to the colours.

For three years past, loungers in the London parks had been familiar with the sight of hungry half-pay officers in threadbare red coats and the hat and feather of their profession.   The poor fellows had had much to put up with during the anti-military reaction that followed the Peace of Ryswick.   Even their half-pay was in arrears.   And the veterans of the Boyne, Steinkirk and Namur had been told to their faces that they were ' the plagues of the nation,' a danger to the constitution and to all honest men.   The habit of showing gratitude to soldiers at the end of a war is a growth of quite recent times, at least in England.   Many officers, rather than beg or go on the highway, had taken service under the Emperor or the Dutch.   Those who remained in England watched eagerly the signs of a change of temper in the country and the chances of a new war with France.   Now once more they found themselves the favourites of their fickle countrymen.   The King, in accordance with the votes of Parliament, was signing commissions for them at the rate of two hundred a day.   The playhouse resounded with their wrongs, advertised by the Whig playwrights.   The army was in vogue again.[145]

But while the moderate Tories co-operated with the Whigs in all that concerned the coming war, they were at one with the High Tories on home affairs.   Neither section of the party could forgive the late dissolution, or the Whig agitation that had preceded it.   When the new House met in the first days of January 1702, the moderate Tory, Harley, was elected Speaker by four votes over the Whig Littleton.   But in the following days the Whigs were in the majority on several election petitions, which in those days were treated by both sides not as questions of evidence but as tests of voting strength in a new House.   A few weeks later, when William was on his deathbed, the Tories begin to win the election petitions, and it was only by fourteen votes that the Commons decided to drop the impeachments against the late Whig Ministers. No one could tell from day to day how the House would vote.[146]

The Tories just succeeded in carrying a retrospective censure on the famous Kentish Petition. But their resolution reflecting on the petitions which had urged the King to dissolve the late Parliament was defeated. The Whigs warmly defended the liberty of the subject to petition, and the rights of the constituencies to express their opinions about the actions of their representatives. The Tories took their stand on the sacrosanct character of the House of Commons, and its right to choose a course uninfluenced by the pressure of opinion from outside. The debate on these nice principles of the constitution, fanned by party passion, went on after the winter daylight failed. Candles were ordered, but as only one was set upon the table, the orators harangued unseen, hurling across the floor language which they would never have ventured to use if their faces had been visible to their opponents. The darkness rang with angry cries, sword hilts were handled as on the day of the Grand Remonstrance long ago ; the scene was compared by alarmed spectators to Milton's pandemonium or the Polish Diet.[147]

Such was the fury of faction during the last days of William's life, in a Parliament happily united on foreign affairs. The last important public act of the reign was the Abjuration Bill. No one in England had regarded the recent Proclamation of the Pretender as a 'formality.' The Tories were fully as angry as the Whigs, and more embarrassed. It was necessary for them to dissociate themselves in the most unequivocal manner from Jacobites in league with the national enemy. In the new Parliament, not only did Seymour insist on the insertion of the Protestant Succession in the Treaty of Grand Alliance,* but an Act of Attainder against the Pretender was passed into law.

Finally the Abjuration Bill imposed the test of a new and

* See p. 151, above.

stricter oath on all Members of Parliament, clergy, and office holders.   It had been part of the compromise on which the Revolution Settlement was based, to respect the tender consciences of Nottingham and other High Church-men who, while perfectly ready to swear allegiance and give true loyalty to William as King ' in fact,' could not swear to him as King ' by right.'   That was a distinction known to the old law of England in the days of the rival Roses, and it helped to give peace to the land under William's rule.   But Louis' insult stirred the nation to such anger, that a new oath was demanded, renouncing the Pretender in less equi-vocal terms.   By the Abjuration Bill of 1702 every person holding a post in Church or State was called on to deny the theory of divine hereditary right, for he had now to take the compulsory oath to William, and afterwards to Anne, as 'lawful and rightful' monarchs, and to abjure the Pretender and his heirs as having ' no right or title whatsoever ' to the Crown.

Nottingham and the High Churchmen had Louis to thank when they were forced to swallow this unpalatable draught.   The fact that Anne had come to the throne before they were called on to take the new oath, no doubt made it easier to conform, in actuality though not in logic. Yet the satisfaction felt by the High Tories at the accession of James II's daughter was qualified, when they found them-selves thus compelled to make a more explicit declaration of Revolution principles under Anne than had been required of them under William.   Those who still hoped for a repeal of the Act of Settlement and a Jacobite restoration after Anne's death ' took it for granted,' like one of Nottingham's correspondents, ' that notwithstanding this oath every man is free to consent to any change that shall be made by Parliament.'[148]

But the new oath tended to prevent the return of Non-juror clergymen to the Established Church in Anne's reign. It was refused wholesale by the Scottish Episcopalians. It was used in 1709 as a further weapon with which to persecute the Roman Catholic priesthood in Ireland.

The Tories in Parliament had assisted at the passage of the Abjuration Bill and, with the exception of the ever

scrupulous Nottingham, they had scarcely ventured to
object to the stricter terms of the proposed oath of loyalty.
The majority of the party had indeed voted against making
the oath compulsory.   But in their days of power under
Queen Anne they never repealed it.   The new test, thus
far sanctioned by the passive consent of the Tory Parlia-
mentarians, aroused the indignant protests of many of their
supporters in the Church and in the country at large.   The
oath indeed was taken, but not without many murmurs
against those who had passed it.   Such was the embarrassment into which the dynastic question was constantly
putting the great party which, but for that question, would
have been decidedly the strongest in the State.   In the reign
of Anne, many Tories, like Swift, tried to solve these difficulties for themselves or their friends, by still affecting
doubts as to the birth of the Pretender, while the Whigs
rejoiced to proclaim him the genuine son of James II, but
excluded from the throne by vote of Parliament on the clear
and rational principles of the Revolution.[149]

On February the twentieth William went for his last
ride in Hampton Court Park.   The intrepid horseman,
who had so often hunted the boar and the stag all
day, and so often ridden unscathed through the
thick of battle, met his end from the stumble of his
horse, Sorrel, on a level stretch of English sward.   It
was only a collar-bone, but death had its bill out against him
on other counts, and his frail body was unable to recover from
the shock.   For more than a fortnight he lay at Kensington
in a fever, slowly dying, while Whigs and Tories wrangled
at Westminster as fiercely as ever, not knowing for some
days after the accident how near they were to the great
change.   On February the twenty-eighth a message came
to them from the King raising larger visions : William's
last message to the two Houses was a recommendation for
a closer Union of the kingdoms of England and Scotland.
He had had the misfortune to be King of both, severally and
at once, and knew from the experience of Darien what
weakness resulted to Britain from the disunion of her two
Parliaments and her two systems of commerce.   William,
who loved England little, understood her interest well.

Feb. 20
(O.S.)
1702

The large successes of the reign of Anne, which laid the foundations of British power and prosperity in the Eighteenth Century, had all been foreseen and advised by the Dutch King—the Grand Alliance, the Continental war under Marlborough, the fleet in the Mediterranean, the acquisition of Gibraltar and Port Mahon, and last but not least the Union with Scotland—these were all policies that he bequeathed.

On the sixth of March, no longer able to write his signature, he was held up in bed to put with feeble hand the stamp of his approval on a commission to pass the Abjuration Bill. The High Tories who had hoped he would die before it passed, considered this the last outrage.[150]

Two days later the end came.* As the news spread over Europe, men's hearts stood still, the Allies fearing that all was lost, the French hoping that all was won without a war. Louis had been promised by his agents great changes for the good in Holland and England as soon as the breath was out of William's body. For some days it was rumoured in French official circles that Anne was having difficulty in securing the succession, and would be in need of all her troops at home. Then the mists cleared, and Anne was seen, seated benignly on her throne amid the enthusiasm of a loyal people ; while in Europe the great machine of the Alliance prepared by William, moved forward to the brisker tune of Marlborough going to the war. If indeed it was a molehill over which Sorrel had stumbled in the Park, the ' little gentleman in black velvet,' toasted by Jacobites, had done his work too late to help either them or their friend King Louis.[151]

* Macaulay's account of the death of William, on the last page of his history, has no references at the foot of the page, as the historian himself died before completing it. I do not therefore know whether he had read the account given by L'Hermitage to the Dutch Government, nor, if he had, whether he considered it a high authority. I think some of it is worth quoting for comparison with Macaulay's narrative. In the first place L'Hermitage states that Bentinck was half an hour late in coming to the bedside of his friend and master owing to the mistake of a valet sent for him by the King. When at length he came, Bentinck found William being held up in bed by attendants. ' Il s'approcha tout prest du roi pour entendre ce que Sa Majesté vouloit lui dire, mais il ne peut entendre que quelques paroles Flamandes qui signifient en Français *pour la dernière fois.* S.M. lui tendit la main et la lui serra, et l'on dit qu'elle (S.M.) la luy porta sur son coeur.' *B.M. Add. MSS.* 17677, x, f. 248. ' Flamande ' we should translate ' Dutch.'

M

In times of desperate difficulty William had done services to England greater than those rendered to her by any save a very few of her native Princes.   But he had been cold to Englishmen, not hiding his preference for his native land and people.   So his meed over here had been admiration always, gratitude sometimes, but seldom love.   He was remembered as the Deliverer, often with religious thankfulness ; but warmth of feeling for him, on this side St. George's Channel, was found chiefly in the army, among the men who had seen his soul taking fire under the stresses of battle.   Uncle Toby, when he remembered the look of William galloping past him at Landen to rally the shaken squadrons for another charge, forgot the King and cried ' gallant mortal ! '

In Anne's reign and for long afterwards, his memory was the plaything of parties—a toast for Whigs, a stumbling block for Tories, a flag of flaming battle in Ireland.   But though opinions about him differed with parties or persons, there was a core of agreement : the central feeling in England was given voice by the West Country Tory member, Sir John Packington, when the news of his death was announced in the Commons.   ' Sir, we have lost a great King ; we have got a most gracious Queen.'

CHAPTER VIII

First days of the new reign. Marlborough again at the Hague. Question of the command. Character and opinions of Queen Anne. Her Church appointments. The dynastic question in 1702. The ' Queen's evil.' Anne and Party Government. Anne and the war. The Prince Consort, George of Denmark. Character of Marlborough. Godolphin as Lord Treasurer.

THE first week of Anne's reign was hardly less momentous than the last. If the dramatic scene at her deathbed cleared the path for the peaceful advent of the House of Hanover, the early hours of her accession ensured that the conduct of the coming war should lose nothing in vigour by William's death, a decision unwelcome to some who stood near the Queen's throne, utterly unexpected in France, and hardly hoped for in Holland.

William died on the morning of March the eighth. It was Sunday, but no one thought it wrong to labour for the salvation of the State. That very day the Queen was proclaimed, and met her Privy Council. She addressed them in a soft, clear, pleasant voice, her chief asset on public occasions. She told the Council, and thereby told the world, that her two aims were the maintenance of the Protestant Succession and the reduction of the power of France. As old Sunderland wrote to the Marlboroughs—' She is now in the King's place, her interest is the same as his was.' [152]

March 8 (O.S.) 1702

The same day the Lords and Commons assembled,* and each voted an address, expressing not only their loyalty

---

* *H. of L.* and *H. of C. Journals.* After the Assassination Plot against William, an Act had been passed to avoid a dissolution of Parliament at the demise of the Crown. The Houses were thereby enabled to sit (for not more than six months) after the King's death, and so thwart all Jacobite plots against the succession.

to Anne and the Protestant line, but their desire to wage the war with the utmost vigour.   On Monday these addresses were presented to the Queen.   On Tuesday, March 10th, only forty-eight hours after William's death, Marlborough had received his instructions as Ambassador Extraordinary from Queen Anne to Holland : he was to go at once to the Hague to revive the drooping spirits of the Alliance and arrange for the opening of the spring campaign.   On Wednesday the Queen, making her first speech to the two Houses of Parliament,

charmed them both, for never any woman spoke more audibly or with better grace.   And her pressing to support our alliances abroad will commute for what the Dutch may take amiss in that emphasis which Her Majesty laid on her *English heart*.   But it did very well at home and raised a hum from all that heard her.[153]

The swift sequence of these steps towards vigorous warfare on the Continent, by no means desired by everyone, least of all by the Queen's relations of the Hyde family, must have been pre-arranged between Anne and the Churchills while William was still drawing painful breath.

The City of London, that fourth Estate of the Realm, whose long purse was destined to maintain the efforts of the Allies and to bankrupt Louis, was eager for the renewal of war in defence of commerce and the Protestant religion. London had never been more united.   During the reign of William the City had been rent by the feud between the Old and New East India Companies, rival claimants for the privilege of trading in the East.   The Old Company was mainly supported by the Tories, the New mainly by the Whigs.   The political reactions of this great quarrel in the financial and commercial world had caused grave embarrassments to government, for, whatever line it took, half the City was in high dudgeon.   In January 1702 the agreement for the eventual amalgamation of the two companies had been signed, in time for the East India trade of the country to face the renewal of naval hostilities with something like a united front.   The agents of the Dutch Government regarded it as an augury of the first importance for the unity of England's effort in the coming struggle.[154]

Marlborough well knew how necessary was his immediate presence abroad.   As soon as the wind permitted him to leave Harwich, he made for the Hague, where he found the Allies in consternation over William's death, and more than half expecting to be deserted by England.   Louis' emissary, Barré, was on the spot, attempting to renew the old-time connections of French diplomacy with the anti-Orange party in the States. A few days after Marlborough's arrival, Barré was instructed to promise that France would negotiate separate terms with Holland if she would desert the Grand Alliance.   What the terms were to be was not said ; they certainly did not include the retreat of the French from the Spanish Netherlands.   The tone of Louis' instructions to Barré was that of a man confident of a revolution in Holland on William's death, and the resurrection of a party prepared to purchase peace by accepting vassalage to France.

But Barré's offer had been forestalled by Marlborough's presence, and by the good news from England.   Assured of the support of Queen Anne's Government, the Dutch nation, without distinction of party, demanded war to recover their lost national security.   Amsterdam, where anti-Orange tradition was strong, took the lead in the patriotic movement.   Indeed the followers of Buys, the Burgomaster of the great City, were not, as Louis supposed, hostile to the late Stadtholderate on account of William's foreign policy; the wealthy burghers of the Republican party considered war a great evil, but they were not for peace at any price, and they were particularly anxious to retain the friendship of England.   Buys was soon on confidential terms with Marlborough.[155]

The Pensionary Heinsius was thus confirmed in power, not as the leader of a party, but as the head of a united nation in the hour of crisis.   Both he and Alexander Stanhope, the English Minister at the Hague, declared in their confidential letters that the situation had been saved by the prompt action of the English Queen and Parliament, and by Marlborough's timely arrival.   Heinsius was on such excellent terms with Milord that he ventured to speak to him about English politics, advising him not to engage in the High Tory policy of a hue and cry against Whigs and Dissenters, but rather, on the model of Dutch statecraft, to incline to 'moderate sentiments, so as to introduce unity among the people' in time of war. Marlborough expressed agreement with his ally's advice.

At the same time Heinsius confessed, in confidential letters to Bentinck, Earl of Portland, that one question still 'gave great embarrassment'—the leadership of the Allied Army in the Low Countries. Queen Anne had made Marlborough Captain-General of the British Expeditionary Force ; but the Dutch and the auxiliaries were the larger part of the whole army : who was to command them now that William was gone ? Various Princes competed, but the Dutch did not want a foreign Prince, because he might resent the orders of their Field Deputies. They were prepared to place their troops under Marlborough, on whose shoulders William had dropped his mantle. But on no account would they accept as their Commander-in-Chief Queen Anne's notoriously stupid husband, Prince George of Denmark, whom she insisted on pressing upon her Allies. It was Marlborough's task to argue for this absurd proposal ; he did so with his usual suave propriety. Who shall say whether he dropped a hint of his real thoughts to Heinsius ? Probably such a hint was unnecessary. But if those serene and perfect features were ever distorted by a wink, it must surely have been while he was urging upon the Pensionary the claims of Prince George to the supreme command. At any rate the Dutch stood firm and saved Europe. Anne struggled for her husband's claims till May ; only then, when the campaign was already beginning, was it agreed that Marlborough should command both the English and Dutch forces as William had designed.[156]

This curious and little remembered episode must be borne in mind in interpreting the character of Queen Anne. The idea, long prevalent, that she was a weak woman governed by her favourites, first by the Marlboroughs, then by Mrs. Masham and Harley, is far from the full complexity of the truth. Never were Sarah and John Churchill dearer to Anne than in the year when she came to the throne. Yet she strove for two months to give to Prince George the supreme command in the Low Countries, in order to please a husband she loved, and to flatter her own sense of what was due from the Powers of Europe to the Queen of England. The appointment would have cruelly frustrated Marlborough's dearest ambition, yet there is no evidence that ' Mr. and Mrs. Freeman ' dared to expostulate with their ' poor dear unfortunate Mrs. Morley ' on this very delicate question. It is doubtful whether Anne had any prompting or support except from her husband, who was fool enough to wish to match himself against the Marshals of France. He was not the choice of the High Tories ; their military favourite was Ormonde, Marlborough's life-long rival, who had been bitterly disappointed the year before when William overlooked his claims to the command.[157] Yet Anne held out alone in her obstinate choice, till the positive refusal of the Allies to submit their armies to her husband's orders forced her to desist. Then, indeed, she consented without demur to Marlborough's nomination. But since she had endeavoured to set Prince George's claims above his, it cannot be argued from her preference for his claims over Ormonde's that she was aware in the spring of 1702 of the immense superiority of his military talents. By the autumn, Anne and all Europe had learnt that Sarah's husband chanced to be the greatest English soldier since Cromwell.

The friendship of Anne Stuart and Sarah Churchill, though partly fostered by self-interest on Sarah's side, was rooted in genuine human affection. Like many friendships, from that of Hamlet and Horatio downwards, it flourished on a contrast of temperaments. It withered when after many years the strain imposed by that contrast became too great.

Anne's mind was slow as a lowland river, Sarah's swift as a mountain torrent. Sarah kept her sharp and witty tongue in constant use. Anne, though she could read a speech well in public, could not carry on a conversation. That disability, together with her ill-health, prevented her from keeping Court. The occasional receptions at St. James's or Kensington consisted of ' Foreign Ministers and Ladies sitting for a quarter of an hour about the Queen in dead silence ! ' ' No Court attenders ever came near her,' but reserved their obsequiousness for her servants, particularly for Godolphin. If people came to the Palace at all, Anne ' never cared to have them come in to her, having little to say to them, but that it was either hot or cold.' Her delight was to sit alone with Sarah, listening in silence to her friend's brilliant talk. Sarah for her part declared that ' to be shut up for so many tedious hours as I have been with a person who had no conversation and yet must be treated with respect,' was often a weariness, but, ' on account of her loving and trusting me so entirely as she did, I had a concern for her which was more than you will easily believe and I would have served her with the hazard of my life upon any occasion.' [158]

Though one of the friends was clever and the other pious, neither had strictly intellectual interests. Sarah indeed did not lack the brains to be a blue-stocking, if time and place had been favourable. But at the Court of Charles II ladies graduated in nothing but gambling and intrigue. There, Sarah tells us, ' I never read, nor employed my time in anything but playing at cards '—and later at the larger stakes of politics. Anne had been taught in the same school. One of her early letters to Sarah runs as follows : ' I am sorry you have so ill luck at dice yesterday. I won £300 but have lost about half of it again this morning.' [159] But in the sad years following the Duke of Gloucester's death and at the time of her own accession, Anne spent a good many hours of her retired life in reading works of devotion ; and she even read some English history to prepare herself for the queenhood. The only exercise of which she was physically capable consisted in driving a *chaise roulante* with two gentlemen walking beside the horses' heads, holding the reins.[160] In this way she ' hunted the hare ' at Windsor, went out to watch great herds of deer driven past her in her own or her subjects' parks, or attended reviews of her troops.

The birth and death of at least fifteen children, few of whom survived infancy, was a closed chapter when she came to the throne. That experience in the past, and ever recurrent fits of gout or dropsy, rendered pain of body and mind her portion in life. She was often swathed in bandages, presenting an object of horrified pity to her subjects when, brought bowing into the presence, they saw their glorious Queen as a much-suffering woman, ' in extreme pain and agony, everything about her in much the same disorder as about the meanest of her subjects.' [161] Shut away in the privacy of ill-health, with a husband dull and sottish though faithful and well-loved, no wonder she leaned on Sarah for company and on religion for comfort. No wonder she liked her dinner, for she had few of the other common pleasures of life. Shortly after the Revolution the royal family had been thus described :

> King William thinks all,
> Queen Mary talks all,
> Prince George drinks all,
> And Princess Anne eats all.

After she had come to the throne, her subjects were pleased to believe that she consoled herself with brandy out of a tea-cup, and jokes were made about Queen Anne's ' cold tea.' [162]

She was indeed no picturesque figure. Yet in that part of heroism which consists of endurance, poor dowdy Queen Anne was no less heroic than her ancestress the Prima Donna of Scottish romance. And certainly the last of the Stuart Queens had many more of the qualities required for the wise ruling of a State. For a dozen weary years the invalid daily faced her office work. She did not leave affairs to her favourites or even wholly to her Ministers. In order to do what she thought right in Church and State, she slaved at many details of government. And the ideas that inspired her were those of moderation, good sense and humanity, for which the Stuart line had not always been conspicuous.

One of her hardest drudgeries was not connected with politics. In those days when so many offences were punishable by death, the royal prerogative of mercy was constantly being called into action. Queen Anne took great pains in reading the disagreeable literature of such

cases, and after faithful examination often directed her
Ministers to grant reprieve.[163]

In the same conscientious spirit she applied her mind to
the more pleasant business of Church appointments.   Here
Sarah at once found that her own influence went for nothing
at all.   For Sarah, if not a freethinker, was a decided anti-
clerical.   The pretensions of the clergy to order men's lives
and thoughts were one of the many things that roused her
to fury.   And the bitterness then commonly displayed by
the High Churchmen towards English, Scottish and Continental Protestants who were not of their communion,
seemed to her equally injurious to the domestic unity and
the foreign interests of Britain.   Sarah thought for herself
about politics, a subject on which in 1702 the ablest married
couple in England agreed to differ.   Sarah was a Whig,
Marlborough was still a Tory.   And each feared and loved
the other too much to quarrel over it.

Queen Anne indeed was no persecutor.   She was determined to be Queen of all her people, and was free from the
itch of hatred for Dissenters and Low Churchmen that
embittered the minds of Atterbury, Sacheverell and Swift.
But in a positive sense she was a devout Anglican, and in
those days politics and religion were to some extent inseparable.   Because she was High Church in religion, she
was Tory in politics.   But she did not allow Tory politicians to dictate all her ecclesiastical appointments, as Swift
was one day to find to his cost.   On Church matters she
consulted Bishops as well as statesmen.   She had, indeed,
no confidence in Tenison, Archbishop of Canterbury,
on account of his Latitudinarian views.   But she constantly
sought the advice of Sharp, Archbishop of York, a High
Churchman of great piety but of equal moderation.

It is not then surprising that Sarah, when solicited for
her good offices by a friend in 1704, replied by professing
her own impotence, and bearing witness to the non-political
character of the Queen's motives in clerical appointments.

I must own to you that I have less opinion of my solicitations
of that sort than any other, because whoever speaks to the Queen
upon that subject, she does always consult with the Bishops before
she disposes of the thing ; and besides Her Majesty has so many

Chaplains who are always importuning her for preferment, that I think they have the advantage of everybody else.[164]

Most of her Church appointments were therefore made on genuinely religious grounds. On first coming to the throne, she vainly pressed Ken, the saintly Non-juror, to reconsider his scruples and return to the Bench. All that she could do was to induce him to receive, as he did most gratefully, a yearly allowance paid him through the hands of his successors at Bath and Wells, to whom this exemplary Christian bore no animosity. A few years later she chose the uncompromising Whig, Fleetwood, as Bishop of St. Asaph. That remarkable man, the originator of the study of economic history in England by his *Chronicon Pretiosum*, lived to see his Whiggish sermons burned by order of the House of Commons at the end of the Queen's reign, and to enjoy high honours under the House of Hanover. His benevolence and assiduity in the Bishop's office, like Burnet's, failed to atone in the eyes of many of his clergy for the friendliness he showed to Dissenters. But Anne was not afraid to call him ' my Bishop ' and to attend his sermons at the time when he was most unpopular with her fellow Tories.

1702

1708

1712

Naturally most of her ecclesiastical appointments went to the High Church. But Archbishop Tenison, though much out of favour with the Queen, outlived her in a most aggravating manner, so that Lambeth was never available for a Tory and High Churchman. Certainly the Whigs had luck about the bishoprics. The Queen was not indeed in all cases obdurate to political considerations, for the links between Church and State were manifold. But in the middle of her reign, owing to the split in the Tory Party, her political advisers were hostile to High Church claimants for preferment, and she herself was alienated by the conduct of the High Flyers in Convocation and in Parliament. In 1705 she was actually induced by two Tories, Godolphin and Bishop Trelawny, contrary to the advice of her mentor Sharp, to give the bishopric of Lincoln to Wake, the learned Whig protagonist of the

Bishops' cause against the lower clergy in Convocation.[165] Seventeen episcopal appointments were made during her reign. In the net result, the rule of the Tory Queen, though it raised Atterbury to the Bench, failed to reverse the moderate Low Church character which the Hierarchy had rapidly and irrevocably assumed in the reign of William.

How did Anne's High Church religion affect her view of the royal office ? Born five years after the Restoration, the offspring of the marriage of James Duke of York with Clarendon's daughter Anne Hyde, she had at Charles II's command been saved from the instructions of her father's Jesuits, to be brought up in the very heart of the Royalist and Anglican atmosphere, during two decades when the Church of England made the Divine Hereditary Right of Kings its most distinctive dogma. Then had come the Revolution, shattering that theory, and rendering those who still held it suspect of disloyalty to the new regime. And now Anne herself was reigning as a consequence of the overthrow of the belief in which she had been so religiously nursed. Her attitude as Queen was a full acceptance of the Revolution in practice, and something just short of complete acceptance of it in theory. Even in her most Tory days at the end of her reign she declared that her right was not divine, and that such an expression ought not to be used of the claims of any mortal to authority over his fellow creatures.*

So far she accepted Whig doctrine. And yet, like many of her Tory subjects, she strengthened her case against her popish brother by dallying with the idea that he might after all be supposititious. Was he her father's son, or had he entered the royal circle in a warming-pan ? One day, in answer to a question of Sarah's :

She told me she was not sure the Prince of Wales was her

---

* In October 1710 the Duke of Shrewsbury wrote : ' Lord President having left with me the City address I read it to the Queen last night. She immediately took exception to the expression that *her right was Divine*, and this morning told me that, having thought often of it, she could by no means like it, and thought it so unfit to be given to anybody that she wished it might be left out.' *H.M.C. Bath*, I (1904), p. 199.

brother, and that it was not practicable for him to come here, without ruin to the religion and country.

At a later date Sarah wrote :

I never could observe that she had any scruples about wearing the Crown, nor any inclination to those that were in that interest if she believed them so, though she always loved the Torrys, because she believed they would be for her against her brother. And I believe to the last [1710–14] Mrs. Masham's Ministers never ventured further with the Queen than to persuade her that it was best for the Protestant religion for him to come after her death.[166]

It is very difficult to determine how far, at various times in her life, she contemplated the possibility of being succeeded by her brother.* But it is certain that she was always resolute to defend her rights in her lifetime against him and his adherents. The Tories were equally stiff in her defence against all comers. In the spring of 1702 they excited themselves with a rumour that some Whig Lords had plotted to exclude her from the throne, and bring over the House of Hanover in immediate succession to William.† The Tory Party regarded Anne as their Queen in a special sense. They would defend her against Whigs, Jacobites or French. But already in 1702 many of the Tories who had the year before passed the Act of Settlement for the benefit of the House of Hanover, were speculating among themselves, in the freedom of the Coffee House, whether after all James III might not succeed Anne, provided the power of France had first been well reduced. They would not take James as the nominee of Louis, but after a victorious war a restoration might perhaps be desirable on an English and an Anglican basis. Such talk was common in High Tory circles in the first year of Anne's reign, and was still more common in the last.[167]

So uncertain, therefore, did it seem who would succeed Queen Anne, and so doubtful was it how long she would live, that the old game of ' insuring ' against a Restoration by secret overtures to St. Germains continued to be played

* See p. 118, above.

† The only scrap of evidence for the alleged plot is the statement made many years later by Dartmouth in his notes to Burnet, iv. p. 540 (299). When the enquiry was made in Parliament in 1702, no evidence was forthcoming from Dartmouth or any other source. *Parl. Hist.*, VI, pp. 18–22.

by the less scrupulous statesmen of all parties. In the spring of 1703, Somers himself, the model of Whig constitutional propriety and reputed honesty, thus 'insured' by making insincere offers of service to the Jacobite Court through the medium of the French Minister Torcy, a strange method of approach for a patriotic statesman in time of war with France ! The Whigs dreaded a Restoration above all things. But as a result of Anne's accession, they felt that the Tories were masters in the land, and might use that mastery to bring back the ancient line after her death. If such an event were unavoidable, the Whigs did not wish to be proscribed and for ever excluded from power under the House of Stuart. After Blenheim they recovered their confidence in the future ; there is no evidence that Somers thus played the knave any time later than 1703.[168]

If for these reasons even Somers was 'insuring,' no wonder Marlborough was doing the same. In 1702, while dealing the French armies shrewd and vigorous blows in the Netherlands, he protected secret Jacobite agents coming into his lines with proposals from Torcy for an agreed peace, and a restoration of the Pretender by consent of the English after the Queen's death.[169]

Anne's view of her high office was not wholly rationalistic. She disclaimed 'right divine,' but she was yet the anointed Queen. Her High Church religion still shed upon the throne a light of something not derived from the vote of Parliament. She moved in a world of royalist sentiment unknown to her predecessor and successor. William had faced unpopularity by refusing to touch for the King's Evil, because he did not believe himself endowed with miraculous powers. Anne revived the practice the moment she became Queen, to the joy of High Churchmen and old Cavaliers. The representative of King Charles the Martyr of course had magic powers denied to a Dutchman. In the course of her reign she must have 'touched' several thousands of her poorer subjects, including little Samuel Johnson, who was brought to her among two hundred others on a March day of 1712. The cures do not seem to have been remarkable. The parents who thought that their scrofulous offspring had the Queen's Evil, hastened to bring them to the Royal healer ; and many more, without a close diagnosis of their children's case, sent them up for the sake of the bit of gold which the Queen tied round the neck of each boy and girl.

Anne seems to have taken a particular pleasure in this old-world performance, dating by tradition from the time of Edward the Confessor :

> I desire [she writes on one occasion] you would order 200 pieces more of healing gold, for I intend (an it please God) when I come from Windsor to touch as many poor people as I can before hott weather coms. I do that business now in the Banqueting House, which I like very well, that being a very cool room, and the doing of it there keeps my own house [St. James's] sweet and free from crowds.[170]

With these notions of her royal office, half of the old world, half of the new ; with a kindly nature, and a due stiffening of obstinacy ; with a fund of moderation and good sense, shading off into stupidity ; and with ' a heart entirely English,' she was not at all ill-suited to fill the throne after William, to be umpire of her subjects' quarrels, and to preside over the period of transition from Stuart to Hanoverian England.

Her reading of the prerogative acknowledged the checks imposed on it by the Revolution Settlement. But she did not accept any more modern constitutional theory or practice. She did not, for instance, hold herself bound to choose her Ministers solely from the party dominant for the time in the House of Commons. William, by hard experience, had been driven some distance in that direction when he sent for a Tory Ministry in 1700. But Anne throughout her reign asserted her right to choose her servants from either party, or none.

> All I desire [she wrote to Godolphin] is my liberty in encouraging and employing all those that concur faithfully in my service, whether they are called Whigs or Tories, not to be tied to one or the other. For if I should be so unfortunate as to fall into the hands of either, I shall not imagine myself, though I have the name of Queen, to be in reality but their slave, which as it will be my personal ruin, so it will be the destroying of all government. For

instead of putting an end to faction, it will lay a lasting foundation of it.[171]

She began her reign so decided a Tory, so strongly prejudiced against the chiefs of the Junto, that the Whigs in 1702 only benefited very slightly by this royal liberty of choice. But in a short while the High Tories had gone so far to alienate her, that her theory of holding the balance between parties became a reality of great importance.

The parties are such bugbears [she wrote Marlborough] that I dare not venture to write my mind freely of either of them without a cypher, for fear of any accident. I pray God keep me out of the hands of both of them.[172]

So long as the Marlborough-Godolphin Ministry was in a middle position independent of both Whig and High Tory, it suited Anne excellently ; but as soon as it was made captive by the Whigs, it lost her confidence.

This battle to maintain the right of the Crown to choose its servants independent of party and of Parliament, was waged by the Queen alone throughout her reign ; first against High Tories, then against Whigs ; now at the instance of her domestic favourites, now in opposition to their demands. It was Queen Anne's personal contribution to the constitutional and political history of her reign. The future was against it, for Parliamentary Cabinet Government was destined to displace the old idea of Ministers chosen by the King. But Anne's stubborn fight for the ancient rights of the monarch in this matter probably enabled England to wage the war effectively in the early years of her reign in spite of the High Tory majority in the Commons, and to get peace at last in spite of the Whig majority of 1708–1710. She could not have carried on this struggle in our faction-ridden island if she had not had the power of dissolving Parliament, and of throwing the weight of the Crown and the Ministers at election time against the party whose predominance she at the moment wished to reduce.

But apart from her High Church religion and her Tory politics, apart from her theory that the queenly office must be kept independent of control by any section of her subjects, there remained Anne's feeling as an Englishwoman and a Protestant. She was Queen of England and heir of the Revolution, and Louis had scornfully defied her in both capacities. She held it her first duty, in the circumstances of her accession in March 1702, to defeat France in war. Whosoever was to be her successor on the throne, he must come in by the choice of England, not of France. War, then, was her first duty. And after the first campaign, she saw that Marlborough was the only person who could lay victory at her feet. Marlborough, therefore, must have a free hand abroad, and if her High Church friends, if her domineering uncle Rochester, if her faithful servant and co-religionist Nottingham, obstructed Marlborough in foreign and military policy, they must be removed out of his way. Her support of Marlborough as war lord between 1702 and 1706 decided the fate of England and of Europe.

Marlborough was a Tory and his wife a Whig, but on everything touching the war there was no shadow of difference between them, or for many years between them and their mistress. All three made themselves executants of the European policy of the late King whom they had loved so little.

The retired invalid's life led by Queen Anne put her much more in the hands of a small domestic circle than was the case with Queen Elizabeth or even Queen Victoria. And the Marlboroughs' influence over her was the greater, because she disliked her Hyde relations, Clarendon and Rochester, who had never been kind to her and who scarcely concealed their Jacobite opinions. Her uncle Clarendon, indeed, refused to take the oaths to her, and was therefore sent away from Court, though she allowed him a pension. Her loved and loving husband, Prince George the Dane, was too stupid or too shrewd to wish to govern her political action. He had become a 'good Englishman,' identifying himself with his adopted country. But his accent still betrayed the foreigner, and he prudently regarded English politics as a mystery too deep for his understanding, a maze wherein if he ventured he would certainly be lost. By those who stood near him the Prince Consort was liked, if not respected ; he was ' mighty easy towards his servants,

N

affected not popularity nor appearing in public.'   And we
have Bishop Burnet's word for it that he was ' free from all
vice '—after his marriage.   It was no vice in those days to
drink like a fish.   As years went on he grew very fat on
England's good cheer.   After many a succulent meal, he
died in 1708—a kindly, negligible mortal.*

There was, therefore, in 1702 no rival influence to
counteract that of the new Queen's oldest and truest friends,
the Churchills.   Of treachery to Anne, Marlborough has
never been accused.   And if in the end Sarah quarrelled
bitterly with her mistress, the breach had its origin in the
too jealous quality of the servant's devotion.

Macaulay adopted his unfavourable reading of Marlborough's motives and character straight from Swift and
the Tory pamphleteers of the latter part of Anne's reign.
Macaulay, indeed, was less often misled by traditional Whig
views than by his own over-confident, lucid mentality, which
always saw things in black and white, but never in grey.
The greatness of his history lies in his account of political
situations and his narrative of the course of events; a public
man himself, he understood these things better than most
historians, and he could make them clear in his own unrivalled manner.   But he was no psychologist, and the artist
in him tended to delineate character by the unsafe method
of dramatic antithesis.   He instinctively desired to make
Marlborough's genius stand out bright against the background of his villainy.   He had blacked in the background,
but did not live to put in the full-length figure of the victor
of Blenheim in all his magnificent panoply.

In place of Macaulay's villain of genius, what do we see
in fact ?   Nothing quite so clear, except indeed the military
genius, which shines the brighter the more closely it is
analysed.   But Marlborough's motives often remain obscure
and his character is not as sharply definable as that of

---

* Compare Burnet's remarks on Prince George's supposed Toryism, with the
Earl of Westmorland's belief that he would have favoured the Whigs if he had lived
longer than 1708.   Both agree that he was a kindly man, and not quite so ridiculous as he has been represented.   *Burnet*, V, p. 380 (515), and *H.M.C. Westmorland*
(1885), p. 50.   See p. 261, below, on his position as Lord High Admiral.   He
was a patron of science and a friend of Newton.   *Proceedings of Brit. Academy*,
pp. 181-2 (Broad on Newton).

Chatham, Nelson or Wellington. Unlike those occasionally talkative heroes, Marlborough kept a very strict guard on both his tongue and his pen. He liked to keep his own secret, and in keeping it from contemporaries he has kept it from posterity as well. He scorned or neglected to answer his libellers or to state his case in memoirs. His correspondence deals with the matter in hand and refrains from discursive remarks. The nearest approach to self-revelation and frank comment on events as he saw them, is to be found in the long sequence of his love-letters to his wife. Otherwise his actions alone speak for him. Sarah for her part told her story in the *Conduct of the Duchess*, with frankness worthy of Pepys and ability worthy of Defoe. She unpacked her heart in words ; but her husband hid himself in the cloud of his mighty deeds.

It would be an error, in reaction against Swift and Macaulay, to picture Marlborough as a public servant of the same integrity and high-mindedness as Wellington. Born in 1650, John Churchill had been brought up in the very worst school of Restoration laxity. His father, Sir Winston Churchill, a West-country squire, had suffered heavily for the royal cause, and John, when still of school-boy age, was sent up to Whitehall to remake the family's fortunes there as best he might. His elder sister, Arabella, was mistress of James, Duke of York. If the brother had been a man of high principle, he would have felt his sister's shame and would not have attached himself to James's clientele. But Churchill had no higher standards than the world in which he found himself, and that world regarded a Prince's mistress as a grand lady. So, too, Whitehall thought that handsome Jack Churchill had done a fine thing when he cut out King Charles in the easy affections of Barbara, Duchess of Cleveland ; nor would that Court have raised its eyebrows very high, if indeed the lady, as rumour

1668–
1670

1672–
1673

afterwards averred, had rewarded her needy gallant with gold. But unlike the other harpies of White-hall, Churchill was hardening his body and training his mind in the profession of arms, in the desert hills behind Tangier, and in Germany under Turenne himself.

A few years later, he married for love a Court lady of unspotted character, whose face and wit were her only fortune. This was not the act of a mercenary or coldly calculating man. And he loved Sarah Jennings, for all her disagreeable humours, every hour till he died. 1678   Between the ages of fifty and sixty he went through his great campaigns at the head of half the armies of Europe, with his thoughts as constantly turning home to Sarah as those of a young subaltern to his mistress. Of all the world's famous soldiers he seems to have had the warmest and most fixed domestic affections. In the campaign of 1702 he writes :

I do assure you that your letters are so welcome to me that if they should come in the time I was expecting the enemy to charge me, I could not forbear reading them.[173]

And as he drew rein on the plateau of Blenheim, before the carnage of that great victory had ceased, he had two thoughts : one for his wife to whom he scribbled a pencil note from the saddle, the other for the wounded and prisoners who depended on his care. He was, like the Duke of Wellington, a humane man in war and in peace, and he was less stern than Wellington to his subordinates. Except the burning of Bavaria no act of cruelty stands against his name. He won Sedgemoor ; others turned it into a butchery. He taught generals how their poor soldiers should be fed, clothed and cared for.

The successful military conspiracy which Marlborough organized against James II at the time of William's invasion saved England from the horrors of a civil war. Macaulay, without denying the public usefulness of his action, regarded it as a piece of selfish treachery on Marlborough's part against his patron James II. But there is no reason to doubt that his devotion to the liberties of England and the Protestant religion was a motive with him at that crisis, as with the rest of his countrymen. And like them he thought that, in time of revolution, conspiracy is a legitimate weapon, and the method of conspiracy is deceit. Probably, indeed, his motives were to some extent personal in 1688 as at other times. He did not like the prospect of holding high command at the goodwill of Jesuit Fathers ; and he had good private as well as public reasons to support a revolution which would secure the reversion of the crown to his wife's devoted friend, Princess Anne.

So, too, when she at length came to the throne, he took pleasure in his position as the greatest subject in England and in Europe. He enjoyed using in the largest field his unrivalled military talents, as everyone who is worth anything enjoys doing the thing he can do best. But it is clear from his letters to his wife that he cared deeply for the cause for which he fought—the cause of England, of Protestantism and of European liberty against the domination of France.*

There are, indeed, bad incidents in his career, particularly in the troubled reign of William III. His deep intrigues with the Court of St. Germains are ugly reading. Whatever his precise motives in these mystifications, he was playing the knave—but so were many others, Whig and Tory, whom it is not the custom to set down simply as villains. Perhaps, like so many others, he was only insuring his head and his fortune against a Restoration which he did not desire but regarded as probable. In judging his actions we must consider the standards of a time when Russell, Shrewsbury and Somers thought fit to masquerade as Jacobite penitents. But when Marlborough sought to strengthen the impression of his loyalty to St. Germains by
1694   betraying to the national enemy the coming attack
on Brest, he touched the lowest point in his career. It is true that the French had previously had warning from others, including his friend Godolphin, at that moment a Minister of King William. And it is probable that Marlborough knew that the French were so forewarned. All this must be remembered. But even so it was a base thing for an English soldier to do.†

Apart from the charge of treachery, it is said that he was uxorious, ambitious and avaricious. He was uxorious in the sense that he lived long and happily with that woman

* *E.g.* p. 205, below, his letter to Sarah of June 10, 1703.
† I think Lord Wolseley's analysis of the Brest affair in Chap. 78 of his *Life of Marlborough* is very fair.

whom no one else could charm or control. His ambition saved his country and Europe. And for every guinea that his avarice drew from England, he gave her back the value of a thousand. Nearly all the other statesmen of the day were engaged in founding families and amassing estates at the public expense. Marlborough only differed from Portland, Rochester, Danby and countless others, in that he gave the public very much fuller value for their money.

The talk about his avarice, grossly exaggerated for purposes of faction, arose in part from little, thrifty personal habits which never go down well in England. They would have passed unnoticed in Holland or France. But the English made it a crime in the man who had given them victory, that he blew out unnecessary candles, and walked home when other rich men would call a coach. These habits of life, innocent, if not actually laudable, he had acquired in his penurious youth, when he was living at Charles II's Court on his ensign's pay, and they clung to him when he grew rich.

Perhaps the secret of Marlborough's character is that there is no secret. Abnormal only in his genius, he may have been guided by motives very much like those that sway commoner folk. He loved his wife, with her witty talk and her masterful temper, which he was man enough to hold in check without quarrelling. He loved his country ; he was attached to her religion and free institutions. He loved money, in which he was not singular. He loved, as every true man must, to use his peculiar talents to their full ; and as in his case they required a vast field for their full exercise, he was therefore ambitious. Last, but not least, he loved his fellow men, if scrupulous humaneness and consideration for others are signs of loving one's fellows. He was the prince of courtesy. It is true that courtesy was one of his chief weapons in political and diplomatic negotiation ; but it would not have been so effective if it had not been genuine, and based on kindly feeling. Old John Evelyn records on one of the last pages of his journal a scene in London society in the winter after Blenheim.

I went to wait on my Lord Treasurer, where was the victorious Duke of Marlborough, who came to me and took me by the hand,

with extraordinary familiarity and civility, as formerly he was used
to do, without any alteration of his good nature.   He had a most
rich George in sardonyx set in diamonds of real value : for the rest
very plain.   I had not seen him for some years, and believed he might
have forgotten me.

Swift might suspect Marlborough of some deep-laid
scheme of avarice or ambition, when he crossed the room
to give pleasure to the old man by speaking to him.   But
what advancement could he hope from Evelyn ?   It is not
so that the incident should be read.

The charm of Marlborough's manners was irresistible,
and he used it to the full to hold together for ten years the
Alliance of touchy Kings, Generals and Councillors.   His
patience was often tried to the utmost by fools of importance
—English, Dutch and German, in the Cabinet and in the
field.   And his patience was as inexhaustible as his courage.
Now patience is not only a weapon but a virtue.

Why, then, was he so hated by the Tories and so ill
defended by the Whigs ?   Chiefly for reasons of faction.
Party spirit raged in the reign of Anne with a ferocity that
devastated social life and human intercourse.   Marlborough
deserted the Tories, yet never fully became one of the Whigs.
Yet in spite of his fall between the two stools of English
public life, he would have found more friends and defenders
if he had ever obtained a hold on the popular affection at
all proportionate to his services.   His soldiers loved him,
because he cared for their wants, and led them to victory ;
they bitterly resented his treatment by the politicians at
the end of the war.   But, outside the army, the common
people had so little feeling for him that they allowed the
Tories to libel him and drive him from the country without
protest.   Patient, courteous, persuasive, humane, he lacked
the spark that kindles devotion.   His unbroken reserve,
though we need not suspect it as a mask for designs invariably evil, acted as a screen between him and the multitude of his day, and still acts as a screen between him and
historians seeking to know him.   He never gave himself
away, to friends in love or to foes in anger.   Except
by his achievements he has never fired the imagination,
like Cromwell or Nelson.   The flame of his spirit served

for light, not heat. He stands on the threshold of the
Eighteenth Century, one of the first-born of the Age of
Reason, the armed champion of toleration and good sense.

In the reign of Elizabeth, Sir Francis Godolphin, of
Godolphin Hall between Lizard and Land's End, had
brought over skilled Germans who had permanently improved the traditional methods of Cornish tin-mining. He
had thus enriched his county and founded the fortunes of
his house. His great-grandson was now to display the
same business qualities as Lord High Treasurer of England,
in supplying the sinews of war for Marlborough.

Sidney, Lord Godolphin, was much more a public
servant than a party politician. He brought to the aid of
the wild factions of the Restoration and Revolution era, the
trained and dispassionate ' civil-service mind.' That indispensable element in the well-being of a State was very little
provided for in the old machinery of Government ; ' Whitehall ' in the reign of the Merry Monarch had a different
significance from the sober associations of the word to-day.
Godolphin was indeed a ' political chief ' in the departments
where he served, but he found no difficulty in continuing
at his duties in all political weathers—under James II until
the actual outbreak of the Revolution, then under the
Tories, and late in Anne's reign under the Whigs. The
intervals when he was out of office were seldom long. He
made his changes of allegiance quietly, with the least possible
amount of apology and protestation. And he was too useful
an ally for anyone to bring up against him his political past.

Unlike many of his Whig and Tory colleagues, he had
no literary tastes. Gambling was his passion, though conducted with his habitual prudence. The professional
libeller, Mrs. Manley, was for once not unfair when she
described him in her *New Atlantis* as ' the greatest genius
of the age with the least of it in his aspect. The affairs of
a nation in his head, with a pair of cards or a box of dice in
his hand, or poring upon a chess board.' Newmarket was
his spiritual home. And not the least of his services to
England was done in the capacity of breeder of race-horses.
The Barb and Arab sires, which he was one of the first to

bring over, altered the appearance and improved the speed and quality of the animal in Eighteenth-Century England, which became the greatest land of horses in history.

In 1698 Godolphin's son, Francis, married Henrietta Churchill, the Marlboroughs' handsome eldest daughter. In January 1701, their younger and still more beautiful daughter, Anne, toasted by half the town as ' the little Whig,' was married to Charles Spencer, son of the Earl of Sunderland. On the death of that veteran rascal in September 1702, his more straightforward son became third Earl of Sunderland and thenceforth was accounted as one of the Lords of the Whig Junto ; yet he was Marlborough's son-in-law. In this manner, when Queen Anne came to the throne, Marlborough and Godolphin had already forged domestic links with one another and with one of the great Whig Houses. These marriages proved of dynastic importance to England and even to Europe. For Marlborough and Godolphin, Tories without zeal, were liable to regard marriage alliances as no less sacred than party ties.*

Nor was Anne without personal friendship for Godolphin. He had stood unobtrusively but firmly on her side in her frequent bickerings with William. In one of the last of these, in the winter before her accession, she had written to Godolphin :

It is a very great satisfaction to me to find you agree with Mrs. Morley [Anne herself] concerning the ill-natured cruel proceedings of Mr. Caliban.[174]

* Sir Winston Churchill, *ob.* 1688.

Arabella Churchill, 1648–1730, mistress of James, Duke of York (**James II**). She bore him the famous **Duke of Berwick** and other children.		Sarah Jennings=**John Churchill** 1660–1744	1650–1722, Duchess of Marlborough	Baron Churchill, 1682 (married 1678)	Earl of Marlborough, 1689 **Duke of Marlborough,** 1702.

Henrietta Churchill=Francis Godolphin, (married 1698) son of **Sidney** Duchess of M. in **Lord Godolphin.** her own right 1722– 1733.	Charles Spencer=Anne Churchill 3rd **Earl of** (married 1701, **Sunderland** *d.* 1716).	John Marquis of Blandford, *d.* 1703.

Charles Spencer
Duke of Marlborough after his
aunt Henrietta's death in 1733.

It appears from Coxe's *Marl.*, Chap. 7, that Marlborough in 1700 had objected to the Whig politics of young Sunderland, but that his objections to the marriage had been overcome by Sarah and by the genuine lovers' devotion of the young couple.

He was destined to be a faithful servant to Anne as Queen. He had not been very faithful to William : in 1694, while at the head of the Treasury, he had preceded Marlborough by several weeks in sending intelligence to France of the intended attack on Brest, and he was constantly in communication with the Court of St. Germains.

In May 1702 Marlborough asked of the Queen, as a condition of his own military service abroad, that Godolphin should become Lord Treasurer.   His reasons were two-fold.   In the first place, he could not be sure of money for the war unless a financier in full sympathy with his exten-sive plans were in control of the national purse, a man not only able to raise the money, but able and willing to see that it got through to the purposes for which it was voted, a thing by no means of course in those days of corrupt and hap-hazard administration.   Secondly, Marlborough could not be sure of the conduct of parliamentary and political affairs during his absence abroad, unless a man in his full personal confidence were Chief Minister.   The head of the Ministry was then the Lord Treasurer—the ' White Staff,' as he was commonly called after the symbol of his office.   If Godolphin were Lord Treasurer he could counteract any disturbing movement by Rochester, Nottingham and the High Tories in the Cabinet, who opposed as a matter of party principle the dispatch of a large English Army to the Netherlands and liked the expedition no better for being under Marlborough's command.   Marlborough, therefore, was in earnest when he said that he would not go abroad unless Godolphin were Treasurer.   Anne was willing enough, but Godolphin declined the post.   He only yielded to his kinsman's positive refusal to serve without him. Once in office, the Treasurer showed no eagerness to quit; in 1710 he was compelled much against his will to surrender the White Staff which he had first handled with such apparent reluctance eight years before.*

---

* Dartmouth, in his notes to *Burnet,* said ' Lord Godolphin would have been more uneasy if the Treasurership had been put in other hands. But he constantly refused everything that he was sure would be forced upon him.' This may be so ; or, again, he may have felt some genuine shrinking from the load of so heavy a responsibility, to which, when once he had assumed it, his broad shoulders soon grew accustomed.   Hugh Elliot, *Life of Godolphin,* pp. 204–207.

It was fortunate for England that financial talent was not then a monopoly of either Whigs or Tories, as it was a monopoly of Tories in the era of Huskisson and Peel. The Whig Montagu, Earl of Halifax, had an initiating genius in finance, a flight beyond the more steady qualities of Godolphin. Montagu had founded the Bank of England and the National Debt to meet the darkest crisis of William's reign. But he was sadly deficient in the arts of mollifying hostility and managing men. Godolphin's more work-a-day talents were fully adequate to carry on the system that Montagu had begun, and steadily to pursue the sound financial road for eight years of European war. England beat France with the purse as much as with the sword, and great credit is due to Godolphin's finance.

But the Lord Treasurer was not merely what the Chancellor of the Exchequer is to-day. He was also, under Queen Anne, something very near to a modern Prime Minister. He was responsible for the principal acts of the Government at home and abroad, and it lay with him to secure the acquiescence of his colleagues in one another's actions, and to instil a certain unity into the policy of the various Cabinet Ministers. King William himself had played this part, at least in foreign affairs. He had been his own Prime Minister: Anne only chose hers. The Queen's sex and her lack of political training threw much of the higher political work on the Lord Treasurer, and helped to approximate his office to that of Prime Minister—a term occasionally used in this reign almost in its modern sense.

The Government was known as ' Godolphin's Ministry ' so long as he was Lord Treasurer ; it began in 1702 almost entirely Tory, and ended in 1710 almost wholly Whig. It derived its coherence not from party loyalty, but from the family alliance of Marlborough and Godolphin and their agreement on public affairs. But without the Queen's friendship and the use of her name, the task of the two kinsmen would have been impossible. Even when supported by the royal authority, the Lord Treasurer had need of all his tact, temper and craft to steer a course for this family Government between the Tory and Whig parties, to keep on terms with one without wholly antagonizing the other. But Godolphin was by nature one of those statesmen whose skill it is to handle perilous material tenderly, and get the work of the country done under grave difficulties, by patient and tactful plodding rather than by eloquence, genius and daring. Godolphin's slow methods eminently suited the political situation at home, while Marlborough's lightning strokes were needed for the war abroad. And the Lord Treasurer found in Speaker Harley a man of ideas and qualities not dissimilar to his own, a public servant and a moderator, who could manage for him in the Commons, as he himself managed in the Cabinet and in the Lords. The methods and the services of Godolphin and Harley were not those of the Pitts, Cannings and Gladstones ; they were those of the Walpoles, Liverpools and Asquiths.*

* The *Godolphin MSS.* and the *Hatton Finch* (Nottingham) *MSS.* in the British Museum show Godolphin in his letters performing the Prime-Ministerial functions of bringing the Secretaries of State and other Ministers into line with a common Cabinet policy, *e.g.* about the War and Scotland. The phrase 'Prime Minister' was occasionally used in Anne's reign. Clerk of Penicuik (*Memoirs, Rox.*, pp. 53, 56, 58) calls Godolphin and Marlborough the Queen's 'Prime Ministers' in the plural, and later speaks twice of Godolphin alone as 'Prime Minister.' And Defoe in his *History of the White Staff* (1714) twice speaks of Lord Treasurer Oxford as 'Prime Minister.' Equally marked uses of the word in its modern sense, and without any implied disparagement, will be found in *H.M.C. Portland*, IV, p. 119, and V, p. 655. See correspondence in *Times Lit. Supp.* throughout March 1930. For Godolphin as guardian of the finances see *C.S.P.Tr.* pp. vii–viii and *passim.*

CHAPTER IX

Two very different types of Englishmen, the Protestant Nonconformists and the Whig aristocrats, combined to form the irreducible minimum of the Whig Party. Others supported or opposed it according as its policies won or lost the general approval of the nation. But the Dissenting Chapels and great Whig Houses never wavered in their party allegiance in good fortune or in bad. This strange political combination of forces, socially so far asunder, was no mere stratagem adopted to meet a passing crisis : it proved to be one of the two enduring elements in English public life from the middle of the reign of Charles the Second to the middle of the reign of Queen Victoria. The Whig alliance and tradition answered to something persistent in the national mind and character, just as the union of the Church clergy and the squires in the equally long-lived Tory Party expressed the other aspect of England's needs and ideals. On questions of foreign policy, of peace and war, of free trade and protection, the two parties in Anne's reign held views which it is possible to regard as the opposite of those which they respectively held in the early Nineteenth Century. But the more enduring instincts and antipathies of religion and of class preserved the core of Whig and of Tory tradition through all changes of party policy and of party fortune, from the days of Somers and St. John to the days of Grey and Peel. On other matters the parties changed policies with the changing circumstances of new eras, but the Tories were always the champions of the Church interest, and the Whigs the critics of Church privilege.

The Protestant Nonconformists* were strongest in the middling classes of society ; they were rich merchants, small shopkeepers, freehold yeomen, artisans and crafts-men—unfashionable folk, living in a world far removed from the parks and mansions of their aristocratic leaders. They followed the Russells, Cavendishes and Whartons all the more faithfully because they themselves were not of social rank to aspire to seats in either House of Parliament, were rigidly excluded from the Universities, and were prevented by the Test Act from taking any considerable part even in local administration. Yet they could not be indifferent to politics. From the age of Elizabeth onwards, the Puritan tradition in England had always been closely associated with Parliament. And, moreover, the Dissenters had to protect themselves against the threat of renewed persecution.

The Tories in Anne's reign complained that even the Quakers voted for the Whigs, the men of peace for the war-mongers ; and old poll books bear out the charge. One Quaker, indeed, was put in the stocks at Canterbury for fixing on the walls of a church some verses against ' Wars and Bloodshed among Professors of Christianity '—

> You kill and slay and take the prey,
> And thank God when murder's done,

—on the day of thanksgiving for the victory of Vigo.[175] But the Quakers as a body, for all their pacifism, had good reason to vote against the High Tories, who were continually attacking them as little better than infidels, and threatening to close their schools, as well as those of the Protestant Sects of more militant tradition. These threats began to cause alarm among all the Dissenting bodies at the beginning of Anne's reign, and at the end of it took shape in the Schism Act.

The Dissenters dreaded the rage not only of the squires

* See p. 58, above.

and parsons, but of the people. For although the High Church doctrine and discipline were little appreciated by the common herd, the cry of ' No Fanatics ' could rouse the *mobile* almost as easily as the counter-cry of ' No Popery.' The surest appeal of both the English parties was made not to the religious instincts of the ordinary man, but to his dislike of the religion of others.

In self-protection against an unfriendly world, the Protestant Dissenters sought refuge as clients of the Whig aristocracy. They did not come empty-handed, for they could offer their patrons good value at election time. They were many of them of the rank of society likely to have votes as forty-shilling freeholders in the counties, or as possessors of one or other of the numerous varieties of fancy franchise in the boroughs. Although they formed perhaps a twentieth part of the nation in numbers, they possessed much more than a twentieth part of its wealth and voting power.

The ' Whig aristocracy ' is a phrase that requires analysis. In the reign of Anne it consisted of rather less than half of the English nobles* and a small but important minority of the untitled country gentlemen. The Whig squire was often richer than his neighbours ; he was frequently connected with commerce or public affairs. Robert Walpole of Norfolk was such an one. But in Anne's reign the chief political leaders of the Whig, as also of the Tory, party sat in the Lords, which was more important in comparison with the House of Commons than it had been in the Long Parliament. To that extent the Whigs under Anne were more ' aristocratic ' than the Roundheads of 1640. But the Roundheads and their Whig grandsons, the Cavaliers and their Tory grandsons, were landed gentry leading rival sections of the middle and lower orders, on behalf of opposing ideals in Church and State. English politics were only to a limited extent a strife between classes.

In Anne's reign hardly one of the Whig noblemen or

---

* The modest majority that the Whigs often obtained in the Upper Chamber in Anne's Parliaments was due to the preponderance of Low Church principles on the Episcopal Bench in consequence of William's numerous appointments. Some of the Peers had, of course, no party allegiance, and Roman Catholics could not sit.

gentlemen was a Dissenter. In ninety-nine cases out of a hundred they conformed to the Church of England and were, therefore, unlike their Dissenting clients, qualified by law to hold office. Some were religious Churchmen of tolerant views, like Addison and Lord Somers ; some were scoffers, like Lord Wharton, the Restoration rake ; or moral philosophers, like young Lord Shaftesbury, whose writings helped, in the more respectable reign of Anne, to render fashionable a serious-minded scepticism suited to a man of culture.

The High Churchmen pointed out the difference between leaders and led in the Whig Party :

> The Dissenters themselves [says a Tory pamphlet of 1705] are not so silly as to imagine that those persons who have of late put themselves at the head of their quarrel do it on any conscientious liking of their doctrine and manner of worship, and that they whom wantonness, unbelief and faction have rendered impatient of the discipline of the Church, can be brought to submit to the sour rules and saucy encroachments of Edinburgh and Geneva.[176]

This was perfectly true, if we add that ' wantonness, unbelief and faction ' were as marked in St. John, champion of the High Church, as in Wharton, champion of the Dissenters.

Besides aristocrats and Nonconformists, certain other classes added to the Whig strength. Army officers, war-profiteers, lawyers, merchants trading oversea, younger sons and persons of all sorts who had to make their own way in the world and found themselves more hampered than helped by the respect paid to antique custom and privilege—all these were more often Whig than Tory. It is significant that in February 1703 the Tories passed through the Lower House a Parliamentary Qualification Bill to exclude all save landowners with a certain annual value of land from sitting in the House of Commons, even to represent the boroughs. The small Whig majority in the House of Lords threw it out in 1703, but it became law in the heyday of Tory power in 1711. It remained on the Statute Book till Victoria's reign, but was rendered a dead letter by legal subterfuges of conveyancing. This Act, which was praised by Swift as a statesmanlike measure, would, if it had achieved its purpose, have closed the doors of Parliament to all save squires ; it would have kept out merchants, professional men including lawyers, and even the younger sons of the landed gentry.   The second Pitt, Fox, Sheridan and Canning would have been excluded from Parliament, if this masterpiece of October Club legislation had not been neatly evaded by the chicanery of successive generations of lawyers.[177]

The Tory Party in Parliament, when it came to be reconstituted by the younger Pitt, extended a welcome to recruits from the mercantile and professional classes—Eldon and Stowell, Rose, Canning and the Peels.   But in earlier times the party marshalled by Harley and St. John firmly believed that the landed interest alone had a right to govern the country.   In Anne's reign the Tories raised perpetual complaints of the intrusion of ' monied men ' into the constituencies and into Parliament, and considered their presence as one of the chief crimes of the Whigs.   According to Swift every form of property, except land, was ' transient and imaginary,' and its owners were not fit to sit in Parliament.*

After more than forty years of unchallenged power, the Whig aristocracy of 1760 could be justly charged with exclusiveness.   But in Anne's reign their faction was fighting for its life against great odds ; they were most of the time in opposition ; the shifting breath of popular favour was their only hope.   They stood, therefore, for the career open to talents.   Out of the five Lords of the Whig Junto, at least two, Somers and Halifax, were self-made men who had risen by their wits into the inner shrine of Whig aristocracy.   And Addison was lifted out of Grub Street and given high office.

In these circumstances young ambition often inclined to the Whigs as being more ready than their opponents to patronize merit independent of pedigree.   But though the

* Swift, in the *Examiner* of March 29, 1711, rejoicing over the passage of the Qualification Bill, says that now ' future Parliaments ' will be ' composed of landed men ; and our properties lie no more at the mercy of those who have none themselves, or at least only what is transient and imaginary.'

Whig party enlisted wealth, activity and intelligence from many quarters, it was a minority party prior to the Industrial Revolution. The landed interest and the Church together made up far the greater part of old England. The parish clergy, in spite of the bishops, were Tory. So were the smaller gentry, particularly in the rural communities farthest removed from the influence of London and the trading world. These classes and their clients, led by one half of the nobility and larger gentry, were in normal times more powerful than the Whig interest. The Whigs could hope to prevail only through the divisions of the majority and through their own closer union.

It may seem strange that the Whigs were the more united party of the two. For they were an alliance of socially heterogeneous atoms, while the Tories were a solid phalanx of squires and parsons, accustomed to co-operate in the governance of village life. Yet the Whigs were agreed on the main political questions of the day : religious toleration for all Protestants ; war with France by land as well as by sea ; the Scottish union ; and the Hanoverian Succession. On all these issues the Tories were at variance with one another. Moreover, while the chiefs of the Whig Junto acted together as one man, the Tory chiefs were divided by acute personal jealousies—Rochester, Nottingham and Ormonde against Marlborough and Godolphin, and a few years later Bolingbroke against Oxford.

Whig members of Parliament were better disciplined than their opponents. Under the orders of the Junto, the Whig body moved and wheeled like a well-drilled battalion throughout the whole of the Queen's reign. There was no repetition of the indiscipline that had injured the party in 1698–1699.* The most malcontent of the Whigs of William's reign, such as Jack Howe, had carried their humours over into the Tory camp. The remaining members had learned, in the fierce struggle against the Tory majority in 1701, the need of supporting and obeying their own chiefs. And the leaders, on their side, had learned better the arts of managing a party. The ' Junto ' of five Whig Lords—Wharton, Somers, Halifax, Orford

* See pp. 111–112, above.

and Sunderland—consulted in private, decided on party policy, and in accordance with these decisions conducted parliamentary operations with great skill. Their chief theatre of action was the House of Lords, where all five members of the Junto sat. Thence the Whigs in the Commons, led by young Walpole and Cowper, took their cue for action.*

The Tories had no such leadership. They never knew in what humour proud Seymour would come down to the Commons, or conscientious Nottingham to the Lords : whom these individualists would attack, or what resolutions they would move. St. John alone could be depended on to show the party sport, and Speaker Harley to enjoin caution. In important divisions the Tory chiefs again and again divided on opposite sides.

The most active manager in the Whig Junto was Thomas, Lord Wharton. In the Lords he led the party with equal energy and craft. But electioneering was his special province. In the *Life of Wharton*, published after his death in 1715, occurs a story that throws an intimate and amusing light on the development of canvassing and electoral methods in the reigns of William and Anne.

His Lordship having recommended two candidates in the Borough of Wicomb, some of the staunch Churchmen invited two of their own party to oppose him and money was spent on both sides. . . . They found my Lord Wharton was got there before them and was going up and down the town with his friends to secure votes on their side. The [Tory] gentleman with his two candidates and a very few followers marched on one side of the street ; my Lord Wharton's candidates and a great company on the other. The gentleman, not

* The social centre of the aristocratic Whigs was the Kit-Cat Club. In Nov. 1703 we read—'The last 4th of this month was King William's Birthday. 'Twas kept with eluminations etc in the chief streets all over the town, and Lord Orford, Lord Sunderland made bonfires. And at the Kitcat 'twas very great. Lord Hartington, Duke of Somerset, etc were there. The glass sent down was to the immortal memory of King William. They had all new cloathes etc, and now I am in the Kitcat, 'tis proper to tell your Lordship that a great number of glasses are chose and a sett number of lady's names are writ on them.' *H.M.C. Rutland, II,* p. 177. The most popular ' toast ' at the Kit-Cat at this time was Marlborough's younger daughter Anne, married to young Lord Sunderland and known in society as ' the little Whig.'

being known to my Lord or the townsmen, joined in with his Lordship's men to make discoveries, and was by when my Lord, entering a shoemaker's shop, asked *where Dick was?* The good woman said *her husband was gone two or three miles off with some shoes, but his Lordship need not fear him, she would keep him right.* 'I know that,' says my Lord, ' but I want to see Dick and drink a glass with him.' The wife was very sorry Dick was out of the way. *'Well,'* says his Lordship, ' *how does all thy children? Molly is a brave girl I warrant by this time.*' '*Yes, I thank you,*' says the woman. And his Lordship continued : ' *Is not Jemmy breeched yet ?* ' The gentleman crossed over to his friends and cried : ' *E'en take your horse and be gone ; whoever has my Lord Wharton on his side has enough for his election.*'

This scene is laid in Buckinghamshire, Hampden's old Roundhead county, which had become the chief centre of Wharton's influence. He had also estates and political interests in Yorkshire, where the Whigs held a surprising number of seats. And he organized the party in many widely scattered shires. At election time he scoured the island, on horseback and in his coach-and-six, giving himself and his unfortunate retinue no rest by night or day. His biographer boasted that 'sometimes thirty members of Parliament were chosen by his procurement.'

In these and similar stories we see the national machinery of party life gradually gaining ground on the purely local choice of Members of Parliament. The party system, by dividing the whole nation into two camps, worked towards national unity, because it obliterated local interests and divisions, such as had often decided elections in earlier times. Neither Whigs nor Tories, it is true, had Central Offices or Central Funds as parties have to-day, but energetic Whig or Tory magnates like Wharton, who had time, money and horses to spare, helped to supply a certain degree of national organization and control, in the aristocratic form suited to the tastes and habits of the age.

Sir Edward Seymour was the Tory magnate who had his finger in most of the electoral contests in Devon and Cornwall. At election time men spoke of Seymour's ' Western Empire.' In Devon, where Dissent was strong, the Whigs, under the flag of the House of Russell, carried most of the seats against him.   But almost all the Cornish rotten boroughs were Tory.*   Indeed, the party had in the same district another electoral chief of great influence, Sir Jonathan Trelawny, Baronet, Bishop of Exeter.   Of the Seven Bishops whom James II had put on their trial, five had become Nonjurors after the Revolution.   Trelawny and Lloyd alone took the oaths to the new regime.   At the beginning of Anne's reign Lloyd of Worcester electioneered for the Whigs, but very much less effectively than his brother of Exeter for the Tories.

Seymour and Trelawny were rival hereditary chieftains of the West, each playing very much for his own hand, on doubtful terms one with another and with the party leaders in London.   Trelawny, though a Tory, had his eye on the main political chances and on the ladder of ecclesiastical promotion.   Before Anne had been a year on the throne, he was complaining to Nottingham that, though he had returned eleven Tory members by his electoral influence, nothing was being done to relieve his ' numerous family from the burdens of a poor Bishopric.'[178]   And even Seymour's more uncompromising High Toryism was a point of personal pride rather than of party loyalty. Wharton's influence, on the other hand, was placed without reserve at the disposal of the Whig party.   He was a member of the Junto, in frequent and friendly consultation with Somers, Halifax and Sunderland ; and he put all his electoral influence and experience into the common pot.

Wharton came of a Roundhead Puritan family, to which he owed his politics and his religious antipathies.   But he owed his scepticism, his engaging manners and his loose morals to the Restoration society in which he had been brought up.   When Anne began to reign, he was a vigorous and attractive debauchee of fifty.   He was also the most cheerful and unblushing of liars.   Swift, like all Tories, ' hated Wharton like a toad,' and declared him ' the most universal villain I ever knew.'   Yet Swift bore testimony to

---

* L'Hermitage, speaking of the last Parliament of William III, said that all the members for Cornwall were Tories, but this proves on examination to be exaggerated ; of the forty-four, I reckon some half dozen as Whigs or Whiggish.

his good humour, which had analogies to that of Charles II, the good humour of a man who has long ago ceased to trouble about his own reputation. After reading one of Swift's fiercest lampoons on him, Wharton would come up to the Doctor and say he was ' damnably mauled,' and then, with the easiest transition in the world, ask about the weather or the time of day.

Without principle in private, he was an example of public loyalty in a slippery age, when half his Whig colleagues and Tory rivals were in secret relations with the Court of St. Germains. Wharton's zeal for the principles of parliamentary government, and of toleration for all Protestants, was a genuine and disinterested passion, and this man, renowned for his falsehood in private life, would have sacrificed everything rather than be false to his party. His colleagues could trust him with their political, though not with their marital honour. Young Lord Shaftesbury, the moralist, who knew Wharton well, wrote :

If I ever expected any public good where virtue was wholly sunk, 'twas in *his* character. I have seen many proofs of this monstrous compound in him of the very worst and best.[179]

Tory swordsmen were set on to challenge him, but he disarmed them one after another, always sparing their lives. The charm of his company was such that he made a practice of luring young noblemen and men of fortune into the Whig party as his boon companions, as did Charles Fox two generations later. But while Fox was a good man with faults, Wharton was a bad man with virtues. He had a great deal to do with the development of our party system, and has left his mark on our history. He was perhaps the most influential Whig of Anne's reign, and he was long remembered. Dr. Johnson in his Dictionary illustrated one of the meanings of the word ' leader ' by his example : ' One at the head of any party or faction, as the detestable Wharton was the *leader* of the Whigs.' *

* In the first edition of this volume I noted here that I felt uncertain as to the truth of the well-known charge against Wharton of indecently profaning a church, because I had never seen the place and occasion of the alleged action stated, except by Swift in the *Examiner*, who was obliged to admit, two numbers later, that the place he had named was wrong. But my attention has now been

The disreputable character of Wharton was balanced by the gravity of his chief colleague in the Junto, the ex-Lord Chancellor Somers. A fine constitutional lawyer, he was the most generally esteemed of the Whig chiefs in Anne's reign. But the Queen had taken a strong prejudice against him, and the Partition Treaties stood against his record in the popular regard ; he was never again destined to have charge of the Great Seal. Such are the curiosities of human character that the respectable Somers, in sending insincere messages to the Court of St. Germains, committed a meanness which the reprobate Wharton would have scorned.

A third member of the Junto was Charles Montagu, Earl of Halifax. Somers had won his place among the hereditary aristocracy by his legal talents, Halifax by his financial genius.* But Halifax was vain and arrogant ; his head was turned by success ; in spite of the great services which he had rendered to England in William's reign, he was neither popular like Wharton nor respected like Somers.

The fourth member of the Junto was Lord Orford. He had great claims on the Whig party and even on the nation at large. He was a Russell, and he was the victor of La Hogue. But he was a cantankerous, selfish, false-hearted man. By the time Anne came to the throne he had deservedly forfeited his influence. In 1702, despite his name and fame, he was already the least important member of the Junto.

The fifth member of this strange, informal Opposition Cabinet was young Charles Spencer, who became Earl of Sunderland on his father's death in September 1702, when he inherited the mansion house of Althorp in Northamptonshire. The new Lord Sunderland, like several other party

called to p. 297 of the late H. A. Evans' *Highways and Byways in Oxford and the Cotswolds*, where the story is told in sufficient detail, wholly different from Swift's. According to Mr. Evans, it occurred at night, when a band of drunken revellers led by Wharton broke into Barrington Church, Gloucestershire. In the *Carte MSS.*, Bodleian, there is a letter of Bishop Frampton (dated Nov. 7, 1682) to Wharton, which trusts he continues to make prayers to God for pardon for his great and horrid offence in the church at Barrington. The story is true.

* See p. 187, above.

leaders in that Augustan age, was a true Mæcenas. He began to collect the first of the great Spencer libraries, just as Harley made the Harleian collection of Manuscripts. In contrast to his unprincipled father, Sunderland was a sincere and straightforward Whig. But he was intemperate and unwise, and not personally popular. Queen Anne disliked him, yet because he was Marlborough's son-in-law he was destined to be the first member of the Junto whom the Whigs succeeded in forcing into her Cabinet.

But in 1702 any such event seemed highly improbable. The Queen filled up her Cabinet and nearly all the lesser ministerial posts with Tories. Only some Court places of no administrative importance she gave to moderate Whig noblemen who were not of the Junto : the Duke of Devonshire became her Lord Steward and the Duke of Somerset her Master of the Horse. But the Junto she regarded, not without justice, as an organization directed to the control of the Queen's government by a party ; such control she would not endure from any Tory combination, still less from a combination of Whigs. Not only, therefore, was every member of the Junto excluded from office in the spring of 1702, but Somers, Halifax and Orford suffered the indignity of having their names omitted from the list of the new Privy Council. Wharton was yet more odious to Queen Anne. She not only dismissed him from the Lord Lieutenancy of his own Buckinghamshire, but took from him the staff of the Comptroller of the Household and handed it in his presence to his personal enemy Sir Edward Seymour.

The only statesmen outside the Tory fold to whom Anne willingly turned for advice were the Dukes of Shrewsbury and Somerset. She trusted them because they were detached from party. In the last years of her reign they were destined to play a decisive rôle, first in helping to deliver her from bondage to the Whig Junto, then at her deathbed in thwarting Bolingbroke and bringing in the House of Hanover. But in 1702 Shrewsbury would make no effort to help the Queen.

The career and character of Charles Talbot, Duke of

Shrewsbury, bear some resemblance to those of Lord Rose-
bery two centuries later. A cultured, super-sensitive
nobleman, self-indulgent but no libertine, a wit in whose
brilliant but weighty conversation everyone delighted, he
was known to all ranks and to both sexes as ' the King of
Hearts,' ' the only man the Whigs and Tories both spoke
well of.' Called upon to lead a party, he saw too clearly
the faults of both parties. He had roused himself once to
take a resolute and active part in bringing about the Revolution. William, who owed his throne in no small measure
to Shrewsbury, employed him in high office. But with all
the ability he had only half the health, will-power and
industry required for an administrator and parliamentarian.
It was said of him that ' he went out of the great Offices
with as much ease as he shifted his clothes.'

When Anne came to the throne he was resident in Italy,
and declined, on his usual plea of ill-health, to return and
serve her. For half a dozen years he lived at Rome the life
of a dilettante *milord*, when he might have been helping to
govern his country in the crisis of the great war. He preferred to spend his time procuring pictures and statues to
be sent home to his friends. Many of the older works of
art in the great mansions of England are pieces which
Shrewsbury picked up in central Italy, while Eugene was
desperately holding his own against the French armies in
the north of the peninsula. On one occasion he sent
Godolphin a plan drawn by the best Italian architects for
the reconstruction of Whitehall Palace. He was on excellent terms with the Lord Treasurer, with Marlborough,
with the Whig Vernon, and the moderates of all parties ;
they corresponded on home and foreign affairs with the
illustrious exile. But, Whig as he was in principle, he was
not on good terms with the Junto, and he incurred the censure of the party in the first years of Anne for absenting
himself from Parliament, at a time when the House of Lords
alone ' stood in the gap for two years together ' against Tory
reaction in the Lower House.

Once, in 1704, his equanimity was disturbed by a
rumour circulating in England to the effect that his long
residence in Rome meant that he was reverting to the

religion of his boyhood. He wrote to clear himself to his kinsman Talbot, Bishop of Oxford :

> I never go to a church unless it is sometimes to look at a picture. I have never been with the Pope. In my discourse among our countrymen I have never omitted to expose the folly and superstition of this religion. Venice excepted, where I fear the moist air would not agree with me, the Pope's dominion is the least Popish of any place in Italy. I have often lamented that there's nowhere in Europe a Protestant country favoured with a warm sun, a blessing the circumstance of my health so much wants.

When, before the Allies had got the upper hand in the war, the Francophile Pope tried to bring about a peace that must have been to the advantage of Louis, he tried to approach Shrewsbury through 'a hermit,' but in vain. In the middle of Anne's reign Shrewsbury returned home, as good a Protestant as when he went away. The most serious outcome of his residence abroad was an Italian Duchess, an eccentric and entertaining woman, duly converted to the Anglican communion, but guarded by a fury of a brother, who was eventually hanged by impartial English justice for murdering his servant in the street.[180]

Charles Seymour, the ' proud Duke ' of Somerset,* had not Shrewsbury's charm, brains or brilliancy, but he, too, was a political Duke of moderate Whig principles, detached from the party and alienated from the Junto. He had the Queen's ear in the first days of her reign, and joined with her moderate Tory advisers in persuading her to express her desire for a closer union with Scotland in her speech to the Houses on March 11th. Thus the policy which had been William's last was Anne's first advice to Parliament. Her message led to a debate in the Commons that divided the Tories. The more pronounced High Churchmen declared against any dealings with the Presbyterian kingdom, and Sir Edward Seymour railed at the Scottish nation in harsh terms. But when the Whigs spoke up for the royal policy

---

* His pride was illustrated by a current anecdote to the effect that when his second duchess tapped him with her fan, he said, ' Madam, my first duchess was a Percy, and she never took such a liberty.' He was sixty years Chancellor of Cambridge University.

of a closer union, they were supported by a number of
Tories connected with the Government.   A Bill
Mar. 27   enabling the Queen to name Commissioners to
(O.S.)   treat with Scotland for a Union was carried by 165
1702   to 119.   But Anne was surprised and hurt by the
reception which her proposal had met with from the Church
party.   It was symptomatic of much that was to come.[181]

Meanwhile, throughout March and April, Lords,
Commons, clergy and officers of the Crown were one after
another taking the necessary oaths to Queen Anne, including
the Abjuration of the Pretender.   Some of the High Tories
had hoped that the Abjuration Bill, so vexatiously passed by
William on his death-bed, would be repealed in the new
reign.   But the old Parliament was still sitting and nothing
was changed.   After some demur, Nottingham took the
oath, and was followed by all other sticklers for the theory
of divine right who recognized the Queen, even if, like the
Bishop of Norwich, they avowed a hope that she would be
succeeded by her brother.*

In the middle of April, King William's body was in-
terred by night in the vault of Henry VII's chapel by Mary's
side : Prince George acted as chief mourner.   Ten
April 23   days later, on St. George's day, Anne was crowned
(O.S.)   with full magnificence.   Unable to walk, she came
1702   privately in a sedan to Westminster Hall, whence
she was carried across Broad Sanctuary in an open chair,
so as to be better seen by the shouting multitudes.   Both
Archbishops were present : Tenison performed the coronation ceremony, but her favourite, Sharp of York, preached
the sermon.   At the end of the service medals were thrown
by handfuls among the grandees in the Abbey, and money
to the mob outside.   The new Queen was popular with
the mass of her subjects, and the Coronation Day was kept
as a high festival in parts of the country distant from
Westminster : at Bristol there was mumming, music and
dancing, closed at night with a bonfire of the Pope in his
robes and triple crown : at Kendal, in front of the town

* See p. 159, above, on the Abjuration Oath.   *B.M. Add. MSS.* 29588, ff. 16-17,
2 ; *Tindal* (1744), III, p. 544 ; H.M.C., R. 3 (*Lestrange*), p. 273.

cross, the Mayor and Corporation drank on their knees health to the Queen and prosperity to the established Church, whereon followed ' illuminations, bonfires and such joy as I have never seen in the town.' [182]

One other ceremony was needed to initiate the reign —the formal Proclamation of War. Already French privateers were attacking Dutch and English commerce, and the Allied army had begun operations on the lower Rhine. Yet even now Rochester protested in the Privy Council that England ought not to declare war ' as a principal.' He argued that we should aid the allies, May $\frac{2}{13}$ 1702 since we had promised to do so, but only as ' auxiliaries ' and not go to war with France in our own name and interest. Rochester had just been admitted by his niece to a seat in the Cabinet and had been confirmed by her in the Lord Lieutenancy of Ireland, of which William had been on the point of depriving him. But instead of going to Dublin, he lingered in England to thwart Marlborough and Godolphin, of whose influence with Anne he was bitterly jealous. When, however, he proposed that war should not be declared, he failed to carry with him either Nottingham or Seymour, representatives of High Churchmanship, indeed, but on patriotic and anti-Jacobite lines.

With the hearty concurrence of both Houses of Parliament, war was proclaimed in front of St. James's Palace gate. On the same day war was declared in Holland May $\frac{4}{15}$ 1702 by the United Provinces. English and Dutch sailors began at once to retaliate vigorously on French privateers and merchant ships.[183]

In the same month of May, Rochester issued from the Oxford University Press the first folio volume of his father Clarendon's *History of the Rebellion*, doing thereby a greater service to High Tory principles than any he was ever likely to do by direct intervention in politics. That epic record of great events, written by one of the chief actors, in the grave and stately speech of an elder world, has a perennial value for all Englishmen, not to be touched by the changing tides of time and faction. But when it first appeared in the early months of the reign of the Tory Queen, it was bound to have a political effect, stimulating the cult of King Charles the Martyr, stirring up anger against the Dissenters as the heirs of the Puritan fanatics, and against the Whigs as the heirs of the Roundhead rebels. Rochester's preface, though written in dignified language, did not fail to point the moral of the story for the passing hour, and went on, rather unnecessarily, to denounce ' the raising of a great number of land forces ' and warlike operations in the Low Countries, where the enemy ' by the strength of his numerous garrisons must be, for many years at least, invulnerable.'

Marlborough, indeed, regarded Rochester as the most dangerous enemy of his plans for the deliverance of Europe. A year later he thus opened his heart to Sarah on the subject :

The conversation that was between Rochester and the Speaker is no doubt the language that Rochester entertains the whole Party with, and if they can once be strong enough to declare which way the War shall be managed they may ruin England and Holland at their pleasure. . . . Our poor country would then be the miserablest in all Christendom for we should not only lose our liberty, but our religion also must be forced, and those gentlemen that would be helping to this would then be as miserable as others, for the French when they are masters make no distinctions.[184]

The debates on the proclamation of war were enlivened in the House of Commons by a vigorous party tournament on the subject of foreigners in the army. The English were only in process of becoming a military nation, and in William's reign they had owed much to the professional knowledge and zeal of the Huguenot exiles, a number of whom were men of birth and breeding, formerly officers of the French army. Besides Marshal Schomberg, who had died at the ford of the Boyne, and Ruvigny, Earl of Galway, who had turned the Irish flank at Aghrim and was still destined to command English armies, there were many regimental officers of like origin. A Tory member now proposed to place a restriction on the grant of com-
May $\frac{2}{13}$ missions to foreigners born, even if they had been
1702 naturalized and had served England in the last war. The Whigs, led by Lord Hartington, protested against the

motion as cruel and ungrateful. Colonel Mordaunt bore testimony to the efficiency of the French-born Captains, who, he declared, kept their companies fuller and better disciplined than those of their fellow officers. The motion was lost by ninety-four to ninety-one.[185]

Besides the question of the war and the Scottish Union, another issue from the first moment divided Anne, Marlborough and Godolphin from the more intransigent members of their party. This was the demand for a clean sweep of all Whigs from the Government service in all its branches.

No such clear distinction existed in men's minds as exists to-day between ministerial posts of a 'political' character which must be vacated at a change of Government, and those parts of the public service which are permanent and non-political—Civil Service, Army, Navy and Magistracy. When a Government changes to-day, everyone knows precisely which places will change hands and which will not ; but it was otherwise in Anne's reign, and to this want of definition was due much of the confusion and anger of political strife among her subjects, and much of her own distress of mind in dealing with infuriated rivals for every kind of office.

In accordance with the principle enunciated in general terms at the time of the Revolution, the judges kept their places through all party storms and changes until, with the accession of the House of Hanover, the Act of Settlement came into operation and gave to every judge an even clearer legal right to keep his place, unless both Houses of Parliament petitioned for his removal for ill conduct.* But except for the judges and the clergy, no other public servant had security of tenure, either by law or by custom. Marlborough, indeed, who had no wish for politics in the army, was able to save military officers from proscription until his own fall in the last years of the reign. Godolphin, for similar reasons of efficiency, threw his shield over Whig financial experts in the Treasury. But the High Tories, led by Rochester and Seymour, called loudly for the dismissal of everyone who was not a Tory from the Civil

* See p. 120, above, clause vii.

Service, the Lord Lieutenancies and the Bench of Justices of the Peace.

The Queen, who had of her own free will done much in this direction, soon began to find such extreme demands unreasonable.   In an evil hour for her own peace of mind she had delivered the Great Seal into the charge of Sir Nathan Wright as Lord Keeper.   He was a poor lawyer, but a keen partisan.   He used his position to dismiss Whig Justices and to substitute Tories wholesale.   But the Queen, urged by Godolphin, was perpetually moderating his zeal, greatly to the annoyance of the extremists.

The Treasurer and the Marlboroughs had it clearly in mind from the first that only a united nation could win the war, and that the Whigs must not be driven to desperation. They knew that many of the ablest and most experienced servants of Government in the provinces were magistrates who had sat on the bench in the last reign, men whom Wright and Rochester regarded as Whigs and wished, in many cases, to replace by fox hunters of semi-Jacobite proclivities.   For the first four years of the reign this quarrel raged high, leaving Anne hardly a day's peace.   Every post in the gift of the Crown was claimed by the High Tories as their party perquisite, a claim rejected by the Tory Queen. She declared that she ' would be the Queen of all her subjects.'   As time went on, Godolphin and Harley discovered from the reports of Defoe and others that many of the High Tory Justices appointed by Wright were using their public position to attack the home and foreign policy of the Moderate Tory Government.   It was largely this that brought the schism in the party to a head.*   The case was

* Here is a report to Harley of 1704 from Richard Duke, in Devon : ' Sir Edward Seymour prevailed with the Lord Keeper (Wright) to throw out several of our most valuable justices, five round me worth £100,000, and put in one of £100 per annum ; he threw out Sir Jo. Elwill, worth £50,000, the most necessary justice in the county, and I desire you may have the honour to rout Sir Edward by inducing the Queen to restore the Justices of this Kingdom county, as has been done in lesser counties.'   Next year Defoe writes to Harley :

' Brentford : lodged at Justice Merriwether's—he was a Justice, turned out of commission in the general displacing moderate men.   Note, Justice Lamb of Acton is now the high-flying and ruling Justice of that side of Middlesex.'

' Tewkesbury, a quiet trading drunken town, a Whig baily and all well.' (H.M.C. Portland, IV, 122, 269–271.)   On Justices of the Peace, see pp. 100–101, above.

the more serious because of the scale of Wright's operations : an enquiry by the House of Lords showed that between 1700 and 1704 several hundred magistrates had been removed from the Commission of the Peace.[186]

In the summer of 1702, the High Tories took advantage of Marlborough's absence with the army abroad to push their policy of exclusion hard. The General Election was coming on, which was expected to put the House of Commons and therewith the control of Government policy into the hands of the High Churchmen. But elections were in many places influenced by the local representatives of the Crown—Lords Lieutenant, Justices of the Peace, Governors of Castles, Bishops and Cathedral clergy—and by expectations of favour to come. Hope of promotion in Church and State was a great reason with many persons of all ranks, from nobleman to tide-waiter, for supporting the Whig or the Tory candidates. Therefore, as the General Election drew near, the High Tories assailed the Queen and her Ministers with urgent demands that a more complete distribution of loaves and fishes among the well-disposed should be made in good time to affect the results of the poll. Nottingham, as the Secretary of State most trusted by the High Tories, was the recipient of such confidences as this on the eve of the election :

My Lord,—
    The six old Commissioners are continued when I particularly excepted against Mr. Pollexfen to my Lord Treasurer, and the two scandalously ignorant Commissioners of Customs are kept in only for being Whigs. . . . Certainly Cornwall did ill in choosing so good members last time, and must now be made sensible of it. . . . It will be difficult enough to make good elections without such discouragements.[187]

In Northamptonshire one of the Tory candidates, Sir Justinian Isham, and the local Tory manager, Griffin, had made early application at Court for the substitution of a Tory for at least one Whig magistrate, ' which will keep the rest in proper awe ' for the election ; a few weeks later both the town and county of Northampton were duly carried by the Tories, and Isham and Griffin rejoiced together that

'Lord Spencer went home very melancholy' to Althorp.[188] Innumerable instances could be given of the close connection which was held by both parties to exist between the patronage of the Crown, the local magistracy and the election results.*

Another equally important influence at election-time was the activity of local noblemen and magnates on either side. In Northamptonshire, only the slackness of Lord Exeter, so it was said, could have lost the County for the Tories ; but he appears to have been brought up to the mark in July 1702. In the same month, in the neighbouring county of Leicester, the Tory candidate, John Verney, writes to his friend Thomas Coke, knight of the shire for Derby :

We have a great many persons towards Melton side that will vote for us ; but the power of the two Lords has carried off from us all the gentry of that part of the country. So that if you will please to permit the freeholders from that part of the country to attend you to Leicester your presence would give great reputation to us ; and I am sure we have a sufficient number in those parts to make a very considerable figure if they could have the honour to be conducted by a person of your quality.[189]

If considerations of this kind went for so much in the free atmosphere of county elections, they went for still more in the close boroughs.[190] In the choosing of Members of Parliament, family influence and personal interest weighed at least as much as Whig and Tory principles. Partly for this reason, there were a very large number of uncontested returns ; perhaps in half the constituencies no poll was taken.

Nevertheless, the Tory enthusiasm of the first summer of Anne's reign, and the expectation of favours to come from that quarter, sufficed to reduce the Whigs in the new Parliament to a shadow of their former strength. The

---

* The connection between electioneering and office-cadging is illustrated in the following letters of September 1710 : Duke of Beaufort to Lord Dartmouth : 'I find the not having the list of Deputy Lieutenants with the Queen's approbation will be of ill consequence to our elections.' And Lord Guernsey writes to Lord Dartmouth asking for the office of Register of the Chancery of the Duchy of Lancaster for ' my cousin Mr. Harvey ' ; it is only £100 a year, but ' will help him with his election at Clitheroe,' because a sign of royal favour helps candidates. *Dartmouth MSS.* at Patshull, see also *H.M.C. Coke* (1889), p. 107.

P

Queen, in her farewell speech to the old Parliament on
May 25th, had said :

I shall be very careful to preserve and maintain the Act of
Toleration, and to set the minds of all my people at quiet. My own
principles must always keep me entirely firm to the interests and
religion of the Church of England and will incline me to countenance
those who have the truest zeal to support it.

The country was not slow to take the hint, and in the July
elections the Queen's name was everywhere used against
the Whigs.

As the importance of the House of Commons had
grown in the constitutional balance of power, there had
grown with it the excitement, corruption and violence of
electioneering methods, sometimes brutal, sometimes sporting and good-natured. If we take a long view of our
national history, we may perhaps believe that the rowdy
noise and fun of the ' Eatanswill ' type of election have done
more good than harm : for they interested the mass of the
people, even in times when the fewest of them had votes, in
the joyous business of choosing and chairing a Member ;
and it is largely for want of popular interest in polling day
that parliamentary institutions in sunnier lands have wilted
and died.

Certainly the electioneering politicians of Queen Anne's
time could not be accused of want of enthusiasm. An Act
of William III punished bribery and intimidation by the
loss of the seat ; but it was a dead letter, except when the
majority of the House of Commons wanted to get rid of
a political opponent. The most corrupt constituencies were
the boroughs with a small electorate of a hundred or fewer
votes. At Thetford ' all is sold : the election there is
among the magistracy, and fifty guineas for a vote is their
price.' [191] At the end of the reign, Atterbury, with some
exaggeration, said of the country as a whole, ' the price of
a vote is as well known as an acre of land,' and complained
that the Tory squires were so exhausted by war taxation
that they could no longer as candidates make head against
the Whig moneyed men.[192] They did their best ; and at
any rate in 1702 their pockets were still full.

But even more prominent than direct bribery was the

power at election time of landlord over tenant, of patron over client, in all ranks and callings. The open poll left small room for independence except to the freehold yeoman, and even he was often a tenant for some other piece of land beside his freehold. Bishops canvassed the clergy of their diocese, and the parson sometimes took refuge from episcopal pressure in the plea that he was unfortunately necessitated to vote according to the wishes of his lay patron.[193]

The recording and counting of votes were often mismanaged by incompetent clerks or falsified in the interest of a party. Sometimes, indeed, both sides ' signed articles to prevent any disputes or disorder, and provided that a gentleman should watch the clerks on behalf of each candidate.'[194] But the returning officer himself could by no means always be trusted. At the Gloucester election of 1702 the Whig candidate, Sir John Guise, complained :

This was a bad time, for there was the Earl of Marlborough, Godolphin and the whole court entirely in the Tory interest and whatever power could contrive to defeat my election was done. But the High Sheriff put the finishing stroke to their design, for, by pretending to make a scrutiny of the bad votes, he shuffled up a return, which return when I petitioned the House against, . . . without hearing my case, Simon Harcourt put the question that Mr. John How was duly elected and it was carried. . . . And here I must take notice that I after sat in the House and saw Simon Harcourt turned out of the House, if possible, with more injustice than he excluded me.[195]

Sham arrests for debt and kidnapping of voters were common. In the 1705 election, the Whig candidates of Great Bedwin kept sixteen doubtful voters drunk at their expense all night before election day, but

would not suffer them to whisper to one another nor to stir out of doors to do their necessary occasions but under the guard of two or three of Sir George Byng's or Mr. Pollexfen's servants. William Darrell sat in the doorway with his legs across the door to stop them from going forth.[196]

Another aspect of election time is given in Defoe's *Review*, where the grazier says to the farmer :

Ay, ay, zooks we mun all vote for Sir Thomas. They say his Baily was with all the tenants t'other day, and kissed all our wives round, and said my Landlord sent him. But they say he shall come and kiss 'em himself before they'll speak for him ; they won't take it at second-hand.[197]

Few people in Anne's reign, or for fifty years after her death, seriously proposed a redistribution of seats so as to get rid of the rotten boroughs. Their existence was indeed sometimes spoken of as a 'scandal' and 'a mighty blemish to the constitution of England.' [198] But neither Whigs nor Tories wished to part with their own rotten boroughs. The spirit of the age was against institutional change. The last person who had adopted parliamentary redistribution was Cromwell, and the last person who had tampered with existing franchises and the charter rights of corporations was James II. In the age of Anne both were considered to be *pessimi exempli*. Parliamentary Reform and Municipal Reform were not public questions of the day.

It would be hard to say which party would have gained most if a Reform Bill such as that of 1832 had been carried one hundred and thirty years earlier. The increase of county seats would have favoured the Tories, who returned the majority of the knights of shire even at elections like 1705, when the Whigs did well. But the increase of the representation of trading towns and of the London area, in place of rotten boroughs, would on the balance have favoured the Whigs.*

As it was, both parties were content to fight in the electoral field as they found it. The Tories, all told, were the stronger party, but their divisions often gave the Whigs a chance in the reign of Queen Anne. In the first year of her successor's reign, Lord Chancellor Cowper thus instructed his Hanoverian master :

* The electoral condition of Old Sarum in this early era is not without interest. Governor Pitt's son Robert, the father of the great Chatham, reports in 1705 to the old man in India :

'My election for Old Sarum was unanimous : and had not Mr. Mompesson opposed your right of bailiwick I should have joined with him. Finding, however, that he intended to take that course I set up Lord Grandison against him. There was a double return, five, including himself, voting for Mr. Mompesson, and five, including one, Carter, for Lord Grandison ; the former, through superior party influence, was duly elected. Carter voted for a garden which I bought for you from Mr. Philips, for £500, of which £100 was paid for the vote, which was pretty dear ; but the other side were ready to give the money I refused for it.' *H.M.C. Dropmore* (1892), I, pp. 16–17.

Give me leave to assure your Majesty, on repeated experience, that the parties are so near an equality, and the generality of the world so much in love with the advantages a King of Great Britain has to bestow without the least exceeding the bounds of law, that it is wholly in your Majesty's power, by showing your favour in due time (before the elections) to one or other of them, to give which of them you please a clear majority in all succeeding Parliaments.[199]

Such, indeed, was the 'repeated experience' under Anne, beginning with the election of July 1702 when she had 'showed her favour in due time' to the Tories. The good Queen held the balance throughout her reign ; she inclined first to one side and then to the other, for much the same reasons as those which swayed the mass of her people, whom in many respects she represented better than many cleverer politicians. But, whether we regard her as leading or as following public opinion, certain it is that the one party who never lost a General Election in her reign was Queen Anne herself.

In every Parliament of Anne there sat a number of members not pledged to Whig or Tory, but inclining to support the Queen's Government as such. Godolphin once calculated that the House of Commons contained 190 Tories, 160 Whigs and 100 'Queen's Servants.'[200] Most of the 'Queen's Servants' would probably have called themselves moderate Tories, prepared to support Marlborough and Godolphin. The division of the House between Whig and Tory was not exhaustive and was not always employed. A contemporary made a list of one of Anne's early Parliaments, in which he divided the members into the following categories—'Churchmen, High-Churchmen, Low Church, Nonconformists, Courtiers and Sneakers.'[201] But the net result of the polling in July 1702 was to put the House of Commons into the hands of the Tories—unless they fell out among themselves.

When the result of the General Election was known, the Queen prorogued the new Parliament till October and went on a tour in the West, which naturally took on the character of a Tory triumph. Prince George's asthma troubled him, and Bath, their favourite resort in less happy days, had

attractions for both husband and wife.   After enjoying a
great demonstration of loyalty and Anglican enthusiasm
in the Sheldonian and in the Colleges of Oxford, the royal
party travelled slowly westward at the end of August.   On
the top of Lansdowne Hill they were met by two hundred
virgins clothed in white, as Amazons, with bows and
arrows by their sides, and attendant shepherds ' with their
crooks and tarboxes, singing and playing on pipes of reeds,'
who accompanied the royal coach into the city of Bath.
The spirit of the Elizabethan pageant was not yet dead in
the land.   The Queen was entertained in Bristol by the
citizens, and yet more splendidly by the Duke of Beaufort
at Badminton ; but she remained at Bath as her headquarters until October 8, surrounded by her principal
counsellors and statesmen.   From this autumn began the
recognition of Bath as indisputably the greatest provincial
centre of fashion, a reputation of which young Beau Nash
and other founders of the City's greatness were not slow to
take advantage.   Its fine public and private buildings, and
the ordering of its social customs dated from this visit of
Queen Anne.[202]

The Western Tour had been a success.   It had shown
something at least of the invalid Queen to her subjects.
It had been rendered cheerful by the hopefulness of a new
reign, by the Tory victory at the recent elections, and not
least by the good news that kept arriving from the Netherlands of the retreat of French armies, and the surrender of
fortress towns on the Maas to the arms of Marlborough.

CHAPTER X

THE sentientious moral philosopher, Lord Shaftesbury, grandson of a greater and less innocent man, held it a proof of the corruption of the age that his own Whig leaders had not opposed King William's wishes for a standing army in time of peace. No man, according to Shaftesbury and his friends, loved English liberties better than William of Orange who came over to save them, but no true patriot could trust even the ' Archangel Michael ' with a military establishment, ' lest his heart should be lifted up and he should turn aside from the commandment, *anglice* the law.' [203]

Such language coming from such a quarter is evidence that anti-military feeling was not mere party prejudice of the High Tories, but was a rooted national instinct, reinforced by recent experience with the Kings and Protectors of the Stuart era. It was no easy matter to reconcile the institution of a standing army with the genius of parliamentary and popular government, and the work was not done in a day. It was due to the device of the annually expiring Mutiny Act, and to the good sense of Ministers under the first two Georges, that the small but efficient military establishment required by Britain's growing Empire became one of the facts accepted by Eighteenth-Century custom. Marlborough's victories helped to make England proud of her soldiers. Yet the treatment of Marlborough himself in the last years of Anne shows how little, even then, the country cared for a red coat, or was dazzled by the glory of war.

The armies of Europe had ceased to be feudal but had not yet become national. They were not raised by conscription. Soldiering was a trade or profession at which a man spent his life, by no means necessarily in the service of the State to which he owed political allegiance. An army was a polyglot epitome of Europe. Long service was the rule, although in England, army-shy, the return of peace meant disbandment and the throwing on to the street of men who had no resources for civil life. Every great army, especially that of the Dutch, and even to some extent those of France and England, consisted largely of foreigners. They were some of them enlisted as individuals, but more by the purchase of their services from German and other Princes who enlisted them in their territories and let them out as a source of State revenue. The cause of the employer was not by any means always the cause of the employed in the trade of war—certainly not in the great Dutch army, except in so far as common Protestantism was felt as a motive in the ranks, in the struggle against the revoker of the Edict of Nantes. But in the native regiments of the French and the English armies there was a strong national feeling.

Of the 40,000 men that Parliament had voted in the winter of 1701–1702 as England's contribution in kind to the first year of the land war, only 18,000 were to be British ; more than half of these were destined for the Low Countries under Marlborough. By 1706 the native British soldiers engaged in Spain, Portugal and the Low Countries together numbered 33,000. In 1708–1709 England's war effort reached its high-water mark, when the Peninsular War engaged 25,000 English-speaking troops, and the war in the Netherlands as many more, while the whole regular army, including home and colonial garrisons, touched 70,000—not counting foreign regiments in British pay, and altogether apart from the armies of other States subsidised by the British tax-payer.[204]

By what methods were Marlborough's men recruited ? Europe was not then subject to conscription. Even the armies of the Grand Monarch were maintained by voluntary enlistment, except that near the end of his reign the militia ballot had to be employed sometimes to keep up the waning military strength of France. On the other hand, compulsion was always used to man the English Navy in wartime, by armed raids of the press-gang on the folk of the port towns and neighbouring villages. But the Army was less popular and was regarded as less essential to our island safety. In 1702 no compulsion was authorized in its recruiting, nor was that task undertaken directly by the State. Each Colonel had to enlist his own men.

The Colonel was in a sense the proprietor of his regiment. It was known by his name. He paid and clothed its rank and file out of the public money allowed to him for the purpose. Abuses were rife under corrupt officers, who made ' false musters,' drawing pay for ' faggot men ' who were not in the ranks at all. The poor privates were often choused of their pay, food and clothing, either by the civilian contractors or by their own officers, under a system peculiarly favourable to such frauds. These bad practices were commonest among the absentee officers of regiments allotted to the dreaded service in the unhealthy climate of the West Indies. They were least common in the Low Countries under Marlborough's vigilant eye.

A normal regiment consisted of a single battalion of 700 to 900 men.[205] The business of replenishing its ranks in wartime was one of the severest tests of a good officer. Six months were spent in the field, but the six winter months, when the operations of war were suspended, were none too long for the drill necessitated by the elaborate line tactics of the day, and for the arduous task of making good the yearly wastage of the ranks through battle, disease and desertion. Directly the regiment went into winter quarters in Holland or Portugal, the Colonel sent over his most trusted officers to England to find the food for powder in the next campaign. A Yorkshire Colonel whose regiment had lost 200 men in 1710, sent home that winter, ' two Yorkshire gentlemen with a good number of sergeants and corporals ' to raise men in the West Riding. The proceedings of Captain Plume and his faithful sergeant Kite, recruiting the yokels of Shropshire in the year after

Blenheim, can be studied in Farquhar's comedy, *The Recruiting Officer* :

If any gentlemen soldiers, or others, have a mind to serve Her Majesty and pull down the French King : if any prentices have severe masters, any children have undutiful parents, if any servants have too little wages, or any husband too much wife, let them repair to the noble sergeant Kite, at the sign of the Raven in this good town of Shrewsbury and they shall receive present relief and entertainment. . . . I love a fellow of spirit, but I scorn to coax, 'tis base : though I must say that never in my life have I seen a better built man. . . . give me your hand then : here's a purse of gold and there's a tub of humming ale at my quarters. 'Tis the Queen's money and the Queen's drink.

Criminals were drafted in wholesale* and the debtors' prisons were emptied into the Army ; bounties sometimes amounting to four pounds for each recruit tempted the needy to enlist. Sometimes the lure of a short service of three years was offered. Yet with all their shifts the most diligent officers found it ever more difficult to keep the old regiments up to strength while Parliament was perpetually voting new ones to be raised. The soldier's life was popularly regarded as an escape only for the desperate, and in the early years of the reign the country was prosperous and work abundant. No wonder then that in 1702 the naval press was abused for the purposes of the land service ; that year over a thousand English recruits deserted to the French lines, and ' alleged one and all that they were pressed for the sea service, and then carried to the Tower, were embarked blindfolded and transported to Flanders.' [206]

To remedy this state of things a series of Recruiting Acts was passed, beginning in the session of 1703–1704,

---

* The following ungrammatical note from Narcissus Luttrell's Diary (March 12, 1705–6, vol. vi. p. 25) may be read with the explanation that ' half-hanged Smith ' was a famous character at this period owing to the unusual experience he had undergone at the hands of public justice :—' Smith, who some time since was half hanged and cut down, having accused about 350 pickpockets, housebreakers etc., who gott to be soldiers in the guards, the better to hide their roguery, were last week upon mustering the regiments drawn out and immediately shipped for Catalonia ; and about 60 women, who lay under condemnation for such crimes, were likewise sent away to follow the camp.'

whereby compulsory enlistment in the Army was rendered legal within certain strict limits. Magistrates were instructed to hand over to recruiting officers persons who could show no means of supporting themselves. Parish constables were to be given ten shillings for every person suitable for the press whom they produced before the authorities. The small privileged class of electors for the House of Commons were specifically excepted from the operation of the Acts, probably to prevent their forcible enlistment by politically-minded magistrates, anxious to remove voters of the wrong colour before the next election.

But the business of enlistment, though thus facilitated by law, was still left to local haphazard and caprice. High-flying Justices, who disliked the war or had taken offence with the officer recruiting for his regiment in the district, would do nothing to help. But magistrates of Moderate Tory opinions, who supported Godolphin and Marlborough, and the remnant of the old Whig bench that had escaped Wright's purge, were zealous to enlist those whom they chose to regard as having no other means of livelihood. The Recruiting Acts were seized on as a chance to rid the countryside of poachers and suspected persons, and to pay off personal or political scores. In the Isle of Ely three Tory Justices of the Peace drafted a well-to-do Nonconformist minister into the ranks, clearly contrary to the law as he had a vote for Parliament. The Court of Queen's Bench had to intervene to obtain his release. Sometimes the mob rose against the recruiting officers, and forcibly set free those whom the magistrates had consigned to their clutches as unemployed. The new 'pressing act' was unpopular, as a weapon of tyranny in unscrupulous hands. Employees complained that if they asked for better wages or food from their masters, they were threatened with being carried before the magistrates and forced into the Army.

Meanwhile, a whole class of bounty-jumpers lived by taking the Queen's guineas in regiment after regiment and deserting each in turn before they could be marched down to the transport ship. The recruiting officers of the rival regiments were careful not to enquire whence volunteers came. Desertion was easy, for there were no barracks

or proper depots.*   Even when these lively fellows had at
length been carried safe to Flanders, many of them slipped
over to the enemy's lines, hoping to get back to England as
exchanged prisoners, and there play the game of bounty-
jumping once more.

The raising of Marlborough's armies was indeed a
harum-scarum, knock-about affair, replete with old English
comedy and tragedy, of which glimpses are revealed to our
later age, accustomed to the machine-like horror of modern
war and its unavoidable roll-call of the whole youth of the
nation.   In those days ' the fife of war ' could still sound
like ' a blackbird's whistle ':

> Here's forty shillings on the drum
> For those that volunteers do come,
> With shirts and clothes and present pay
> *When over the hills and far away.*
>
> We then shall lead more happy lives,
> By getting rid of brats and wives,
> That scold on both night and day,
> *When over the hills and far away.*
>
> Come on then, boys, and you shall see
> We every one shall Captains be,
> To whore and rant as well as they,
> *When over the hills and far away.*
>
> The constables they search about
> To find such brisk young fellows out ;
> Then let's be volunteers I say
> *Over the hills and far away.*
>
> *Over the hills and over the main*
> *To Flanders, Portugal and Spain,*
> *Queen Anne commands and we'll obey,*
> *Over the hills and far away.*[207]

* The want of barrack accommodation in England caused many difficulties.
The Mutiny Act of 1702, besides complaining that officers and soldiers destroyed
a great deal of game, orders the Justices of the Peace to find them quarters in the
inns, and to fix the prices the soldiers were to pay.   They were not to be quartered
in private houses except by consent of the owner.   Officers were to be cashiered if
they took money for excusing the quartering on any inn ; presumably therefore
these compulsory guests were disliked by inn-keepers as keeping away more
paying customers.   *Stats. of Realm*, VIII, pp. 211–214.

Such were the sorrowful chances of recruiting for the regular army bound on foreign service. There was no such difficulty in filling the ranks of the stay-at-home Militia of the shires and towns, trained a few weeks in the year and officered by civilian Justices of the Peace. That force was popular with everyone, and in particular with the Tory squires. Therefore it was raised by a well regulated system of compulsion, which would not have been tolerated for the army proper. The burden fell on the willing shoulders of the country gentlemen : the Militia was their own force and they were ready to pay for it without any of those murmurs with which they paid the heavy land-tax to support the war. Every rich landowner was called on to supply, in person or by deputy, a horseman fully armed ; every landowner of moderate means, a foot soldier ; while the small landowners were bound in groups, each of which had to send one militiaman to the muster.

The squires armed and paid men to serve for them in the ranks, but themselves competed eagerly for the officers' commissions. The manor-house walls were hung with Militia weapons, which the Muster-Master of the Deputy Lieutenant had the right to inspect. The Militia, therefore, cost the State but little. It was a capital force, the country's pride, the guardian of our free constitution. There was nothing to be said against it, except that, as realistic Whigs pointed out, one regiment of Louis's veterans would easily drive before it the Militia of three English counties.[208]

At the opening of the Thirty Years' War, battles had been fought by troops fighting in close column. Even the cavalry charged in column six or more deep ; they trotted up, handling their musketoons, or huge ' dag ' pistols, and slowed down to let them off, before offering to draw their swords. In the pictorial art of the Seventeenth Century, the battle-pieces, from those of Wouverman downwards, frequently depict horsemen firing their pistols as they swerve their horses round for retreat ; and such was the commonest manœuvre of the cavalry of the period.

A worse way of employing mounted men could hardly have been devised. To permit men to fight from horseback with firearms instead of hand-to-hand weapons, is to throw away the power and speed of the animal, by checking its charge just before the moment of impact. And if any shooting is to be done, the column is the worst formation, either to give or receive fire. Gustavus Adolphus, indeed, reduced the cavalry formation from column of six to line of three deep, and taught his cavalry to charge home, though even he permitted his men to fire their pistols at close quarters provided they did not break the pace of their charge. Rupert and Cromwell each made his troopers fight in this ' Swedish ' fashion ; three deep they charged in with pistol and sword upon columns of hostile cavalry, who halted to fire their dags at a distance and then broke before the onset of fast-trotting horses and cold steel.

In the wars of Queen Anne, battles were still lost by cavalry halting to fire, as did many squadrons of French horse at Blenheim. The English, without breaking their pace, rode in on them sword in hand. Marlborough would not let his troopers fire their pistols at all, as even Cromwell's men had often done. The Duke ' would allow the horse but three charges of powder and ball to each man for a campaign, and that only for guarding their horses when at grass, and not to be made use of in action.' [209]

We may then think of Marlborough's cavalry as fighting in line three deep, charging, not indeed at a gallop, but at a brisk trot,* and using no weapon but the sword. In his early campaigns his cavalry had no body armour ; in 1707 he gave them a cuirass in front, but none at the back. Dragoons had a double function : they could charge sword-in-hand like the cavalry ; or else as mounted infantry they could ride to the scene of action, leap down and picket their horses, and use their muskets to contest broken ground. At Barcelona, Peterborough used dragoons in siege warfare.

The Infantry too, when the Thirty Years' War began,

---

* Marlborough's orders to the English cavalry for the decisive charge at Blenheim were ' to advance gently until they came near them and then ride *on a full trot* up to them.' *Parker's Memoirs* (1746), p. 92. See also Taylor, *Wars of Marlborough*, II, pp. 386–387.

fought in dense columns. The principal weapon had been the mass of long pikes in the centre. The musketeers, also in column, fought on both sides of the pikemen, dangerously exposed to the charge of cavalry, against which the club end of the musket was a poor defence. Gustavus set the fashion of reducing the depth of the infantry, and at Naseby ' the poor foot ' fought in battalions not more than six deep. But so long as the pike was the chief weapon, the column was the natural formation rather than the line. The real revolution in infantry tactics only occurred at the end of the century, when the invention of the ring-bayonet enabled the musketeer to be as it were his own pikeman, to fire his shot through the ring that fastened the bayonet to the gun, and next moment to stab the enemy with the same weapon.

With the introduction of the ring-bayonet in William's wars, the proportion of each regiment to be armed with the pike had rapidly diminished. But in the first campaign of Marlborough there were still some pikemen in the army of each nation engaged. In the English regiments of 1702 they numbered one to every five musketeers. The tallest men were selected for the service, and given half-a-crown every time they could break a pike on the parade ground ' to induce a brisk and smart motion in charging.' Two years later pikes had disappeared.*

Marlborough's Infantry, therefore, from the Blenheim campaign onwards, were armed with the firelock and ring-bayonet, and arrayed in long lines, usually three deep, sometimes two or four. When surrounded by the enemy's horse, a well-drilled regiment of foot could form hollow square and move safely away in that formation.[210] And even without forming square, infantry were brought up, as in the allied centre at Blenheim, to play a deciding part in the main action between the cavalry of the two armies,

* February 9, 1704, Lord Portmore writes to the Duke of Somerset, about troops destined for Portugal:
' I have the honour of receiving an order from your Grace directing the store-keeper to deliver 450 firelocks, in lieu of the like number of pikes which some of the regiments which come from Holland have, as they say, left behind, by his Grace, the Duke of Marlborough's allowance.' *H.M.C. Somerset* (1898), p. 118 ; *Peter Drake's Memoirs*, pp. 50–51 ; *Fortescue*, I, p. 584.

a thing unheard of in the time of Rupert and Cromwell, and rendered possible only by the bayonet.

The line tactics of the early Eighteenth Century were superior to the practice of most armies in the time of Napoleon, when the French and every Continental Power in imitation of them had gone back to the more primitive method of the infantry column. The line formation demands excellent drill and strict discipline. The great conscript armies of France under the First Republic were not sufficiently trained to be able to manœuvre properly in line. Even in Napoleon's time they kept the field all the year round and had little time for drill. But the forces of Marlborough and of his antagonists were small, professional armies, who kept the field only half the year and spent six months on the parade ground, learning the difficult manœuvres of the period.

The English did not therefore enjoy under Marlborough the advantage which they enjoyed under Wellington, of fighting in line against enemies clubbed in the clumsy column. Both sides were in line. But the English had a fire-drill superior to the French. They were taught to fire by platoons, while the French fired by ranks. And the English aim was much the more deadly. Marlborough laid great store on fire-drill and marksmanship, which he caused to be practised strenuously in winter quarters. The effect of the simultaneous volley of an English platoon, two or three deep, was shattering to the enemy's ranks and nerves.[211]

The ' grenadiers ' had not then given their name to the First Regiment of Foot Guards. Every regiment in the army had a company of grenadiers, armed with hand-grenades and axes, as the song recalls ; it was their business to lead the attack on fortified places or other obstacles. They were in some sort ' storm troops,' and specially selected for their athletic qualities and their dash.

Marlborough's use of his field artillery, commanded by the famous Colonel Blood, played an important part in his battle tactics. The waggoners who dragged the guns into position were not soldiers, but rustic carters in peasants' dress, for the artillery service was as yet only half militarized.

But Colonel Blood, his officers and gunners were as good artillery men as ever served, and the difficulties of ground which they overcame in the passage of the Black Forest and on the day among the marshes of Blenheim, proved them also to be expert and energetic engineers. Their field-pieces fired cannon-balls at long range, and at close quarters ' cartridge ' or ' partridge ' shot, as grape was then called. The heavy siege trains were a separate service, sent up from the base, as far as possible by water, when required against a particular town.

Marlborough was in direct command of all the batteries in his army, placing them with the greatest care on spots selected by himself. In the moderate-sized armies of that day there was no large unit, like the modern Division or Army Corps, comprising smaller units of all three arms under a subordinate command. Without any intermediary, Marlborough sent his orders to each Brigadier or Colonel, or rode up with them himself to point the way.

Any more elaborate system would have hampered Marlborough's genius, that shone most brightly in the smoke and uproar of actual conflict. The modern Divisional system of orders interpreted by subordinate Generals, would have made sad work for him in those days of big-wigged Princes and Lords jealously stickling for their rank and rights, even on the battle-field. The complete freedom enjoyed by Marlborough to move any of his troops in detail himself, if he saw fit to do so, was one of the secrets of his invariable success whenever action was joined, when, in Addison's words, he

> Inspired repulsed battalions to engage,
> And taught the doubtful battle where to rage.

The limitation of his freedom to attack the enemy when and where he wished was diplomatic rather than military. The right of the civilian Field Deputies, and yet more often the right of the Dutch Generals themselves, to veto any order that would have brought the troops of the States General into action, ruined his plans half a dozen times, by preventing him from fighting under conditions which would have rendered victory certain. Marlborough, though

Commander-in-Chief of the Dutch and other allied forces in the Netherlands, had not, therefore, on all occasions complete control over his foreign troops in that region, though he enjoyed it on the Danube.

Bolingbroke, who having been Secretary at War in the year of Blenheim knew something of the army, long afterwards wrote in his essay on the *Study and use of History* :

> What I remember to have heard the Duke of Marlborough say, before he went to take on him the command of the army in the Low Countries in 1702, proved true. The French misreckoned very much, if they made the same comparison between their troops and those of their enemies, as they had made in precedent wars. Those that had been opposed to them in the last [William's war] were raw for the most part when it began, the British particularly ; but they had been disciplined, if I may say so, by their defeats. They were grown to be veteran at the peace of Ryswic, and though many had been disbanded, yet they had been disbanded lately : so that they were easily formed anew, and the spirit that had been raised continued in all.

But in the operations of 1702 the army was only in process of being ' formed anew,' and its discipline was proportionately bad. The misconduct of Ormonde's landing party at Cadiz that year was a European scandal. And before Marlborough arrived in Holland, English regiments were plundering Dutch villages as if in an enemy country. On June 9th our agent in Rotterdam wrote to Nottingham, ' My Lord Marlbury goes next week from the Hage to the Army, where he is extreamly wanted to keep our men in order.' In the following year the Allies still made occasional complaints of the plundering habits of the English as contagious to other nationals.[212] But these murmurs died away as Marlborough established his hold. In the march to the Danube of 1704, the well-behaved English regiments maintained week after week their popularity with the allied populations through which they passed. Nor did discipline degenerate in the later years of the long protracted war. No such scenes as those that dimmed the glory of the capture of Badajos and San Sebastian in

Wellington's day stained the reputation of Marlborough's men.*

The good conduct of the army was secured by the double method of rigorous punishment and of careful supply of food, clothing and comfort. Military executions were not rare. Still more common were military floggings —things of terror, as we know from Corporal Trim's account of the unfortunate ' grenadier in Mackay's regiment ' who was ' whipped to death's door,' and ' begged to be shot outright.' Recorded history supports the novelist. In 1712 a guardsman had killed his Colonel's horse to steal the hide ; he was ordered 12,600 lashes, and received the first 1800, of which he nearly died. A sentence of such extreme ferocity was indeed exceptional, and occurred only after Marlborough had been dismissed from the command of the forces. In civil life flogging was still the common punishment of the poorer classes, including women, and for that reason flogging in the army and navy was not yet, as in a later age, denounced as an outrage on humanity and a degradation to the service.[213]

Marlborough would not have reduced his men to proper discipline merely by ceremonial lacerating of their flesh. He took great trouble about everything connected with the supply and comfort of the troops, and he had his reward. Well fed, well clothed, well shod, well drilled, the English army came to be recognized as the best on either side in the war. This was due very largely to the care which the Duke deigned to bestow on small prosaic things behind the scenes, in days when troops were too often neglected, starved, ragged and unpaid. Part of his ' genius ' consisted in ' an infinite capacity for taking pains.' †

The connection between army and navy has often been a weak link in England's armour. Although Marlborough had unusually sound and penetrating ideas as to the

* ' Marlborough's army seems to have been better conducted than Wellington's,' *Fortescue*, I, p. 572. The ' burning of Bavaria ' in 1704 was deliberate policy ordered by Marlborough, who employed chiefly foreign troops in that bad business.

† The wounded, including the enemy prisoners, received more care from Marlborough than from other generals of the day. But medical practice, even in time of peace, was rudimentary, and nursing was a science unknown.

co-operation of the two services, which governed his successful strategy in the Mediterranean, and triumphed at Vigo, Gibraltar and Minorca, he does not seem to have secured proper conditions for soldiers at sea. In January 1704 Admiral Rooke vainly protested against the absence of proper transports, and the consequent crowding of whole regiments upon the men-of-war, 'especially without beds,' for the long voyage to Spain. In the winter of 1706–1707 nearly half of a large body of troops sent thus to Valencia perished of hardship and disease before they landed. And in 1708 private John Deane, a God-fearing and well-educated man, who trusted and loved Marlborough and was no grumbler, described the lot of the soldier at sea as ' Pox above board, plague between the decks.' He tells us, in words impressive in their simplicity, how, even off the coast of England, they lay ' under many inconveniences having only the bare deck to lie upon, which hardships caused abundance of our men to bid adieu to the world.'

In the Spanish Peninsula, far from the Duke's protecting hand, our troops suffered terribly from exposure, climate and bad food, which slew far more than the sword in that unfriendly land, where even our allies, the Portuguese, hated us. In Gibraltar, after it had passed into English hands, the authorities spent money on fortifying the rock with batteries, but for many years erected no barracks for the soldiers. The garrison continued to die there of disease and exposure for many seasons after the Spaniards and French had raised the siege of 1705. In the West Indies, the men died like flies from tropical diseases and gross neglect, forgotten by the War Office and often by their own absentee officers. In short, during the wars of Queen Anne, those were luckiest whose service kept them nearest to Marlborough himself.[214]

If the Duke had not had political as well as military authority, if Godolphin had not been in charge of the national purse on his behalf, he could not as a mere General have coped with cheating civilian agents and contractors and procrastinating Treasury officials. Even as it was, the fight was uphill. In the infancy of paper credit and financial science, the difficulties of the Treasury were great, even under the best management. It was customary to leave soldiers and diplomats unpaid for years together, with disastrous results to the prestige of the country abroad. In 1702 many officers had not touched money due to them for services in the last war. Lord Cutts, when left in command in Holland during Marlborough's absence in the winter of 1702–1703, failed to receive his pay and was ignominiously harassed by the dunning of Dutch tradesmen. Michelborne, the military governor of Londonderry during the siege of 1689, where he had lost his wife, his seven children and his fortune, was still in 1704 petitioning the State for arrears acknowledged as due to him for that memorable service. He was the national hero of Protestant England, yet in Anne's reign he was a prisoner in the Fleet for debt, because he was a creditor of the State. And the widow of Micaiah Browning, who had broken the boom on the Foyle in his own ship, the *Mountjoy*, and lost his life in the action, petitioned in vain for nine years' arrears of her pension—and was in 1703 'paid as much as is due in the queen's time.' Such was the Treasury as paymaster.[215]

That this shameful state of things was somewhat improved in the course of the long wars of Anne, instead of getting very much worse as might have been expected, was due to the earnest efforts and close co-operation of Marlborough and Godolphin. Yet in 1712 the embarrassed father of the diplomat John Molesworth, after vainly visiting Godolphin's successor at the Treasury, writes : ' I am told I shall not be paid a day sooner than the other envoys when they come in course. There is two and a half years due to them all. In the meantime we must maintain Jack out of our estate.'[216]

The warfare of that age was far less destructive than the warfare of the Twentieth Century, partly from the inferiority of the weapons used, but chiefly because of the small proportion of the world's manhood which it was then possible to withdraw from production and maintain in the field. Europe was too ill-organized and too poor to pay a heavy blood-tax, and her credit system was too primitive to draw

large drafts on the wealth and happiness of future generations.   Man was still so much more valuable than the
machinery he used, that his human rights were seldom
forgotten by the War-lords.   Prisoners, for instance, were
rapidly exchanged, by an excellent system, honestly worked
throughout the war.   The French and English authorities
saw their advantage in exchange, because it was difficult to
get recruits and impossible to keep prisoners alive without
great expense.   The same difficulty of raising men, before
the age of conscription, made governments and generals
unwilling to risk lives in battle, or to expose them to the
inevitable wastage of winter campaigns.   Only Marlborough saw that battles won as he could win them would
save lives in the end.

Plundering by the soldiers was naturally commoner in
enemy than in allied country, but systematic destruction was
seldom resorted to.   When Louis ravaged and burnt the
Palatinate in 1688, when the Allies ravaged and burnt
Bavaria in 1704, there was in each case an outcry that had
its effect.   The War of the Spanish Succession went on for
a dozen years—that was indeed the worst of it, and was one
of the chief causes of the decline of Holland.   But the war
did not ruin the districts where it was fought—the Netherlands, the Rhine Valley, the plain of the Po, or Spain—as the
Thirty Years' War had ruined Germany, and as the Four
Years' War of our own day made a desert of the seat of
operations and ruined the whole of Europe.   A battle, or
manœuvres to avoid a battle, trampled the crops of two or
three villages—no more.   A heavy bombardment or a siege
might unroof a few score houses.   But trade by land went
on very much as in peace time, even between countries at
war with one another, in spite of England's protest against
Dutch trade with France.   The war on commerce at sea
was a more serious matter for merchants.

It was not the custom to make armies support themselves by pillage.   The universal brigandage of the ill-
disciplined bands of the Thirty Years' War was never
repeated ; civilization had taken a step forward out of
that quagmire.   Nor had military science yet adopted
Napoleon's system of supporting armies by the systematized

plunder of invaded territory, so as to make penetration more
rapid.   On the contrary, a chain of supply bases was formed
by an advancing army, and each of these bases had to be
filled up with supplies and stores from the rear, before the
invading forces could move further into the land.[217]   Partly
for this reason the movement of the armies of Louis XIV
and his adversaries was slow compared with Napoleon's lightning darts across Europe.   Consequently, Marlborough's
march on the Danube, carefully, though secretly, prepared beforehand, surprised the French, and aroused the
admiration of the world.

The general character of this slowly-moving warfare,
especially in the highly fortified Netherlands, was a war of
sieges.   To the military mind of that age, a campaign
meant a summer of sieges, with field armies manœuvring
to cover or break up investment, followed by a winter of
recruiting and drill.

But Marlborough had other views.   Like Gustavus and
Cromwell before him, he knew that the enemy's towns and
fortresses would fall fast enough if the enemy's armies were
first destroyed in the open field.   But this unorthodox
system of war by battle caused doubt, hesitation and panic
among all the allied Generals and Princes, except Eugene.
And it met with most opposition of all from the Deputies
and Generals sent with the Dutch troops to see that Marlborough, to whose charge they had been somewhat rashly
committed, did not spend their valuable lives too fast.

The attitude of the Dutch to their large army of well-
disciplined and well-paid mercenaries from all the Protestant
countries of Europe, was the attitude of a careful trader to
the stock in which he has invested his money.   Those
expensive regiments must not be hazarded in battle.   Dutch
military history had been full of lost battles, from the time
of William the Silent's first defeats by the Spaniards, down
to William III's Landen and Steinkirk.   Such adventures
were therefore suspect to the mind of the careful Hollanders.
Their one great soldier, Maurice of Nassau, had taught
them, a hundred years before, the bloodless strategy of
covering sieges as the principal use of armies in the field.
If Louis XIV had the splendid military engineer, Vauban,

the Dutch had his rival Cohorn, both still active in 1702.

Only the Pensionary Heinsius partly saw the force of Marlborough's reasoning, when he argued that to recover the Spanish Netherlands at the rate of a couple of successful sieges a year, would mean another Thirty Years' War. Louis was the man in possession—he held Italy, Spain, the Netherlands and parts of Germany. It was for the Allies to extrude him from these positions before the inevitable exhaustion of the combatants put an end to hostilities. Therefore, Marlborough's risky method of warfare by battle was the only possible hope of salvation to Europe, since her liberties had no longer, as in the last war, to be guarded from French aggression, but had now to be wrested back from the already triumphant enemy.

(See Appendix C, below, 'War then and now.')

CHAPTER XI

Opening of the war in 1702. German Princes and the Empire. Affairs
on the Rhine. Marlborough's campaign of 1702. Reconquest of the
Lower Rhine and Maas valleys. Venloo and Liège. Character of Cutts.
Bavaria joins France, September 1702.

[For this Chapter see the maps at the end of the volume.]

THE principal cause of trouble in Europe was the political
unity of France, over against the political non-existence of
Germany and Italy. Germany was a geographical expression for several hundred sovereign Principalities, many of
them the size of an English nobleman's estate. Except
Bavaria, which was on the point of joining France, the only
two German-speaking States with large and formidable
armies were Austria and Brandenburg-Prussia, and they
lay so far away to the East that their troops had great
distances to march before they could operate on the French
border at all.

Austria, moreover, was distracted by constant trouble,
or fear of trouble, with Turks, Poles and Swedes, and by the
running sore of the Hungarian rebellion. Yet the whole
weight of the war against France in Italy rested on Austria's
empty treasure-chest and ill-organized army, until the defection of Savoy from the French cause at the end of 1703.
England and Holland, who ere long undertook the war in
Spain, never sent their own troops into Italy ; and in the
spring of 1702 they were fully occupied in protecting
Dutch territory from invasion.

In these circumstances, the war of the Rhine depended
chiefly on the armies of the smaller German Princes, since
Austria was engaged in Hungary and Italy, and England

and Holland nearer home. The attitude of the German Princes was therefore of vital importance.

The only political union known to the Germans of that day was the famous Holy Roman Empire, a loose confederacy of sovereign powers, with the Emperor as unpopular chairman. Leopold's real power lay in the fact that he was also hereditary ruler of the Austrian territories in the East—a great recruiting ground for armies where men were to be had cheap. But that hereditary position of the House of Hapsburg in the lands of the Lower Danube caused the Emperor to be regarded with all the more jealousy by the republic of German Princes over whom he presided. The Empire was divided constitutionally into ' Circles '—Westphalia, Swabia, Franconia, the Upper and Lower Rhine, and half a dozen more. Each Circle debated in its Diet whether it should remain neutral or take a side in the war that had begun between Austria and France. The adherents of Louis argued that the question of the Spanish Succession was a private quarrel between the Houses of Hapsburg and Bourbon, and that if the Empire fought in Austria's quarrel it would become Austria's slave. Leopold replied that it was the duty of the Circles to stand by the rights of the Empire, whose feoffs in Italy, particularly Milan, had been wrongfully seized, and whose Netherland territory had been invaded by France ; and that the power of Louis was a danger to the independence of every German Prince.[218]

In 1701 the Circles hesitated to respond to the Emperor's call to arms. Each Prince waited to see how he was personally affected by the new situation. But in the winter and spring of 1701–1702 the decided action of England and Holland, the subsidies they offered to fighting Princes, and the ever-increasing dislike and fear felt by Germans for the insolence of French diplomats and soldiers, brought a strong nucleus of Princes into the Alliance.

Foremost among these was Frederick Elector of Brandenburg, faithful by family tradition to the Protestant and anti-French cause in Europe, and personally gratified by the recognition of his brand-new title of King of Prussia, wrung from the unwilling Emperor as the price of alliance in the war ; the Maritime Powers readily acknowledged his Kingship and paid his excellent troops.

George, Elector of Hanover, was influenced by his expectations of the English succession. His neighbour and kinsman, Anthony Ulric, Duke of Brunswick-Wolfenbüttel, had formed an alliance with Louis, and was raising troops to fight for him. But in March 1702 Anthony's Principality was invaded by his watchful cousins of Hanover, and Wolfenbüttel was compelled by military duress to join the Alliance.[219]

This prompt action against French intrigue in the heart of Northern Germany counterbalanced the defection of the Elector Bishop of Cologne and Liège, who had successfully invited French troops into his territories.*

The Bishop's brother, Max Emanuel, Elector of Bavaria, though acting wholly in the interest of France in his capacity as Spanish Governor of the Netherlands, still maintained a show of neutrality as German Prince. He had not yet declared on which side he would employ the forces of Bavaria, reckoned at 45,000 troops, more numerous and no less stalwart than the contingent contributed by Prussia to the allied cause. Max Emanuel had permitted the Imperial armies to cross Bavarian territory, and as late as August 1702 he was still negotiating with Godolphin and with the Emperor, though probably only to amuse them, as to the terms on which he would consent to terminate Bavarian neutrality and serve the Imperial cause either in Hungary or the Italian plain.[220]

The delay of Max Emanuel in declaring for Louis, whatever its motive may have been, rendered it possible for many of the smaller Princes, whose territories lay between Bavaria and France, to join the Grand Alliance in the spring of 1702. The Electors of Mainz and Trier, the Landgraves of Hesse-Cassel and Hesse-Darmstadt, Lewis, Margrave of Baden and the Elector Palatine all took the field ; a German army of the Rhine came into being.

The active alliance of so many Rhenish Princes with Holland and England brought into painful prominence

* See p. 156, above.

the fact that the French were astride the Rhine at Kaiserswerth and Bonn, barring communication along the great waterway between Holland and her allies in South-West Germany.   An army of Prussians, Palatines and Dutch therefore laid siege to Kaiserswerth, the first operation of the war north of the Alps.*

The main French army, 60,000 strong, under Marshal Boufflers, endeavoured to raise the siege ; Boufflers lay near Xanten in the King of Prussia's territory of Cleves. But Kaiserswerth was on the east bank of the Rhine and the French dared not cross the river in the presence of the main Dutch and English forces.   The Allies lay at Kranenburg, watching Boufflers, partly to cover the siege of Kaiserswerth, and partly to protect the approaches to Dutch territory.   At this early stage of the campaign their numbers were not half those of Boufflers' army, and Marlborough was still in England, smoothing out the political arrangements of the new reign.   In his absence the Allies were commanded by the Earl of Athlone, one of William's Dutch generals, best known in English history as Ginkel, who had completed the conquest of Ireland after the Boyne.

May
1702

Boufflers decided that the best way to raise the siege of Kaiserswerth was to invade the Dutch territory by the route of the Rhine and Waal, along which the armies of Louis had entered in 1672. Athlone, ill informed by his scouts, was taken off his guard.   Boufflers made a sudden dash from Xanten for Nimuegen ; if he had been able to seize it behind Athlone's back, the English and Dutch armies would have been cut off from their base and Holland exposed to the invader. Athlone retreated at full speed from Kranenburg and only just reached Nimuegen before the van of Boufflers' army.   In the rearguard action outside the town, the English troops were engaged for the first time in the war and came well through the ordeal.†

June 10
(N.S.)
1702

* *See Map VIII at end of volume.*

† According to Captain Parker, who was present : ' If Boufflers had won the race not a man of our small army would have escaped ; all must either have been killed or taken. At the same time Nimuegen must also have fallen into their hands which would have opened them a way into the heart of the very province of Holland.'   *Parker*, p. 64.

By so small a margin had the blow failed which might have proved fatal to the allied cause. But a miss is as good as a mile. Holland was safe, though frightened through and through. A few days later Kaiserswerth fell. The allied army received large reinforcements. Last but not least, Marlborough at length arrived to take the command.

The first of Marlborough's many letters to Sarah from the war which was destined to be known by his name, was written on a morning of mid-May, on board ship, as the Margate coastline was vanishing from sight :

It is impossible to express with what a heavy heart I parted with you when I was by the water's side. I could have given my life to have come back, though I knew my own weakness so much that I durst not, for I knew I should have exposed myself to the company. I did for a great while, with the perspective glass, look upon the cliffs in hopes I might have had one sight of you. If you will be sensible of what I now feel, you will endeavour ever to be easy to me, and then I shall be most happy.

Was she not always ' easy ' to him ? On that point she has kept her secret from posterity. At her request, he burnt her letters as fast as he received them. In the *Account of her Conduct* which she gave to the curiosity of mankind, she readily exposed herself and her friend the Queen and their most intimate mutual relations. Only for her husband and for the nature of their life together she showed, by her silence, a reverence that she displayed for no one and for nothing else.

At the Hague Marlborough was detained some weeks, before it was finally agreed, chiefly owing to the efforts of Heinsius, that he should have the command of the Dutch and other allied armies, as well as of the English.* Many of the Dutch Generals had no wish to serve under him. Athlone, with the support of many of his fellow countrymen, aspired to the post, and was chagrined at the promotion of the Englishman over his head. It must be remembered that Marlborough's European reputation as a soldier was yet to make. He made it first in the short remainder of the campaign of 1702. At the end of the year Athlone said

* See p. 166, above.

with admirable generosity : ' The success of this campaign is solely due to this incomparable chief, since I confess that I, serving as second in command, opposed in all circumstances his opinions and proposals.'   One of Marlborough's most notable victories was the conquest of Athlone.[221]

At the beginning of July, nearly half-way through the normal fighting season, he arrived at the front, to take over at Nimuegen the command of an army now as large as that of Boufflers, some 60,000 men, of whom 12,000 were English.   His first object was to manœuvre the French field-army out of the strongly entrenched position that Boufflers had taken up between the Rhine and the lower Maas.   There, in the territories of Cleves and Cologne, his presence was a threat to Holland, whose inhabitants ever since 1672 had lived in terror of invasion down the great waterways from the East.   Till the French could be shifted from that region, the Dutch would never consent to any serious operations against the Spanish Netherlands.[222]   So long as Boufflers remained in Cleves, the Allies were held to the defensive, and so long as Louis could hold them to the defensive he would be victor in the war, for he was the man in possession, and need only retain what he already had, to rise the winner.   Unless the Allies could take the offensive, there was no purpose in their having gone to war at all.

July 2
(N.S.)
1702

All this was realized by Marlborough, who saw the remedy.   If he crossed the Maas at Grave and boldly marched south, on the west side of the river, the French army would be forced to evacuate the territory between Maas and Rhine, and come racing home to save the Spanish Netherlands.   For the weakness of Boufflers' fine advanced position in Cleves lay in his communications.   His supplies came from Brabant and the Liègeois ; they were already threatened and hampered by the Dutch garrison in Maastricht, and if Marlborough moved south from Grave he would cut the line on which the French army depended for its food.

This reasoning was certain and simple.   Yet Marlborough had the greatest difficulty in persuading Athlone and their High Mightinesses the States General to give him leave to advance.   They feared that, if he moved off south, Boufflers would make another pounce on Nimuegen. Marlborough had to spend three precious weeks in messages to and from the Hague, persuading the Allies that the way to save Holland from all fear of attack during the rest of the war was precisely to take the offensive in a southern direction, and so force Boufflers to retreat once for all into Spanish Brabant.   'I shall soon deliver you,' he said, ' of these troublesome neighbours.'

At length leave was obtained.   Crossing the Maas near Grave, Marlborough moved southwards across the marshes and heaths of Dutch Brabant into the Bishopric of Liège.*   The result he had prophesied instantly followed.   Boufflers retreated in haste from the territories of Cleves and Cologne, which were never again during the war infested by a French field-army.   Already, without a shot fired, an immense success had been achieved. ' Our marches have already had the desired effect,' wrote Marlborough to Godolphin, ' which was their repassing the Maas, which had we done sooner, would have been much better.'

July 26 (N.S.) 1702

Boufflers had good reason to be in a hurry : to reach his lines in Spanish Brabant he had to march right across the front of Marlborough's advancing army.   As the French hastened by forced marches from Bree to Sonhoven, they were caught in the flank on the open heathlands at Peer, and could have been attacked under circumstances which must have resulted in their complete defeat.   But the Dutch Field Deputies stopped Marlborough at the very moment he was moving into battle.   It may be doubted if a man ever underwent a more bitter disappointment.   But without any sign of annoyance, he invited the Deputies to ride forward with him ' to see the enemy pass over the heath, which they and most of the General Officers did, and saw them hurrying over it in the greatest confusion and disorder imaginable.   Upon this they all acknowledged that they had lost a fair opportunity of giving the

Aug. 2 (N.S.) 1702

* If the Dutch had consented he would have turned further west and invaded Spanish Brabant, threatening Brussels. But that had proved too bold a proposition to win their consent.

enemy a fatal blow.'   Nevertheless, on the very next day they refused to allow Marlborough to attack the French at Sonhoven, in a position so badly chosen that Berwick, the ablest of the French Generals present, declared they must have been totally destroyed if they had been attacked by the Allies.[223]   Thus twice fortunate, Boufflers escaped into Spanish Brabant where he was joined by reinforcements.

A fortnight later, Marlborough had once more, by skilful manœuvring, drawn the French army into striking distance in the same region of open heaths near Helchteren.   This time the Dutch General Opdam refused to advance to the attack when ordered, on the excuse of the ground being marshy.   The next day it was the turn of the Dutch Deputies to save the French, by prohibiting the attack which the Dutch General had thwarted by his disobedience the day before.

Aug. 23 (N.S.) 1702

By this time even Marlborough's temper was disturbed. His secretary, Cardonnel, described him as ' much out of humour.' [224]   Yet even now he was capable of writing from Helchteren to Godolphin :

Aug. 27 (N.S.) 1702

I believe we should have had an easy victory, for their whole left was in disorder.   However, I have thought it much for her Majesty's service to take no notice of it, as you see by my letter to the States.   But my lord Rivers and almost all the general Officers were with me when I sent the orders [to Opdam], so that notwithstanding the care I take to hinder it they do talk.

The feeling between Dutch and English rose high, and a disastrous breach was only prevented by Marlborough's instinct for the tactful management of Allies, which he practised as an essential part of the art military.

On four several occasions in the month of August, Marlborough had been prevented by Dutch Generals or Deputies from giving battle, under circumstances which would very probably have led to the reconquest of the Spanish Netherlands in 1702 instead of four years later after Ramillies.   At Ramillies the French army was drawn out on ground of its own choosing, in circumstances much less favourable to the Allies than those offered on the heathlands of the northern Liègois.   Time has its revenges.   Between the battle of Ramillies and the Treaty of Utrecht, the Dutch had much to complain of in their treatment by English Whigs and Tories, in the protraction of the war and the circumstances of the peace. But if they had allowed Marlborough to win the war at an earlier stage, they might, with the help of the moderate Tories, have obtained a ' good peace ' before the exhaustion of Holland's resources had rendered her the plaything of English factions.

So Marlborough was not permitted by his Allies to begin the conquest of Spanish Brabant and Flanders in his first campaign. But he found time that autumn to reduce the fortress towns of the Maas valley. The sieges of Venloo, Ruremond, Stevensweert and Liège were carried through in the face of Boufflers, who was unable to hinder the operations.

The English army won golden opinions at the taking of Venloo in September. Venloo lies on the east bank of the Maas, but the key to it was the fort of St. Michael on the west bank. Fort St. Michael was an elaborate earthwork fortress of the smaller size ; traces of it can still be seen on the meadow by the riverside to-day. It was quite capable of holding up the besiegers for a few days. But 1500 English, in obedience to the orders of Lord Cutts, nicknamed the ' Salamander ' because his element was fire, were set on to capture the outer works. They shortened proceedings, contrary to all the rules of siegecraft, by pursuing the defenders from post to post till they had captured the whole fort. Captain Parker, who took part in this memorable escalade, has left his comments:

Sept. 18 (N.S.) 1702

Thus were the unaccountable orders of Lord Cutts as unaccount-ably executed, to the great surprise of the whole army and even of ourselves, when we came to reflect on what we had done. However, had not several unforeseen accidents occurred, not a man of us could have escaped. In particular, when we had penetrated as far as the wooden bridge, had the officer drawn the loose plank after him, as he ought, we must all have fallen into the moat which was ten feet deep in water. And again, when we had passed the bridge which was 120 feet in length, and had got on the faussebraye, had there been six or eight feet of stone or brick under the sod work (which is always practised in our modern fortifications) or had the Governor

R

kept the grass, by the help of which we climbed, close mowed, as he ought to have done, what must have been our fate ?   But everything fell out fortunately and Lord Cutts' orders were crowned with success.[225]

It is possible that Cutts, who knew more about storming parties than any man in the army, had judged the chances coolly and the legitimate risks aright.   Early in life he had been the first to plant the Imperialist standard on the walls of Buda.   He had served William at the head of attacking parties at the Boyne, Limerick, Steinkirk, Brest, Namur and been wounded again and again.   ' Tall, lusty and well-shaped, an agreeable companion, with abundance of wit, affable and familiar, but too much seized with vanity and self-conceit,' the ' Salamander ' was always in the public eye and always in debt.   A poet and a wit, one of Dicky Steele's many friends and one of Swift's many enemies, a Cambridge gentleman and five times Member for the County, he seems almost as Elizabethan as Peterborough himself ; but he was more of a soldier by profession.

Ruremonde fell next and Stevensweert, placing the whole waterway of the Maas up to the outlying Dutch city of Maastricht in the hands of the Allies.   Still not content, Marlborough prolonged the season of warfare to attack Liège.   He was welcomed by the inhabitants of the city, who had no more love for their Bishop than in the days of Quentin Durward.   But on the hill overhanging the city stood the Citadel, whose extensive and formidable earth-works, duly faced with brick, still remain very much as when Marlborough besieged them.   Marlborough effected a breach in five days and stormed the fortress on October 23.*

---

* These sieges were regarded as great exploits in England. Several years later the actor speaking the Prologue to Farquhar's *Twin Rivals*, flattered the patriotism of the audience with these lines :

> ' So Don and Monsieur, bluff before the siege,
>   Were quickly tamed at Venloo and at Liege.
>   'Twas " *Viva Spagnia*," " *Vive la France* " before,
>   Now " *Quartier, Monsieur*," " *Quartier, ah Señor !* " '

There were a few Spanish troops in the Netherlands.

Here ended the first campaign. Marlborough returned to the Hague by the waterway of the Maas which he had opened. It nearly cost him dear. A raiding party of irregulars from Guelder, a town in alliance with the French, surprised his boat as it was gliding down the river at night. It was the chivalrous custom of the age for generals to give passes to their opponents. Marlborough had none, but his servant, Stephen Gell, slipped into his hand in the darkness a French passport really made out for his brother, General Charles Churchill. With impassive mien he handed it to his captors. They failed to recognize him in the darkness, and let him go on, after plundering the boat and securing the escort. The rumour that Marlborough was captured got abroad, spreading joy in France and consternation in Holland. When he arrived safe at the Hague the whole population turned out to meet him with shouts and tears of joy. He had won the heart of the Dutch people, who, whatever some of their rulers might think, recognized in Milord the man who had saved them from France. He gave Stephen Gell a pension of fifty pounds a year.[226]

The results of Marlborough's campaign of 1702 may be summed up as the expulsion of the French from the valleys of the Maas and lower Rhine. The navigation of the Maas from Liège downwards was in allied hands. On the lower Rhine, only Bonn held out for the French, an isolated post, reduced in the following year. In those days of bad roads, waterways were to generals what railways are to-day. The march on the Danube two years later was only rendered possible by the work of 1702—the freeing of the Rhine and Maas valleys for the movements of the Allied army, and the release of the Dutch mind from all fear of invasion from that quarter. Moreover, the Elector Bishop of Liège and Cologne had been signally punished for his desertion of the cause of the Empire : he had lost both his provinces, where the constitutional party, represented by the Chapters, welcomed the Allied troops. The diplomatic prestige of the Alliance had thereby been enhanced at a moment when such encouragement was sorely needed. The year's campaigning in Italy and the upper Rhine brought the Allies small success, beyond the capture of Landau and Eugene's bare victory of Luzzara—if victory it was. And in September a blow fell which threatened the fundamental structure of the Alliance ; Bavaria took the field for France in the rear of the Allied German Princes of the Rhine.

It appears probable that the Elector of Bavaria's nego-tiations with England and Austria in the summer of 1702 had been carried on either to distract their attention from his real designs, or to raise his price with France.* Ever since the spring he had been drawing subsidies from Louis, who grew impatient at his long delay in throwing off the mask. But Max Emanuel frankly avowed to his patron that he would not take the risks of defying the German cause in the heart of Germany, unless he was promised something very tangible as a reward in case victory crowned the French arms. His terms were a vast increase in the territories of Bavaria, and for himself nothing less than the Imperial dignity. The House of Hapsburg was to be dethroned and the Holy Roman Empire reconstituted under the House of Wittelsbach, with Bavaria in place of Austria as the leading State. But in effect the Empire would become a Protectorate of France. Max Emanuel's letters show that he designed to subject Germany to France in order to gratify his personal ambition. The scheme was indeed Napoleonic, but fortunately for Europe the Napoleonic genius was not on the side of the conspirators.[227]

By the Bavarian Alliance Louis was enabled to pass from the defensive to the offensive. He need no longer confine his ambition to keeping the whole Spanish Empire as his perquisite ; he could advance across Central Europe and end the rivalry of centuries by destroying the House of Hapsburg. He could dethrone Austria from the leadership of Germany in favour of a vassal of France. Militarily Vienna would be taken between two fires ; the Hungarians were already knocking at its gates from the east. French and Bavarians would now march upon it from the west.

That would be for next year's campaign. All that was

* See p. 235, above.

necessary in the autumn of 1702 was to establish communication between Bavaria and the French armies, sufficient to
prevent the conquest of the rebel German State by the
troops of the Empire. This was effected in September;
while Marlborough was reducing the fortresses on the Maas,
the Bavarian army unexpectedly attacked the territory of its German neighbours. The Free Imperial
City of Ulm was seized by an old-fashioned ruse,
cleverly executed by Bavarian officers, who entered disguised as peasants, overpowered the burgher guard, and
opened the gates to their comrades without. Ulm was,
in the tradition and feeling of its citizens, an outpost of
Protestantism on the Upper Danube, strongly opposed to
French ambition and Bavarian intrigue. But now, under
military duresse, it became a place of arms where the well-
appointed Bavarian army could await the arrival of the
French forces from Alsace. Between them lay the pine-
clad mountains of the Black Forest, but the routes across it
were inadequately guarded by the Allies. Communications
of a sort between France and Bavaria were established that
autumn. In face of this fact, the capture of Landau by the
Allies was of small account. For a train had been laid
which should result next year in the fall of Vienna.[228]

Sept. 8
1702

CHAPTER XII

WHEN the War of the Spanish Succession began, it seemed to many that the command of the sea had passed with the Empire of Charles II into the hands of France. The Mediterranean, recently open to the commerce of England and of all nations, had become a French lake : the ports and islands of the Spanish and Neapolitan kingdoms were occupied by the soldiers of Louis and his grandson. French troops were already in Naples, quarrelling with the inhabitants. The French fleet from Toulon patrolled the coasts of the inland sea, unchallenged. Tuscany, Savoy and the Papal States were submissive to Louis, and though Venice was neutral she was so impotent that the enterprising French captain, Forbin, ran into the very port of Malamocco and burnt an English vessel in the middle of the Venetian shipping. In these circumstances, many Englishmen spoke of their Turkey and Levant trade as a thing already lost.[229] Spanish America was officially closed to all commerce save that of a French Company, and a great French fleet under Châteaurenault was cruising in the West Indies to enforce the embargo.

But if we look forward ten years to the end of the war, matters wear a very different face. Queen Anne's Admirals are policing the Mediterranean like Nelson after the Nile, reliant on their own impregnable bases of Gibraltar and Port Mahon. The harbours of Portugal, Italy, Turkey and North Africa are in the hands of allied or friendly

powers. The action off Malaga in 1704 was the last
occasion on which the French Grand Fleet ventured to
encounter the English, and three years later it was destroyed
in Toulon harbour. After Malaga, the campaign against
commerce was the only form of enemy activity at sea. The
Spanish-American trade was lost to France, and at Utrecht
was officially assigned to an English Company. In the
words of Admiral Mahan : ' the demands made by England
as conditions of peace in 1711 showed her to have become
a sea-power in the purest sense of the word, not only in fact,
but also in her own consciousness.'

In the course of the Queen's reign, not the French
enemy alone but the Dutch ally were finally left behind in
the race for sea-power. The Republic, which in the time
of the De Witts had been well-nigh defenceless on land,
but had fought the united French and English navies on
equal terms, began the Marlborough wars with a military
force rising to 80,000 men. A great Dutch army was
kept up till the end of the war, but the Dutch fleet was
allowed to shrink from fifty-five ships of the line in 1702
to forty in 1711. The financial strain of protecting their
land frontier told as heavily on the Dutch as on the French,
and sealed the doom of both their navies. Holland became
England's client, trusting her maritime security to British
power and good faith. Towards the close of the war, the
Tories made the decline of the Dutch naval contingent a
subject of diplomatic complaint abroad and political agitation
at home ; but it was greatly to the advantage of England to
be left without a rival at sea. The statesmen of the United
Provinces, in excusing their default, pointed out that
England had incomparably greater commercial interests to
defend, particularly in the Mediterranean—an argument no
Dutchman would have used thirty years before.[230]

The erection of British naval and commercial supremacy
on a footing that proved permanent for more than two
hundred years, might not unreasonably be regarded as the
most important outcome of the reign of Anne. But it passes
little noticed in English popular tradition, being associated
with no stirring name like the Armada, La Hogue or
Trafalgar ; no supreme seamen like Drake, Blake or Nelson.

Even the heroism that won and kept Gibraltar for Queen Anne lies in the shadow cast by Eliott's later defence of the Rock.

This great but noiseless revolution in sea-power was accomplished by the victories of Marlborough's arms and diplomacy on land ; by the maintenance of England's fighting navy at full strength during the time when French and Dutch were perforce disarming at sea ; and by the wise application of an amphibious strategy in the Mediterranean, dreamed of by Cromwell, conceived by William, and executed by Marlborough,* through the agency of such capable seamen as Rooke, Leake, Shovell and Byng. It was because Marlborough regarded the naval war as an integral part of the whole allied effort against Louis, that English sea power was fixed between 1702 and 1712 on a basis whence no enemy has since been able to dislodge it.

If the idea of a standing army was unpopular, there was no corresponding prejudice against the navy. Both political parties were in favour of a powerful war fleet. The liberties of England were thought to be threatened by the red-coat and protected by the blue-jacket. A song, popular in the Seventeenth Century, reflects this feeling :

> I care not for your martial men who do the State disdain,
> But I care for your sailor lads who do the State maintain.

The sons of the Cavaliers nursed resentment against the New Model Army and against all soldiers for their sake, but not against Blake's fleet which had defended the Regicide Republic and chased Rupert's privateers, the Dutch and the Spaniards in turn. And so it happened that when in 1698 Parliament cut down the army in England to 7000 men, the fleet had been maintained on a peace footing of 15,000 men with a proportionate number of good ships in commission. When war broke out again the navy had not, like the army, to start again from the bottom. A few weeks before William died, the House of Commons voted that the number of seamen should be increased to 40,000 for the first year of renewed hostilities.

* See p. 129, above, and *Corbett*, II, *passim*, e.g., pp. 471–474.

The navy, as the more essential service of the two, also enjoyed the right, denied to the army, of forcibly seizing any of the subjects of the land, to man the Royal ships in time of war. The sight of honest citizens waylaid, knocked down and marched off manacled to serve the Queen at sea, was strangely out of keeping with the free and lawful spirit of the English polity. The interruption of trade was even more loudly complained of, for merchant fleets ready to leave port often lost so many of their crews to the press-gang that they could not set sail. The demand for a just and scientific naval conscription was raised by Admiralty officials like Burchett, the successor of Pepys' traditions in the post-Revolution world. But in the age of Anne it was not easy to carry out big administrative reforms. The body of efficient Civil Servants was not large enough to tackle the initial task of compiling a register of seamen for the whole country. And since all agreed that the navy must be manned in war time, the abuses of the press-gang, with its arbitrary and haphazard methods, went on through the days of Rooke, Shovell and Leake to the days of Nelson.[231]

The naval campaign of 1702 was played out in the two widely distant theatres of America and Spain. Each became the scene of a dramatic episode long remembered in popular tradition—Benbow's last cruise and the conflagration in Vigo Bay. They were linked together by the trail of the Spanish treasure ships across the Atlantic, which gave a certain unity to the maritime operations of the year.

Throughout 1701 the expectation of coming war, which kept European statesmen from their sleep, made American planters and backwoodsmen no less uneasy. The prospect of war with France and Spain, for the first time united as allies, alarmed every English-speaking household from Barbados to Hudson Bay; and the most anxious of all were the English of the rich West Indian islands scattered about in an archipelago that was still very largely Spanish and French. The buccaneers from the English colonies had, for more than a generation past, dealt alternately as traders and as robbers with the Spanish Americans of the isles and the mainland.   If French fleets and armies from Europe now took a hand on the side of Spain, the smuggling trade was like to be stopped, and the plundering exploits of Morgan and Sharp bitterly avenged on their countrymen.

Admiral Benbow, a rough and loyal sailor of the ' tar-paulin ' breed, better loved in the foc'sle than on the quarter-deck, was familiar with the West Indian station.   He was sent out again by King William in the summer of 1701 to cruise with a small squadron round the Leeward Islands and Jamaica, in expectation of events.   His arrival at first greatly cheered the English colonists.   But when Château-renault arrived at Martinique in January 1702 with forty warships, mostly of the line, Benbow's squadron was heavily outclassed.   Châteaurenault was only waiting for the declaration of war to fall on Barbados and the English Leeward Islands.   Benbow fixed his base at Port Royal in Jamaica, where his men took ill and died apace ; he reported to the Secretary of State that ' scarce one in three of our Europeans live here twelve months.'   And, indeed, the French fleet was losing men from disease as fast as the English.

At length, in July 1702, the news of the declaration of war arrived, having taken two months to cross the Atlantic. Fortunately for the English planters of the Leeward Islands, the French Admiral had, ere that, moved west to Cuba and Vera Cruz, leaving our defenceless colonies intact. Another more urgent task had called him away.   The Spaniards had very few warships in either hemisphere capable of putting to sea, but they had a fleet of armed treasure galleons ready to sail from Vera Cruz, which could safely start for Spain if the French war fleet acted as convoy. Châteaurenault, with great difficulty, persuaded the sus-picious Spaniards to put themselves under his charge, and in the middle of July set sail for Europe with thirty battle-ships, guarding the precious galleons, a moving magnet to the imagination of seafaring men all the world over. Benbow, in no force to attack such a fleet, sent word home of their departure, fluttering the dovecots at Whitehall and Portsmouth with visions of Spanish gold that at once began to cast a spell on our naval strategy in Europe.

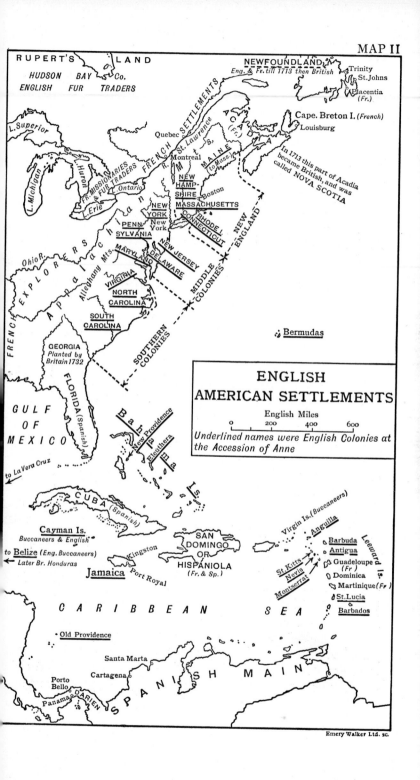

MAP II

RUPERT'S LAND
HUDSON BAY Co.
ENGLISH FUR TRADERS

L.Superior

NEWFOUNDLAND
Eng. & Fr. till 1713 then British
Trinity
St.Johns
Placentia (Fr.)

Cape. Breton I. (French)
Louisburg

FRENCH SETTLEMENTS
Quebec
R. St. Lawrence
Montreal
MAINE (to Mass.)

In 1713 this part of Acadia became British, and was called NOVA SCOTIA

FR. MISSIONARIES & FUR TRADERS
L.Michigan
Huron
L. Erie
Ontario

NEW HAMP-SHIRE
MASSACHUSETTS
Boston
NEW YORK
New York
RHODE I.
CONNECTICUT
NEW ENGLAND

Ohio R.
FRENCH EXPLORERS
Appalachians
PENN-SYLVANIA
Alleghany Mts.
MARYLAND
NEW JERSEY
DELAWARE
MIDDLE COLONIES

VIRGINIA
NORTH CAROLINA

SOUTH CAROLINA
SOUTHERN COLONIES

Bermudas

GEORGIA
Planted by Britain 1732

FLORIDA (Spanish)

GULF OF MEXICO

to La Vera Cruz

Bahamas
New Providence
Eleuthera

ENGLISH
AMERICAN SETTLEMENTS
English Miles
0   200   400   600
Underlined names were English Colonies at
the Accession of Anne

CUBA (Spanish)

Cayman Is.
Buccaneers & English
to Belize (Eng. Buccaneers)
Later Br. Honduras

Jamaica
Kingston
Port Royal

SAN DOMINGO OR HISPANIOLA (Fr. & Sp.)

Virgin Is.(Buccaneers)
Anguilla
Barbuda
Antigua
St.Kitts
Nevis
Guadeloupe (Fr)
Dominica
Martinique (Fr)
Montserrat
St.Lucia
Barbados
Leeward Is.

CARIBBEAN   SEA

Old Providence

Santa Marta
Cartagena
Porto Bello
Panama
DARIEN

SPANISH   MAIN

Emery Walker Ltd. sc.

Benbow, left behind with his little squadron in the West Indies, addressed himself to a more prosaic task.   Château-renault, whose name the honest English Admiral rendered as *Shatternoe*, had detailed a small squadron under Ducasse to sail to Carthagena and Porto Bello, there to establish the French Company now enjoying the rights of the *Asiento* trade,* and to ' destroy the trade of the English and Dutch on that coast.'   Benbow determined that the enemy should never reach Carthagena on such an errand.   Leaving his base at Port Royal, he came up with them off Santa Marta, and at once engaged them in a running fight, as they sailed westward along the Spanish Main.

Aug. 19
(O.S.)
1702

The English squadron, all told, had a superiority of more than a hundred and twenty guns.   If battle had ever been fairly joined, Ducasse was doomed, for the common seamen on the English ships were eager for battle.   Unfortunately, four out of the seven captains were of a different mind.   The flagship *Bredah*, the gallant little *Ruby* and the *Falmouth* did their duty.   The other four refused to obey Benbow's signals to join in the action.   For six days they followed, for the most part at a distance of several miles, watching their Admiral and his consorts keeping up the battle against odds—the enemy still making every effort to escape.

Once, indeed, Captain Kirby of the *Defiance* found himself close up against the enemy ; even then he refused to fire because, as he afterwards boasted to the Court Martial, the French held him in too much respect to fire at him. His crew reported that he was in bodily fear, ' dodging behind the mizzenmast and falling down on the deck on the noise of a shot.'   Some at least of the other Captains were men of proved courage, and it is, therefore, generally presumed that they were in a conspiracy of personal rancour against Benbow.   It is said, though on no certain evidence, that he had given them the rough side of his tongue in Jamaica.   But he behaved with only too much gentleness to them during the action, and no explanation of their conduct or account of their alleged wrongs appears in the

* See p. 139, above.

report of the Court Martial.   There is still a certain element
of mystery about the affair.   Burchett of the Admiralty,
a competent judge and a friend of Benbow, blamed him for
not summoning the recalcitrant Captains on board his ship
and placing them under arrest.   Rightly or wrongly, he
did not venture to take this course, presumably for fear of
further treachery or desertion.

At length, at early dawn of the sixth day of this strange
battle, Benbow had his ' right leg broke to pieces by a chain
shot.'   Thereupon, he ordered the ship's carpenter
to rig him up a cradle on the quarter-deck, and sat
there directing the fight as though nothing had
happened.   Later in the day, Kirby came on board
and, without so much as asking after the wounded Admiral's
health, demanded that the battle, in which he had taken no
part, should at once be broken off ; Benbow, instead
of arresting him, summoned the other Captains to the
Bredah to consult, and all followed Kirby's lead, signing
a paper advising that the action should be brought to an end.

Aug. 24
(O.S.)
1702

So the dishonoured squadron returned to Port Royal in
Jamaica where Benbow at once had his Captains tried by
Court Martial.   Kirby and Wade were condemned
to death, carried to England and shot on board ship
in Plymouth Sound, the Queen refusing to pardon
them.   Several months before his betrayers suffered the last
penalty Benbow died in Jamaica.   According to
Admiral Whetstone's report, ' his leg never being
set to perfection, which malady being aggravated
by the discontent of his mind, threw him into a sort of
melancholy which ended his life.' [232]

April
1703

Novr.
1702

There are some gestures which redeem mistakes.   Like
Cranmer's hand held in the fire, old Benbow's cradle on the
quarter-deck prevents posterity from enquiring too closely
what else he had done or left undone.   No incident of the
war took such a hold on the popular imagination, or was
longer celebrated in alehouse song :

> Says Kirby unto Wade : ' We will run ; we will run,'
> Says Kirby unto Wade : ' We will run.
> For I value no disgrace, nor the losing of my place,
> But the enemy I won't face, nor his gun, nor his gun.'

Brave Benbow lost his legs by chain shot, by chain shot,
Brave Benbow lost his legs by chain shot.
Brave Benbow lost his legs, but on his stumps he begs,
' Fight on my English lads, 'tis our lot, 'tis our lot.'

While the surgeon dressed his wounds, thus he said, thus he said,
While the surgeon dressed his wounds, thus he said :
' Let my cradle now in haste
On the quarter-deck be placed,
That mine enemies I may face till I'm dead, till I'm dead.'

Although the shame of the action is the most notorious in our naval annals, it was not in that period unique. Six years later, again in the West Indies, two captains failed Admiral Wager in a celebrated action. They were court-martialled and broke, which was thought ' a very favourable sentence,' for talk about their conduct had been ' enough to concern any true Englishman.' [233]

1708

In view of these facts, we must be content to read patiently, though without full agreement, the opinion of a witness most friendly to England, Mocenigo, the Ambassador of Venice. Four years after Benbow's battle, and two years before Wager's, he reported to his Republic that the maritime power of England must be considered as permanently greater than that of France, owing to the number of men and ships. But the French navy, he adds, is better organized, has ' better discipline and more numerous officers,' so that ' a French ship will always defeat an English ship of the same class.' The last statement was even then demonstrably untrue, but the fact that it was made by a well-informed Venetian diplomat in London shows that the quality as distinct from the quantity of the English marine was not yet fully established in the eyes of the world. The opinion expressed by Sir Cloudesley Shovell to the Secretary of State in 1702 is probably nearer the real truth :

The misfortune and vice of our country [writes the Admiral] is to believe ourselves better than other men, which I take to be the reason that generally we send too small a force to execute our designs. . . . To fight, beat and chase an enemy of the same strength I have sometimes seen, but have rarely seen at sea any victory worth the boasting when the strength has been near equal.

It was not yet the age of Nelson. [234]

The weakness of the English navy, such as it was, lay not in the men but in some of the officers. It was a weakness which the fine Admirals who served Queen Anne—Rooke, Shovell, Byng and Leake—were busy eradicating. They succeeded so well that posterity has difficulty in believing that the English naval officer under the later Stuarts was not on all occasions what he has been for two hundred years past. The politics of a country with an unsettled dynasty had something to do with the evil. In William's reign the Jacobites had correspondents in the navy and counted on disaffection among a section of the officers, though not, as they admitted, among the crews.[235] Actually, Jacobite hopes had been disappointed, but fear of possible treachery of this kind was constantly present as a demoralizing factor. More important, probably, was the friction between the 'tarpaulin' captains who had spent their lives at sea, and the gentlemen who owed their rank to solicitation at Court or in the lobbies of Parliament. But that cause of friction, as old as the voyages of Drake, was now diminishing, and the day was not far distant when every officer in the King's navy would be both a gentleman and a sailor, a man of education bred to the sea since he was a lad.

Against the crews no one had a word to say. Though many of them were pressed men torn from their trades and families, though they were poisoned with bad food * and drink, exposed undefended to storm and pestilence, their country could count on their constant and devoted service, their skilled seamanship, their light-hearted courage. Fortunately, the proportion of officers worthy to command such men was on the increase. Though the common sailor was, by modern standards, grossly neglected and ill-treated, he had no feeling against his officers as a class, and moreover

* In January 1703–1704 one of the agents for the victualling service gave evidence how ' from January before King William died till November last was twelvemonth, he cut several hogs full of matter and stinking corruption for the sea service, which flew in his face when he chopped them, so as to make him spew and his nose to bleed. He saw those hogs salted and packed up.' On the other hand, Sir Cloudesley Shovell (a trustworthy witness) gave evidence that his fleet in 1703 has been well provisioned ' and I have never known fewer complaints.' *H. of L. MSS.*, 1702–1704, pp. 270, 286. No doubt there were variations.

it was much less difficult for a common seaman to rise to be captain or even admiral, than it became in the days of a more regulated naval system.

In Anne's wars we may think of the common sailors working and fighting, not in any uniform, but in sea-slops of the most variegated description, and the Captains in blue coats, full-bottomed wigs, three-cornered hats and sometimes in cuirasses in time of action. The warships were much the same in build, size and weight of gun-metal as those of Nelson a hundred years later.[236]

Only less important in war time than the Royal Navy were the privateers. A great deal of the fighting, and particularly of the commerce destroying, which would have been done in later times by the King's ships, was done by vessels authorized by government to make war on the enemy, but fitted out and armed by private capital as a venture at once remunerative and patriotic. Parliament passed new laws to encourage privateers, by permitting them, for the duration of the war, to employ a larger proportion of foreign seamen and of foreign-built ships than were allowed under the Navigation Laws ; to take the whole value of the prizes they made ; and to import their captured goods for sale under specially easy terms at the custom-house. Thus encouraged, they swept the seas of enemy commerce.[237]

There were, indeed, some disadvantages to the public in this system. The easier discipline on board a privateer, and its reputation as the road to wealth through jolly adventure, attracted men to desert to it from the Royal Navy and the mercantile marine. 'The privateers which are commissioned by the government,' complains Admiral Whetstone from the West Indies, ' have slockstered away several of our men, notwithstanding we use all the care we can to prevent it.' Some privateers did not distinguish very closely between the merchant ships of the enemy and those of neutrals, allies or English ; and turned regular pirates as soon as the war was over.[238]

In this war, as in more modern times, there was no lack of a fighting spirit in the merchant service, altogether apart from the privateers. Trading ships carried guns, and often gave a good account of themselves when attacked by the French. A London skipper came into port at Jamaica ' with more prisoners than he had crew,' having fought two actions on the way out. And an enemy attack in the same seas was foiled by the crew of a small Liverpool ship, who beat off the assault of superior numbers by strewing broken bottles for the bare feet of the boarding party and sweeping the deck with musketry fire.[239]

While privateering was the secondary part of the English naval warfare, it was the principal maritime effort of the French, when their Battle Fleets had become port-ridden in Brest and Toulon. In King William's war, after the English victory at La Hogue, Jean Bart and other French privateers had been the sea-heroes of their nation rather than the unlucky Admirals of the Fleet. And so it was again in the wars against Queen Anne. The French State supplied much of the material for private enterprise against allied commerce, even letting out the King's ships for the purpose. And successful corsairs like Forbin and Duguay-Trouin were made much of at Versailles. Forbin became a favourite with Louis himself—and, being a person of ' Provençal vivacity,' took liberties with the Ministers on which the Marshals defeated by Marlborough would certainly not have ventured.

Dunkirk, commanding the English Channel, was a name of terror to the allied merchants ; it sent out its commerce-destroyers singly and by squadrons. Sometimes as many as a hundred privateers were at sea from that one port. The Dutch navy undertook to patrol the North Sea against the Dunkirkers, while the English navy guarded the Channel and the coasting trade between London and the Tyne. In the very first year of the war the New-castle colliers had to wait for convoys which were not ready at the agreed time, with the result that trade was dislocated and coal rose to a prohibitive price in London.[240]

1702–
1703

Ostend, on the same coastline as Dunkirk, was an enemy base till Marlborough took it after Ramillies. In 1702, six French war-galleys, whose oars were a strange sight in

s

those waters, took advantage of calm weather to row out from Ostend and capture a Dutch warship of fifty guns ! St. Malo also was constantly full of privateers, building or fitting out, and of English merchant ships brought in as prizes.[241]

Between 1702 and 1708 the English lost 1100 merchant ships to the enemy. But in the same period 175 French privateers were accounted for—answering to the list of German submarines destroyed in our own day. In the later years of the war the danger to commerce was in the main overcome ; the merchants' complaints ceased after 1708. In 1712 the tonnage of British ships clearing outwards was greater by one-fifth than in the year the war began, a striking improvement over William's war in the matter of defence of our seaborne trade.[242]

The East India Company maintained its own naval and military establishment and did not reckon on the presence of the Royal Navy in the Eastern seas. But the trade of the American colonies had to be protected for the most part by the Queen's ships. The task was no sinecure, for Martinique was a transatlantic Dunkirk. And again and again, from 1702 onwards, squadrons from England were sent through the Newfoundland fogs to protect the fishing settlements on that coast, and the cod fleets at work there from the small seaports of Dorset, Devon and Cornwall. The French settlements of Newfoundland, especially Placentia, were better populated, fortified and garrisoned than those of our colonists, who suffered from the jealousy of the fishing fleets from home ports. In spite of the frequent cruises of English squadrons in those waters, the French in the first years of the war reduced the English and Colonial fishing fleets off Newfoundland to a mere fraction of their number in time of peace.[243]

The American colonists, though active as privateers, paid nothing towards the elaborate convoy system or the upkeep of the Royal Navy, on which their trade largely depended in wartime. That was one aspect of the old colonial system. Another was the right of the Mother Country in return to put what restriction she would on the trade and manufacture of the Colonies. A third aspect of these curious arrangements was the leave so frequently taken by colonists to break the restrictive laws.

Nevertheless, England's main effort at sea was not directed across the Atlantic. It was not off the Spanish Main but off the Spanish coasts in Europe that the Grand Fleet manœuvred and fought.

After the victory of La Hogue in the late war, the British islands were safe from invasion, and the Channel no longer required defence against the Brest Fleet, but only against privateers. The strength of the English and Dutch navies could be sent farther afield. Whither, then, should it be directed ? Marlborough decided to renew the policy formulated by William in the last year of his life ; the late King had held that the proper opening for the war would be to send the allied fleets to Spain, in order to encourage Portugal to join the Allies, to open the Straits, and to secure English naval power in the Mediterranean by the seizure of Cadiz or Gibraltar.

This Mediterranean strategy, which our great naval historian, Julian Corbett, has pronounced to have been rightly chosen in the interest of English sea power, was not universally approved. There was a ' blue-water school ' which considered that we ought to have little or nothing to do with the Continental war, but wage an oceanic war on our own account against the enemies' colonies and their supply of American gold. The motive behind this policy, at least in its more extreme forms, was quite as much dislike of our Allies as love of our navy. Those who hated the Dutch could not bear that we should fight by their side in Europe, or continue any part of the policy of William of Orange. This view of Rochester and the High Tories already in 1702 came into collision with the war plans of the Moderate Tories and Marlborough. It was the view which Swift preached ten years later in the *Conduct of the Allies* in retrospective criticism of the way in which Marlborough had by that time won the war.

According to the general tenor of these doctrines put forward in different forms by different writers, we ought to have sent few troops or none to the Continent, and no ships to the Mediterranean or the Spanish coast.   We ought to have made our chief effort in the West Indies, stopping the enemy's trade and seizing his colonies and, above all, way-laying the Spanish treasure ships from Panama.   If that were done, it was argued, Louis and Philip would, for want of money, soon be obliged to abandon the war in Europe. If the war had been against the King of Spain alone this reasoning would no doubt have been true.   But how far France depended on the arrival of the Spanish treasure ships it is exceedingly difficult to say.   She had not depended on them in the war against King William, when Spain had been her enemy, not her ally.   Marlborough believed that Louis could have amply recouped himself for captured Spanish treasure ships and lost French sugar islands by occupying Vienna and the Hague, as he would almost certainly have done but for the intervention on the Continent of the English army and General.   Quite certainly the Allies could not, without the help of Marl-borough's generalship and his English troops, have expelled the French from Bavaria and the Netherlands ; nor from Italy, without the help of English subsidies and the English fleet in the Mediterranean.   And if the Franco-Spanish power had been permitted to dominate Europe like Napoleon's in later days, English sea power could not long have survived in selfish isolation, however many colonies we had meanwhile seized beyond the Atlantic.   Therefore, even from a purely maritime point of view, our active support of the Allies on the Continent and in the Mediter-ranean was justified for the years 1702–1706.   Even for our colonial Empire, this system proved the best.   Marl-borough won Acadia and Newfoundland in Germany, and the *Asiento* on the plains of Ramillies.   After the victories of 1704–1706 much of Swift's criticism begins to be true ; but applied to the early stages of the war much of it is erroneous.[244]

Admiral Sir George Rooke had, through all changes of the political scene, retained the confidence and favour of William III, who realized that he had no abler or more loyal seaman, no public servant who dipped his hands less in the public purse. But, though highly competent to manage a fleet and to conduct any given operation, Rooke was cautious to a fault, sulky and unimaginative. It was never more than an even chance that he would seize an opportunity when it offered. It was he, even more than Kirke, who had been responsible in 1689 for the long inactivity of the fleet off Lough Foyle, which caused the unnecessary martyrdom of the defenders of Londonderry. His unenterprising temper had wedded him to the doctrine that the Grand Fleet should cruise within easy reach of the Channel and that any squadron detached as far as Spain must be certain to be back home before the autumn storms began. He had no sympathy with the policy of William and Marlborough that part of the fleet ought to be able to re-fit and even to winter in southern Europe, and that therefore England ought to seize and fortify naval bases in the Mediterranean. But, in spite of his limited views, William chose him to execute the designs against Cadiz and the Straits with which the naval war was to begin ; and after the King's death, Marlborough, though no less intent on these large designs, continued to employ the unwilling and recalcitrant Admiral.[245]

The alterations that took place at the Admiralty, on the substitution of a Tory for a Whiggish Ministry at Anne's accession, compromised the hopes of the year by delaying till late in July the departure of Rooke for Spain. But the political and personal changes made no difference to the outline of our naval policy as William had planned it. It would, indeed, have been otherwise if Rochester and the High Tories had controlled Anne's naval strategy. Fortunately the Prince Consort became nominal Lord High Admiral, with George Churchill as the most influential member of his Council. Marlborough, therefore, controlled the big decisions. He had to yield to his brother George, a more eager Tory partisan than himself, on a few changes of the lesser commands, particularly as to the shelving of the able Captain George Byng for political reasons, contrary to the promises made him by the elder of the Churchills. But the great strategical designs against Spain and the Mediterranean were persevered in,

1702

despite the protests of Rooke, who was still employed to execute them.[246]

During the last months of William's reign, while men were wondering how soon the inevitable war would be proclaimed, a stream of secret information had been pouring into Whitehall about the undefended condition of Cadiz and Gibraltar. It was known, indeed, that two French engineers had been drawing up plans for the repair and extension of Charles V's fortifications of Gibraltar, but those best acquainted with the ways of Spanish officialdom were confident that nothing would be done—and, in fact, nothing was done till, three years later, the Rock passed into hands better able to defend it.[247]

Meanwhile our allies were clamouring for the presence of the English fleet in Mediterranean waters. Wratislaw, the Emperor's able envoy in England, urged that the sight of Rooke's topsails would effect a revolution in Naples, win south Italy from the precarious grasp of Philip V, overawe the Francophile Pope and encourage Savoy and the other Princes of Italy to change sides. Prince Eugene, in command of the Austrian army in the valley of the Po, more modestly pleaded for a squadron to protect the passage of his supplies from Trieste across the Adriatic.[248]

April 1702

But Marlborough knew that without a base in the Iberian Peninsula nothing big could be done inside the Straits. A bold stroke on the coast of Spain might not only put Gibraltar or Cadiz in the hands of the Allies, but would encourage Portugal to join the war and to place the great harbour of Lisbon at the disposal of our fleet. The Methuens, father and son, England's energetic representatives at that Court, were clamouring for a naval demonstration against Spain to support their arguments with the hesitating King of Portugal.

Rooke, therefore, was instructed to take Cadiz. He was sent with the English and Dutch Grand Fleets, carrying 10,000 English infantry * and 4000 Dutch. The English soldiery were under the command of James Butler, Duke of Ormonde, one of Britain's grandees, inheriting great cavalier

* Of these, 2400 were the newly raised force of Marines.

traditions and the leadership of the Protestant Church
interest in Ireland.   This good-natured and honourable
man was well fitted to play the part of popular Duke and
political figurehead, but the attempt made to pass him off
as the High Tory military hero, the rival of Marlborough,
was foredoomed to fail.   He was weak enough to accept
the rôle and to follow the lure of a vain ambition till it led
him to ruin and the tragedy of a long exile.   But when the
gallant armament sailed in July 1702, the sun shone
brightly on the fortune of the most popular nobleman in
the British Islands.

On August 12th, according to the home reckoning used
by the Navy at sea, the armament appeared before Cadiz,
and at once the weakness of its leadership became
evident.   Rooke was sick and sulky, opposed at
heart to the whole enterprise : he insisted on
nothing himself, but allowed the Council of War to
quarrel to its heart's content.   In those days Admirals in
command of fleets were more bound by their Councils than
in Nelson's time.   ' Was I to engage the confederate fleet
without a resolution of the Council of War ? ' he asked
indignantly of the Committee that afterwards enquired into
these miscarriages.[249]   A score of generals and admirals,
English, Dutch and German, met in Rooke's cabin off
Cadiz on August 13th and quarrelled till they had rejected
every reasonable proposal, and agreed in sheer weariness to
the one course which was certainly wrong.

If the Allies had had the spirit of Drake and his fellows,
off that place, with such a force, they would have adopted
one of two plans.   Either they would have sent ahead a
squadron to force its way past the forts of the Puntales into
the inner harbour and destroy the French and Spanish fleets
therein, before the enemy had time and warning to throw
a boom across the mouth.   That course was suggested by
a captain who offered to carry it out himself.[250]   Or else
they might, under cover of a bombardment by the fleet,
have landed the army on the narrow neck dividing Cadiz
from the mainland, and taken their chance of capturing the
city at a rush while it was still surprised and ill-garrisoned.
The third defensible course consonant with their instruc-

Aug. 12
(O.S.)
1702

tions was to sail away at once and attack some other place,
if Cadiz was too strongly defended.

Ormonde, who was by no means lacking in personal
courage, argued in favour of a military landing on the
isthmus and a direct attack on the city.   But Rooke's
entourage had been alarmed by false accounts given them
by captured Spanish fishermen to the effect that a powerful
garrison of regular troops was already inside the walls.   The

MAP III

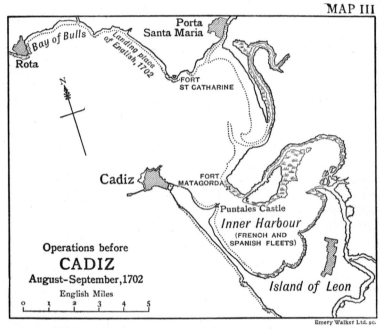

Operations before
CADIZ
August–September, 1702

English Miles
0   1   2   3   4   5

Emery Walker Ltd. sc.

fatal decision was reached to land the troops between the
Bay of Bulls and Fort St. Catharine, far away from Cadiz
and far away even from the Puntales forts and the harbour;
to seize the open villages of Rota and Porta Santa Maria,
and to sit down there to see what would happen next.   The
landing was effected in face of slight resistance from Spanish
troops and batteries : the loss chiefly consisted of twenty
men drowned in the swell of the surf.   But when they
had landed and captured Fort St. Catharine, no real
strategical object had been gained.   Marlborough's comment on this proceeding is the verdict of posterity :

What can be said for staying 26 days at Port St. Mary? For if Cadiz was to be attacked, they should not have staid there. And if the taking of Cadiz was not thought feasible, then they should not have lost time, but have reimbarked to have attempted what was in their instructions.[251]

But the month spent at Santa Maria was much worse than wasted. It was grossly misused, with disastrous and lasting effects upon the attitude of Spanish opinion towards the Allied cause. Although England and Holland had not yet bound themselves by treaty, as they did in the following year, to make the Austrian Archduke Charles King of Spain, they hoped to do so if the Spaniards proved agreeable. Prince George of Hesse, who knew something of Spanish conditions from his experience as Governor of Catalonia in former years, accompanied the fleet to see that the interests of Austria were not overlooked. The English issued promises and invitations on behalf of Charles as King of Spain in the villages that they occupied : but this system of policy met with little or no response except among the beggars of the region, and the cause of Charles III became associated in the Spaniards' minds with the scandalous conduct of Ormonde's troops, who plundered Santa Maria to the bare walls, sacked the churches with heretical glee, raped women, and even nuns.

Ormonde's limitations as a commander became only too apparent. In face of the misconduct of his troops, he was equally distressed and helpless. Sir Henry Belasys, his second-in-command, and Sir Charles Hara took a lead in the plunder. The officers even went so far, in their deplorable meanness of soul, as to place guards in the street to take the spoil from the privates and store it all away for their superiors. To add to the irony of the situation, though all Spain was horrified and alienated by the story of the conduct of the allied army, the chief losses fell upon rich English and Dutch merchants doing business under Spanish names, through whom the trade of Cadiz with America had long been conducted. They complained pitifully that they had been robbed of property of great value, besides having their future residence and work in Spain rendered impossible by their compatriots' conduct. When the fleet and army finally departed, they ' carried away,' as the sufferers wrote, ' for the major part their countrymen and allies' goods,' and ' left behind them such a filthy stench among the Spaniards that a whole age will hardly blot it out.'[252]

The latter part of the month spent by the army on shore was devoted to a feeble attempt to take the fort of Matagorda, on the north side of the Puntales, with a view to facilitating the entry of the fleet into the harbour to destroy the enemy's ships. But by this time the Spaniards and French were reinforced and in good heart. The land on which the batteries were set up against the Matagorda was spongy and malarious. Rooke declared that, even if the fort were taken, the fleet could not penetrate into the harbour because of the corresponding fort on the other side of the Puntales entrance. At last it was decided to break off operations against Cadiz. The troops were re-embarked, all save a few companies of Irish Catholics who seized the occasion to desert and seek service in the French army, after having taken a leading and profitable part in the sack of Santa Maria.

Sept. 15–16 (O.S.) 1702

Ormonde and Prince George of Hesse wished to land again at Vigo or some other point of importance in Spain, and winter there with part of the fleet and army. But Rooke was all agog for home, and for once asserted his authority at the Council of War. The autumnal gales, he declared, would be upon them unless they hurried back to England. Belasys and Hara, anxious to lodge their ill-gotten gains in safety, voted with the sailors against Ormonde's demand for another landing in Spain.[253] Loaded with plunder and infamy the great armament set sail for England. The Admiral and the General, though both on the same side in politics, were now scarcely on speaking terms ; Ormonde thought that but for Rooke's veto he could have taken Cadiz ; and Rooke, himself as honest as the day in all that concerned money, had written to Ormonde in bitter terms of the plundering by the soldiers on shore.

It is remarkable that the two most disgraceful actions on the part of our countrymen in the whole long War of the Spanish Succession, Benbow's battle and the affair at Cadiz, took place during the same days on the two sides of the Atlantic. It was fortunate for the allied cause that an accident on the way home gave Rooke's fleet and Ormonde's army an opportunity, of which gallant use was made, to retrieve the prestige of England at sea. Methuen's pessimistic letters from Lisbon to Admiral Rooke in September clearly show that if the failure before Cadiz had not been redeemed at Vigo, Portugal would not have entered the war on the allied side in the following year.[254]

It was August weather on the ocean, while day by day the Spanish treasure galleons, under the convoy of the French warships, had been drawing nearer to Europe—unseen on the watery waste, but never out of the thoughts of men in London, Paris and Madrid.* Arrived at length off the coast, Châteaurenault would have had the galleons run for safety into a harbour of France. But the Spaniards refused to take a step which would have put Philip's gold into the hands of Louis. The flotilla, therefore, put into Vigo Bay in Northern Spain in the middle days of September. There it lay for several weeks, unknown to Rooke and Ormonde farther down the same coast. The bulk of the treasure—that part which belonged to the Spanish crown—was unshipped and taken up the stony paths of the hills on the backs of mules ; a residuum belonging to private persons and a great quantity of merchandize remained in the galleons, and most of the French war fleet remained to guard them.

Rooke, in his ignorance, was sailing past the mouth of the harbour in his hurry to be back home before the autumn storms which he dreaded so much. But already messengers from London and from Lisbon were scouring the seas to find him. Actually the word was brought to him by one of his own ships. The *Pembroke* had stayed behind the fleet to water at Lagos. There her Captain, Thomas Hardy, had stumbled on the great news. The Chaplain of the *Pembroke*, a Jersey man like his Captain, spoke French well ; he scraped acquaintance with the French Consul in Lagos, who could not forbear a boastful hint that the

* See p. 250, above.

treasure ships were snug in a harbour of the coast. Thus put on the alert, the Chaplain fell in with another stranger who proved to be a messenger from the Imperial Embassy in Lisbon with official confirmation of the fact. At once Captain Hardy gave chase to his Admiral, and caught him up on October 6 (O.S.), in time to prevent him from crossing the Bay of Biscay.

Rooke sent ships to explore the mouth of Vigo Bay and report. They returned with the correct information, gleaned from a friar whom a landing party had seized, that the fleet was at the head of the bay protected by a strong boom and batteries, that the King's part of the treasure had already been landed, but that much wealth was still on board the galleons. Another of the inevitable Councils of War was held, fortunately this time without the participation of Belasys and Hara ; ' the two knights ' had at length been put under arrest, by orders from the home government which Ormonde ought to have forestalled on his own responsibility weeks before. Even so, the decision to attack was only carried by a majority which included the Dutch Admiral. Vigo Bay was by this time a harder nut to crack than Cadiz would have been if Cadiz had been assaulted on the first arrival of the fleet.[255]

Oct. 10 (O.S.) 1702

On the evening of October 11th the English and Dutch warships ran up the fiord for ten miles between the hills, past ' Bayona's hold ' at the mouth, past the two castles of Vigo city that fired at them as they sailed by unheeding, intent only on what they should find in the inmost lair at the end of the long bay.

The tragedy of the French and Spanish fleet was to take place in a theatre worthy of the event. Vigo Bay, after running to a narrow passage not much more than half a mile broad at the promontory of Randa, suddenly opens out into the spacious harbour of Redondela, circled by ranges of wild, bare Galician mountains. There the estuary comes superbly to an end, and there lay the treasure ships and the French fleet. Châteaurenault had blocked up the entrance from shore to shore with a boom of masts strongly lashed together. At the north end of the boom was a battery, of which traces can still be seen.

At the south end of the boom the defences were still more formidable. Randa Fort can be found by the curious to-day much as it was left after the battle, but surrounded now by a peaceful grove of trees, a forgotten monument of English valour in a strange land. A strong stone tower, with inner platforms and embrasures constructed for cannon, stands some little way up from the sea. The space between the tower and the water's edge is occupied by an outer ward

MAP IV

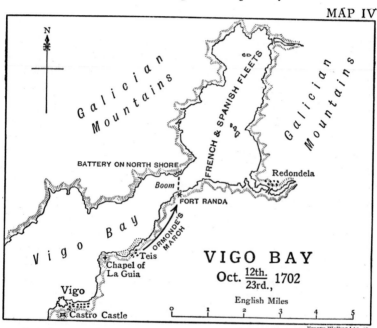

VIGO BAY

Oct. $\frac{12th.}{23rd.}$ 1702

English Miles

Emery Walker Ltd. sc.

or fortified enclosure ; at the bottom of it, along the rocky shore, runs a long platform on which stood a battery to command the straits. Châteaurenault had landed ships' guns at either end of the boom. The Randa fortifications had been armed with more than thirty cannon, the northern shore with rather less.

The leading ships of the Allies, in attacking the boom on the morning of October 12th, were therefore liable to receive a flanking fire at close quarters from both shores, besides the broadsides of seven French ships of the line ranged inside the boom to fire across it at the assailants.

But the spirit of the Allies at Vigo was very different from
their spirit at Cadiz. Shame at their recent disgrace, and
the sight of the top-sails of the treasure ships roused the
hero or the devil in every man. Rooke, indeed, lay in his
berth, ill of gout, far down the bay. The active command
fell to Vice-Admiral Hopsonn, who in the *Torbay* led the
attack on the boom, in a spirit not unworthy of the *Mountjoy*
at Londonderry. Behind him pressed a strong squadron of
his English ships, and of Dutch under Vice-Admiral
Oct. 12   Van der Goes. They were met by a terrible fire
(O.S.)   from the ships behind the boom and the batteries
1702   on either shore. The *Association*, of ninety guns,
laid her broadside along the battery on the north shore and
soon silenced it. The more formidable batteries of Fort
Randa were being assailed by the English infantry.

Early that morning Ormonde and some 2000 men had
landed on the sandy shore near Teis, a couple of miles lower
down. They marched straight to Fort Randa, over hill-
sides broken by ravines, pine-woods, vineyards and old stone
hamlets. Many thousands of Spanish militia were roaming
about and firing, but it was not an occasion when guerilla
tactics could avail. The fort was reached, with its formidable array of guns and several hundred French, described as
'seamen' or 'marines.' Ormonde marched on foot with
the main body, sending Lord Shannon with the vanguard of
grenadiers to begin the assault. The wall enclosing the
outer ward was stormed, and the seaward battery silenced in
time to assist the breaking of the boom by the ships. The
tower, which could only be entered up sixteen steps, held
out a little longer, defended by 300 French, ' the grenadiers
plying them briskly with their hand-grenadoes as soon as
they appeared on the wall ' and finally charging up the steps
and capturing the fort and its garrison.

Meanwhile, the *Torbay*, favoured by a breath of wind,
crowded on all sail and crashed at the boom. It cracked,
and Hopsonn's flag-ship floated through the wreckage in
among the enemy beyond. The breeze fell, and for an
anxious period of time no other vessel could follow. The
Torbay was assaulted by superior numbers, and a blazing
fireship was laid along her side. She caught fire ; most of

her crew leapt overboard, and she would have been burnt to the waterline had not the fireship, loaded with a valuable cargo of snuff from the Spanish Indies, suddenly blown up. A great cloud of snuff enveloped the flag-ship and partly extinguished the fire. A few sneezing and gallant men who had stuck to the ship were thus enabled to get the better of the flames.

Meanwhile, the breeze had risen once more, and other English and Dutch ships followed the *Torbay* through the gap, or hacked fresh passages in the boom with blows of the axe. Then was put to the test the opinion of the Venetian Ambassador that ship for ship the French navy was the better. Châteaurenault's sailors did not think so. Setting fire to their vessels, they sought safety on shore—after a very ' mean ' resistance in the judgment of the English Admiral. For a loss of some two hundred men, the Allies destroyed or captured the whole of the enemy's fleet. Night fell, and all through the night the waters of the bay reflected the burning ships. The air was filled with the roar of cannon and musketry, varied by louder explosions as the flames reached some magazine, and masts, men and merchandize went hurtling through the night sky. The English and Dutch worked with fury to quench the flames and save their prizes. When day dawned, they were still at the work; but there was no longer a French or Spanish vessel but had been either captured or destroyed.

The loss of the galleons was not likely to be made good in the idle shipyards of Spain. But far more serious was the loss of ten French line-of-battle ships taken and five burnt, besides frigates and smaller craft. For this was the opening year of a war in which Louis thought himself bound to keep up his armies in preference to his fleet. Even more important was the recovery of the Allied prestige, lost at Cadiz and now dramatically regained; for that secured the entrance of Portugal into the war, and the opening of Lisbon as a naval base for the Maritime Powers.

As to the treasure, which had drawn on the battle, there is no clear evidence how much was taken, either in gold or in merchandize. Much certainly, but nothing like what had been hoped. Rooke was informed by one of the captured Captains that the King's treasure, which had gone up-country beforehand, was worth three millions sterling, and it is not improbable ; if it had been captured by the allied fleets, the feeble war-effort of Spain in the next few years would have been feebler still.   In that respect the affair of Vigo had been a failure.   The belief that other great sums went to the bottom in the burning ships, whether true or false, has inspired prospectuses and dredging operations by hopeful company promoters in the Eighteenth, Nineteenth and Twentieth Centuries.   The wealth captured and destroyed was much of it the property of the Dutch merchants who carried on the trade between Spain and her colonies ; the news that the treasure fleet had got safely to Vigo had caused joy in many quarters in Holland, and the subsequent story of the battle was received in Amsterdam with mingled feelings.[256]

A few days were spent in salvaging and in making the captured ships ready to sail.   The Galician peasants stood round the shores of the bay, sometimes aiming their muskets at the victors as they worked, and continually shouting abuse at them as ' English dogs, rogues, heretics and cuckolds.'   ' Captain Martin, where he lay in the harbour, had a good deal of it from a neighbouring hill, the seamen making sport of it to call names with them,' till ' a volley of small arms spoilt the joke.'

Ormonde wished part of the fleet and army to winter at Vigo, but Rooke would not hear of it.   So they all sailed home, to be hailed as heroes for Vigo, and questioned as culprits for Cadiz, to quarrel with one another, and to divide the blame, the fame and the spoil.   Ormonde was at the height of popular favour.   Wherever he appeared in an English street, he was followed by cheering mobs.   Rooke would have met with a like reception, but the gout which had kept him from the battle still kept him indoors when he got home.[257]   He was well pleased with his luck.   For he had won his contest against Marlborough and the Admiralty by evading their desire that he should seize a port and gain permanent control of the Straits, and yet he had come home covered with glory.   Two years later they beat him, when he took Gibraltar.[258]

CHAPTER XIII

The Session of the winter 1702–3. The Fall of Rochester. Lords and
Commons. Peer-making, limited. The Occasional Conformity Bill.
Defoe in the Pillory. Relation of politics to religion. The Convocation controversy. The Cabinet and its machinery. Nottingham
as Secretary of State.

THE year's success in the Netherlands and on the coast of
Spain was celebrated by the first, as it proved, of many
thanksgivings for victory to be held by Anne and
her subjects at St. Paul's. The Mayor and Aldermen in procession conducted the Queen from
Temple Bar, followed by both Houses of Parliament.
The long line of coaches defiled for hours through the
streets. The guns of the Tower fired salvoes. There had
been no ceremony of the like pomp, men said, since the
times of Elizabeth. The glories of the Age of Anne had
begun.[259]

Ormonde was the hero of the day, for Rooke was ill in
bed, and Marlborough only returned to England a fortnight
later. But already Marlborough overtopped his rivals in
fame. Vigo might atone for Cadiz, but it could not blot
it from men's memory, or even prevent a damaging official
inquest ; whereas the career of victory on the Maas, as every
Englishman knew, had been limited only by the timid inter-
ference of Dutch Deputies and Generals. That winter
Marlborough was still a Tory hero, and already a national
hero. The Queen raised him from Earl to Duke. The
newly elected Tory House of Commons * voted that he
had ' retrieved the ancient honour and glory of the English
nation.' The Whigs divided in vain against the word

---

* See pp. 208–213, above, for the General Election of July 1702.

T

retrieved, which had been chosen to cast a retrospective slur on William's campaigns in the Netherlands.

The Queen settled £5000 a year on the new Duke from the Post Office revenue, but she could only do so for her own lifetime. She asked the House of Commons to legislate so as to prolong the grant to him and his heirs for ever. This they refused to do, although they assigned the immense portion of £100,000 a year for life to the Prince Consort. There may indeed have been good reasons of public policy against a perpetual grant to any man's heirs. But one motive for the refusal was that the High Tories, who looked on Rochester as their chief, could not bear to see the Churchills monopolize the Queen's favour, which they thought should go in more liberal measure to her relatives of the House of Hyde. Rochester made no concealment either of his personal jealousy of Marlborough, or of his political opposition to the war on the Continent. When the Queen directed him to return to his post as Lord Lieutenant in Ireland, he still delayed his departure. He preferred to linger in England and lead the malcontents against his Cabinet colleagues. By this time Anne had had enough of her uncle's humours. In February 1703 he was forced to quit her service, the first of a long line of Tories who followed one another into retirement for half a dozen years to come. The fall of Rochester eased the situation for the Godolphin Ministry for awhile—but not for long.

The attack on William's memory and the prosecution of his Whig Ministers were pursued together by the newly elected House of Commons. But since Halifax and Orford were Peers, the Upper House saw to it that they had fair play. The charges against William's great financial adviser, Halifax, broke down on examination. Indeed, the outcry against the late Whig Ministers as corruptionists, though it had served its turn at the General Election, received a set-back from the public investigation now made into the nation's accounts, from which the Tory pot emerged as black as the Whig kettle. But the Commons found one victim. An Irish Peer, Lord Ranelagh, almost the only Whig who sat in this Parliament for a Cornish borough, was expelled from the House on a charge of peculation as

Paymaster-General of the Army—it is not clear with what degree of justice. The truth as to the charges against him and against Russell, Lord Orford, were obscured by the rancorous quarrel between the two parties, which soon developed into a clash between the two Houses.[260]

The Commons had the privilege that posterity may envy them of listening with delight to young St. John's lost philippics against Whigs and moderates. But the leaders of the House showed more vigour than skill. Sir Edward Seymour, relentless in his pursuit of the feuds of the last reign, had not the temper for tactics. The day before the House adjourned for Christmas, the country gentlemen were some of them, we may suppose, excited by seasonable good cheer and by the prospect of a week's holiday on their estates. At any rate they passed that day a series of remarkable votes. The first was a motion of Seymour's to resume all grants made by William. His Irish grants had been resumed by the Act of the Tory Parliament of 1698. The new proposal would have carried the war against the estates of certain Whig and Dutch noblemen into England as well—where the security of property was normally greater and where such a measure would have been more of a shock to society than in Ireland. Young Robert Walpole replied by moving to resume all grants made in the reign of James II, and though the proposal was voted down, it considerably damped the Tory ardour for resumptions. Seymour's proposal went no further.

The next division on that noisy evening showed 135 votes to 80 in favour of the principle that no one holding office under the Crown ought to sit in the House of Commons. But a few minutes' reflection, and perhaps a little lobbying by anxious Ministers, reminded the honest squires that almost all 'placemen' at that moment were Tories : Seymour himself was Comptroller of the Household. When therefore it was proposed to proceed with the measure on the lines just decided, the House went back on its opinion by 138 votes to 77.*

(In the left margin beside the paragraph above:) Dec. 23 1702

* *H. of C. Journals*, XIV, p. 95 ; *Parl. Hist.*, VI, pp. 143–144. Office-holders were to be excluded from the House of Commons under the Act of Settlement, Clause VI, see p. 120, above, as soon as the House of Hanover came to the throne. But this clause was fortunately modified in 1705 before it took effect.

And so, on second thoughts, the Constitution was permitted to grow unchecked in the direction of Ministerial representation in the Lower House. But such rash voting shows how little the Commons yet understood their future place in the English polity. The House still regarded itself as the critic of government which it had been in the past, not as the seat of government which it was to be in the future.

In the reigns of William and Anne all the leading Cabinet Ministers were found in the Upper House. There sat the five Lords of the Whig Junto ; there sat Marlborough and Godolphin, Rochester and Nottingham. When, after the political landslide of 1710, Harley and St. John came in their turn to rule the nation, they both hastened to take Peerages. Sir Robert Walpole was the first of our rulers who preferred to govern the country from his seat on the front bench of the House of Commons, and to go up to the Lords only when he left office. It is not then surprising that in Anne's reign, when all the chief Ministers were away in another place, the Commons acted according to their own sweet will, often with little regard to the wishes of Government. The idea of Government was personally associated no longer with the Court, but with the House of Lords ; and against the House of Lords the Commons nourished a tradition of jealousy almost as strong as that which it nourished against the Court.

Throughout the Stuart era the Upper Chamber represented continuity and moderation, while the House of Commons, though more vital and creative, was the seat of the alternate violence of Roundhead and Cavalier, Whig and Tory. The balance of parties in the Lords was always so close that it could be decided by the unattached Peers of moderate views. But whereas in the days of the Exclusion Bill and the Convention Parliament, there had been a small Tory majority, by the end of William's reign there was a small Whig majority, or at any rate a majority that could be relied on to pour cold water on the Tory heats of the Lower House. This change was ascribed to the numbers of Low Church Bishops whom William had been able to appoint to the numerous sees vacated by death and by the Nonjuror

Schism.   The High Tories looked to the new Queen for
a remedy.   Though she could not make vacancies in the
Episcopal Bench, she could create a large batch of Tory
Peers.   But her own good sense and that of her Moderate
Tory advisers made her content with a creation of four
Tories and, at Sarah's special request, one Whig,
Feb.–   Lord Hervey, who came in as a client of the Marl-
March   boroughs by no means in opposition to Government.
1703   Even against this discreet exercise of the Prerogative
the Whigs raised an outcry.   The question of the right of
the Crown to 'swamp' the House of Peers so as to alter
its political complexion, was to come up again nine years
later over the Treaty of Utrecht.[261]

Of many conflicts between the two Houses in the winter
session of 1702–1703, by far the most serious took place
over the Occasional Conformity Bill.   The accession of
Anne and the General Election in the summer had given the
signal for a High Church revival.   The Doctrines of divine
hereditary right and non-resistance were preached again in
many pulpits, as being compatible with loyalty to Anne,
1702   though not to William.   In June Dr. Sacheverell
had delivered at Oxford a sermon that struck the
note for the High Tories in the new reign.   He took for
his thesis the dependence of government on religion ;   the
throne was based on the altar ;   heresy and schism must lead
to rebellion ;   finally the orator declared that ' rather than
strike sail to a party that is so open and avowed an enemy
of our communion,' he would ' hang out the bloody flag of
defiance '—an expression that ran round the country and
became a catch-word of the day.   Above all, Sacheverell
thundered against ' occasional conformists '—' insidious persons who can creep to our altars,' only to qualify themselves
for office in order the better to destroy the Church.
   The indignation of the Tories against Dissenters in
general and occasional conformists in particular, had been
brought to a head by an incident that occurred near the
end of William's reign.   A Lord Mayor of London,
Sir Humphry Edwyne, who had presumably qualified for
the office he held by taking the communion according to

the rites of the Church of England, had the imprudence, or impudence, to ride in state to his Presbyterian Chapel on Sunday, in his Mayor's robes, with the sword and insignia of London borne before him.   The political literature of the age of Anne is full of the incident.   The Tories were never tired of harping upon it.   Swift's *Tale of a Tub* tells ' how Jack's tatters came into fashion in court and city : how he got upon a great horse and ate custard '—custard being a traditional dish at the Lord Mayor's feast.   Sir Humphry must have been sorry he had been so foolish.   He certainly brought down the vials of wrath on the heads of his coreligionists for years to come.

The Occasional Conformity Bill proposed to punish with heavy fines, that might mount up to be ruinous, holders of municipal or national office who, after qualifying by taking the Anglican Sacrament, afterwards attended a Nonconformist service.   Informers were to have the whole fine.

The Test Act of 1673, though passed primarily to keep Roman Catholics out of office, incidentally hit Dissenters. By the Test Act no one could hold State or municipal office unless he had first taken the Communion according to the rites of the Church of England.   The Test effectively barred out Roman Catholics, in whose eyes such communion was a deadly sin.   But the Dissenters were divided on the question.   Many of them indeed thought it wrong for religious reasons to communicate according to the rites of a prelatic Church.   Others, while not regarding it as sinful, thought it mean to communicate for no other purpose than to qualify for office.   On the other hand, as Bishop Burnet reminded the House of Lords, many worthy persons made a religious habit of attending sometimes the Church, sometimes the Chapel, wherever the gospel was well preached ; Baxter and other moderate Presbyterian Divines had defended Occasional Conformity as permissible on religious grounds.   Burnet had been coached in these arguments during a visit he received from the famous Dissenting minister, Calamy.

Then, as now, there were many Church of England people who liked occasionally to attend Nonconformist services.   Under the Bill, such persons, if they held office, would be at the mercy of servants, spies and ill-wishers threatening to inform against them. Queen Victoria, by Anglican standards, was an ' occasional conformist,' for she went to Presbyterian services in Scotland. Anne's own husband, Prince George of Denmark, was an occasional conformist, for he had Lutheran services in his own chapel. In 1702 his wife sent him to the Lords to vote for the Bill, but as he passed into the Tory lobby he whispered to Wharton the Whig : ' My heart is vid you.'

On the other hand, it was not unnatural that even moderate Tories should have felt indignant at the practice of Occasional Conformity for political reasons. By the Revolution Settlement of 1689, the agreed compromise that gave peace to England, Dissenters were granted legal toleration for their worship, but were to remain excluded from State and municipal office. Moderate Tories held that even if, as Burnet said, some humble folk innocently loved to hear the word in both Church and Chapel, it was nevertheless an evasion of the intentions of Parliament when a Dissenter, who never otherwise darkened the doors of the Parish Church, approached the altar in order to qualify as Mayor or Alderman. It might, indeed, be called a legal evasion of the law. But it is more doubtful whether the practice should have been so hotly denounced as a blas-phemous hypocrisy by legislators who themselves insisted on keeping a religious rite as a political test. The High Tories did not consider it blasphemy when Freethinkers and rakes of their own party, like St. John, knelt to receive the necessary passport into the Queen's service.

Whatever might be thought of the arguments for and against the Bill on its merits, there were other important motives for pressing or opposing it. The Tories pressed it in order to monopolize the borough corporations more completely, and diminish the Whig vote in Parliament and the Whig influence in towns. The Whigs opposed the Bill for analogous reasons. But many Moderate Tories, above all Godolphin and Marlborough, thought the measure untimely, not for any domestic or party reasons, but because it divided the nation at the most dangerous crisis of a war on which England's independence was staked.

In the winter of 1702–1703, the Bill, fathered by St. John and by Bromley, one of the members for the University of Oxford, passed by large majorities in the Commons, and came up to the Lords.   The opposition to it was led by Wharton and Burnet, a strange couple but both sincere in their advocacy of the cause of Toleration and Protestant union.   Archbishop Tenison voted with them. It would not be possible to throw the Bill out on second reading, supported as it was by the Commons and the Queen heartily, and by her chief Ministers nominally. But amendments were passed which the Commons would never accept.   One amendment cut out the municipal officers from the Bill, confining its scope to State officers alone.   This change was so drastic that it would have been hard to maintain it in face of the Commons, if the issue had been narrowed down to that.   But by reducing the excessive money fines proposed in the Bill, Wharton hoped to set the two Houses at issue on a disputed point where each was most sensitive.   He succeeded admirably, for the Commons could not endure that the Lords should amend their finance, nor the Lords that the Commons should deny them the right to do so.   A conference of the two Houses was held, but agreement could not be reached.

The Bill was therefore lost, to the indignation of the High Churchmen, who asserted, not without reason, that Marlborough and Godolphin had done little to help the measure except vote for it.   The line of cleavage in the Tory Party on foreign affairs and the conduct of the war was thus widened by a difference of attitude on the chief domestic question of the day.

Feb.
1703

The small majority of the Lords who had carried the final vote to disagree with the Commons, were so well pleased with themselves that they took the unusual step of printing and publishing the proceedings.   Such an appeal to the opinion of the country was the more remarkable, because both Houses were at that time absurdly jealous of the publication of their debates, though the reason for such secrecy had passed away with the passing of the King's power to punish members for their speeches in Parliament.[262]

The once famous controversy over the ' Occasional Bill,' that so fiercely shook the political and religious world of its day, is so far removed from the mentality of our own that it is now chiefly remembered for its effect upon the fortunes of an obscure inhabitant of Grub Street. To the careless Gallios of our later age all this noise and fury is chiefly significant because it set Daniel Defoe in the pillory.

In politics Defoe was a man of principle but not of party ; in consequence he was often surprised to find himself alone upon a desert island. His principles were religious toleration, trade and British interests in the world. His hero was William of Orange, whom he loved in a more intelligent and a more disinterested manner than many who shouted his name. For violences of sect and faction Defoe had an instinctive dislike, partly because the extremes of denominational and party zeal seemed to him to be perpetually clashing with the true interests of the country. Add to these peculiar opinions the shifts natural to a hunted and friendless man, and we get the true explanation of Defoe's tergiversations in politics, and, above all, the secret of the devotion that he came to feel for Robert Harley. The one was a Dissenter and the other a Tory, but they were both suspect to their nominal friends, alike for their moderation and for their sly, underhand ways.

The relations of Harley and Defoe began, unpropitiously enough, over the Occasional Conformity Bill. On that burning controversy Defoe characteristically wrote two pamphlets, the first of which ruined him with the Dissenters, and the second with the High Churchmen. In the first, entitled *An Enquiry into Occasional Conformity*, he denounced the practice with an obvious sincerity that irritated his co-religionists, although he also expressed deep indignation at the brutality of the High Church outcry against all Dissenters. In the second and more famous pamphlet, entitled *The Shortest Way with the Dissenters*, he parodied the violence of the High Church writers. ' It is cruelty to kill a snake or a toad in cold blood, but the poison of their nature makes it a charity to our neighbours to destroy these creatures.' Unfortunately for Defoe, his irony was taken in earnest, and for some days the town

believed that Sacheverell had been outstripped in zeal by
an unknown champion of the Church. For Defoe's
political pamphlets, like all others at that period, appeared
anonymously.

When it became known that it was a hoax, the anger of
the High Churchmen was intense—and not unjustified.
Defoe had been playing with edged tools and his genius for
literary make-believe had for once been sadly misemployed.
Speaker Harley as interpreter between the Tory House of
Commons and the Ministry, reported to Godolphin that it
was 'absolutely necessary for the service of the Government' to discover and punish the author. When Defoe's
identity was revealed, he was prosecuted and received
sentence to stand three times in the pillory and be imprisoned
during the Queen's pleasure.

Defoe had offended all sections of the powerful. The
Moderate Tory Ministers were angry with him for causing
them embarrassment ; the High Churchmen regarded him
as their worst enemy ; even the Dissenters resented the
criticisms in his first pamphlet and the disastrous maladroit-
ness of his second.

And yet his punishment in the pillory was turned by the
Londoners into an ovation. His non-party attitude was
perhaps not so unpopular with the multitude as
July   party men affected to suppose. The 'integrity and
1703   good nature' of the English people prompted them
to throw flowers instead of rotten eggs at the man whom
Church and State had united to crush. But the imprison-
ment 'during the Queen's pleasure' that followed meant
ruin to him—unless he could shorten it by making his
peace with some important member of government by an
offer of notable services. He was destined ere long to find
the needed protector in Harley.

In Newgate, then, let us leave him for the present,
bringing out ever fresh editions of his *Hymn to the Pillory* :

> Hail ! Hiroglyphick State Machin
> Contriv'd to punish Fancy in.

The immediate popularity of the poem gave him revenge on
his enemies, without thereby increasing the chance of his

own deliverance.   From Newgate, too, he wrote to his friend William Paterson, his complaints of misprision by the political world :

> Even the Dissenters, like Casha (*sic*) to Caesar, lift up the first dagger at me ; I confess it makes me reflect on the whole body of the Dissenters with something of contempt, and gives me the more regret that I suffer for such people.   Shall I own to you that the greatest concern I have upon me is that the government whom I profess I did not foresee would be displeased, should resent this matter ?   I had it not in my thoughts that the Ministers of State would construe that as pointing at them which I levelled only at Dr. Sacheverell, Dr. Stubbs and such people.   Thus like old Tyrell who shot at a stag and killed the King, I engaged a Party and embroiled myself with the Government.[263]

The motive behind the party passions and political manœuvres of the age of Anne was religious, or if not religious in the higher sense, at least denominational.   The world of Marlborough and St. John, of Defoe, Swift and Sacheverell does not appear religious in the same sense as the world of Laud and Baxter, of Cromwell and George Fox. The chief actors in Anne's reign, even when they are beating the drum ecclesiastic, do not seem to have essentially religious minds.   Doctrine and ritual are no longer undergoing transmutation in the crucible of war and parliamentary debate.   The House no longer divides on Arminianism or the use of the surplice.   The doctrine and ritual of the Church of England has become a fixed quantity that no one proposes to alter.   The Dissenting Sects hold with easy minds the doctrines that their grandfathers sought after sorrowing, and reached with doubts and divisions, groans and tears.   And the Puritans no longer aspire to capture the Church of England.   Controversy, therefore, has limits set within which it must move.   Yet within these limits the rivalry of Church, Dissent and that vague *tertium quid*—Free Thought—is the very pulse of the machine of politics.   As in the Ireland of to-day, so in the England of Anne, although men no longer debated doctrine and ritual as the subject-matter of politics, the framework of the rival political parties was formed on a confessional basis, and dislike of the smell of one's neighbour's religion seemed the prevailing passion in man as a political animal.

The last year of William's reign and the first four years of Anne were filled with the noise of the Convocation controversy. Not only were the Upper and Lower Houses of Parliament divided against one another, Whig against Tory, but precisely the same division set the High Churchmen of the Lower House of Convocation against the Low Church Bishops of the Upper House.

At this period a definite attempt was being made to revive Convocation as an integral part of the Church and State system of the country. If the attempt had been conducted with moderation it might have been successful and beneficent. But in the hands of the extreme political High Churchmen, the Lower House, by violently attacking the Bishops and the Whigs, became a sounding-board for High Tory politics. Their political acrimony gave an incentive and an excuse to the Whig Government of George I's reign to relegate Convocation once more to the limbo of an assembly that never meets.

Convocation had not played a prominent part in the religious struggles under the earlier Stuart Kings. The Anglicans had depended on the Crown; the Puritans on Parliament. In the days of Laud, neither party in the Church had used Convocation in the way the Presbyterian party in Scotland had used the Scottish Church Assembly. For Convocation was a purely clerical body, representing the clergy alone, whereas the Scottish Church Assembly had a large lay representation, like the English Church Assembly of our own day.

Convocation, therefore, had played little part in the controversies of James and Charles I's reigns. At the Restoration, the Lower House of Convocation had deprived itself of future political importance by voluntarily surrendering its right of taxing the Church for State purposes. From 1664 onwards the House of Commons taxed the clergy, and the clergy were in return allowed to vote for Parliament. Thenceforth, throughout the reigns of Charles and James II Convocation was not suffered to meet for the discussion of business. But after the Revolution, William III summoned it and appealed to its members on behalf of a scheme of Comprehension. He wished to obtain its blessing on a proposed parliamentary alteration of the Prayer Book, designed to 'comprehend' Moderate Dissenters, that is to induce them to return to the fold of the Church. But the clergy of the Lower House were hostile to the scheme, which had indeed enemies in many other quarters, Whig as well as Tory. William was vexed at the failure and did not summon Convocation in the middle period of his reign.

But in the closing years of the century the Convocation question was forced to the front of politics by the writings of a new High Church champion, Francis Atterbury, a controversialist of much higher stamp than Sacheverell, but unfortunately no less extreme.

In his *Letter to a Convocation Man*,* Atterbury claimed that the clerical assembly was an essential part of the Constitution of Church and State, on a par with Parliament both in its importance and its independence, and that even the King had no more right to prevent the meeting of Convocation than to prevent the meeting of Parliament. According to Atterbury, it was because it had not sat for some years past that infidelity and Socinianism had made such alarming strides. Let it only meet, and it would soon set the laity to rights as to what they were to believe and to read.

This claim for the rights of Convocation was one of the chief war-cries of the Tories in the reign of Anne. It was a new policy on the part of High Church. Under the early Stuarts the High Anglicans had looked to the Crown, and after the Restoration to Parliament also, to maintain them against their enemies. But now times had changed. Neither Crown nor Parliament were any longer allies on whom the Church party could count on all occasions. Therefore Convocation was to be set up again, with vague but ambitious schemes for the control of thought and morals.

Indeed, since the Revolution, the High Church could

---

* That Atterbury was the principal author of this famous *Letter* appears from his own statement to Hearne (*Collections*, III, pp. 279–280). See also Beeching's *Atterbury*, pp. 53–56.

not even trust the Bishops.   Atterbury, therefore, claimed that the Lower House of Convocation, where the parish clergy were represented, depended not on the Archbishop but on the Crown alone.   The clergy in Convocation, he pleaded, were not subordinate to the Bishops any more than the Commons were to the Lords.   Such was his analogy, a dangerous one for an episcopal Church.   It laid the High Church party open to the charge of practical Presbyterianism, which the Whigs scoffingly flung in their teeth. It was a topsy-turvy situation.   The Episcopate, once the *bête noire* of the Puritans, now shielded Dissenters and Low Churchmen from persecution.

In 1700 William III, in coming to terms with Harley and the Tories, had consented to summon Convocation again.   In 1701, and again in each year of Anne's reign, as often as Parliament met, Convocation met also.*   Led by Atterbury, the majority of the Lower House plunged into violent courses chiefly against the Upper House.   Burnet of Salisbury, outspoken, tactless and formidable, was the broad butt at which the High Churchmen loved to shoot.

1701   His very innocent book on the Thirty-nine Articles was attacked as heretical by the Lower House. And other latitudinarian writers were placed under the same ban.   It was openly said that if the Bishops would not act against false doctrines, their clergy would act for them. The Bishops, alarmed at what they regarded as a mutiny against their authority, prorogued the sittings of the Lower House through the action of Archbishop Tenison.   Thereupon Atterbury claimed that the Archbishop had no power to prorogue the Lower House, and it continued sitting in spite of the prorogation.

An important minority, however, broke away and obeyed the Bishops.   It would be a mistake to suppose that the whole of the Parish Clergy were extreme High Churchmen.   But a majority of their representatives took the high line in this quarrel.

* There was, of course, a Convocation of Canterbury and a Convocation of York, meeting separately.   It was in the southern Province that the great struggles took place, and historians of this epoch usually speak of the Convocation of Canterbury as ' Convocation ' for short.

The dispute over the right of prorogation, begun in the last Convocation of William, swallowed every other issue in the early Convocations of Anne. The learned aspect of the controversy was illuminated by writings of Wake and Gibson against Atterbury. Precedent did not appear to be on his side.

Thus the energy of a revival that might have been most useful to the Church, was wasted in bickerings between the Bishops and their clergy, which ungodly Whigs watched with delight. The affair added greatly to the bitterness of politico-religious controversy, and to the discontent of the High Church and the High Tories with the Ministry in the first years of the Queen's reign. The Queen, Marlborough and Godolphin did their best to keep out of the conflict, but their impartiality was itself an offence to Atterbury's followers, who had called on the Crown to resume powers said to have been usurped by the Archbishop. When in the session of 1702–1703 the Lower House of Convocation appealed to the Queen to interfere, Her Majesty, for all her High Churchmanship, gave them no answer. This, as well as the loss of the Occasional Conformity Bill, counted in the minds of zealots against the Ministers and even against the Queen herself. In January 1703 Nottingham vainly attempted to mediate behind the scenes in a correspondence with Tenison. The failure of the Ministry to do anything in the matter was one of the causes of the break up of the Tory Party in the year of Blenheim.[264]

The reign of Anne was marked by an important constitutional development—the growth in unity and power of the Cabinet Council. King William had directed Foreign Affairs himself, and he had been his own Prime Minister, holding together Cabinets of mutually antagonistic Whig and Tory statesmen by the imposition of his own will. Anne, being a woman and an invalid, had to leave many more decisions to be made by the agreement of her Ministers. The Cabinet, therefore, grew in importance, and at the same time the need for political unity and joint responsibility among its members was increasingly felt.

It was found in the very first years of the reign that the same Cabinet Council could no longer contain High Tories and Moderate Tories, who hated each other personally and differed as to the conduct of the war. The 'confidential servants of the Crown' had no longer a royal master to keep them in order and override their differences. Some other principle of unity was required. Party loyalty like that of the Whig Junto might give it. Failing that, Godolphin as Lord Treasurer began to impose his personal authority, and so to approach the position of Prime Minister —a name by which he was occasionally called.*

Nevertheless, the Queen was almost always present at the Cabinet Councils, though her power of controlling them was limited by her disabilities of health, sex and understanding. Meetings were held wherever Anne happened to be. In August 1703 we find Godolphin writing to Nottingham to collect the views on Scottish policy of those 'Lords of the Cabinet Council' who were then in London, and send them down to him at Bath in writing, 'upon receipt of which Her Majesty intends to call together those Lords who are here' and come to a decision by the help of the Cabinet's advice. At meetings in London, Cabinet Ministers were 'summoned to attend the Queen.' It was George I's ignorance of the English language and indifference to English affairs that first occasioned the absence of the sovereign from his own Cabinet Council.[265]

The 'Lords of the Cabinet Council,' as they were called, were not necessarily Peers. They consisted, then as now, of the chief officers of State. The year before Anne's accession the experienced Sunderland named ten posts, the occupants of which ought to compose the Cabinet.† But

---

* See p. 188, note, above.

† Archbishop, Lord Keeper (or Lord Chancellor), Lord President, Lord Privy Seal, Lord Steward, Lord Chamberlain, First Commissioner of the Treasury (or Lord Treasurer) ; two Secretaries of State ; Lord Lieutenant of Ireland when he is in England ; and, 'if the King would have more,' the head of the Admiralty, and the Master of the Ordnance. In Anne's reign Marlborough attended the Cabinet in the latter capacity. *Hardwicke*, II, p. 461. *H.M.C. Portland*, IV, p. 669, and *Salomon*, pp. 352-356, show there was little change from this list by the end of Anne's reign.

The Cabinet appears to have originated from two independent bodies, the All-purposes Committee of the Privy Council, and the Cabinet or private meeting

there was no absolute rule, and the Archbishop of Canterbury, who was reckoned in the list, was certainly not always present—towards the end of the reign very seldom. These great officers, 'the Lords of the Cabinet,' usually met once a week in the Queen's presence, and at other times to prepare business without her.

Besides these meetings of the Cabinet, the two or three greatest managers met privately to decide on policy, as so often happens in the case of over-large committees. In November 1703 Godolphin wrote to Harley, ' It is necessary above all the rest that the Duke of Marlborough and you and I should meet regularly, at least twice a week if not oftener, to advise upon everything that shall occur.' [266] Since Harley was at that time Speaker and not in the Cabinet at all, it would be a misnomer to call such a meeting ' an Inner Cabinet.' But no doubt the knowledge that Godolphin, Marlborough and Harley were arranging the affairs of the nation in private conference was one of the things that drove first Rochester and then Nottingham into revolt, and made the position of the High Tories in the Cabinet impossible.

The older, larger and less homogeneous body, the Privy Council, also met frequently and transacted much executive business which is now left to various departments of State. But it no longer initiated policies of any importance that had not been previously sanctioned by the Cabinet. Only in case of some grave emergency like a dynastic crisis, it was always possible that the Privy Council might assert its ancient authority once more.*

Next under the Lord Treasurer, who controlled finance and was beginning to assume the rôle of a Prime Minister, the most important administrative office in the Cabinet was

of the King's Confidential Servants—not a legally recognized body at all. In Anne's reign these two bodies are practically identical in personnel. See articles in *E.H.R.*, October 1912, January 1914, April 1914, April 1916, April 1917, and *Am. Hist. Rev.*, July and October 1913.

* By Clause IV of the Act of Settlement (see p. 120, above) the Privy Council was to be restored to its ancient position as the real organ of government, in place of the more modern Cabinet. But that clause, only to come into force when the House of Hanover came to the throne, was repealed in 1705 and was therefore never operative.

that of Secretary of State, who dealt with almost everything except finance. There were two Secretaries of State, one usually of the Civil Servant type, for if both Secretaries had been politicians claiming to guide high policy, they would have collided, since their spheres overlapped. In 1703 Sir Charles Hedges, Secretary for the Northern Department, was the modest administrator ; Nottingham, Secretary for the Southern Department, was a statesman who considered himself on a par with Godolphin and Marlborough—an issue that was yet to be tried. It would be impossible for the two kinsmen to carry on the war without the co-operation of Nottingham, for as Southern Secretary he dealt with the South European countries and with the Colonies ; the Northern countries of Europe and Scotland were the province of Hedges as Northern Secretary. There was no general Foreign Secretary. The two Secretaries of State also shared the duties of the Home Department, and each could issue orders to the Admiralty and the War Office, although there was a Lord High Admiral and a Secretary at War, not to mention the Commander-in-Chief.

It seems strange that government could have been carried on under such a shapeless system of overlapping departments. The Secretaries were in a sense subordinate to the Treasurer, but his power over them was that of influence, not of authority. In the last resort the Queen must be called in to judge the disputes of her servants. Godolphin, however, exercised his influence on the heads of the other departments with watchful industry and tact. Rochester, indeed, had soon proved impossible and the Queen had dismissed him. But the final breach with Nottingham was postponed until 1704.

CHAPTER XIV

War Taxation and the National Debt. The Squires and the Land Tax. Dutch and English trade with the enemy. Neutral Rights. The Methuen Treaties. Port *versus* Claret. The Portuguese Alliance and revised war aims. The Peninsular War, Lisbon and the Mediterranean. Nottingham's Foreign Policy. Victor Amadeus. Savoy joins the Alliance. The Great Storm of 1703.

THE close co-operation of England and the United Provinces, by which alone the power of Louis could be kept in check, had been secure throughout the last war because the greatest statesman in Europe was both Stadtholder of Holland and King of England. After William's death a like result was attained, only in a less degree, by the friendship between Marlborough and Heinsius, the Grand Pensionary. This good understanding with the Calvinist Republic was disagreeable to the High Tories, the more so as they saw it leading England month after month into larger military commitments on the Continent, and ever more extensive subsidies to German Princes.

1689–1697   William's war had lasted nine years and had cost England an average of three and a half millions a year. The War of the Spanish Succession 1702–1713 was destined to last a dozen years and to cost her an average of four millions a year or more. William's finance Minister, Charles Montagu, had, with the help of the City magnates, devised the machinery of the National Debt and the Bank of England, by which the last war had been financed. The same machinery was employed by Godolphin for the War of the Spanish Succession. William's war had run up a National Debt of fourteen and a half millions. To this was added another twenty-one and a half millions debt for Anne's war ; and since the total cost to England by this second struggle was over fifty millions, more than half must have been defrayed out of annual taxation, which also bore the interest on the debt.[267]

The Tory squires had special reasons for objecting both to the National Debt and to the method of taxation in time of war. They complained that the deeper the Treasury became indebted to the great moneyed men of the City, many of whom were Dissenters and few of whom were Tories, the more the Queen's Government was inclined to listen to the advice of the 'moneyed' as distinct from the 'landed' interest. Year by year Godolphin, in his capacity of Lord Treasurer, was drawn into closer communion with the City, and the Queen herself was ever more deeply pledged to that section of her subjects. Conversely, those who lent money to the State tended to become Whiggish, because if the Pretender returned he would repudiate loans to the governments of the Revolution.

Moreover, as the landowners complained, it was they who were charged with the cost of a policy which they disliked and in which the moneyed men found their profit. The interest on the National Debt, the subsidies to the Continental Allies, the maintenance of the English army— all objects of malediction to the up-country squire of that day—were paid for to a very large extent out of the Land Tax. Even if the High Tories were short-sighted in grumbling about expenses necessary for a modern State aspiring to independence and expansion, they were more justified in complaining of the peculiar incidence of taxation in that era. The direct taxes, a large proportion of the whole, were not evenly assessed on all wealth, but fell with disproportionate weight upon the land.

Attempts had indeed been made in the reign of William, and were made again in the first year of Anne, to levy an Income Tax on the salaries of officials and the profits of professional and business men, side by side with the Land Tax on the squires. But there did not then exist the machinery of the Inland Revenue requisite to make the necessary calculations for the assessment of profits and incomes ; and the tax-payer was unwilling to help any such inquisition into his private affairs. So the Income

Tax of four shillings in the pound on personal property, voted in 1702, was a failure and fell into disuse.* The whole burden remained on the landlords, whose acres could not be hidden away from assessment.

The method of raising the Land Tax appears very singular to our modern notions. Each year of the war a new Act declared that two millions were to be raised by what was called a 'four-shilling Land Tax.' This annual Act contained a schedule of the counties and principal towns of England, with the amount that each was to pay, making up in all the two millions required. The local authorities had to produce these sums, and did so by charging four shillings in the pound, nominally on the annual value of land, really on certain old assessments which were often not half the true value. The so-called 'four-shilling Land Tax' was in its actual effect nearer a two-shilling tax on the real annual value of most estates in Queen Anne's day. Many properties escaped far more easily than others, owing to the antiquity of the assessment. When peace returned in 1713, the Land Tax fell to a nominal two shillings in the pound, half the war-time rate.

Since it was beyond the ability of the State in that age to make an up-to-date assessment even of the land, it is no wonder that the more difficult assessment for a general Income Tax proved impossible. If it had been within the power of the administration to levy such a tax on all kinds of property, Godolphin would have been only too glad to propitiate the Tory squires by laying a share of the burden on the moneyed and professional men. It was his political interest to do so. But how to do it puzzled the Treasury officials, and even the Tory economist Davenant regarded the difficulty as insuperable. It was the younger Pitt who first successfully levied an Income Tax in addition to the old Land Tax, to fight the war against Revolutionary France. The statesmen of William and Anne tried to raise such a tax, and failed for want of official machinery.[268]

The Whig merchants, therefore, escaped too lightly from the burden of the wars against Louis. But the Whig

* It had been reckoned to produce £800,000 and actually produced £300,000, after which it was abandoned.

landed aristocracy paid its share. John Hervey, in 1703, the year when he was made a lord, drew £5250 in rents alone, of which he tells us nearly half went in 'taxes, repairs and charges of the house and garden.' Nine years later he wrote, 'I am sure the war has cost me above £40,000.'

Such grandees were often more Whiggish, or at least more ministerial, than the generality of squires, and owing to their frequent visits to London were better informed about foreign countries. Therefore they complained of war taxation less than their more rural neighbours, who regarded Europe much as a Western American farmer regards her to-day. It was the murmurs against the four-shilling Land Tax in the smaller manor houses that consti-tuted the chief danger to the ministerial policy during both the wars against Louis.

In the early years of Anne's reign harvests were good and corn prices low, so that the common people did not suffer as they had suffered during the wars and bad harvests of William's reign. That helped to prevent the renewed war from becoming generally unpopular, until prices doubled about the time of Malplaquet. But although the lowness of corn prices postponed discontent among the masses, it did not enhance the profits of those who grew corn for the market, and the squires considered themselves less able to pay the Land Tax on account of low prices. 'We have meat and drink sufficient, but we receive little money,' wrote one country baronet. Northern squires complained that all their ready money had gone to the tax-gatherer, and that unless the Vigo Treasure was as great as rumour said, there would be very little specie for the ordinary business of the countryside. Others 'were alarmed at taxes, and thought with King William all should cease.' A supporter of the war said the country gentlemen were unwilling 'to groan under the weight of four shillings in the pound,' unless the new war showed a better list than the last of victories won and towns taken.

Could Marlborough in the field deliver the goods in time to stop the mouths of his Tory critics at home? In the first two anxious years of Anne both the success and the popularity of the new war were doubtful. Especially when

1703 failed to repeat the military successes of 1702, Ministers walked on a razor edge at home and abroad. Then came the turning point of Blenheim, bringing two-fold relief, foreign and domestic. For the capture of an army and a Marshal of France seemed to the country squires, as a correspondent wrote to Harley, ' more for their four shillings in the pound than ever yet they saw.' [269]

The somewhat divided feelings with which the Tory majority in the Commons regarded the war and the Dutch Alliance, found a natural vent in protests about allied trade with the enemy. The State policy of England differed from that of Holland in this matter. Under the influence of Whig politics and mercantilist economics, England had endeavoured to put a stop to her own trade with France even in time of peace. But Holland lived by trade, and not least by trade across her southern border. Amsterdam, the financial centre of the world, continued to remit money to France by bills of exchange, undeterred by the outbreak of war. It was commonly said in England that France could not have fought either the war against William or the war against Anne, without the money that came from Holland and the horses that came from Holland and Germany in return for French wines. The Dutch replied that neither could they fight a long war unless their trade was maintained, and that the English themselves were constantly smuggling goods into France.

In January 1703 this controversy grew to a head. The House of Commons voted an increase of 10,000 men for the next year's campaign in Flanders, as requested by Holland, but only on condition that the States General compelled their subjects to break off trade and correspondence with the enemy. Marlborough was determined to keep friends with the Dutch in order to win the war, but he was, for the same reason, most anxious to stop the trade with France. He took, as mediator, a strong middle course. The States General, guided by Heinsius, was ready to meet the English demand half-way. But the federal constitution of the United Provinces left the Government with but feeble control over the smuggler-privateers of Zeeland or the capitalist houses of Amsterdam. ' Whatever the States General may resolve, they will never be able to hinder their people from trading where there is hope of gain,' wrote Alexander Stanhope, Queen Anne's Envoy at the Hague.

However, in accordance with the English demands, a Treaty was signed in April between England, the United Provinces and the Emperor; the three Powers bound themselves to prevent their subjects from trading with the enemy except in certain specified goods. The prohibition was to run from June 1703 for twelve months, since the Dutch refused to sign for more than one trial year.

During the agreed period of prohibition there were many infractions of the pact by the subjects of all three signatories. June 1703– June 1704 Ships from Irish ports drove a regular trade with Brest, under colour of being taken by privateers, really by collusion with the French Government, to whom they paid ten per cent. on their cargo. Evidence was given before the House of Lords proving that ' the French fleet was victualled from England and Ireland.' ' Owling ' of English wool to France went on as briskly and as illegally as ever from Sussex and East Anglia.   But these English lapses from the path of allied righteousness did not prevent our privateers from seizing Dutch ships which they caught running cargoes into Spanish American ports.

If English and Irish practice was irregular, so was that of Zeeland and Amsterdam. Nevertheless Dutch trade with the enemy was so far curtailed that the States General declared themselves desperately impoverished, and unable to continue the war any longer on a basis of prohibition. They absolutely refused to renew the pact for another year. England had to submit.   In the winter session of 1704– 1705, the public was rejoicing over Blenheim and the influence of the Whigs and Moderate Tories had increased. They were therefore able to prevent the House of Commons from quarrelling further with the Dutch on the subject. For the Whigs, though more anxious than the Tories to stop English trade with France in peace as well as in war, were as anxious as Marlborough himself not to ruin the prospects of the Alliance in order to punish the Dutch for holding a different view of their own interest.

After this unsuccessful experiment in agreeing to stop trade with the enemy, England and Holland agreed better in another policy—that of trading with Spain and Spanish America. After our proclamation of Charles III as King of Spain in 1703, the territories of which he pretended to be King were treated by England and Holland technically as Allied countries. In the middle and later period of the war, the French and Spaniards of Europe were prevented by our control of the sea from visiting Spanish America, where commerce was carried on by the English and Dutch in constant rivalry with one another. But the trade was less lucrative than it would otherwise have been, because the English privateers could not be induced not to attack the property and alienate the sympathies of Spanish-American colonists.

The international position as regards neutral rights in the War of the Spanish Succession was complicated by the fact that another war was going on among the Scandinavian and Slav States of the Baltic seaboard. In that eastern war England and Holland were neutrals, whereas Sweden, Denmark, and Poland were neutrals in the war against France. It is true that Denmark had hired out a most excellent army for the service of the Western Allies ; the charge of the Danish Horse enabled Marlborough to win Ramillies. Yet Denmark, no less than Sweden, claimed the maritime rights of a neutral in the French war. England and Holland could not afford to break with the Danes, whose armies they required on loan, nor with Charles XII of Sweden lest he should fall on the rear of their German allies. Moreover Scandinavian naval stores were essential to the very being of the Maritime Powers.* We could not, while claiming our own rights as neutral traders in the Baltic, press too closely the right of search against Baltic neutrals in the war nearer home. For these reasons, the Danes were permitted to trade with France, except in contraband of war, including horses. And the formidable King of Sweden was treated with similar respect. Neutrals whose favour we had less reason to court, like Genoa and other Italian States, after our fleets had occupied the Mediterranean basin, were more effectively prevented from trading

* See p. 9, above.

with France. But in one way and another French trade, though blocked in many avenues, was never devoid of outlets, some recognized and some unrecognized by the governments of the Grand Alliance.[270]

The year 1703 was marked by no warlike successes by sea or land.* This unproductive campaign would have been fatal to the Alliance in its race against time, had not the year, so barren in martial achievement, been singularly fruitful in diplomacy. In May Portugal ceased to be neutral and joined the enemies of France, and in October Savoy abandoned the French for the Allied party. Neither event would have occurred but for the skilled application of English naval, diplomatic and financial pressure.

John Methuen and his son Paul, successive envoys to Portugal in the last years of William and the first years of Anne, were the chief architects of those famous Treaties which are still known by their name in economic and political history. The Methuens thoroughly understood not only England's interests in the country to which they were accredited, but the inner workings of its Court and the mind of its people. Their first duty was to prevent the King of Portugal from joining the French side. After the disbanding of the English army in 1698 had been followed by the acceptance of Charles II's will by Louis on behalf of his grandson, the impression in the Iberian Peninsula of the weakness of England and the strength of France was for a time overwhelming. King Peter II of Portugal was on the point of acknowledging the Pretender as King of England, in accordance with the solicitations of France and Spain, with whom he had formed an alliance. The Methuens were just able to persuade him to watch events a little longer before taking the plunge into war against the Allies.

It would be necessary for Portugal to take one side or the other. Like Italy in 1915, she was between the Devil and the Deep Sea, and neutrality was as dangerous for her as intervention. If Portugal stood neutral and let the French and Spanish power establish its hegemony in

---

* See the next chapter for Marlborough's Campaign of 1703.

Europe, the little Kingdom would be the merest vassal of Louis and his grandson, lucky if she were not annexed once more to Spain as in the days of Philip II. And whether she remained neutral or joined the side of France, in either case she would be in danger of losing her trade and her colonies, for the English fleet could sweep her shipping off the sea, and cut her communications with her American, African and Indian possessions.*

Could she then with safety join the Allies? Her own army was useless against the French. Would English and Dutch troops come in sufficient numbers to protect her eastern frontier against Bourbon invasion? In 1701 England seemed helpless, and the answer in the negative. With difficulty the Methuens kept up their end at Court against the formidable Franco-Spanish party. The King was less favourable to France than were his Ministers. Then the news of Vigo turned the tide of opinion in Portugal. The power of English ships and landing parties had been demonstrated in dramatic fashion. Perhaps after all the Portuguese could trust the Alliance to defend their eastern border, provided the Maritime Powers would commit themselves to the policy of a Peninsular War on the grand scale by undertaking the expulsion of Philip V from the throne of Madrid.

Oct. 1702

Six months of intrigue and negotiation followed, ending in the signature at Lisbon of the Methuen Treaties, commercial and political. They form the most important group of diplomatic documents signed between the Grand Alliance of 1701 and the Peace of Utrecht. They changed the war aims and the war

May 1703

* 'The late King [of Portugal] made the [Methuen] Treaty and broke his alliance with France because he was told he could not stand neuter, the French could not protect his port and trade ; therefore he joined with us. The same reasons subsist still with much greater force : the French have no fleets at sea and we are in possession of these seas, and these people can have no trade but under our protection. Though their trade is certainly beneficial to us, yet 'tis so more to Portugal. All their gold, sugars and tobaccos are the returns of our own manufactures, which our people give them on credit, to be paid for upon the return of the Brazil trade. Three parts in four of the corn expended here and all the dried fish is imported by the English, so it is plain these people live by us.' Thos. Leffever to Lord Dartmouth, October 13–24, 1710, Lisbon. *Dartmouth MSS.* at Patshull.

strategy of the Allies.   They remained the basis of England's power in southern Europe till the days of Nelson
and Wellington, and affected her commercial policy down
to the era of the Great Reform Bill.

The origin of the Methuen Treaties can be sought far
back in the commercial history of the two countries, and in
the conditions of the marriage of Charles II of England to
Catharine of Braganza.   But the bargain struck in 1703
began a new era in Anglo-Portuguese relations, because it
was successfully followed up by the taking of Gibraltar and
Port Mahon and by the permanent establishment of English
power in the Mediterranean, based on the free use of the
harbour of Lisbon.[271]

The commercial part of the Methuen Treaties bound
Portugal to remove her existing prohibition on English
cloth, and admit it at an easy rate.   In return, England
undertook to admit Portuguese wine at rates that should
always be less by one-third than those charged on French
wine.   English merchants and manufacturers were delighted
at a bargain that found a new vent for their cloth, and sheep-
breeding squires and yeomen were well pleased.   The cloth
manufacture of Portugal was destroyed by English imports,
but the country found salvation in reorganizing itself as a
huge vineyard to supply the English table with port.

A vested interest in the Methuen Treaty grew up
during the war, so strong that, at the height of the reaction
against the war policy ten years later, the powerful Ministry
that made the Treaty of Utrecht failed to carry the Commercial Treaty with France through a House of
1713   Commons that took a Tory view of every other
subject.   To admit French claret at an easier rate than
port would have meant breaking the Methuen Treaty and
losing the Portuguese market for our cloth.   A pamphlet
of that year asserts that :

'Tis the Portugal trade that has supported us in the war, and
without it we should soon find the peace more burdensome than the
war.   But I need not to talk to a West Countryman, who for several
years has seen so much Portugal gold in the Fairs, markets, shops,
and amongst the gentlemen's Stewards, how advantageous the
Portugal trade is to England.

Very possibly a French trade might have proved even more 'advantageous,' but the country refused to sacrifice the Portuguese bird in the hand in hopes of greater advantages that would at best have to be shared with France. The French trade was pronounced dangerous by the school of political economy then prevalent. And so, throughout the Eighteenth Century, port came into the country more lightly taxed than claret.* Port was patriotic and Whig and woollen ; claret was Francophile and Jacobite—patriotic only in Scotland. The gout that consequently afflicted the English upper class so sorely in the days of Fox and Pitt was one of the by-products of the Methuen Treaty, of Whig policy, of mercantilist economics, and of the exigencies of the great war in the early days of Queen Anne.[272]

But in the spring of 1703 Marlborough and the Methuens were not thinking of their descendants' gout or taste in wine, but of the way to obtain the Portuguese alliance, and the Lisbon harbour for the war fleet. King Peter's terms were irreducible. Not only must great English and Dutch armies be sent to the Peninsula, but as a pledge of allied sincerity not to desert him, they must proclaim the Austrian candidate as Charles III of Spain, and he must come in person to the Peninsula to fight for his inheritance. These demands raised for some months considerable difficulty, because the Emperor Leopold was most unwilling to send his dearly loved younger son to the other end of Europe, to a barbarous land under a bodyguard of heretics. ' The Imperial Ambassador in Portugal,' wrote Secretary Hedges, ' shows himself very indifferent in the matter and says that the Emperor will not need Portuguese help.' Certainly Leopold was an aggravating mortal. He had plunged all Europe into war rather than forego any portion of his family's claim on the Spanish Empire, and now he was ' indifferent ' to his one chance of placing Charles on the throne of Madrid.

---

* The Portuguese possession of Madeira also began to supply us with its wine, the companion of port. In 1705 Queen Anne established a Consul General in ' the islands of Maderas ' ' to aid and protect our merchants ' there, as an outcome of the Methuen Treaty two years before. *P.R.O.* (S.P.), 104, 130 ff. 260–262.

But Viennese lethargy was coerced by the more energetic purpose of London ; after all, the English and Dutch were the paymasters of the Alliance, and could call the tune. At length the Emperor consented to sign the military part of the Methuen Treaty, whereby he promised that the Archduke Charles should go to Portugal. As soon as he arrived, but not before, King Peter undertook to acknowledge him as Charles III of Spain and begin the Peninsular War on his behalf. England, Holland and the Emperor pledged themselves to send 12,000 'veteran troops' ; and the 28,000 Portuguese, promised by King Peter, were to be mainly paid for and armed by the Maritime Powers. Austria, in truth, contributed nothing more than the person of Charles. For, although by the Treaty she undertook to supply one-third of the 12,000 allied troops in Spain, England at once took over her share. A readjustment of the Brazilian frontier with French Guiana favourable to Portuguese claims was also to be arranged at the peace.

Such was the political and military section of the Methuen Treaties. It placed the harbour of Lisbon at the full disposition of England's fleet and so enabled her to take and keep Gibraltar and Minorca, to dominate the Mediterranean and to assist effectively in the liberation of Italy from the French power.

In so far as the Portuguese alliance gave the Allies entry to the Mediterranean it was pure gain, indispensable to victory over France. But in so far as it drew them into a war inside the Iberian Peninsula it was a more doubtful boon. They gained indeed Portugal, Catalonia and the Eastern Provinces of Spain as active friends, but they roused up Castile and Central Spain from habitual sloth to active resistance, against which the English and Dutch spent the strength of armies that might have fought elsewhere. It is true they thus compelled Louis to send troops to Spain. But as the French were on the inner line they could keep troops in Spain more cheaply than the Dutch or English. It was a question similar to the vexed question of the ' sideshows ' in the World War of our own day.

More certainly disastrous was the deflection of the moderate war aims defined by William in the Treaty of

Grand Alliance,* to the misleading policy of placing on the throne of Madrid a candidate who, though popular in Catalonia, was odious to the great body of the Spanish people. This increase in the allied programme was dictated by the desperate need to purchase the support of Portugal at the worst moment of the war. It served its purpose, but in the end it protracted the world struggle long after it had been won. The vain endeavour to turn Philip off his throne added, perhaps, four years to the war.

The fatal formula ' no peace without Spain ' became the Whig shibboleth after Ramillies, and it took the whole strength of the reunited Tory party to overcome it and give peace to Europe at Utrecht. But in the early years of the war, Nottingham, the High Tory Secretary of State, was the staunchest supporter of the policy afterwards regarded as peculiarly Whig. In 1703, as Southern Secretary, he was active in pushing through the negotiations of the Methuen Treaty. In this matter, as in so many others, this most conscientious of English statesmen took a line of his own : Nottingham wanted a great military effort to be made by England in the Peninsula, whereas other High Tories wanted the war to be confined to the sea and to coast raids. But he did not agree with Marlborough's policy of fighting on a large scale with English troops in the Netherlands and Germany ; he wished them to be sent instead to Spain. In 1703, therefore, while the Methuen Treaty was amaking and the preparations for the coming Peninsular War were on foot, Nottingham was able to co-operate heartily on those matters with Marlborough and Godolphin. But in the following spring, when the question arose of sending English troops into the heart of Germany, the difference between the Secretary's view of the war and that of the two kinsmen would alone have sufficed to bring on a Cabinet crisis.[273]

The activity of Nottingham in foreign affairs was not confined to Portugal. It was his policy to stir up the mid-European powers to save themselves by their own exertions, so that the English army could be concentrated on Spain. His Secretaryship was marked by great efforts to induce

* See pp. 146-147, above.

Savoy and Bavaria to change sides.   And at his instigation,
as also at that of Marlborough, our Minister, Stepney, at
Vienna was constantly urging the Emperor Leopold to
grant concessions to the armed Hungarian Protestants and
Constitutionalists, so as to face westward against France
with his eastern door safely closed behind him, and his
hereditary dominions united.   But the Emperor, under
Jesuit advice, was obdurate, and when pressed used only to
reply by raising the analogous case of Ireland, and pro-
testing against the infamous penal laws still being added to
the Statute Book in England's Hungary.

If Nottingham could have won the Elector of Bavaria to
change sides, and Leopold to be humane and reasonable in
his dealings with his subjects, the English army need never
have gone to the Danube.   But though he succeeded with
Portugal and Savoy, he failed with the Emperor and the
Elector.   And that failure doomed his own scheme of war
strategy and made him impossible in 1704 as a colleague of
Marlborough, who held that if the Emperor would not save
himself, it was England's interest to go to his rescue.[274]

Victor Amadeus, Duke of Savoy, would have won the
approval of Macchiavelli, both for his ends and for the means
by which he attained them.   It was his life-long endeavour
to keep the foreigner out of his principality—since to keep
him wholly out of Italy was no longer possible ; to preserve
the real independence of Savoy-Piedmont by balancing
Austria against France ; to observe no faithfulness except
to this patriotic end ; to use subjects, allies and daughters
as mere pawns in the game ; to dodge perpetually like a fox
and now and again to strike like a lion.   Just as England
sought the balance of power in Europe, so the Duke sought
the balance of power on the Alpine watershed.   He was
a ' trimmer ' in the sense of Savile, Marquess of Halifax :
he ' trimmed ' not towards the victor of the hour but against
him to hold the balance even.   No party could trust him in
the hour of triumph.

In 1703 the position of the Allies was so desperate that
Victor Amadeus saw that it was time for one of his periodic
desertions from the stronger to the weaker side.   Louis

could not believe that the Duke, twice his kinsman, meditated a treachery so dangerous and apparently so contrary
to his interest.   One of his daughters was married to the
Duke of Burgundy, ultimate heir to the throne of France ;
another to Philip, King of Spain.   The French armies were
in and around the Savoyard territory, which constituted their
land route to Milan, Naples and Sicily.   Surely, if ever a
man was attached by interest and by fear to the French
cause it was Victor Amadeus in 1703.   Moreover, he had
recently been angry with the English for rejecting the
claims of his House in favour of the Hanoverian succession.*

But the Duke was in no good humour with the French.
Their Generals were insolent to him ; their soldiers treated
Italians as inferior beings.   His daughter at Madrid was
quarrelling with the Court of France over the personality
and power of her female favourite the Princess des Ursins.
Above all, the real object of the Duke's statecraft was not
to find the path of immediate safety, but the road of ultimate
independence.   If French power were permanently established in Italy, Savoy would be surrounded by lands ruled
from Versailles, and its Duke would be a vassal of the Grand
Monarch.   Victor had other dreams for the future of his
House.   Austria must be re-established in the Milanese :
for only then would Savoy be independent, holding the
mountain passage between the two rival powers, like Afghan-
istan between England and Russia.

Richard Hill, our envoy at Turin in 1704, thus explained the policy of the Court to which he was accredited :
Victor Amadeus ' hopes the Germans may have a greater
force in the country than the Spaniards used to have and may
be always at hand to support him on that side, as the French
may do upon occasions on the other side.'   Hill added that
the Italians of the Milanese ' do perfectly hate the French
and abhor their government.   They are used to the
Spaniards ; born and bred under that gentle or feeble
government.'   It was French government to which the
nominal Spanish Province of Milan had in reality been subjected ever since the death of Charles II of Spain.

But Victor would not change sides unless he had a

* See pp. 116–117, above.

x

reasonable chance of preserving himself from the vengeance of the French. The foothold of Prince Eugene's Austrian army in the plain of the Po, feeble in 1701–1702, was feebler still in 1703. The secret negotiations begun at Vienna for a change of sides by Savoy, produced from Leopold many promises of military aid and offers of additional Italian territory as good as those made by France. But what was the chance of performance by an out-at-elbows Emperor, with Hungarian, Bavarian and French armies at that moment in different parts of his Austrian territories? Stepney, the well-informed English Minister at Vienna, disbelieved in the whole negotiation, which he regarded as another fox-trick of Victor's, signifying nothing. ' It does not seem probable,' he wrote, ' that the Duke of Savoy should resolve to deprive his daughter of the kingdom of Spain. I can hardly think for my part that he is in earnest.' Stepney ' never had any opinion of the Duke's honesty ' ; he was a ' Proteus ' whom it was impossible to catch ; as late as September 1703 the English Minister regarded the whole negotiation as ' banter.'

Yet for once the wise Stepney proved mistaken. In the atmosphere of Vienna, every allied effort might well seem hopeless which depended on the Emperor's aid. But the Duke of Savoy did not depend on Vienna alone. The English fleet, under Sir Cloudesley Shovell, with Leake as his energetic lieutenant, was sent into the Mediterranean in 1703, ' above all to induce the Duke of Savoy to declare for the House of Austria,' wrote Nottingham to Heinsius, as well as to encourage the Imperial party in all the States of Italy and to get into touch with the revolted Protestants of the Cevennes. Shovell sailed too late to do much, but he showed the flag off the coasts of Italy, unchallenged by the Toulon fleet. Through the Savoyard ports of Nice and Villafranca, the Duke was in direct communication with the power of England. Godolphin's promise of financial aid to the tune of 800,000 crowns a month was certain to be carried out ; and the English Ministry's undertakings, to put the Emperor in a way to resume military operations powerfully in Italy, were honestly meant and were ultimately fulfilled.

Yet for all the promises of Nottingham, Marlborough and Godolphin, the danger in which the Duke would stand if he defied France was so great that he hesitated from month to month. Finally, in the autumn, Louis got wind of the negotiations and ordered the 5000 Savoyards in the French army to be disarmed and arrested. This stroke, instead of frightening the Duke, rendered him desperate and bold. He took the plunge and publicly joined the Allies. It is possible that he thereby saved Vienna from capture. But he almost lost Turin. In July 1704, when Marlborough was already on the Danube, the plight of Savoy was such that Hill in Turin thought Victor would still be obliged to sell himself back to France. 'The Duke,' he wrote, 'will lose his country, or we shall lose the Duke.' In Italy, as elsewhere, Blenheim came just in time to save the allied cause from utter ruin.[275]

Oct. 1703

The return of Savoy to the English alliance at once revived a policy, dear to English statesmen of all parties, of arming the Protestants of Southern Europe against their French persecutors. Victor Amadeus appealed to the most hardy and war-like section of his subjects, the mountaineers of the Vaudois Valleys, to supply him with recruits against Louis, whose influence at Turin was always so fatal to their welfare. Huguenot refugees from Switzerland and France swarmed to his standard. At the same time the Duke and his English allies put themselves into communication with the 4000 Huguenot rebels of the Cevennes hills, who, rendered desperate by their wrongs, were waging a terrible war of mutual atrocity against the power of Louis in the very heart of France. The Cevennois had their agents in Switzerland, in London, and now at Turin. Their number, though not their courage, was exaggerated in the minds of the Allies. The idea of a combination of these French rebels with the Savoyard army and the English fleet against Toulon was already floating through Marlborough's mind. But the time for such an attempt was not yet. Turin had first to be placed out of danger, and the French expelled from Milan.[276]

At the close of November, English naval supremacy

was nearly broken and the war lost by the sudden, brief and
unprovoked intervention of a neutral power. The
Great Storm, without rival in the recorded history
of our island, fell for two days on the Channel and
the South of England. The wind blew from west-
south-west, ' resembling thunder at a distance and being
attended with terrible flashes of lightning.' The battleships of Shovell and Leake, just returned from the Mediterranean, were lying in the Downs and off the Gunfleet.
Another squadron was off the coast of Holland, waiting
there to take up ' King Charles III ' bound for his kingdom
of Spain. To avoid being dashed on shore, most of the
English fighting fleets ran out to sea. So did thousands of
merchantmen of all sizes. For a week to come the North
Sea was covered with English shipping, in every variety of
peril. Only after many days was it possible to tell what
proportion of them would ever come back. It was said
that ' if the storm had not been at its height at full flood and
in a spring tide, the loss might have proved fatal to the
nation,' as the ships would have been driven on the sand-
banks that were mercifully covered when the hurricane
first fell.

Never was English seamanship put to a harder test and
never were ships better handled. On that awful night, and
the no less awful day that followed, England was saved by
the skill and courage of the crews of innumerable vessels,
fighting the greatest naval battle of the war against no
mortal foe. At Versailles the courtiers believed that the
English had lost their fleet. At home men and women
waited in an agony of suspense for the return of the ships.
One by one the survivors came in, battered, with broken
masts and rigging in shreds. Happily the winter was still
in front, so that the dockyards had many months in which
to repair the ships before next year's campaign. The
Royal Navy had lost Admiral Beaumont, 1500 seamen and
15 warships varying from second to sixth rate, besides
smaller craft. The total losses of the merchant service
were never estimated, but amounted to several hundred
craft of all sorts.

The pride and resolution of the country rose to the call.

The Navy was well loved and it was well supported in its hour of need. On the first of December, the Commons, to the dismay of the enemies of England, voted supplies to make good all losses, and insisted that the quota of ships in commission next spring was not to be diminished. Next year, indeed, Gibraltar fell to the English sailors and marines, and was preserved by the only full-dress naval action of the war, the battle with the French Grand Fleet off Malaga. Within a fortnight of the storm, Alexander Stanhope wrote from the Hague, ' I have read with no small pleasure the votes of the House of Commons and addresses to Her Majesty on the occasion of our losses, which will certainly make both Her Majesty and the nation more considered and respected all over Europe.' *

Between sea and land stood the Eddystone lighthouse on its rock. The upper part consisted of wood, but it was then regarded as a great engineering feat and was a blessing to mariners. By the strangest of chances ' the ingenious Mr. Winstanley,' who had been responsible for its erection, had crossed over to see after some repairs and was there on the unlucky evening when the storm began. Signals were made for help, but no boats could put out from shore. Night and hurricane closed round the Eddy-stone. In the morning the rock was bare ; the lighthouse and its occupants were gone.[277]

The storm on land was less dangerous to the State than the storm at sea, but the destruction that it wrought was no less dramatic. The south-west, where the hurricane first struck the island, bore the full brunt. Kidder, Bishop of Bath and Wells, was killed with his wife as they lay in bed in Wells Palace, by the fall of a chimney-stack. The saintly Ken, the Nonjuror whom Kidder had succeeded, records that he narrowly escaped a like fate. Of great cities, Bristol suffered the worst. Its port was filled with wrecked shipping. Its famous underground warehouses were swamped by the inrush of the tide before the wind, and so much property was destroyed that the loss was computed at

---

* It is pleasant to note, in the Journals of the House, that the Commons at the same time voted that the families of the drowned seamen should be relieved—a matter by no means of course in those days.

over £100,000.   For days afterwards, boats from Bristol were rowing through the countryside, rescuing families off roofs and tree-tops.

Starting from Cornwall, the Great Storm traversed England in an eastern direction with a touch of north. Trees went down in battalions ; the lead roofs on cathedral and parish churches were rolled up like carpets ; in many places scarce a chimney remained standing, not a roof uninjured. Boats were flung out of river beds, carriages thrown over hedges into the fields.

I bless God we are all well [wrote Lady Rachel Russell] but the chimney where my son and his wife lay fell, and the bricks and soot coming down the chimney made them rise at six o'clock and come to my drawing-room.   The wall of the garden fell next the field, and all the trees beat one side to the very ground.   But at Stratton my loss is worse in all respects, corn and hay dispersed hanging on the trees, and the fir-grove entirely tore up by the roots.   Hampshire is all desolation.   I hear of many killed in country as well as town. Lady Penelope Nicholas killed in her bed in her country house, and he in the same bed saved ; a piece of timber falling between his legs kept off the bricks.

In London the damage was reckoned at a million pounds. On the morning of November the 27th, Londoners peering through the storm saw their streets like those of a city bombarded, piled high with the rubbish of fallen chimneys and roofs.   It was fortunate that, after the rain on the first night, three dry weeks followed, most unusual at that time of year ; otherwise the roofs of South England could not have been patched up before the contents of the houses had suffered fatal damage.

At midnight on the 26th Queen Anne had stood watching through the windows the downfall of trees of historic tradition in St. James's Park.   At the same hour, one of the most venerable of her subjects, old John Evelyn, father of arboriculture in England, was listening to the uproar of the uneven battle between the great wind and his beloved oaks at Wotton—'Wood Town no longer' as he mournfully said.   At morning there they lay, 'like whole regiments fallen in battle by the sword of the conqueror, and crushing all that grew beneath them.'   Evelyn lost

2000 great trees that night ; a neighbour lost 1300, New Forest 4000 'brave oaks,' Forest of Dean 3000 more. The elms of South England fell, as it were, without a struggle. But in those days there was hope of the future, for though elm and oak might fall, men planted others—as they seldom will to-day.

The fury of the storm lessened as it passed northwards. It died out somewhere in East Anglia. Ely's long roof was torn to shreds. But at King's Lynn on the Wash the damage in the town was only reckoned at £1000, and the loss in the harbour at no more than £3000, though it included seven or eight ships. The North was but little affected.

So England survived by land and sea. It was a sad but thankful Christmas. Normal life had surely returned when on December 16 'the pious Robert Nelson' was discussing with other members of the Society for Promoting Christian Knowledge 'whether acting the *Tempest* upon the next Wednesday after the late dreadful storm, at the new play-house in Little Lincoln's Inn Fields, was proper or seasonable ? ' England was herself again.[278]

CHAPTER XV

THE year 1703 was Marlborough's year of sorrow:
domestic calamity stood prelude to a fruitless campaign.

The Duke's family affairs, like all else that he touched,
bore the mark of his sure mastery over life: forty-four
years of happiness with the cleverest woman in England,
who quarrelled sooner or later with everyone else, was in
itself no mean achievement. His political power was
increased by the splendid yet happy marriages of his handsome daughters. His second son Charles had died early,
but John, Lord Churchill, Marquess of Blandford, had
reached the age of seventeen, beloved and admired, with
his mother's wit and his father's sweetness of temper. 'He
is not only the best-natured and most agreeable but the
most free-thinking and reasonable creature that one can
imagine at his age,' wrote Godolphin. What a place this
young Marcellus seemed born to fill in Eighteenth Century
England !

Given to sober companions and proficient in the classics,
Blandford had passed from Eton to King's,* where, though
admitted as a ' nobleman,' he pursued his studies with zeal.
His tutor was that adventurous clergyman, Francis Hare,
afterwards the Duke's Field Chaplain on the Danube and

---

* In Blandford's day the Kingsmen lived in buildings on the site of the present
(1930) Cambridge University Library, on the north side of King's Chapel. The
present King's buildings, other than the Chapel, did not exist.

in Flanders. Blandford was burning to serve a campaign under his father ; but Sarah interposed : her son must stay yet awhile at college.

She had better have let him go. The smallpox, with its wonted humanity, chose for its prey the youth with the brightest prospects of any man at Cambridge. Blandford's parents hurried down, but could only watch him die. In a side chapel of King's, his tomb of white marble, prodigal of inscription, bears witness to the frailty of human hopes.

Feb. 20
1703

Jactat genus et nomen inutile.

A few weeks later Marlborough wrote home to Godolphin, after a review of the allied forces on the Rhine :

I have this day seen a very great procession, and the thoughts how pleased poor Lord Churchill would have been with such a sight have added very much to my uneasiness. Since it has pleased God to take him, I do wish from my soul I could think less of him.

Common sorrow had drawn him closer than ever to his wife. In April he wrote to her from the siege of Bonn :

If you had not positively desired that I would always burn your letters, I should have been very glad to have kept your dear letter of the ninth, it was so very kind, and particularly so upon the subject of our living quietly together, till which happy time comes I cannot be contented.

They still hoped for a male heir :

Pray let me have in every one of your letters an account of how you do. If it should prove such a sickness as that I might pity you but not be sorry for it, it might yet make me have ambition.

Heavens ! What then is ambition, if Marlborough lacked it ? But we need not strain at the chance outcry of a man in grief. There is more need of interpretation for the following letter that he wrote to the Duchess in August.

You and I have great reason to bless God for all we have, so that we must not repine at his taking our poor child from us, but bless and praise him for what his goodness leaves us. The use I think we should make of this his correction is, that our chiefest time should be spent in reconciling ourselves to him, and having in our minds always that we may not have long to live in this world. I do not mean by this that we should live retired from the world : for I am persuaded that by living in the world one may do much more good than by being out of it, but at the same time to live so that one could cheerfully die when it shall be His pleasure to call us.

This might pass as Oliver Cromwell's to his Elizabeth, but it is Marlborough's to Sarah. It cannot be conscious hypocrisy, for the woman to whom alone it was addressed insisted on no such sentiments ; nor can it be mere custom, for such was not the conventional language of the Whitehall where he and his wife were brought up. It must represent one of the genuine moods of this most secret man.[279]

Sick at heart, Marlborough had crossed to Holland in March, and by great efforts got the Dutch early into the field. But their Generals were less willing than ever to undertake the downright attack on the French lines in the Netherlands, without which Holland could not hope to obtain her chief object in the war. Athlone, who had been converted by the events of last year's campaign to recognize the genius of the English commander,* had unfortunately died, and his successors with one consent began to make excuse why there should be only a defensive campaign. All that Marlborough could get leave to do was to besiege Bonn in good time before the enemy were moving. It fell, the last of the Rhine fortresses that the Archbishop of Cologne had betrayed to the French, and its fall opened the great waterway to the Allies and so rendered possible the operations of the following year, which no man then foresaw.
Marlborough in person pressed forward the siege at Bonn.† The operations were covered by an army under Overkirk, the best of the Dutch Generals, holding an entrenched camp under the walls of Maastricht against the relieving army coming from the direction of Brussels under Marshals Villeroi and Boufflers. Overkirk would have been surprised and overwhelmed at Maastricht but for the delay of the French before the little walled town of Tongres, where two battalions, one of Dutch and the other of Scots

* See p. 238, above.   † *See Map VIII at end of volume for this campaign.*

in the Dutch service, endured bombardment by an army
for a night and a day, before they surrendered.
May 15 During the breathing space thus obtained, Overkirk
(N.S.)
1703 ably prepared his defences, which Villeroi cannonaded
but dared not assault. Marlborough, having that
very day taken Bonn, hastened back and all was well.

The Duke valued so highly the services of the Scottish
and Dutch defenders of Tongres, that he insisted upon
their being exchanged for the next batch of French
Aug. prisoners whom he captured three months later on
1703 the fall of Huy.   That fortress, high up the Maas,
near Namur, was the last town held by Joseph Clement, the
Elector Bishop of Cologne and Liège ; all his territories
had now passed into the hands of the Allies he had betrayed,
who indignantly remembered that he owed these very
provinces to their diplomatic support of his candidature in
the days of William of Orange.   Retribution had been
swift in the case of Joseph Clement ; it hung on a slower
foot in pursuit of his brother, Max Emanuel of Bavaria.*

Bonn, Huy and the fortress of Limburg were all
Marlborough's trophies for the year 1703—a miserably
inadequate counterpoise to the great Franco-Bavarian thrust
along the Danube that threatened the very heart of the
Alliance at Vienna.   But all the efforts of the Duke to
make headway in the Netherlands had been shipwrecked
on the folly or ill-will of the Dutch Generals, who proved no
less obstructive than the year before.   In July Marlborough
had devised a plan for a surprise attack on Antwerp.   The
Dutch Generals Cohorn and Opdam were to attack it from
the west and Marlborough from the east.   But Cohorn,
better at a siege than a campaign, gave the enemy warning by
avaricious plundering raids into Western Flanders.   Opdam
allowed himself to be surpised at Ekeren, and ran
July 29 away from his army, leaving it to be extricated and
(N.S.)
1703 brought off by Slangenburg, a man of courage and
resource but of vile temper and bitterly jealous of
Marlborough.   The scheme against Antwerp had failed.

From Antwerp to Namur the French were constructing
' lines,' like those of Torres Vedras, but ninety miles long,

* For these Wittelsbach brothers see p. 156, above.

to protect their occupation of the Spanish Netherlands. The line consisted in some sections of impassable rivers, elsewhere of continuous earthworks. Marlborough, back on the Maas in the neighbourhood of Huy, proposed to force these lines near the Mehaine, at a point where the earthwork barrier was still incomplete, not far from the future battlefield of Ramillies. A formal remonstrance was signed by Marlborough and a dozen English, German and Danish Generals, demanding that the attack should be made, and pointing out the reasons to expect success. But the Dutch Generals refused to concur, in spite of the willingness on this occasion of their civilian Field Deputies. William Cadogan, the burly Irish giant in whose staff-work Marlborough confided, wrote of the Dutch that 'the resolution and vigour the Deputies show were enough to put their Generals out of countenance, if they were not equally incapable of shame and reason.'[280]

Aug. 24 (N.S.) 1703

Taking two years of experience together, the dominant fact of campaigning in the Netherlands was this, that the Dutch Generals would not let Marlborough fight. He wrote to his friend Heinsius that he would 'much sooner die' than fight another campaign under the same conditions, and that he 'had the spleen to a very great degree.' The anger of the English army spread to the home front. The High Tories found fresh fuel for their campaign against the Dutch alliance and fresh proof that the war on land was a waste of men and money. Among the Ministers, Nottingham, Seymour and Jersey were agreed that the English troops should leave the Netherlands. Marlborough was coming to the same opinion, but in a different sense. Might not his army instead of taking ship either for England or Spain, march southward along the Rhine on some enterprise of pith and moment?

As early as August 11, 1703, he wrote to Stepney at Vienna that the Dutch Generals were impossible, but that a campaign on the Moselle next year might yield better results. It would open a road into France not, like the Netherlands, studded thick with fortresses. Marlborough asked Stepney to see whether the Emperor would support his plan by representations at the Hague and elsewhere, so as to obtain for him ' a good body of troops to winter on the Moselle,' and take Trarbach and Trier, as a preliminary to a speedy opening there next spring. The desperate straits of Vienna would not permit this particular plan to materialize, but the idea of turning south, from co-operation with the Dutch to co-operation with the Austrians, held the seeds of the Blenheim campaign.[281]

The summer of 1703 nearly witnessed the fall of Vienna, and with it, as an inevitable consequence, the collapse of European resistance to the ' universal monarchy ' of Louis XIV. The instigator of the attempt was Villars, the greatest French soldier of the war. His gasconades, his hearty good-fellowship, his obvious enjoyment of life, his sudden tempers, his blunt utterances of the thought that was within him, endeared him to the French soldiery, but rendered him odious to prickly princes, formal courtiers and bigoted priests. He would have been more at home in the armies of the First Republic : Murat would have found him a man after his own heart, and Napoleon would have used him to the full. But in 1702, though fifty years old, Villars was still a General of lower rank. His victory that October over the German Princes at Friedlingen, near Basle, led to his elevation as Marshal of France. But since this honour was shared with a group of nonentities, he wrote to the Minister in no courtier's vein : ' I hear that his Majesty has just made ten Marshals. It would be more to the point if he had made ten generals fit to command.' [282]

However, after Friedlingen it was impossible to over-look the value of this rough diamond. That victory, won near the borders of Switzerland, rendered possible for the following year the junction of the French armies of Alsace with the Bavarians on the Danube. In 1703 Louis XIV entrusted to Villars the task of crossing the Rhine and the passes of the Black Forest, and joining the Elector of Bavaria for a stroke at the heart of the Empire. Not waiting for the usual season for operations to begin, Villars in the depth of winter seized Kehl, the bridge-head across the Rhine opposite to Strasburg. But even his ardent spirit felt the necessity of waiting till

Feb.
1703

near the end of April before attempting the difficult passage
of the Black Forest.*

The safe arrival of Villars and his army on the Upper
Danube early in May seemed to presage the speedy ter-
mination of the war in a blaze of glory for the Sun King.
On June 1st, one of his servants wrote to a Scottish nobleman bidding the Jacobites press the Government hard in
the Edinburgh Parliament, because the junction of Villars
with the Bavarians would enable France to bring the Dutch
to a separate peace and send help to Scotland.[283]   There
was consternation among the Princes of Germany at
Villars' arrival on the Danube.   The Diet of the Empire
was sitting hard by at Ratisbon for the express purpose
of declaring war on France.   The usual strife was going
on between the Catholic and Protestant parties in the
three Colleges of Electors, Princes and Towns ; the Protestants of the Diet appealed to Queen Anne, and she replied
' Her Majesty regards herself as the Chief of the Protestant
interest.'   A few weeks later Ratisbon was occupied by
Bavarian troops, and the Diet continued to sit under the
armed duresse of its enemies.[284]

The family, the Ministers and the subjects of the
Elector of Bavaria disliked the part that he was forcing
them to play.   They had no love for the French, who
plundered them and all other Germans without mercy.
The Bavarian peasants thought it hard to be exposed to the
miseries of war ' for the sake of the French whom they look
on as their natural enemies.'   De la Colonie, who was
serving in the Bavarian army, describes himself as ' a solitary
Frenchman in a regiment where it was customary for the
officers to hate all our nation,' against whom they had been
fighting all their lives.[285]   Yet so much stronger was the
instinct of obedience to the Prince than the still nascent
instincts of race and nationality, that from beginning to
end of the War of the Spanish Succession the fine Bavarian
army remained loyal to their Elector and his French friends,
throughout long years of disaster and exile.

The reason why Max Emanuel clung to the French cause

* For these Franco-Bavarian operations of 1703 *see Maps IX and X at end of
volume.* See also Marlborough's letter to Heinsius, May 24, 1703, in Appendix
A, below.

against the wishes of his servants and his subjects, was personal ambition to fill the Imperial throne in case of victory, and the assurance that, even if rebellion had bad luck upon the Danube, he could still look forward to a great career as Governor of the Spanish Netherlands. It never occurred to him as possible that Marlborough would conquer both Bavaria and Flanders.

In May 1703 all the omens were favourable to the Elector's ambition. He made Villars welcome as the saviour of his throne and family. But this warmth was little reciprocated. In the previous November, before ever he crossed the Rhine, the Frenchman had conceived a deep distrust of Max Emanuel's loyalty. Since the Elector never ceased to negotiate with the Allies even after he had drawn the sword for France, these suspicions were not unnatural ; but they were in fact unjust, as his subsequent conduct showed. The habit of negotiating secretly with one side while remaining essentially loyal to the other, was at that period common among the Princes of Europe, as well as among the statesmen of England.[286]

For a few weeks after Villars' arrival on the Danube, the appearance of harmony prevailed, for the Elector agreed at first to the French Marshal's daring plan of an immediate march on Vienna. Villars had been there in former years in a diplomatic capacity, and had noted the weakness of the defences. 'We can easily lodge ourselves on the counter-scarp the first day,' he wrote home to the King ; in his opinion it would be 'an affair of eight days' to take the capital of Austria. The siege cannon could come down the Danube, of which the fortresses were one after the other falling without resistance into Bavarian hands. The Hungarian rebels were already almost at the eastern gate of Vienna. Austria's Treasury was empty, and her armies on the Rhine and in Italy could not return in time. They could be held in play respectively by Tallard and Vendôme. Such was Villars' opinion of the situation at the beginning of June 1703. But Max Emanuel was not the man to put it to the touch ; and, according to Villars, he was surrounded by advisers who were at heart in the interest of the Emperor. After a short period of agreement with the bolder plan, he

changed his mind and carried off his army into Tirol, to
the intense disgust of the French Marshal, who was left
to guard the communications on the Danube against the
gathering hosts of Germany.

Even in his anger Villars confessed that the invasion of
Tirol was the next best plan to the immediate march on
Vienna. For what should stop the Bavarians from reaching
the Brenner Pass, and joining hands there with Vendôme
coming up from the plain of the Po ? They could return
together to join Villars on the Danube and resume the
march on Vienna, late indeed but in greater strength for
the reinforcements from Italy.[287]

Max Emanuel had, however, a political as well as a
military reason for thus turning aside into the Alps. He
would add Tirol to his Bavarian territories and so
June-July become possessor of the road between Germany and
1703   Italy, as befitted a Prince aspiring to the Imperial
Crown. He reached Innsbruck, where the townspeople
swore allegiance to him as their lord. The prospects seemed
so bright that Villars wrote him a merry letter asking for a
Duchy in Bohemia from the future Emperor.

Suddenly a blow fell from a quarter of which the conspirators had never dreamt. The loyalty of the mountain
peasantry of Tirol to the House of Hapsburg blazed up in
a flame, like that which Andreas Hofer kindled against
a similar invasion of the French and Bavarians in the time
of Napoleon. Max Emanuel's line of communications and
retreat lay along a single road that meandered through
perilous defiles. Their rocky sides were now occupied by
chamois hunters, the best cragsmen and shots in Europe.
In the last days of July the Bavarian army had to fly for
its life and was glad to win its way back to Munich without worse catastrophe than the loss of a few detachments,
who got little quarter.

The Elector had returned to Villars, but had not brought
the expected aid from Italy. In July Vendôme on the Po
had received orders from Louis to effect a junction with the
Bavarians by way of the Brenner Pass, ' and finish the war
by carrying it into the heart of the Empire.' The resistance
of Austria in Italy was almost negligible that year, for

Eugene had been recalled to Vienna to make head against the Hungarian rebels as best he could, short of money and short of men. But Vendôme wasted precious weeks round the Lake of Garda, partly because of rumours that the Duke of Savoy was about to join the Allies, as in fact he did two months later.* Vendôme's delay was fatal. In August the Bavarians lost all the remaining fortresses that they had garrisoned in Tirol, and it was no longer possible for a French army to pass from Italy to Germany athwart the resistance of the mountaineers.[288]

Though cut off from Italy, Villars and the Elector made good their position on the Danube. On September 20th they inflicted a severe defeat on the army of the German Princes near Hochstädt and Blenheim.† Thanks to the Tirolese diversion, the Empire had been reprieved for one campaign, but its prospects for the next year seemed desperate. In December 1703 the talk at the Austrian capital was that the Court would have to be carried to Gratz in Styria, while the French and Bavarians shook hands with the Hungarian rebels in the streets of Vienna.[289]

These expectations would have been realized if in 1704 Villars had been in Bavaria and Marlborough not. But in the winter the hot-tempered Villars finally quarrelled with the Elector and threw up his command of the French army of the Danube. He was succeeded by Marsin, a commander of talent greatly inferior in every respect except his ability to get on well with Max Emanuel. They were soon hand in glove, and their armies manœuvred as a single unit.

Meanwhile Louis sent Villars for the fighting season of 1704 to command the army of the Cevennes, engaged in the task of quelling the resistance of the 4000 Huguenot peasants—the Camisards as they were called—who were holding out against their persecutors in their native hills. Villars, a rational man, who would have been happier in the age of the Encyclopædists, saw the folly of this unnecessary civil war in the heart of France at the crisis of

---

* See pp. 305–307, above.

† The German army was drawn up behind the rivulet of Gremheim, about two miles to the east of the French position behind the Nebel in the battle of Blenheim next year: the pursuit passed over part of the ground of the later battle.

a foreign struggle. He had the boldness to offer the Camisard leaders terms and toleration. He thought he had stopped the war, but the bigots at Versailles repudiated the sensible arrangements he had made, and things went on much as before, until gradually the resistance of the Camisards was worn down. English promises of help often got through to them, but never the help itself.*

And so, during the campaign that turned the fortune of the war, Louis's one great soldier was removed from the decisive scene of affairs. Afterwards, on the Moselle in 1705, and at Malplaquet in 1709, Villars prevented Marlborough from breaking into France. If he had been opposed to him in 1704 on the banks of the Danube, it is not likely that any such complete victory as Blenheim would have been scored for the saving of the allied cause.

Prince Eugene of Savoy, thirteen years younger than Marlborough, was a French-speaking Savoyard Prince of Alpine blood, brought up at the Court of Louis XIV. As a lad not yet of age, he had dared to quarrel with the Grand Monarch for two reasons : first because Louis had harassed his father and mother with a long and vindictive persecution—so at least Eugene had been taught to think ; in the second place, because he had ordered Eugene himself to be a priest when he wished to be a soldier, and angrily refused to listen to the young man's expostulation. In his mania for arranging other people's lives, Louis refused to allow Eugene to be a soldier of France. He never did a worse day's work for the French army. It was not so easy to put the Alpine eaglet in a cage : Eugene escaped from Versailles to Vienna in order to pursue the profession of arms and to be avenged on Louis. Though more personal in its motives than the steady purpose of William III to thwart the same man, Eugene's determination to humble the Grand Monarch was neither less persistent nor less successful. Cold and ascetic in a profligate age, Eugene had a soul of fire for his profession ; without a country and

1663–1736

1682

* See p. 307, above, and note 276, below, on the Camisards, also Villars' *Mémoires* for 1704.

without wife or family, he pursued honour and fame with the zest of a young knight-errant, during a military career of fifty years.

The desperate danger of Vienna, due to the incompetence of Leopold and his lay and clerical advisers, at length forced them to entrust the fate of the Empire to Eugene. The obscurantists of the Imperial Court could no longer dispense with his hand on the helm. In the winter of 1703–1704 he was brought back from Italy and placed at the head of the War Office at Vienna as President of the Council of War, to reorganize the forces of Austria so far as her straitened means permitted. These means were eked out by English subsidies.

Marlborough and Eugene were not yet personally known to one another, except by reputation. But the world-wide fame of the Savoyard Prince, as the conqueror of the Turks, was one reason why the Englishman entertained the notion of staking his own and his country's fate on a plan which involved close co-operation with the Austrian army. As a colleague, Eugene would be as good as the Dutch Generals were bad. It would be useless for Marlborough merely to exchange Slangenberg for Lewis of Baden. But Eugene was now at the head of the military counsels of Vienna, and might next year himself take the field in Germany.

It is commonly said, and has been often repeated by English historians on insufficient evidence, that the plan for Marlborough's march to the Danube had been pre-arranged in correspondence between himself and Prince Eugene in the winter of 1703–1704, and that the project was for some time a secret between these two men. But their great friendship was the result, not the cause, of the Blenheim campaign. And if they corresponded during the preceding winter, their correspondence has not seen the light.

The method by which the great campaign was planned was somewhat different, more gradual and less dramatic. In so far as any one person persuaded Marlborough to bring the English army to Bavaria, it was not Eugene, but Wratislaw, the Emperor's able envoy in England. As early as October 1703, Eugene, Wratislaw and the Emperor were agreed in the desire that the Allies' chief effort in 1704 should be made in Bavaria. They knew the Dutch would be hostile to any such plan, and that the Imperial General on the Rhine, Lewis of Baden, would be lacking in the necessary initiative. Marlborough was their only hope, and Wratislaw laid personal siege to him all through the winter both in England and at the Hague.

Marlborough was from the first not unfavourable to such a plan, if indeed his own favourite scheme of invading France by the Moselle valley, which he had formed as early as August 1703,* had to be postponed owing to the more urgent danger to Vienna. Moreover, Marlborough was uncertain until the actual moment of action came in April 1704, whether or not it would be possible to elude the hostility of the Dutch Government to his departure with the army on such an enterprise. It is clear from Wratislaw's correspondence with the Emperor that the complicated argument on these issues went on all winter with varying fortunes, and that only at the last moment, at the beginning of April, had Marlborough finally made up his mind that the attempt must be made to carry his army at all hazards to the Danube.

The merit and the genius of Marlborough lay, not in conceiving the idea of the march to the Danube, an expedient so obvious that it was urged that winter, not only by Eugene and Wratislaw, but by the independent judgment of the Elector Palatine, ever zealous in the cause of the Empire. Marlborough's genius lay not in conceiving the plan, but in executing it. And his moral superiority appeared in assuming single-handed the responsibility of carrying his army into Central Europe without the leave of the States General or of more than two or three of his English colleagues. It was easy for the German soldiers and statesmen to ask him to come. It was another matter for him to consent to go, and to effect his most difficult departure.

* See pp. 316–317, above.

APPENDIX TO CHAPTER XV

The Origin of the Idea of the March to the Danube

ENGLISH historians, including such excellent modern biographers of Marlborough as Frank Taylor and Mr. Atkinson, have neglected the most important available evidence on the growth of Marlborough's plan, which is to be found in *Klopp*, XI, pp. 41–42, 91–112, and *Feldzüge*, pp. 50–58, based upon the Austrian archives, particularly on Wratislaw's letters to the Emperor.

But while accepting Wratislaw's account of his frequent conversations with Marlborough and of what Marlborough said on those occasions, we may still ask whether or not Eugene was all the while in correspondence with the Duke on the same subject. I think not. There is a remarkable absence of any indication of this in Eugene's, Marlborough's and Wratislaw's known correspondence. And it seems impossible to square with Wratislaw's accounts of what Marlborough said to him in January, February and March, the theory that the Duke had already made a separate agreement with Eugene to lead the English troops to the Danube. If he had, he or Eugene would surely have told Wratislaw ; for Wratislaw was perfectly in Eugene's confidence in the matter, and both were working together for that object.

The historian has, however, to take note of the following passage in Coxe's *Marlborough*, chap. 21 (ed. 1818, i, p. 234) :

Through the agency of Prince Eugene, with whom he had secretly arranged the whole campaign, he induced the Emperor to write a letter to the Queen, claiming assistance, etc. (*Letters from Eugene to Marlborough, in the Blenheim Papers* ; also *Vie du Prince Eugene*, t. 2, p. 156.)

This method of dealing with a subject so important is not worthy of the learned Archdeacon's usual documentary fullness and care. The *Vie du Prince Eugene* to which he refers is, I think, *Histoire du Prince Eugene*, 1741 (and 1777), Vienna, 5 volumes. In volume II of that work, pp. 145–146 (not 156), there is a letter purporting to be from Eugene to Marlborough asking him to come to recover Bavaria. It is in inverted commas but in *oratio obliqua*, and the authority for it is given as *Vita e campeggiamenti del Principe Eugenio* (Venice 1738). The letter is there, in the *Vita*, sure enough, but in Italian, in *oratio obliqua* and *not* in inverted commas ! It may possibly be based on some genuine original, but as the letter bears no date it throws no light on the question when and how Marlborough came to his decision. The letter is not to be found in the official Austrian collection of his correspondence and is apparently quite unknown to modern Austrian historians.

As to Coxe's vague reference to letters on the subject from Eugene to Marlborough in the Blenheim Papers, it is strange that the Archdeacon, who published so much, did not publish these. No such letters are to be found in his voluminous transcripts of the Blenheim Papers in the British Museum. They are not mentioned in the *Hist. MSS. Com.* Report on the Blenheim Papers. And I have reason to think they are not in Blenheim at all. But certainty on this point will be obtained when Mr. Winston Churchill produces his anxiously expected life of Marlborough. If he has found them at Blenheim, we shall know more. Meanwhile, I am sceptical as to the existence of these letters and as to Eugene's alleged part in persuading Marlborough to come to Bavaria, except indirectly through Wratislaw. Austrian historians know nothing about it, and so far the English historians have produced no evidence of it that bears scrutiny.

The letter of Marlborough to Heinsius of March $\frac{7}{18}$, 1704, which I have printed below, in Appendix A, so far as it goes, supports the idea that the Moselle was in the minds of Eugene and Marlborough as much as the Danube, even as late as the middle of March, and that there was still no fixed plan in Marlborough's mind until the end of that month.

The position of Vienna was certainly alarming enough in 1704 to call for direct assistance. On February 13, Whitworth wrote ' I must own we live at the discretion of the Hungarians as to the suburbs, where they may arrive with little opposition in twelve hours' time.' (*Add. MSS. St.* 7064, f. 130.) The only hope was the Treaty with the Hungarians which the English were perpetually pressing the Emperor to make. If such was the situation in February, before the French and Bavarian armies took the field on the Danube, what was likely to happen in the summer, unless help came from England and Holland!

CHAPTER XVI

IN 1702 it might well have been supposed that the new
reign and the new century in England were both to be
dominated by the Tory Party and the ideals for which it
stood in Church and State. Queen Anne was of that
inclining, and so were the majority of her subjects. Marlborough was prepared to win the world war and lay its
laurels at the feet of his royal mistress and his Tory colleagues. The more distant future, too, was secure, if the
siren lures of Jacobitism could be avoided and the voices
from the past forgotten ; for the House of Hanover was
as yet no more inclined to the Whigs than to the Tories,
who had passed the Act of Settlement in 1701. The long
period of quiet national growth and Hanoverian stability
which we associate with Walpole and the Whigs might
have been associated with the Tories, if, in Anne's reign,
they had held together as a united party in support of their
Queen and their General. All that was asked of them was
to acquiesce, for the duration of the war, in a system of
toleration and moderate measures at home. That system
was implied by the Revolution in which they had taken part
and the Act of Settlement which they had so recently voted.
But the High Tories could not accept these conditions.
They wished to restore the atmosphere of ' good King
Charles's golden days,' to give Whigs and Dissenters the

bad time that was their due, and to ignore the Revolution while enjoying its benefits. If Marlborough would not help them to realize these ideals, so much the worse for Marlborough and his war. If the House of Hanover would not help them, so much the worse for the House of Hanover and its chances of succession.

On these issues, as well as on the personal rivalry of great noblemen, the party split in two, once in 1704, and again, yet more fatally, in 1714. In both these years of decision the schism between High and Moderate Tories was as broad as the difference between Tory and Whig. The political history of the Queen's reign cannot be understood merely in the terms of controversy between the two historic parties.

It was the custom under the good Queen Anne, as soon as the armies of Europe went into winter quarters, for the politicians to meet at Westminster for their annual wrangle. The session was usually over by the end of March, and, if the Government survived so long, Marlborough could then go back to the war with the confidence that Parliament would not meet again till October, and that Godolphin's Ministry was safe for another summer and would support him through another campaign. If Parliament had sat while the armies were in the field, the burden of carrying on the war under such conditions of insecurity at home might have been too much even for Marlborough's iron nerves. In particular, if it had been sitting in May 1704 he could hardly have ventured to steal the British army and run away with it to the Danube.

The session of November 1703 to March 1704 was one of the stormiest of the reign, because the Tory Party was in process of splitting in two, with the fierce mutual reproaches usual on such occasions. Swift, who was in London on one of his visits from Ireland, watched the heats of that winter with detachment, though still calling himself a Whig and even writing in secret against the Occasional Conformity Bill a pamphlet which he did not publish :

I observed the very dogs in the streets much more contumelious and quarrelsome than usual ; and the very night before the bill went up, a committee of Whig and Tory cats had a very loud and warm debate upon the roof of our house.   But why should we wonder at that, when the very ladies are split asunder into High Church and Low, and out of zeal for religion have hardly time to say their prayers ?   To cool your insolence a little [he wrote to a Tory friend] know that the Queen and Court, and House of Lords and half the Commons almost, are Whigs ;   and the number daily increases.[290]

The 'Queen and Court' were not Whigs, but Swift calls them so because they were in process of quarrelling with the High Tories.

Already, before Parliament met in November, the position of Nottingham, Jersey and Seymour in the same war ministry with Marlborough had become almost impossible.   In August, when it was rumoured that Prince Eugene was about to visit England, Jersey had written to Nottingham :

1703

> I cannot look upon this Prince's journey hither any otherwise than as a contrivance of Comte Wratislaw with his friends the Whigs to extort subsidies which I fear this nation cannot bear.

Jersey was a Jacobite at heart, but even Nottingham was declaring for a 'defensive' system of warfare.   In October he took 2000 English troops from the Netherlands and sent them to his favourite seat of war in the Peninsula, without the knowledge of Marlborough and to his subsequent great indignation.   When Parliament met in November, Marlborough's secretary and personal friend, Cardonnel, wrote that the voting of supplies for war was ' like to go on very well,' and that ' Sir Edward Seymour and his gang are the only people to make bustle.   The Duke of Marlborough and he are quite out.'   So much indeed were they ' out ' that in June the Duke had written to Sarah :   ' We are bound not to wish for anybody's death, but should Sir Edward Seymour die it would be no great loss to the Queen nor the nation.'

Sarah, as a good Whig, urged him to turn to her political friends.   But Marlborough still thought, like the Queen, that ' either of the parties would be tyrants if they were let alone,' and preferred to be ' governed by neither party, but do what I think best for England, by which I shall disoblige both parties.'

I do own a great deal of what you say is right, but I can by no means allow that all the Tory party are for King James, and consequently against the Queen : but the contrary, I think it is in her power to make use of almost all, but some of the heads, and to the true interest of England.

Unfortunately, 'some of the heads' were his ministerial colleagues.[291]

The touchstone of party was still the Occasional Conformity Bill,* which loomed larger in the minds of many politicians than the approaching crisis of England's twenty years' struggle with France. In the middle of December the Commons passed it again by a large majority. John Verney, knight of the shire for Leicester, wrote :

We carried up our Bill to-day in great state to the Lords. I believe we were 200 that attended it. But all the bustle we have made about it had no effect. The Bishops, I hear, divided, against it 14, for it 9. The Prince [George] was not there.

The debate in the Lords went more openly against the principle of the Occasional Conformity Bill than last winter. Bishop Burnet took the lead in opposition, again expounding the Dissenters' point of view as he had learnt it from Calamy's coaching. Lord Mohun, who was endeavouring in these years to live down his reputation as a murderous brawler and rake and to blossom out as a Whig statesman, 'did not stick to say that if they passed this Bill they had as good tack the pretended Prince of Wales to it.' This year the Lords felt strong enough to reject the Bill on second reading by 71 to 59. Anne had withdrawn from it her active support. Her husband was allowed to absent himself. The Queen's Speech had contained a significant sentence against 'heats or divisions' and in favour of 'perfect peace and union' in face of the national enemy—phrases that were a signal to placemen in the Lords. This new wartime

Dec. 14 (O.S.) 1703

* See pp. 277-283, above.

doctrine of the Queen's was preached by the Tory pamphleteer Davenant : his latest pamphlet, *Peace at Home and
War Abroad* condemned the Bill as inexpedient, and
preached the comfortable doctrine that the Dissenters
were less powerful, less zealous and less united as a result
of toleration. The tide had turned against the zeal of High
Church, and continued to ebb for several years to come.

Marlborough and Godolphin, indeed, voted for the Bill
and even carried hypocrisy so far as to enter their ' protests '
in the Journals of the House against the rejection. For
Marlborough had written to Sarah :

> I must be careful not to do the thing in the world which my
> Lord Rochester would most desire to have me do, which is to give
> my vote against this bill. But I do most solemnly promise that I will
> speak to nobody living to be for it.

But these shifts did not save Marlborough and Godolphin
any more than Davenant from the fury of the baffled High
Churchmen. Nor did they spare the Queen herself, who
had bitterly disappointed them. A popular satire of the
year treats of their grievances against her :

> And yet the Whigs vote for the Queen
>   More heartily than we do ;
> And is not this as sad a thing
>   As any man can see to ?
> We thought when their Dutch king was dead
>   We should have leave to smite 'em,
> But now our hands are so tied up
>   We cannot gibeonite 'em.
> Thus sorrowfully must we sing
>   Or mournfully may say—
> Our Queen is so much like their King,
>   Alack and well-a-day.[292]

During the remainder of the session, both before and
after Christmas, the anger of the High Tories expressed
itself in a number of Parliamentary moves, some of which
were voted down by a combination of Whigs and governmental Tories in the Commons, and others vetoed by the
Lords, bolder than last year in their Whiggery in spite of
the recent creations of Tory Peers.* The Recruiting Act,

* See p. 277, above.

which enabled Justices of the Peace forcibly to enlist the unemployed,* was opposed by the Seymour group in the Commons as contrary to the liberties of Englishmen, but was carried through both Houses to Marlborough's great relief. The increased estimates for the year were also accepted and honoured. And a dangerous project, favoured by Nottingham and Seymour, for 'tacking' the Occasional Conformity Bill to Supply was postponed till the following autumn. The increase in the numbers of the army was voted, amid murmurs that would have become an uproar if Seymour and his friends had dreamt that it was to be taken to the Danube. The usual attack and defence of Ministers past and present added the spice of personality to party heats. The Whigs attacked Nottingham for the alleged sheltering of Jacobite spies. The High Tories continued the attack on Orford for alleged malversation in the late reign, and the Lords finally exonerated him. Above all, the famous case of Ashby v. White arose out of an electioneering squabble in Aylesbury, a borough of Wharton's, and led to one of the most noisy constitutional controversies that ever brought the two Houses of Parliament into collision.† On these troubled waters Queen Anne

Feb.
1704

poured the oil of her Bounty‡ to the poor clergy, in hopes that it would avert from herself and her Ministers some at least of the indignation of the Church that she loved so well and yet so wisely.[293]

While such matters were occupying the minds of English public men almost to the exclusion of the crisis in Europe, Marlborough was secretly and slowly coming to his great decision. The determination to carry the English army to Bavaria did not spring from his head like Pallas fully armed, nor was it posted to him in a letter from Eugene. It was not made, but grew. Gradually and with many hesitations, as a result of many discussions of other plans with Dutch, Germans and English, under the pressure

* See p. 219, above.
† I shall tell the story of *Ashby* v. *White* in the next volume, as it came to its crisis in the session of 1704–1705.
‡ See pp. 47–48, above, for Queen Anne's Bounty.

of Wratislaw's ceaseless iteration that Vienna, if unaided, would fall in the spring, he came to admit the necessity of substituting the Danube as his field of action for his own favourite idea of an invasion of France through the Moselle valley.   But the Moselle scheme continued to serve in public as a blind to the Dutch, to the French and to the world at large.   For the concentration of troops and stores along the Rhine as far south as Coblentz pointed to the Moselle, yet would serve equally well for a march on the Danube.   It is therefore difficult to determine the precise week when the Moselle ceased to be Marlborough's real objective, while continuing to be paraded as his professed goal.   From the evidence we have, it would seem that as early as January he contemplated the likelihood of going to the Danube, but that until April he felt no certainty of being able to overcome the opposition of the Dutch.

In the middle of January, amid the peril and discomfort of winter storms that delayed other passengers, he crossed to the Hague, and there in the course of the next month divulged the Moselle plan, as a secret, to the Dutch Government.   The States-General took objection even to that not very distant removal of Marlborough's army from their frontier.   But Heinsius again came to the rescue and eventually secured their acquiescence. At the same time Holland and England made arrangements to assist the German Princes with men and money to save the Empire.   But nothing as yet was said to any Dutch statesman about the English going to the Danube.

Jan.-Feb.
1704

During this February visit to the Hague, Marlborough wrote to the Duchess in a mood of despondency, not at all like a man with a great design ready formed, which he is certain of being allowed to attempt.

For this campaign I see so very ill a prospect that I am extremely out of heart.   But God's will be done.   In all the other campaigns I had an opinion of being able to do something for the common cause ; but in this I have no other hopes than that some lucky accident may enable me to do good.[294]

After the Duke's return to England towards the close of February, Wratislaw renewed his representations of the certainty of the fall of Vienna unless something more drastic was done in the Danube valley. It seems to have been in the course of the month of March that Marlborough finally decided that it was necessary that he himself should carry relief to the tottering Empire, at every military and diplomatic risk. To the last he feared that the Dutch, if thus deserted, would make a separate peace with France. But Wratislaw argued that the States-General, however frightened or angry they might be, could not withdraw from the war till the following winter, and that if, meanwhile, the Empire were saved in the summer and Bavaria conquered, the Dutch would again take heart of grace. Marlborough pointed out that the Dutch would not in any case let him take their siege-train to the Danube, and Wratislaw promised that the Princes of the Empire would supply him with siege cannon if he would bring powder enough, and, of course, his own field artillery. This arrangement was actually carried out. By the first days of April the march to the Danube had been arranged between Marlborough and Wratislaw. As part of the plan, the Emperor was to be pressed to release Prince Eugene from his duties at the War Office, and to send him to take the field in Germany as the colleague of Marlborough and of the Imperial Lieutenant-General, Lewis of Baden. On account of his hereditary position and territories on the Rhine, it was impossible to deprive that jealous and incapable Prince of the right to play the part of Lepidus in the triumvirate that was to save the Empire.[295]

For the present, the secret was kept between Marlborough, Wratislaw, the Emperor and Prince Eugene. Presumably the Queen and Godolphin knew that he was going to take the English troops wherever it was necessary to save the Empire, but there is no proof that they yet knew he was going as far as the Danube. And it is certain that Sarah did not yet know. The Moselle would serve excellently to cover the early operations of the campaign. For many reasons secrecy must be observed to the last possible moment. If the French Generals on the Rhine suspected that Marlborough was going to Bavaria by a flank march across their front, they could move forward across his path, or get to Bavaria before him. If the Dutch knew whither he was bound, they would veto the project as regards all the allied troops in their pay. If Marlborough's own colleagues, Nottingham and Seymour, knew, they would raise wild alarm at home. But the Queen and Godolphin were staunch. Anne graciously received and graciously answered Wratislaw's Memorandum on the desperate straits of the Empire ; in her reply she commissioned Marlborough, in concert with the States-General, ' to send a speedy succour to His Imperial Majesty and the Empire.' What the nature of this succour was to be was not stated in her letter ; she left that to the servant in whom she trusted.[296]

Apr. 2
(O.S.)
1704

Next week Marlborough sailed from Harwich on his great adventure. He was far from easy as to the position that he left behind him at home, and on his last evening ashore he wrote to Godolphin complaining that Nottingham was bitterly hostile to them both, that he was in favour of tacking the Occasional Conformity Bill to Supply, and that he was ' doing Her Majesty all the hurt that he is capable of.' In the weeks that followed, the quarrel in the Cabinet came to a head, and the Queen had to make her choice between the High and the Moderate sections of the Tory Party. The crisis was not precipitated by Godolphin, who was far from certain of his position, especially with the Duke oversea. Nottingham made the first move by demanding the dismissal of the two moderate Whig peers, Devonshire and Somerset, from the Privy Council. Anne refused. Nottingham thereupon proffered his own resignation. The Queen, though very angry with her old friend and fellow-churchman, was loath to part with him. But at the instigation of Harley, Godolphin and Sarah she dismissed Jersey and Seymour, whom she had come to dislike. In the end she had to let Nottingham go as well.*

Apr. 8
(O.S.)
1704

For some years to come the dark, tall, melancholy figure of this honest but opinionated man remained in the back-

* The crisis went on confusedly for some weeks, and it is difficult to put an exact date to it. As early as April 22 Hedges writes officially to Ellis : ' A Cabinet must be summoned to attend the Queen to-morrow, and all are to be summoned as usual, except the Lords Jersey, Nottingham and Sir Edward Seymour.' (Add.

ground of English politics.   Nottingham had been known as ' Dismal ' in the world of cheerful reprobates among whom his political life was passed.   He had served England faithfully in times very difficult for a man of nice conscience, first under Queen Mary and then under Queen Anne.   The elder sister, in deep distress of mind amid servants of doubtful loyalty, wrote to her William, absent at the Boyne :

> Lord Nottingham appears to be sincere, though he does not take much pains to persuade me of it on all occasions, as others do, for he never spoke but once of himself.   Yet I confess I incline to have a good opinion of him.   It may be his formal, grave look deceives me.   He brought me your letter yesterday, and I could not hold, so he saw me cry, which I have hindered myself from before anybody till then.

After 1704 Nottingham never again held a dominant position in any government, though he once again held high office.   His room was taken by younger men of suppler mould, like Harley and St. John, to whom ' Church principles ' in politics were not a matter of religious conviction, but a force to be evoked or withdrawn as suited best the needs of national welfare or personal ambition.

It did not occur to Queen Anne that because she had quarrelled with some of her High Tory servants she must, therefore, call in their Whig rivals.   The places of the fallen ministers were taken by Moderates of their own party. And a few High Tories still remained in office, like Wright and the Duke of Buckingham.*   The Godolphin Ministry was reconstituted to support Marlborough in carrying succour to the Empire, but, unlike many war ministries in our history, it did not rest on a ' broad bottom.' It stood on the narrow middle way of Moderate Toryism. Its strength was that it represented the national feeling of the moment ;   its weakness that most of the politicians were against it.   The Whig and High Tory leaders were

---

MSS. (E.) 28895, f. 316).   Yet Nottingham's final resignation is said not to have taken place till May 18. (*Coxe*, Chap. XX, I, pp. 229–230 ; *Feiling*, pp. 373–374.)

As regards Nottingham's character as a man and a gentleman, the terrible accusation made against him by Defoe to Harley in 1704 (*H.M.C. Portland*, IV, p. 88) ought not, I think, to be believed, in view of his general reputation, without other evidence.

* See Appendix B, below, the Godolphin Ministry.

angry at being out in the cold, and only the happy circumstance that the Houses would not meet again till autumn concealed the narrow basis of Parliamentary support on which the Queen's Government now stood.

Feeble attempts to placate the High Tories by dismissing Whig magistrates continued throughout the critical summer of 1704. In June Harley wrote to the party managers in Westmorland that orders had been given to Lord Keeper Wright 'to remove Fleming,' the Whig Squire of Rydal Hall, from the bench. After announcing this sop, Harley adds, apologetically, that the Duke's march into Germany is the only thing to save the Empire. But these tactics failed to appease the High Tories and infuriated the Whigs, who could not see why they should still be excluded from all share of power, since the Cabinet would next session depend upon their votes. The High Churchmen, led by Rochester and Seymour, declaimed against the waste of English blood and treasure in the cruel wars in High Germany, and threatened the impeachment of Marlborough.[297] Like much else then at hazard in England and in Europe, the Godolphin Ministry could only be saved by a great victory on the shores of the Danube.*

In the extrusion of the High Tory chiefs and the reconstruction of the Government, the Speaker, Robert Harley, had been scarcely less instrumental than in the still greater change in the opposite direction which he conducted six years later. Both in 1704 and in 1710 Harley was guided by a correct sense of the needs and wishes of the country and of the Queen, and on both occasions he worked by his usual method of secret whisperings in the lobby and the back-stairs.

In the reconstructed Ministry the gaps were filled up by Harley and the Tories he brought with him, sworn first

---

* A popular ballad-monger next winter expressed the situation in simple terms :

> The Duke the Victory did obtain,
> Or else h'had got a Tartar.
> If he had been beaten back again
> Perhaps he had been shorter.

that is, by his head. (*Poems on Affairs of State* (ed. 1707), IV, p. 120.)

and foremost to win the war, prepared therefore to be profuse in protestations of devotion to Sarah and her lord, and
not to resent some measure of political understanding with
the Whigs.   Harley himself became one of the two
Secretaries of State : since the other was still the serviceable
and unpretentious Hedges, Harley took Nottingham's place
as the leading Minister for home and foreign affairs, under
Godolphin's general control.   He retained the Speakership
as well until the dissolution of 1705.

The new Secretary of State was more active than most
who held that office in seeking information as to the political
opinion in the provinces, and in devising means to influence
that opinion through journalism.   Perhaps because he himself was so little of an orator in Parliament, Harley realized
sooner than any of his colleagues or rivals the relation
of public opinion to political power in post-Revolution
England.   It was not only the Queen, but her subjects
whom he approached by the back-stairs.   He found the
observer, agent and journalist he wanted in Daniel Defoe,
a man of shifty and secret ways like himself, of moderate
views and kindly nature like himself, like himself of Puritan
upbringing, but with a style of writing as lucid and telling
as Harley's was slovenly and confused.

Defoe had not stayed long in the prison where his
Shortest way with the Dissenters had sent him.*   Before the
end of 1703 Harley and Godolphin had effected his release.
And Harley now employed him to travel round England
and report.   Moving about under an assumed name, he
communicated with the Secretary of State by stealth.
Defoe was still so unpopular with all parties in Church and
State that Harley dared not own him in public.   Moreover,
both men loved mystery for its own sake.   Defoe became
Harley's Man Friday, and remained so for long years to
come, through many changes of men and measures.   As
early as 1704 he was writing to his master to urge him to
make the Secretaryship of State a ' Prime Ministry without
a grievance,' by reforming the lax methods of the office, by
courting popularity with all men, by cultivating the middle

* See pp. 281–283, above.   On the date of Defoe's release, see *Times Lit. Supp.*,
January 26, 1928.

classes, and by protecting the Dissenters. More precise were the reports sent in by Defoe of the political conduct of local magistrates. He showed that in case after case the High Tory Justices of the Peace, whom Wright had appointed in such numbers, were actively working against the Queen's Government, and undermining its position with a view to the next General Election. On the other hand, magistrates more Whiggishly inclined supported the war and the Ministers who waged it. These reports must have helped to draw Harley still further away from his old political connections.

But although Defoe's real name and employer were concealed, it was obvious, wherever he went, that he had some political business in hand and that he openly consorted with Dissenters. He was suspect to the high-flying magistrates in ' Seymour's Western Empire ' of Devon and Cornwall, who threatened to enlist him under the new Recruiting Act as an unemployed rogue ; he was forced sometimes to protect himself with Harley's ' pass.'

Nor was Defoe less diligent to serve his patron in the capacity of journalist. He preached the cause of national unity to win the war, in his able *Review*, appearing three times a week, which he wrote single-handed including the ' correspondence.' While the ordinary newspapers gave news with little comment, the *Review* was profuse in comment with little news. For some years its only rivals in this field were its ally the Whig *Observator* and its enemy the *Rehearsal*, conducted on High Tory lines by the Jacobite Charles Leslie. Of the three, the *Review* was the most moderate in tone and became the most influential. It was only towards the end of the Queen's reign that Swift, Steele and Addison, with their *Examiners*, *Tatlers* and *Spectators*, imitated and surpassed the example of Defoe.[298]

Meanwhile, the vacant places in the reconstructed Ministry were filled up by men of the new Secretary's choosing. Seymour was replaced by Thomas Mansell, a dependent of Harley's, a wealthy and popular Welsh squire. And Harley's friend, St. John, became Secretary at War.*

* See Appendix B, below, the Godolphin Ministry.

Henry St. John had run up his price in the political market by serving as the brilliant spokesman of inarticulate High Tory squires, accustomed heretofore to the old-fashioned ponderosities of Seymour. It is easy to understand why Disraeli felt a special interest in his career. The young deist was in truth no fanatic, and was well able to curb his High Church zeal at the call of patriotism or ambition. In May 1704 both motives appealed to him to change his part, to leave his rustic friends grumbling on the back benches while he pushed his own and his country's fortunes. He became Marlborough's faithful and efficient servant at the War Office. He was twenty-five years of age with the world before him ; his wit, his personal beauty and charm and his rare ability endeared him to the Duke. Two such brilliant men never before or since controlled the military forces of England. If Bolingbroke was to prove the Peterborough of politics rather than the Marlborough, that was still hid in the future. For the present he was content to feed politically out of the hand of his friend Harley, whom he afterwards learnt to hate and despise ; while towards Marlborough the young man felt a hero-worship which future events never wholly extinguished in his mind. More than thirty years later, Bolingbroke wrote of the chieftain he had once broken and exiled :

I take with pleasure this opportunity of doing justice to that great man, whose faults I knew, whose virtues I admired ; and whose memory, as the greatest general and as the greatest minister that our country or perhaps any other has produced, I honor.[299]

CHAPTER XVII

Gloomy prospects of the alliance in the Spring of 1704. Marlborough's march to the Danube. Storming of the Schellenberg. Occupation and devastation of Bavaria. Arrival of Tallard and Eugene: the lists set.

THE success of England and her allies in the War of the Spanish Succession, which curbed 'the exorbitant power of France' for eighty years to come, influenced the whole tone of Eighteenth Century civilization in a thousand ways. The defeat of Louis is one of the most prominent facts in history. We are, therefore, apt to forget how very near he came to attaining world-power, by the retention of the whole Spanish Empire as a field of French influence, and by the virtual annexation of the Netherlands and of Italy as jewels in the French Crown. He was never nearer to success than in the spring of 1704. Nothing but the accident of Marlborough's genius, and some lucky turns of fortune in the field that year, diverted the paths of destiny.

If Marlborough had not gone to the Danube, it is likely that the French and Bavarian armies, aided by the Hungarian insurgents, would have taken Vienna, as they had so nearly done the year before. Possibly, owing to the absence of Villars and the presence of Eugene, Vienna would again, in 1704, have escaped capture. But even so, after another inconclusive campaign, the liberation of Europe from French predominance would still have been as far from realization as on the day when the sword had first been drawn. Not to win meant, for the Allies, to be beaten. The Treaty of Grand Alliance had rightly defined the issues of the war : it would be lost if the French remained in Italy or in the Netherlands.* Yet, after two

* See p. 146, above.

years' fighting, they were not only still in the Netherlands, and still in Italy, but in Bavaria as well.

In Italy, it is true, the Allies had gained one advantage ; Savoy had passed over to their side.   But Eugene had been recalled from the valley of the Po to save Vienna, and the English Minister at Turin expected that Victor Amadeus would shortly be deposed or forced to change sides once more.*   In the neighbourhood of the Netherlands, Marlborough had, in his first campaign, won back the Bishoprics of Cologne and Liège, which the French had occupied two months after the Treaty of Grand Alliance had been signed. But he had made no headway at all towards the recovery of the Spanish Netherlands themselves.   Worst of all, he had no prospect of doing so, for on half a dozen several occasions the Dutch had prohibited him from fighting a battle.   The march to the Danube was not merely an expedition to rescue Vienna and conquer Bavaria ; it was also the way chosen by Marlborough to escape from the tutelage of his enemies among the Dutch Generals, and so recover freedom to stake the issue of the war on the wager of battle.   He knew that, unless something great were done, discouragement and war-weariness would presently dissolve the Alliance.   He knew that his time was short, unless he could change the whole atmosphere of the war and set the expectations of friend and foe running in new channels.

Time was on the side of France if the Allies failed to strike an effective blow.   A defensive war would serve the purposes of Louis, who had the prize already in his possession.   Spain could not desert France.   And Louis, though severely feeling the financial strain, was sole master of all the resources of his own kingdom.   But Marlborough was dependent on the temper of Parliament and of the English people, Heinsius on the States-General and Dutch opinion, the Empire on the humours of a dozen Princes, any one of whom might refuse again to hire out his troops for another year.   Already in May 1703 Marlborough had written, with more truth than grammar, ' you see how little the Empire dose for themselves.'   England and Holland paid for almost all that was done.   And already the Dutch were

* See p. 307, above.

crying out under the burden : in November 1703 Heinsius wrote to Bentinck that the gallant little Republic had to borrow money at high interest, and even to pay interest on interest, for every new war expenditure or subsidy to the Allies, whereas the more fortunate English were still able to establish funds based on taxation to meet and partially extinguish any new borrowings.[300]   Only success could keep the Alliance much longer in being, and in the year 1703 there had been no military success at all.   While the Diet at Ratisbon sat under the guard of Franco-Bavarian bayonets, the thought was spreading in the circles of the Empire that the war was already lost.

The domestic crisis in England at the moment of Marlborough's departure had, indeed, brought into office an able and united war ministry of Moderate Tories. But they had no majority of their own in the House of Commons, and would fall as soon as the Houses met in the autumn, unless, before the time for Parliamentary reckoning arrived, Marlborough had achieved a success sufficient to dazzle the Whigs and the multitude, and to stop the mouths of the High Tory opposition.   Meanwhile, Scotland was threatening England with invasion and civil war.   A few days before the news of Blenheim reached our distracted island, the Scots Parliament extorted England's surrender ; Queen Anne unwillingly consented to sign the Act of Security, a measure abhorred of all men south of the Border except those few who were more Jacobites than Englishmen.*   The hold of the reconstructed Godolphin Ministry on Britain was feeble indeed, more like that of the drowning sailor on the spar he has clutched, than of the pilot's hand on the rudder.   And so things drifted on all summer, until that happy day in August, when the tidings burst on London that Marshal Tallard was a prisoner in the Duke's coach.†

April–
May
1704

---

* This and other Scottish matters will be treated together fully in the next volume.

† Chatham's redoubtable grandfather, Governor Pitt, wrote from Madras in September 1704 : ' I like not the face of our public affairs abroad or at home. God send a miracle to save old England at last.' A month before he wrote this at the other side of the world, his prayer had been answered on the shores of the Danube. *H.M.C. Dropmore* (1892), I, p. 12.

On the April evening when Marlborough reached the Hague, the trees were putting on their spring green around the Vyver and in the Bosch, and the diplomats and generals of half Europe were patrolling those pleasant alleys in eager dispute as to the plans of the coming campaign.   The Duke came from England accompanied by Austrian Wratislaw, with whom he was now in secret conspiracy to bring about an English campaign on the Danube.   It would be necessary for Marlborough to take with him to Bavaria not only Her Majesty's forces, native and foreign, but a number of regiments in the pay of the States-General.

April $\frac{10}{21}$
1704

But how was this to be done ?   Merely to mention the word ' Danube ' to the States-General would have provoked an angry refusal, besides letting the whole world, including the French Marshals, into the secret.   When the Duke first arrived at the Hague, the Dutch were so far from contemplating the reconquest of Bavaria that they were calling back from South Germany some foreign regiments in their pay, in spite of loud remonstrances from the Princes of the Empire.   The first struggle was to induce the States-General to leave those troops in their southern stations.

After an initial victory on that point, came the real tug-of-war ;   Marlborough asked leave of the Dutch to go himself on the Moselle campaign.   He had adumbrated the plan during his visit to the Hague in February.*   But now, in April, the Moselle had become, in his own mind, merely a ruse to deceive friend and foe, a half-way house to the Danube.   Writing from the Hague on April 29 (N.S.) he explained his real intentions to Godolphin, who was now, perhaps for the first time, let into the full secret :

By the next post I shall be able to let you know what resolutions I shall bring these people to ; for I have told them I will leave this place on Saturday.   My intentions are to march all the English to Coblentz, and to declare here that I intend to command on the Moselle.   But when I come there to write to the States that I think it absolutely necessary, for the saving of the Empire, to march with the troops under my command and to join those in Germany that are in Her Majesty's and the Dutch pay, in order to take measures

* See p. 333, above.

with Prince Lewis for the speedy reducing of the Elector of Bavaria.
. . . What I now write I beg may be known to nobody but Her
Majesty and the Prince.*

Even Sarah was still left in the dark.   The day before,
he had written to her :

I am hagged out of my life, so that I long extremely for Monday,
when I intend to leave this place. . . . I shall go myself to Coblentz,
to take care that the cannon and other things that are there may be
forthwith sent to Treves.

But it was not for Treves on the Moselle that the
'cannon and other things' were destined.   Possibly the
Duke took the view of Shakespeare's *Brutus* as to the
chances of a great secret remaining hid with even the most
devoted of wives.   Some difference—political perhaps—had
clouded his domestic bliss at the moment he left England,
but Sarah was now kind again, and even wrote proposing
to follow him to the field.

You will see [he replied on May 5], that what you desire is
impossible, for I am going up into Germany, where it would be
impossible for you to follow me.   But love me as you now do and
no hurt can come to me.   You have, by this kindness, preserved
my quiet, and I believe my life ; for till I had this letter, I have been
very indifferent of what should become of myself.   I have pressed
this business of going up into Germany in order to leave a good name
behind me, wishing for nothing but success.   I shall now add, that
of having a long life, that I may be happy with you. . . . I do this
minute love you better than ever I did before.

Against the proposal of Marlborough to go himself
with the main force as far as the Moselle, the States-General
put up a strong resistance.   Their plan of campaign was
that only 15,000 men should be sent to the Moselle, while
the rest of the English and Dutch armies stayed under
Marlborough to guard Holland.   The representatives of
Zeeland loudly opposed his departure for Coblentz, lest
their province should be exposed to invasion.

At length the patient Duke saw that the moment had

* Viz. the Prince Consort.   *For this chapter see Map IX at end of the volume.*

come to force the issue. He announced to the Dutch
May 1–2 Government his positive intentions of marching to
(N.S.) Coblentz with all the troops in Her Majesty's pay,
1704 with or without the consent and aid of his allies.

I am very sensible [he wrote to Godolphin], that I take a great
deal upon me. But should I act otherwise the Empire would be
undone and consequently the confederacy. . . . If the French
shall have joined any more troops to the Elector of Bavaria, I shall
make no difficulty of marching to the Danube.

The announcement that he was going to Coblentz, with
or without their aid, had an excellent effect on the Dutch.
Heinsius had been working on his behalf all this while, and
now carried the day. The States-General not only sub-
mitted to Marlborough's decision, but allowed him to carry
off many of their troops, under Generals such as Goor who
were his personal friends, and would help and not hinder
his plans. And when, a few weeks later, the States found
he had deceived them and was bound not for the Moselle
but for the Danube, they made little remonstrance, and
never dreamt of recalling the army he had obtained under
false pretences. It is true that by that time their fears had
been calmed by the fulfilment of a prophecy he had made :
he had told them that, as soon as he marched south, large
French armies would leave the Netherlands to follow him
—and it was so. But English historians should acknowledge
that, in the decisive year of the war, the conduct of the
Dutch towards Marlborough and the common cause was,
from the first week of May onwards, both wise and
magnanimous.

Meanwhile, Wratislaw was bombarding the authorities
at Vienna with impassioned appeals to initiate at the other
end of Europe the movements that were to meet the deliverer
of the Empire half way. Marlborough would not go, unless
Prince Lewis of Baden, the Imperial General on the Rhine,
agreed to the plan of operations on the Danube. With
some difficulty his consent was won by pressure from
Vienna. But those who knew Prince Lewis best, trusted
him least as a colleague in a great crisis. Wratislaw
insisted that Eugene must be liberated from the Vienna
War Office, and sent to take the field at the head of the other

army of the Empire, with a commission superior, in case of
need, to that held by Prince Lewis. This also the Emperor
Leopold granted in the middle of May, speaking of it as
a heavy sacrifice, made in grateful recognition of Marlborough's efforts to save the House of Hapsburg. One of
Wratislaw's letters to the Emperor that month throws light
on the thoughts and temper of the Duke, as well as on those
of the writer :

> I once more beseech Your Majesty, in God's name, not to lose
> a moment of time, for the execution of these plans depends on time,
> and on their execution depends the survival of your house. Marl-
> borough, who has come in while I write these lines, assures Your
> Majesty that he and his whole army will march into the Empire,
> resolved to sacrifice their lives or overpower the Elector, for if this
> does not happen he will be lost both in England and Holland for ever.
> But if he sees Your Majesty is not in earnest to beat the Elector, he
> will be obliged to retire at once with his troops.[301]

Owing to his successes in the campaigns of 1702–3,
Marlborough now enjoyed the free use of the Maas valley
below Namur, and of the Rhine valley as far up as its
junction with the Neckar. Otherwise he could hardly have
ventured on the dangerous operation of carrying his army
from the borders of Holland to the neighbourhood of
Mannheim and Heidelberg. In so doing he had to cross
the front of the French Marshals and their armies, without
any effective covering force between. Speed was the
essence of the business, and speed was much increased by
the fact that the heavier part of the baggage and artillery,
and the hospital stores, which the Duke had carefully collected, were able to come up by water the whole way from
the borders of Holland, through Coblentz and Mainz, as
far up as Mannheim. The troops, indeed, had to plod
through the muddy roads of the Rhineland, and to take
with them some at least of the field artillery. It was a rainy
May, and the difficulties overcome by Colonel Blood in
dragging his guns up the hill roads above Coblentz without
delaying the advance of the infantry, show how greatly the
speed of the army was increased by the dispatch of the
heavier weights by the waterway.[302]

Coming from Holland, the army crossed the Maas by a bridge of boats constructed at Ruremonde, and made *rendez-vous* at Bedburg, whence the great march officially began.* The Duke's friend and secretary, Adam Cardonnel, writing from Maastricht, reckoned the army at 40 battalions and 80 squadrons, 'upwards of 40,000 men, very good troops,' which the enemy would 'not be able to match for goodness.' Of these 16,000 was computed, perhaps with some exaggeration, to be the number of native British troops.† The army would be enlarged, as it passed south and east across Europe, by German, Danish, Prussian, and other nationals, for whose co-operation in the great design elaborate arrangements had been made beforehand in the correspondence of Marlborough and Wratislaw, Prince Eugene and Prince Lewis of Baden. With the Germans, the southward march of the English army was highly popular. One by one the Princes of the Empire, whose troops were involved, were, at Marlborough's instance, let into the secret of their destination for the Danube ; in the middle of May the truth was told to the Elector Palatine, and a few days later to the King of Prussia. The States-General were informed only in the first week in June, when concealment was no longer possible, though Heinsius had known for at least a fortnight, perhaps for more.[303]

There were two stages in the deception of Europe. Until Coblentz was reached and passed, all the world expected the English would turn thence up the Moselle valley. At Coblentz great stores had been collected as though for this purpose, but they were sent on up the Rhine after the southward course of the army. But even when the Rhine and Lahn had been crossed, when Coblentz and the rock-fortress of Ehrenbreitstein had sunk from the sight of the marching columns, it was not even then guessed by friend or foe that the Danube was the goal. Alsace, it was now

May 12
(N.S.)
1704

---

* *See Maps VIII and IX at end of volume.*

† *Add. MSS.* (St.), 7063, ff. 48–49; *Coxe*, Chap. xxi, I, p. 240. The native British troops present at Blenheim were not more than about 9,000 (14 battalions and 14 squadrons), see *Coxe*, Chap. xxvi, I, p. 289. At the beginning of a campaign a battalion of infantry might be 700 and a squadron of cavalry 150. By the middle of a campaign 500 and 120 effectives would be a safer reckoning.

conjectured, was the field of operations chosen by the Duke. A bridge of boats, which he caused the Princes of Germany to throw over the Upper Rhine near Philipsburg, confirmed the Alsatian hypothesis. In that belief, the Dutch sent after him from the Maas seven more battalions and twenty-one squadrons—a friendly act for which he sent warm thanks.* Villeroi had relieved the fears of the Dutch for their frontier by hastening with his army from the Netherlands to the Moselle ; thence he passed southward to join Tallard in Alsace. Marlborough was drawing the whole war in his wake, away from the North Sea into the heart of Europe.

Tallard, meanwhile, had not been inactive on the Upper Rhine. He had, by a bold and clever piece of strategy, outwitted Lewis of Baden, slipped round the German guard on the passes of the Black Forest, and delivered in the Upper Danube valley the year's recruits for Marsin's French army of Bavaria. They were mostly conscript militia, undrilled and ill-armed, ill-fed and over-driven on the march through the mountains, but they numbered 12,000 men. Tallard returned to his own army in Alsace, where he was joined by Villeroi and the army from the Netherlands. The two Marshals spent precious weeks watching, in bewilderment, the southward progress of Marlborough, speculating as to his still uncertain destination, and corresponding with King Louis at Versailles as to the course to be adopted. Their inaction gave the Duke his chance to make the unexpected wheel to the left at the Neckar, and carry his army across to the Danube.

Marlborough's mind had been finally made up on May 23, in the neighbourhood of Bonn and Sinzig, when the ill news arrived that Tallard had safely delivered Marsin's recruits ; the report that reached Marlborough doubled their real number. In grave alarm for Central Germany and Vienna, he then and there dismissed the possibility of any alternative scheme that would keep him

---

* As late as June 19 he wrote from the passes of the Black Forest to Heinsius : ' I beg you will take care that I receive no orders from the States that may put me out of a condition of reducing the Elector, for that would be of all mischiefs the greatest.' And Heinsius took care. See *Heinsius MSS.*, Appendix A, below.

longer on the Rhine.   From Sinzig onwards, he rode ahead
with the Allied cavalry on the route that led most quickly
to Bavaria, leaving the infantry and guns to follow, a few
days behind, under his brother, General Charles Churchill.[304]

In this mood, and in this order of march, he passed from
Coblentz over the hill roads to Mainz, and finally crossed
the Neckar in the neighbourhood of Heidelberg.   Till they
reached the Neckar, his troops and officers, even his own
brother, did not know whither they were bound.   But all
were in the highest spirits.   Every man felt that he was
marching under a great chief towards a great destiny.   This
time no Dutch Generals would spoil the sport ; somewhere,
therefore, at the end of the long road lay battle and victory.
The German Princes and peoples of the famous and lovely
lands through which they passed turned out to welcome
their deliverers.   The English, as they wound round the
wooded hills crowned with the castles of old romance, as
they passed through shouting towns and wondering
villages, signalled their goodwill to all and sundry, and had
smiles and winks ready for the fraüleins, ' some of them
much handsomer,' Lieutenant Pope wrote home, ' than we
expected to find in this country.'   The Rhine wine, too,
was plentiful, and even the so-called beer had qualities of
its own.   Altogether, the march was a soldier's paradise,
tempered by rain.   But happy as they all were, the red
columns kept up, as they moved along, a running fire of
' oaths and profane language,' harrowing the soul of
Cameronian Colonel Blackader, who found ' an army a sad
place to be in on Sabbath.'

' Notwithstanding the continual marching, the men are
extremely pleased with this expedition,' wrote Marlborough
from Mainz, to Lord Treasurer Godolphin : ' so that I am
sure you will take all the care possible they may not want.'
And never did army, in that era, ' want ' so little.   The
elaborate preparations of their General's forethought waylaid his men at every turn.   When they reached a great
river, a bridge of boats was waiting for them, prepared,
at the Duke's special request, by the Prince of the land.
Every day the troops marched in the grey of the summer's
dawn, and several hours before noon reached their camping

ground for next night, having covered their day's march of twelve to fifteen miles.   But the Commissaries were at the *rendez-vous* before them, with food for man and beast, so that, in the words of Captain Parker, who saw it all day by day, ' the soldiers had nothing to do but to pitch their tents, boil their kettles and lie down to rest.'   ' The remaining part of the day's rest,' wrote Sergeant Millner, ' was nigh as good as a day's halt.'

When the Elector of Mainz reviewed the infantry, he came at the end of the long line to the Battalion of Guards ; ' observing not only their order, but their cleanliness, and their arms, accoutrements, clothes, shoes and linen,' he said to General Churchill, ' Certainly all these gentlemen are dressed for the Ball.'

Contrary to the custom of the wars in High Germany, Marlborough caused everything to be paid for on the nail, ' and to prevent any failure herein he ordered the Treasurer of the Army to be always in cash to answer Bills, and duly to have a month's subsistence beforehand.'   With this object, he had established large credits with the bankers of Frankfurt and Nüremberg, whence specie was conveyed to the army as it drew near the Danube, and in the subsequent campaign upon its shores.   Shoes reached them by the same route, so that the infantry had been completely reshod before they set foot in Bavaria, ' because shoes and other necessities would not be so easily found in an enemy's country.'

As he passed further and further away from English politics and Dutch leading-strings, the Duke's spirits rose. He was no longer, as at the Hague, ' hagged out of his life.' At Coblentz he had written to Sarah :

If flattery could make me happy, Count Wratislaw, who came to me yesterday, has said so much from the Emperor that I am ashamed to repeat it to you ; but I hope the Queen will find the good effects of it.   For it is certain if these troops I bring had not come to his assistance, he would have run great risk of losing his Crown, which he seems sensible of.   I have also the satisfaction of receiving marks of the friendship of the Dutch Generals in Flanders.[305]

It was at Wiesloch, in the plain just south of Heidelberg, that he took his strategic turn to the east, left the Rhine valley and its French armies behind him, and made off boldly for the Danube. The route lay through pleasant farmlands, between wooded hills. In a few days he struck one of the upper reaches of the Neckar, and skirted Stuttgart to the north. At Mundelsheim, half-way between Rhine and Danube, Prince Eugene rode into Marlborough's camp, and the two rivals in fame, destined ever afterwards to be friends without one thought of jealousy, first met face to face. Marlborough confided his impressions to Sarah : ' Prince Eugene has in his conversation a great deal of my Lord Shrewsbury, with the advantage of seeming franker.' A long secret conference ensued that evening, in the course of which Eugene revealed his distrust of the jealous temper and timid strategy of Prince Lewis of Baden. He imparted a secret of state, which Marlborough sent on to Godolphin in cipher :

June 10 (N.S.) 1704

> Prince Eugene has in great confidence told me the Emperor had given him full power in case he and I should have reason to suspect Prince Lewis acting with zeal for the common cause, to take such measures as not to leave him with the army.

But so desperate an expedient was only to be used in the last emergency. As yet the two friends shrank from offending their colleague, a reigning Prince with troops of his own.[306]

Next day Eugene and Marlborough rode on to Gross Heppach where a review of the cavalry was held.

> His Highness was very surprised to find them in so good a condition after so long a march, and told his Grace that he had heard much of the English Cavalry and found it to be the best appointed and the finest he had ever seen. But, says he, money, which you don't want in England, will buy clothes and fine horses, but it cannot buy that lively air I see in every one of these troopers' faces. To which his Grace replied that that must be attributed to their heartiness for the public cause, and the particular pleasure and satisfaction they had in seeing his Highness.

And so they bowed their big wigs to mingle with their horses' manes, in stately compliment to one another. It was in these honeymoon days that Wratislaw brought an offer from his master Leopold, to make the English Duke a Prince of that Empire for which he had already done so much. Marlborough, with characteristic prudence, declined the glittering prize till he had fully earned it.[307]

While they were still at Gross Heppach, Prince Lewis joined their councils, and the parts were allotted. Eugene should go to the Rhine and do his best to keep the superior forces of Tallard and Villeroi amused in that region, while Marlborough and Prince Lewis reduced Bavaria and compelled its erring ruler to change sides. A few days later the English General received full powers from Secretary Harley to make any treaty he chose with the Elector.[308]

Marlborough would greatly have preferred to take Eugene to the Danube, but it was known that Prince Lewis thought it was due to him that he should go there. To prevent jealousy, the Duke and he agreed, after the fashion of the Roman Consuls of old, that each should command their united forces on alternate days. It might be wagered that the first battle would be fought on one of the days ascribed to Marlborough. Eugene had put him on his guard, and he was at great pains to propitiate his colleague ; Secretary Cardonnel reported :

We joined the Prince of Baden two days ago, and there seems to be a pretty good harmony between him and my Lord Duke.

So they parted awhile from Eugene, and pushed forward, ever east and south. Since they had left the Rhine, the heavy baggage and artillery could no longer come by water. The cavalry still marched several days ahead of the foot. The greater part of their way still passed through pleasant and gently undulating farm-country, less difficult than the passes of the Black Forest further south by which alone Tallard would reach the Danube from Alsace. Only when they approached the watershed was the road mountainous ; there the long, narrow, wooded, defile beyond Geislingen was threaded, slowly and with labour, while the rain poured down on cursing men and sliding horses, struggling to move guns and waggons stuck deep in the mud. If the enemy at Ulm had sent out even a small force to dispute the pass, the result might have been disastrous.

At length the table lands at the pass top were reached,

and the army began to descend into the valley of the Danube. Though it was the last week in June, the rain still fell in sheets, and Marlborough wrote to Sarah :

As I am writing, I am forced to have fire in the stove in my chamber. But the poor men, that have not such conveniences, I am afraid will suffer from these continual rains. As they do us hurt here, they do good to Prince Eugene on the Rhine [by immobilizing the superior forces of the French in that region], so that we must take the bad with the good.

The weather caused sickness, but the invalids, well-cared for in hospitals that were set up at Heidenheim, soon recovered and rejoined the ranks. When the united army under Marlborough approached the Danube at Elchingen close to Ulm, the condition in which the soldiers reached the term of their long march greatly added to their fighting strength.[309]

All Europe and all England had eyes turned on the Danube in astonishment and expectation. At home, opinion was divided. The fury of the High Tory leaders knew no bounds at the rape of the English army, vanished into the depths of German forests on the Emperor's quarrel. In the middle of June it was reported :

There is a greater party forming against my Lord Treasurer and My Lord Marlborough than ever there was against King William's Ministers.

Sir Edward Seymour swore that when the Duke came back they would run him down as hounds do a hare. But outside the ranks of professed politicians, high hopes filled many an English heart that summer. Thomas Coke, the Member for Derbyshire, himself a Moderate Tory, wrote to the Duke in June that the country gentlemen were ' more cheerful about the war ' and more reconciled to the land tax by the news of his great march. Even William Penn, the venerable Quaker, felt a concern for the Duke of Marlborough, bound on ' this mighty march to the Danube with so prodigious an artillery requiring 2000 horse to draw it,' to ' give a turn to the French affairs ; and *may England, poor England, ever prevail.*'[310]

In the last week of June, the joint forces of the Elector of Bavaria and of the French Marshal Marsin were awaiting Marlborough on the Upper Danube. The French had amused themselves that winter and spring by pitilessly robbing the Germans of the towns and villages of Swabia. According to de la Colonie, one of their own countrymen who was there, ' the post of Provost-Marshal was non-existent in this campaign ' ; and on arrival at any fresh camping ground they sent out organized parties to pillage the country. Marlborough, therefore, with his well supplied and well disciplined troops, was welcomed as a deliverer by the German populations, everywhere except in Bavaria.[311]

The Franco-Bavarians at Ulm were inferior to the united forces with which the English and their allies had arrived to overwhelm them. A large part of the Elector's army was scattered about in garrisons in his Bavarian territories, as far away as Munich and the Tirolese frontier, whence they were never withdrawn till Blenheim was lost and won. But Max Emanuel, though overmatched for the moment, was yet in a position far from desperate. If he could hold out a month, Tallard would come from the Rhine with another great French army. Marlborough had got a start, but he had no time to waste. Meanwhile, every fortress on the Danube, from Ulm down to Ingolstadt, was garrisoned by French and Bavarians. And the fortified camp on the north shore of the river, between Dillingen and Lauingen, could shelter their field army until Tallard's arrival. Thither Max Emanuel and Marsin repaired, to avoid giving battle ; Marlborough and Prince Lewis, not daring to attack a position rendered impregnable by redoubts and inundations, passed round Dillingen to the north, by wooded and hilly ways, through Balmershofen and Amerdingen, in the direction of Donauwörth. The infantry had overtaken the cavalry at Gingen, and the Duke, on reviewing them, was delighted at their condition and spirit after footing it all the way from Holland.

Three weeks before, Marlborough had, with remark-able foresight of the position he would find on the Danube, already determined to seize Donauwörth and ' there settle

a magazine for the army.' *   His task was to induce Max
Emanuel to change sides before Tallard came to the rescue.
An agent of the King of Prussia was still in the Bavarian
camp, negotiating with the Elector for this purpose, but
the Duke believed that the only chance of bringing him to
close with the Allies' offers was to invade his territories.
That, he hoped, would induce him to abandon the French
alliance, already highly unpopular with his subjects and
Ministers.   But in order to enter and occupy Bavarian
territory, Marlborough must rush past the enemy's main
army at Dillingen, leaving it between him and his old line
of communications.   He must, therefore, form new communications, to obtain supplies from the friendly States of
Central Germany, by way of Nördlingen and Nüremberg.
And he must have a fortified bridge-head and magazine on
the Danube, by which these supplies could cross so as to
reach him when he was in Bavaria, south of the great river.
He had selected Donauwörth to serve this purpose, and he
must capture it at every cost.[312]

The enemy also were well aware of the importance of
Donauwörth.   From their camp at Dillingen, the Elector
and Marsin detached 12,000 troops, including 7,000 of
the best Bavarian infantry, three regiments of French
infantry, twelve squadrons of cavalry and fifteen cannon.
This force, under the command of the principal Bavarian
General, the Piedmontese Count D'Arco, was charged
with the defence of Donauwörth.   It could only be conducted on the heights of the Schellenberg, a high
domed hill that overshadowed the eastern walls of the
town.   The steep slopes and the broad open plateau on
the summit were covered at that season by growing crops.
The Schellenberg had been a place of importance in
war since time immemorial.   After the battle, the
inhabitants of Donauwörth flattered the victors by telling them that the hill had been attacked a dozen times
in history and only once before captured—by the great
Gustavus himself.   The statement was as questionable as
most local legends, but in any case the veritable earthwork fort of the Swedish king still crowned the edge of

* *Coxe*, Chap. xxii, I, p. 249, to Godolphin, June 8 (N.S.).

the Schellenberg plateau, on guard over the town and its northern approaches.

D'Arco had several days in which to fortify the hill. With the help of French engineer officers, he started to repair and strengthen the two miles of old entrenchments that connected the fort of Gustavus with the Danube on one side and with the city walls on the other. But as he had no belief that Marlborough would venture to attack him, he was tardy in beginning the work and negligent in pushing it on. So little, indeed, did he scent danger, that when a French officer impudently applied for leave to pursue his amours at Munich, he let the truant go, almost on the eve of battle.

When the unexpected assault took place, the bastions, the curtain, and the ditch were fairly complete on the long east face from the shore of the Danube up to the wood on the hilltop. In the shorter section extending from the wood to the fort, the angle where Marlborough's fierce attack was delivered, the earthwork had been more hastily made up with fascines of brushwood thinly covered over with soil. Here the English visitor can still trace the faint outline of bastions and curtain, once deeply dyed with the blood of his fellow-countrymen ; further on the star-shaped fort of Gustavus, still nearly complete, encloses to-day a peaceful grove. The third or western section of the lines ran steeply downhill from this fort to the city walls, by way of the Calvary since erected in memory of the battle. In this last section there was very little to show by way of defences,* but to compensate for its structural deficiency, the west end of the line could be protected by a flanking fire from the fortifications of the town.

Such was the strength of the Schellenberg. But its very size might on this occasion be a source of weakness. Could D'Arco's 12,000 men hold so long a line against the greatly superior forces of the Allies until the arrival of the rest of the Franco-Bavarian army ? The Elector, indeed,

---

* In the local museum at Donauwörth is a large painting of the town and neighbourhood, dated 1725, in which the lines round the Schellenberg are represented as extant to the north and east of the fort, but non-existent between the fort and the town.

MAP V

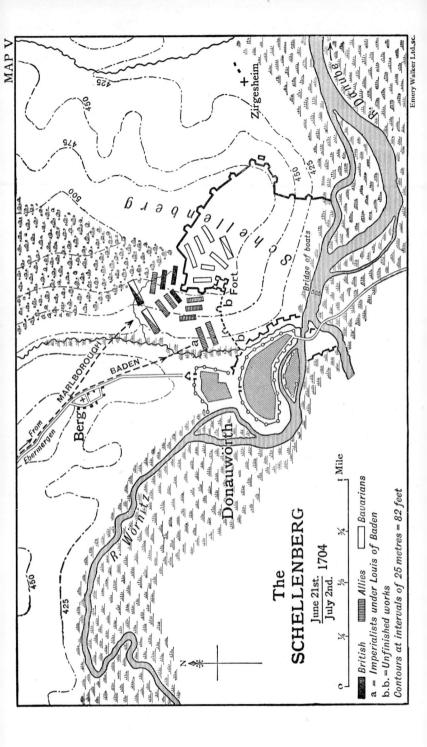

Zirgesheim

R. Danube

Bridge of boats

Schellenberg

Fort

b

a

b

From
MARLBOROUGH
BADEN

A

Berg

From
Eberrmergen

R. Wörnitz

Donauwörth

N

The
SCHELLENBERG

June 21st. 1704
July 2nd.

██ = British   ▒▒ = Allies   ☐ = Bavarians
a = Imperialists under Louis of Baden
b.b. = Unfinished works
Contours at intervals of 25 metres = 82 feet

0   ¼   ½   ¾   1 Mile

Emery Walker Ltd.sc.

was hastening from Dillingen to Donauwörth, having got wind of the allied movements. It was a race against time, a game which Marlborough was peculiarly fitted to win. July 2 was one of the alternate days when it was his turn to command. When authority for the next twenty-four hours passed into his hands at midnight, fifteen miles of execrable road divided his sleeping army from the Schellenberg. But he knew that, unless he stood upon its conquered summit before night fell, it would never be taken at all, and he would never set foot on the southern shore of the Danube. For on the morrow Prince Lewis was most unlikely to take the responsibility of attacking. And in the course of that morrow not only would the earthworks be completed, but the main Franco-Bavarian army would arrive to defend them.

And so, at three o'clock, scarcely waiting for the summer dawn, the Duke took the road with an advanced guard of 5,800 picked troops who were to begin the assault. The rest of the army started at five.

July 2 (N.S.) 1704

The roads, very different from those of our own day, were deep in mud, and the forced march demanded a continuous effort of will and muscle. It would have been an ill preparation for battle at the close of day if they had not been seasoned troops, kept in condition by the constant care of their great captain. The engineers went ahead to improve the worst passages for the cannon, and to throw a bridge of boats across the Wörnitz, side by side with the stone bridge at Ebermergen.

Marlborough himself, riding far ahead, examined the enemy's position at nine in the morning. He observed through his telescope that a camp was being prepared on the other side of the Danube from the Schellenberg, evidently for the reception of the main Franco-Bavarian army next day. About the same hour a messenger reached him from Eugene that Tallard was gathering his forces at Strasbourg to cross the Black Forest and join the Elector. There was indeed no time to be lost. It wanted twelve hours before dark, and those hours were his, though his men were still cursing and struggling in the mud, miles away behind the Wörnitz.

Prince Lewis joined him in his morning reconnaissance, and together they closely examined the enemy's lines under fire from his cannon, and laid the plan to be executed that evening as soon as their troops should arrive.   Marlborough had been courteously careful to consult the Prince the night before as to the proposed attempt, and both commanders did their duty well that day.   Baden was indeed a competent, though an unenterprising officer, fit to be second in command but, unfortunately, aspiring always to the chief rôle.   On a day of his own responsibility, he would never have ordered the attack on the Schellenberg. Indeed, Marlborough's decision to attack that evening was, we are told, taken against the opinion of most of the generals.

It was between five and six o'clock that the advance guard and Colonel Blood's artillery reached the scene of operations.   There would just be time before nightfall to storm the position on its north side, where the attacking army found itself, but there would not be time to pass round the wood on to the east of the Schellenberg and develop simultaneous attacks on the far-flung lines from more sides than one.   For this reason the Allied army lost much of the advantage of superior numbers ; the front of attack must be relatively narrow, for want of time to deploy to the full extent.   Even the wood on the hill-top had to be avoided, as the brushwood was too dense for orderly operations ; therefore the attack could not be developed on the flat summit of the Schellenberg, but had to be delivered mainly up the steepest part of the slope immediately to the north of Gustavus' fort, where the entrenchments followed the very edge of the plateau.   The English, on the extreme left wing of the Allied attack, skirted the wood as closely as possible without passing through it.*

The plan agreed upon was that Marlborough, with his own polyglot army of troops in English and Dutch pay, should assault the angle between the fort and the wood so fiercely as either to carry it at a rush or, at least, to draw thither the whole of the enemy's force.   An hour later Lewis of Baden's Imperialists would be arriving on the

* I think the end of the wood was a trifle further back than its present extent (1930), though not much.

scene.   They would then be able to march straight in,
near the town walls, over the uncompleted lines, which
would, it was hoped, be stripped by that time of all
save a handful of defenders.   This scheme of operations,
dependent on the ardour of Marlborough's containing
attack, would be costly of life, but it was the only way to
take the Schellenberg before dark, and therefore the only
way to take it at all.

Under cover of the smoke of the village of Berg, which
the enemy had set ablaze, Colonel Blood erected his
batteries on that opposing hill, and began to fire across the
valley at the death-angle between the fort and the wood.
The English cannon balls plunged at long bowls into the
ranks of the enemy's reserve, and, according to de la
Colonie, killed eighty grenadiers of his regiment before the
infantry fighting began.   An Imperialist battery soon
afterwards took up its station beside the English.

At six o'clock, Marlborough's advanced guard of
pickedmen—English, Scots, Dutch, Hanoverians, Hessians,
and other German nationals—moved to the attack, up and
along the steep slopes of the Schellenberg.   A forlorn hope
of fifty grenadiers of the English Guards was led on in front
of the rest by Lord Mordaunt, Peterborough's eldest son,
who alone with ten others of that gallant company survived
unwounded.   The battalions coming on behind were
mowed in swathes ; scores and hundreds fell together.
A battery of guns in the death-angle tore their closed ranks
to pieces with grapeshot.   Musketry volleys from the
earthworks did frightful execution.   The Dutch General
Goor, deservedly a favourite with Marlborough, fell dead
at the head of the Hollanders.   Those English who reached
the trenches raised a hoarse hurrah ; even in that moment
of universal uproar it struck a chill into the enemy commanders, one of whom ordered his drums to beat lest
the islanders' cheer should discourage his men.   Next
moment assailants and defenders were at handgrips on the
parapet, ' tearing at the muzzles of guns and the bayonets
which pierced their entrails,' as the same officer described
it.   The Bavarians charged and drove the assailants down
the hill and along the woodside.   But the English Guards,

though already cruelly mauled, drove them back in turn within their lines.

Under cover of the Guards' charge the broken assault was rallied in hollow ground out of sight of the enemy. For awhile the defenders could only see the tops of the standards round which the Allies were gathering for another attack.   Then it came, as bloody and as unsuccessful as the first.   Again the red-coats of the English and the blue-coats of the Dutch service advanced side by side in perfect order, their general officers leading them on foot, sword in hand.   Again they were mowed down in hundreds round the death-angle.   The German General, Styrum, fell, mortally wounded.   Again the attack reeled back, followed by the Bavarian sortie.   Lumley brought up the English horse and again drove back the pursuers.

Twice the assault had failed to carry the lines, but it had done its work.   The Bavarians and French had been concentrated in thousands to defend the death-angle, and the line between the fort and the town was no longer held by more than a skeleton force.   The Prince of Baden's Imperialist infantry were arriving on the scene.   He led them straight at the lines, passing within musket shot of the town.   The cannon of the city fortifications played on their flank, but the French infantry, whom D'Arco had ordered to be put into the covered way beneath the walls, had, by some misunderstanding, never been placed there, and the cannon fire alone could not stop the advance of Baden's men.   Almost unresisted in front, they crossed the lines of the Schellenberg at their weakest point.   Wheeling to the left, with their backs to the enemy cannon on the wall, they marched up the steep slopes into the flank and rear of the Bavarians in the death-angle.   A charge of cavalry down the hillside failed to break their ranks.   Up they came, bringing on their bayonets the well-planned victory.

The moment of the day had come.   The allied infantry on the hilltop moved forward to their third attack on the death-angle, this time with better fortune.   The approach of fresh troops on their rear at last aroused the instinct of self-preservation even in the firm breasts of the Bavarian infantry.   The kaleidoscope of battle was shaken, and in a moment the broad plateau was covered by thousands fleeing for their lives, while the British, Dutch and German foot rushed after them, the islanders crying out ' Kill, kill and destroy.' Lord John Hay's Scots Dragoons or ' Scots Greys ' had dismounted, to follow their noble Colonel over the enemy trenches as part of the final infantry attack ; then remounting their white horses, they headed the pursuit over the top of the Schellenberg.

Marlborough entered the captured lines with the fore-most squadrons of the English cavalry. These he let loose upon the flying foe, while he called off his exhausted foot to rally round their standards, secure the position, and lend aid to the surgeons amid the piles of wounded. Galloping forward once more, he reached the southern edge of the plateau, and in a moment the full panorama of victory was revealed. It was near sunset, but there was light enough to see, beyond the Danube, the vast open plains, deep in standing corn and circled with dark forests, those southern plains which the capture of Donauwörth would open to his advance. To the south-east lay the straight, wooded line of the Lech, marking the boundary of Bavaria, now at his mercy. At his feet stretched the broad, silver ribbon of the Danube, which he had come so far to find, henceforth for ever associated with his name. The bridge of boats, which D'Arco had laid across it below the town, was breaking up beneath the weight of madly-struggling fugitives ; many had crossed ; many were drowning in the river or trying to steer the drifting boats ; many who had been cut off on the northern shore could be seen running for their lives among the reed-beds or the corn, vainly endeavouring to avoid the rise and fall of the sabres of the red-coated horsemen. Looking to the east, Marlborough could see another dark mass of fugitives near the village of Zirgesheim, straining to escape from the pursuing squadrons into the wooded hills beyond. Only to the west he could detect a few battalions, who had found their way into the streets of Donauwörth, crossing the Danube by the town bridge in tolerable order. Then darkness fell and the scene was blotted out. And, with the darkness, sheets of rain descended in pitiless brutality on the maimed and dying men, gathered from all the four quarters of Europe to perish together on that tragic hill.

With the return of daylight all the wounded who could be moved were sent off to the hospitals that the Duke had had prepared beforehand at Nördlingen in readiness for the battle. The Allies confessed a loss of 1,400 killed and 4,000 wounded : these figures included 1,500 of the pick of the English and Scottish armies. Of the British engaged every third man had fallen. Of the general officers of the Allies no less than seven had been killed as they marched at the head of their troops to the attack, and nine wounded, including Prince Lewis of Baden ; most of them were German princes and noblemen, a class that had well borne its part that day.

D'Arco tried to minimize his disaster by dwelling with truth on the greater number of the Allied losses in the actual conflict at the death-angle. But in the pursuit and dispersion that followed, his own losses had risen to an unknown quantity of great dimension. There were at least 2,000 prisoners, and the drowned and the deserters were very numerous. According to the French marshals, those few who rejoined the standards arrived without arms and in a state of complete demoralization. ' I have ruined the best of the Elector's foot,' wrote the Duke to the Duchess. When he allowed his chaplain and historiographer, Dr. Hare, to claim that only three out of the twelve thousand defenders of the Schellenberg were left in service, this estimate, though too precise to be certain, was not inconsistent with the general tone of the reports that reached Marshal Tallard. D'Arco's fifteen field pieces, his baggage, and his stores were prizes to the victor, besides Donauwörth, its fortifications and cannon ; for, contrary to the Duke's expectation, the town was at once abandoned after the battle by the enemy, who left after an ineffectual attempt to set it on fire. Marlborough had won his bridge-head over the Danube and secured a line of communications by which his supplies from central Germany could reach his army as it advanced into Bavaria. He had put himself between the French and Vienna. He stood, moreover, between the Elector and his unfortunate country.[313]

It was a notable victory, and it rang through Europe. Shrewsbury wrote to Marlborough from Rome, ' In this holy, ignorant city they have an idea of you as of a Tamerlane ; and had I a picture of old Colonel Birch with his whiskers, I could put it off for yours, and change it for one done by Raphael.' And he added, to another friend, ' A year ago I was so ill in the opinion of the Pope that it was a crime to go near me ; now that they fear the Duke of Marlborough and his red-coats should come to Italy, His Holiness does nothing but commend me.' At Vienna, wrote Stepney, ' the whole Court is quite changed,' and the British minister was loaded with exultant congratulations. Ratisbon was hastily evacuated by the Bavarian troops, and the Diet of the Empire sat there liberated from the armed force of the anti-German party. Neuburg also was evacuated, and except for Ingolstadt the whole line of the Danube from Donauwörth down to Vienna was once more in Allied hands. ' It is very plain,' wrote Marlborough two days after the battle, ' that if Her Majesty's troops had not been here, the Elector of Bavaria had now been at Vienna.' To the generality of Englishmen at home, as to Lord Hervey, ' the news of the late noble action on the Danube was too full of wonder to let one speak at all upon't at first hearing.' Martial victories of this kind over a foreign foe were new to the islanders, recalling dim traditions of Crecy and Agincourt.

Such were the moral and material effects of the Schellenberg, even before Blenheim decided the still uncertain issue of the struggle on the Danube. Till then, the French kept up their spirits by speaking of the immense losses of the Allies at the death-angle. The High Tories took up the same tale to disparage the Duke ; nothing alienated him more from his old political associates than to learn that Rochester and his friends ' took the action at Donauwörth not to be a victory.' Up till this time he had been accustomed to complain to Sarah that ' your friend the *Observator*,' the ultra-Whig paper, was ' malicious ' towards Moderate Tory government, while devoting most of its space to exposing the iniquities of ' Jacks,' Non-jurors and ' Highflyers,' and paying little attention to the Duke's operations of war.   But on the news of the Schellenberg, the *Observator* discovered the necessity of supporting Marlborough, and did full justice to that victory and afterwards to Blenheim, while it treated with scorn the news of the capture of Gibraltar by the Tory Rooke, as ' an amphibious relation of taking a Spanish town.' [314]

The victory of the Schellenberg put a sharp end to friendly relations with Prince Lewis, who was jealous of the fame his English colleague acquired that day.   The Duke clearly perceived that he would never again get the Prince's consent to fight a battle.

But if Prince Lewis was turning hostile, the rest of the army was devoted to Marlborough.   A week after the victory he wrote to Sarah :

I have the pleasure to find all the officers willing to obey, without knowing any other reason than that it is my desire, which is very different from what it was in Flanders, where I was obliged to have the consent of a Council of War for everything I undertook. [315]

Throughout the month of July the Prince and the Duke, in spite of growing alienation, had a single object in common —to occupy Bavaria and so compel Max Emanuel to change sides, as the price at which he might have back his hereditary dominions.   Negotiations for this purpose were going on all the time.   The Elector had been deeply depressed by the disaster of the Schellenberg.   As a soldier of old experience in the Turkish wars, he knew a defeat when he saw one, and for the first time felt real alarm for the ultimate outcome of the campaign.   For a fortnight after the battle he was inclined to listen seriously to the diplomatic offers of the Allies, backed by their military occupation of a large part of his territories.

The invasion of Bavaria was the more easily effected because, since Neuburg and Ratisbon had fallen into Marlborough's hands, he could fetch supplies and ammunition from central Germany across the Danube by a number of different routes.   He was always anxious about the feeding of his Englishmen.

Our greatest difficulty [he wrote to Godolphin on July 6], is that of making our bread follow us ; for the troops that I have the honour to command cannot subsist without it, and the Germans that are used to starve cannot advance without us. The Duke of Würtemberg has sent orders to his country for two hundred waggons, to help bring our stores, and I have promised to pay them for a month, which time I hope will finish our business in this country [by a Treaty with the Elector.]

To the Duchess he wrote : 'I have it now in my power that the poor soldiers shall not want bread.' But the British soldier does not live by bread alone.

His Grace [so his Chaplain records] was at the same time providing Beer for the Army at Aicha. The furnaces and other conveniences for brewing being out of order, His Grace commanded the inhabitants to repair them and to set all their brewers to work.[316]

He had solved the problem of food supply, but the question of siege guns and ammunition proved more difficult. By great efforts he had brought his own field batteries all the way from Holland, but for heavy cannon it had been agreed that he should depend on German supply. At the siege of the walled market town July 10– of Rain, commanding the entrance to Bavaria, 16 (N.S.) the big guns arrived late, the ammunition for 1704 them was short and the German gunners unskilful, protracting the siege of the little place for several unnecessary days. For lack of a proper siege train the Duke had most reluctantly to abandon his original design of besieging Munich, by which he had hoped to bring the Elector speedily to terms.[317]

Max Emanuel, meanwhile, had taken up an impregnable position at Augsburg, outside Bavarian territory, on the west shore of the Lech, where the Allies from the east bank could not come at him. Marsin's French army was with the Bavarian, and from Augsburg they could easily move to join Tallard as soon as he debouched from the Black Forest. Marlborough and Prince Lewis marched by way of Aicha to Friedberg opposite Augsburg, where they lay from July 22 to August 3 watching the enemy across the river and at least preventing him from entering Bavaria or drawing from it any supplies.

While Marlborough was lying thus on the banks of the

Lech, reduced to relative impotence by the want of an adequate siege train, the politico-military situation had become decidedly less hopeful than it had been a fortnight before. The first effects of the Schellenberg had been exhausted. Tallard was on his way, bringing to the Elector the relief promised him by Louis XIV of 35,000 more French troops. As soon as Max Emanuel was persuaded that help was really coming, he broke off the treaty with the Allies on the very day that an agreement was expected. For three years past he had so many times come off and on in bargaining with both sides, that Marlborough and Prince Lewis did not yet despair ; but for the moment they had failed.

July 15 (N.S.) 1704

Partly, perhaps, from natural indignation with this slippery negotiator, the Allied commanders intensified the policy of devastating his territory, which they had already begun on July 12, before the breakdown of the parleys. On the 16th, in announcing to Heinsius the temporary failure of the treaty, Marlborough added : ‘ We are advancing into the heart of Bavaria to destroy the country and oblige the Elector one way or the other to a compliance.’

It is clear from this that he hoped to appeal to Max Emanuel through the sufferings of his people—a political proceeding of doubtful morality. It was also a military measure intended to prevent the French and Bavarian armies from being able to support themselves from the produce of the Elector’s territory—‘ to deprive the enemy as well of present subsistence as future support on this side,’ as he wrote to Stepney.

A man of proved humanity in the conduct of war, Marlborough was secretly ashamed of a method which recalled the more thorough-going proceedings of Louis XIV’s generals in the Palatinate in the dozen years before, which had raised a universal outcry. He confessed his feelings to his wife :

We sent this morning (July 30) 3,000 horse to his chief City of Munich, with orders to burn and destroy all the country about it. This is so uneasy to my nature that nothing but an absolute necessity would have obliged me to consent to it. For these poor people suffer only for their master’s ambition. There having been no war in this country above sixty years, their towns and villages are so clean and neat you would be pleased with them.*

He had not, indeed, the heart to carry out such a policy to its logical conclusion.

It was with great reluctance [writes his Chaplain], that his Grace saw all the country on fire about him, and therefore he ordered a stop to be put to it, in hopes that the peasants would return to the villages that were yet standing, and reap the corn which was beginning to be shed as it stood, and whole fields were thereby spoiled and lost. His Grace also spared the woods, which are stately and numerous in this country, consisting entirely of tall fir trees and pinasters.

But since the Elector could hardly have supported his troops on fir-cones there seems no particular merit in that piece of forbearance.

Accounts differed as to the actual amount of damage done. De la Colonie, a French officer in the Bavarian service writes :

I followed a route through several villages said to have been reduced to cinders, and although I certainly found a few burnt houses, still the damage was as nothing compared with the reports current through the country.[318]

The Elector cared for none of these things. He had recovered his hopefulness after the first shock of the Schellenberg. He had decided to pin his faith on the arrival of Tallard. With a little constancy he might not only recover Bavaria but dethrone the Hapsburgs and make Munich instead of Vienna the seat of the Empire. He felt no enthusiasm for the French cause as such, for he had fought against Louis XIV in previous wars. But if he rejoined the Allies now, though he would make sure of his Bavarian inheritance, he could never be Kaiser, and he would lose the governorship of the Spanish Netherlands, a lucrative

* Captain Parker, who was there, tells us in his *Memoirs* (p. 85) that ' the Duke of Marlborough would not suffer any of the troops that were immediately under him to go out on that burning command.' This may well be so, but I think the English took part in the daily destruction as they passed along the route. On July 19 an English officer, Noyes, writes : ' Hitherto we burnt and plundered almost all the villages right and left, which indeed are very frequent and very fine in this country. In this last march particularly we entirely burnt a mighty pretty village with a noble church and cloister ' (*Cam. Univ. Lib. MSS.; Add. 40. doc. no.* 17).

and delightful office, to which he had grown accustomed through long years, and which he now held by the goodwill of France. He had learnt to love the Netherlands almost as much as his hereditary German territory on the Danube. It never occurred to him in July 1704 that Marlborough would ever drive him out of Brussels as well as out of Munich.

But while he was ready for the present to abandon much of Bavaria to the enemy, in the hope of a speedy and triumphant return, he was not thorough-going in his acceptance of the situation from a military point of view. His wife and family were at Munich, and he left large forces in his capital and other favourite spots in the delightful regions of southern Bavaria, to protect them, not only against Marlborough, but against Austrian detachments that were returning from Italy through Tirol. In July he sent 8,000 more troops from Augsburg to join these defenders of his property, reserving only a fraction of his army to join to the French under Marsin and Tallard. These half-and-half methods were false strategy. Since he had chosen to fight his way back to his territories, he ought to have drawn out every man to swell the ranks of the Grand Army in the day of battle.[319]

Meanwhile Tallard was arriving. His passage of the Black Forest had been unopposed, but had been conducted in a manner that augured ill for the quality both of the commander and of his troops. When the empire of the world depended on his movements, and perhaps on his speed, Tallard wasted a week before the utterly unimportant town of Villingen, and failed to take it after all. And his troops, like Marsin's before them, did as the French seem always to have done in Germany during this war—plundered to their hearts' desire ; according to one of Tallard's officers, the peasantry of the Black Forest were rendered so desperate that they killed as many as a thousand marauders before the French army reached the plains of the Danube.[320]

In the first twelve days of August affairs moved rapidly towards the grand climax, which was utterly unexpected by everybody except Marlborough and Eugene.

The English army, although the Duke described it at the end of July as 'full of courage and desiring nothing more' than a battle, hardly hoped for such luck, and was beginning to suffer from a sense of inconclusiveness and failure. Even Adam Cardonnel, the Duke's familiar secretary, fell a prey to the general dejection, and on August 7 wrote home to Matt. Prior :

> We have made no great progress since our success at Schellenberg, except that it be burning and destroying the Elector's country, wherein we have not been sparing ; our last march was all in fire and smoke. We are now going to besiege Ingolstadt, and I wish to God it were well over that I might get safe out of this country.[321]

On the day that Cardonnel was writing in this mood, Tallard was effecting his junction with Marsin and the Elector at Biberbach, ten miles north of Augsburg. If Eugene had behaved as any ordinary general would have done in the circumstances and remained on the Rhine with his army to watch that of Villeroi, Marlborough and Prince Lewis would have been overmatched upon the Danube and the war in all probability lost. But Eugene played Blucher to Marlborough's Wellington. Taking with him a force of 18,000 men including the magnificent infantry of Prussia, he came by rapid marches along the north shore of the Danube, parallel with the route of Tallard. To save the Allied cause in the principal theatre of war, he deliberately ran the risk of leaving an inferior force on the Rhine.

The time, therefore, was short. In a week or two Villeroi would cross the Rhine, make himself master of Würtemberg, 'ruin the circle of Swabia,' and send on fresh forces to join the great French armies already gathered on the Danube. Moreover, the Elector had at last sent orders to the large Bavarian detachments on the Tirolese border to rejoin the main army. Marlborough and Eugene must defeat Tallard and Marsin at once, or all south Germany would be lost, and the boasted march on the Danube would prove as dismal a failure as Seymour and Rochester had foretold. The Allies, indeed, could not maintain themselves in the Bavarian territories they had ravaged, while the largest army in Europe threatened their communications with central Germany.   For already on August 10, Tallard, Marsin and the Elector had recrossed to the north shore of the Danube at Dillingen, threatening to march thence upon Eugene's isolated force that lay between Höchstädt and Donauwörth.

The crisis was now at hand.   Prince Eugene visited the Duke's camp near Schrobenhausen and the two friends secretly laid their plan.   They knew that they must at once fight and win a battle, or Europe would be permanently subjected to the power of the Grand Monarch.   The Hungarian rebels were ravaging Austria within thirty miles of its capital.   In Italy, the Duke of Savoy was in desperate straits, appealing to Vienna for the protection of which that city itself was in such sore need.*   To save Germany and Italy a battle must be fought, if necessary at considerable odds.   But Lewis of Baden, in his present temper, would never agree to attack a powerful army in a strong position. The two friends, therefore, thought it cheap to secure his absence from their counsels at the price of 15,000 men. With no less a force he was induced to undertake the honourable task of besieging Ingolstadt, the only enemy stronghold on the Danube between Vienna and Dillingen. Marlborough and Eugene consented to ' cover ' the siege for their princely colleague—a very modest function to all appearance!

So Prince Lewis went off contentedly to sit down before Ingolstadt.   Relieved of the incubus of his share in the command, Marlborough, from the neighbourhood of Rain, hastened to recross the Danube and, on August 11, joined Eugene's forces at Münster on the northern shore, where his friend's smaller army was threatened by the united forces of the enemy, coming from Dillingen by way of Höchstädt.

---

* *P.R.O., S.P.*, 105, 73, ff. 86, 106.   On August 16, three days after Blenheim had been fought, but one day before the news reached Vienna, Stepney, the English Minister there, wrote to Hill, the English Minister at Turin : ' To-morrow, we are to consider what representation may move the Duke of Marlborough to concert with Prince Eugene some means of sending you a present succour from the Empire. But I am afraid they will say our own child is first to be christened.   And if their campaign ends with the taking of Ingolstadt, we shall have almost as uneasy a neighbourhood as you are likely to have this winter.'

The day before he recrossed the Danube, the Duke wrote to Heinsius and to Godolphin in exactly similar terms :

> When Prince Eugene and I are joined our army will consist of 160 squadrons and 65 battalions.   Prince Lewis has with him for the siege 31 squadrons and 24 battalions.*   The French make their boast of having a great superiority, but I am very confident they will not venture a battle. But if we find a fair occasion we shall be glad to venture it, being persuaded that the ill condition of our affairs in most parts requires it.[322]

Whether the forces that the two French Marshals and the Elector had with them on the day of battle were a few thousands more or less than those of Eugene and Marlborough can never be ascertained with certainty.   Approximately, the opposing forces at Blenheim were equal in number, over fifty and under sixty thousand a side, but the French had a very decided advantage in artillery.

The reasons that made it imperative for the Allied Generals to fight ought to have made the French no less determined to refuse battle.   Tallard knew this as well as Marlborough or Eugene.   A diplomat of high intelligence, whose advice, if it had been taken by Louis XIV, would have prevented the formation of the Grand Alliance,† he well understood the situation of Europe in August, 1704.   He believed that if a battle could be avoided till the troops went into winter quarters, the war was practically won. Not only the Netherlands and Italy, but Baden and Würtemburg were now in French hands, and Bavaria would certainly be recovered if only they would sit still for a few weeks.

But Tallard, though he lacked nothing in intelligence, was wanting in firmness.   His training as a diplomat made him dread an open quarrel and seek always for a compromise.   But in war, compromise is less often possible

---

* Compare the very similar figures in *Feldzüge*, p. 496.   At this stage of the campaign, it is likely a squadron on the average contained about 120 effective cavalry and a battalion not more than 500 infantry.   In that case, Prince Lewis had about 12,000 infantry and 3,700 cavalry and Eugene and Marlborough fought Blenheim with about 32,500 infantry and about 18,000 cavalry.

† See pp. 135–136, above.

than in diplomacy. One must fight or one must avoid a battle ; half measures are impossible. Unfortunately for Tallard, he was associated with Marsin and the Elector of Bavaria, who both fancied themselves as soldiers of old experience, and were both eager to win immortal laurels by delivering the decisive blow of the war on a stricken field.*

Unfortunately, too, no one was in supreme command. The army moved under the orders of a Triumvirate. Tallard afterwards wrote that the lesson of Blenheim was ' to have only one man in command of an army.' He himself could give any orders he liked to his own force of nearly 35,000 men, but Marsin and the Elector were equally supreme over their joint army, which was probably less than 25,000, as the Bavarians present were a mere handful. Tallard, therefore, if he had had the requisite strength of character, could have refused to move the majority of the troops, without whom his colleagues could not have offered battle. But he was fatally influenced by a number of considerations : he was only one to their two ; one of them was a Prince for whose favour all the diplomatists of Europe were contending ; the feeling of the great body of French and Bavarian officers was all for a battle, and the forward party threatened him with ' a hundred letters ' denouncing him at Versailles if he refused to fight. Under these pressures only a really strong man would have held out. Tallard consented to a series of compromises between the policy of refusing and the policy of seeking battle, which finally landed them all in the disaster. He was dragged into the battle of Blenheim by others, very much as Aberdeen was dragged into the Crimean War.

Tallard's intention, when the joint force first crossed from Biberbach to the north of the Danube, was to remain

---

* I have adopted Tallard's own account of these disputes between himself and his two colleagues. (*Pelet* IV, pp. 562–566, printed in *Select Docs.*, pp. 118–121). It is first-hand evidence and very detailed. Some partisans of Marsin and the Elector afterwards declared that those two had wished not to fight and had been overruled by Tallard (*Select Docs.*, p. 133 ; *Colonie*, p. 224). But these assertions were not made by anyone present at the conferences, and Marsin makes no such claim in his narrative, which slurs over the subject of these councils before the battle, see his letter in *Lediard, Marl.* I, p. 409 ; see also pp. 424–425 for a witness in support of Tallard's story. Neither is Tallard's account of the matter at all flattering to his own strength of character : it does not read like a made-up tale.

in the impregnable fortified camp at Dillingen until winter.
But his colleagues would not hear of it, and soon persuaded
him to move to Höchstädt, in the hope of falling on Eugene's
18,000 men before Marlborough had had time to join him.
At Höchstädt was another position, almost as impregnable
as that of Dillingen ; the broad marshes round the Pulverbach could not have been forced by the Allies as the smaller
marshes of the Nebel were forced two days later.   At
Höchstädt, therefore, Tallard very wisely proposed to
remain.   Another fierce quarrel ensued.   The Elector
wished to march straight ahead and attack Eugene even if
Marlborough had already joined him.   It was agreed as
a compromise that they should move forward by the great
road across the Pulverbach marshes, and occupy the plains
between Lutzingen and Blenheim.   There they could lie
protected by the Nebel marshes till they had discovered
what was the real force of the enemy before them—whether
Marlborough was with Eugene and whether Baden was
there also.   And so, in the greatest confusion of counsel,
divided between offensive and defensive ideas of strategy,
ignorant of the force of the enemy and still more ignorant
of the amazing intention of the enemy commanders,
Aug. 12   the great host took up as a camping ground a position
(N.S.)   which was destined to prove a battlefield and the
1704   grave of the military reputation of the old French
Monarchy.

Tallard, clinging to caution till the last, the more so as
he wrongly believed Baden's army to have joined those
of Marlborough and Eugene, proposed that entrenchments
should be thrown up on the road where it crossed the Nebel,
and that the little stream should be dammed up to deepen
the water of its marshlands.   Both proposals were laughed
out of court by the more prominent of the French and
Bavarian officers, who had come to regard Tallard as an
old woman.   But he so far had his way as to set his own
men to fortify the approaches of Blenheim village.

So the army set up its tents on the great open stubble-
field, four miles in breadth, that stretched, unbroken by
a hedge, from the Danube at Blenheim to the pine-clad
hills above Lutzingen.   While the quartermasters were

marking out the site of the camp, and while the columns of white-coated French infantry were moving at leisure over the plain to take up their appointed stations, two telescopes were directed upon the scene from the steeple of Tapfheim church, five miles away.   Marlborough and Eugene had ridden out from Münster to see whether or not the enemy's main army had come out from behind the marshes of Höchstädt, and whether it was in a position where it could, with reasonable hazard, be attacked.   What they saw filled them with a sober exaltation, and then and there they formed their great resolve.   It stands on record that very few of the more responsible officers in the Allied army would have ventured to attack such a force so posted, except the two men of military genius who happened to be in sole command.*

* Cardonnel, the Duke's Secretary, wrote : ' The Duke of Marlborough no doubt knew the necessity of a battle better than any of us, for I believe, had the opinion of a majority of us prevailed, we should not have been for it under our circumstances ' (*Select Docs.*, p. 111, from *Add. MSS.*, 28918, ff. 287–288).

And Lord Orkney, one of the very best of Marlborough's subordinates, wrote : ' I confess it is entirely owing to my Lord Duke, for I declare, had I been to give my opinion, I had been against it, considering the ground where they were camped and the strength of the army.   But his Grace knew the necessity there was of a battle.'   *E.H.R.*, Ap. 1904, p. 311.   For the Tapfheim tower episode, see *Dispatches*, I p. 396.

The day after the battle, Hare, the Duke's chaplain, wrote home to a cousin : ' Almost all the generals were against my Lord's attacking the enemy, they thought it so difficult.'   *H.M.C., Hare MSS.* (1895), p. 201.

APPENDIX TO CHAPTER XVII

The 'Geography' of the March to the Danube

A piece of literature about the campaign of Blenheim which will probably survive even the stirring couplets of Addison's *Campaign*, is the conversation in *Tristram Shandy* between Corporal Trim and Uncle Toby on the uses of geography in war.

What business, added the Corporal triumphantly, has a soldier, an' please your Honour, to know anything at all of *geography* ? . . . Thou wouldst have said *chronology*, Trim, said my uncle Toby ; for as for geography, 'tis of absolute use to him. . . . Is it else to be conceived, Corporal, continued my uncle Toby, rising up in his sentry-box as he began to warm in this part of his discourse—how Marlborough could have marched his army from the banks of the Maes to Belburg ; from Belburg to Kerpenord—(here the Corporal could sit no longer)—from Kerpenord, Trim, to Kalsaken ; from Kalsaken to Newdorf ; from Newdorf to Loudenbourg ; from Loudenbourg to Mildenheim ; from Mildenheim to Elchingen ; from Elchingen to Gingen ; from Gingen to Balmerchoffen ; from Balmerchoffen to Skellenbourg, where he broke in upon the enemy's works, forced his passage over the Danube, crossed the Lech—pushed on his troops into the heart of the Empire, marching at the head of them through Friburg, Hockenwert and Schonevelt, to the plains of Blenheim and Hochstet. Great as he was, Corporal, he could not have advanced a step, or made a single day's march without the aids of geography.

All these places that Uncle Toby mentions will be found in Map IX at the end of this volume, except Schonevelt, which is close to Rain in Bavaria. The forms of the names used by Sterne are some of them variants on those given in my map :

Belburg	=	Bedburg
Kerpenord	=	Kerpen
Kalsaken	=	Kühlseggen
Mildenheim	=	Mundelsheim
Friburg	=	Friedberg

CHAPTER XVIII

BLENHEIM

AN hour after midnight, on August the 13th, the armies of
Marlborough and Eugene were aroused by beat of drum
to break up their camp at Münster.* Crossing the
Aug. $\frac{2}{13}$ Kessel Bach by pontoon bridges which had been
1704 laid the day before, they moved westward in eight
columns, threading a passage between wooded hills and
the marshlands of the Danube. The mists of dawn
streamed up, a white shroud through which sounded the
tramp of the invisible army of silent, half-awakened men.

Near Schwenningen they were joined by several
battalions of English, posted there overnight to guard the
mouth of the pass. Now in nine columns, they debouched
into the great plain where the battle was to be fought.

As the sun, rising over the tree-tops, began to disperse
the fog, the many-coloured ranks of horse and foot and the
teams slowly dragging the fifty-two cannon, spread like
the ribs of a fan, across the open country in full view of
the French. The Danish and Prussian infantry and the
Austrian cavalry passed on, under Eugene's command,
toward their distant positions on the right wing, some
of them as far as the fir-clad hills north of Lutzingen.
Marlborough's larger army—English, Dutch, Hessians,
Hanoverians, of all arms, together with the Danish cavalry,
took the shorter routes that led them to the banks of the
Nebel, opposite Oberglau and Blenheim. The two Allied
armies together numbered about 52,000, of whom about
9,000 were British ; but there were very few regiments,
even in Eugene's command, that were not paid for, wholly
or in part, by Holland or by England. The hostile army
was equal, or a little larger, in numbers.

* For this chapter see Map VI, p. 375, above.

The appearance of the heads of the first columns had spread no great alarm among the enemy. Such as were already astir at six o'clock thought that the red-coats moving in the mist must be a reconnaisance, sent out to cover the retreat of the main army up the Kessel to Nördlingen. For the French had made up their minds overnight that the Allied army would seek to retire northwards to its bases in Central Germany, abandoning Bavaria and the Danube. They were still divided on the question whether or not they ought to prevent such a retreat by advancing to attack a foe, who already, as they imagined, knew himself worsted in the campaign. False information, derived from prisoners, that the army of Prince Lewis had joined those of Eugene and Marlborough, still made them uncertain as to the wisdom of taking the offensive.* But the idea that the Allies would attack them was not in their thoughts that morning. Tallard himself wrote that he could see the enemy moving and that they were probably retiring to Nördlingen. Even after the mists had dispersed, revealing not a reconnaisance but the whole army of the Allies, there were French officers who believed that Marlborough was taking this road to Nördlingen, across their very front. That would indeed have been a manoeuvre of ludicrous rashness, but anything seemed to them more likely than that anyone would dare to attack the Grand Army, posted behind marshes, in a line strengthened by fortified villages, and protected on one flank by the forest and on the other by the Danube.

By seven o'clock, however, the real intentions of the Allies could no longer be in doubt. The Flemish Count, Mérode-Westerloo, then serving in a high position in the French army, had gone to sleep, light of heart, in a barn on the eastern outskirts of Blenheim. Awakened by his terrified servant, he saw through the open doorway the whole plain on the opposite side of the Nebel flooded with

---

* Tallard had been opposed to taking the offensive (*see* pp. 373–375, above), yet Hare relates (*Add. MSS.*, 9114, f. 104) that the day after his capture Tallard told Marlborough ' if his Grace had deferred his visit' (meaning his attack) ' a day longer, the Elector and he would have waited upon his Grace first '—and that they would have done so on August 12th but for the false information about Lewis of Baden's presence given by the prisoners.

sunlight and covered by the squadrons and battalions of the enemy. It was the surprise of his life. All around him the French were springing to arms. A cannon was fired to recall outposts and foragers, who hastened to rejoin the army, after having set the villages of Unterglau, Weilheim and Schwennenbach ablaze. Along a battlefield four miles in length, the Allies saw the white-coated infantry whom they had challenged, forming into battalions, while squadrons wheeled into long lines, and in front of the gathering army of France aides-de-camp and general officers chased and crossed each other at the gallop, along the edge of the marshland that alone divided the rival armies.

The fact remained that the French had been surprised, in a strong position certainly—so strong that Marlborough's best officers wondered at his boldness—but not impregnable if only mistakes were made in the dispositions for its defence. And mistakes were made, of which the worst, the inadequate number of French infantry in the centre, resulted, in part at least, from the fact that they had been thus surprised. For they were drawn up in the order of their encampment, not in an order of battle adapted at leisure to the proper defence of the actual ground.

The order of encampment that proved so fatal to France was that of two armies lying side by side. The larger army of Tallard stretched for a distance of two miles. The rest of the position, including the villages of Oberglau and Lutzingen, was occupied by the other French army under Marsin—which included as an integral part the few Bavarians whom the Elector had with him, numbering some 2,500 infantry and as many horse. Tallard to the south and Marsin to the north, had each camped according to custom with his cavalry on the wings, except that the cavalry of Tallard, for whom there was no room between Blenheim village and the Danube, were all encamped together on his left wing which composed the centre of the two united armies. Therefore all the cavalry of Tallard and half the cavalry of Marsin were spread in long lines over the great central plain, stretching for two miles between Oberglau and Blenheim. It was indeed a magnificent ground for the operations of horse, a cornfield already reaped and harvested, unbroken by hedge or house or ditch or tree ; and here the greatest cavalry action of the century was about to take place. But whereas Marlborough was sending thither great forces both of horse and foot, Tallard never sufficiently corrected the original fault of the order of encampment. He had only nine battalions of infantry posted among the many squadrons of the centre. There were indeed three more brigades of infantry a little to the west of Blenheim, but they were shortly afterwards moved into the village itself, without his knowledge and with disastrous results.*

Indeed Tallard's worst shortcoming was his failure to control the course of the battle once it had begun. If he had remained in close contact with his own army near Blenheim he could have rectified the mistakes in his original dispositions, instead of permitting others to make them worse in his absence. But when the action began, he rode over to the left wing of the united armies to see how Marsin's men were doing against Eugene. It was neither his place nor his business, and the real crisis of the day did not lie there. He left his own more urgent duties to subordinates, who mismanaged them worse than heart could conceive. The shortness of his sight, unredeemed by spectacles, was thought to have added to his helplessness that day.

In strong contrast to Tallard's want of control, was the hold that Marlborough established and kept over the battle. He always appeared where he was most needed ; and where he was not present he was admirably served by subordinates, such as his brother, Charles Churchill, Cutts, Lord Orkney, and the Prince of Hesse who commanded the cavalry in the pay of Holland.

If the small number of infantry supporting the horse in the centre was one blot in the plans of the defence, another was the refusal to take full advantage of the Nebel marshes that covered the front. If infantry had lined the edge of the marsh from Oberglau to the mills above

---

* The 'three brigades' probably contained nine battalions, but they must not be confused with the 'nine battalions' further to the left.

Blenheim, the Allies could not have crossed there at all.
And even without infantry, if the French cavalry *en masse*
had charged those who first got across, before they had
formed their battle ranks on the western shore, the Allies
would have been hurled back into the marsh.   But they
were allowed to cross and form up unhindered, and even
then were attacked in sections only, by isolated charges of
French horse, who, through defect in the supreme command,
were not fighting on any harmonized system.

Two explanations were afterwards advanced by the
French.   One was that their chiefs believed the marsh to
be wetter and more impracticable than it proved.   The
other was that Tallard deliberately wished the Allies to
cross, in order to thrust them back into the marsh : the
more of them who came over, the more he would destroy.
It was said that he had a clearly conceived plan for drawing
them across the Nebel in the centre between the villages of
Oberglau and Blenheim, where the infantry were massed
and whence they could debouch on to the two flanks of
those who had been so rash as to invade the French side of
the stream.   This plan was partially realized, at the crisis
of the battle, by the sortie from Oberglau, repulsed only
by the personal activity of Marlborough.   The corresponding sortie from Blenheim was prevented altogether,
because the Duke's original plan was based on a full-dress
attack to be made upon that village by the English and
Dutch infantry, as the initial operation of the day.

From seven o'clock till noon the two armies watched
one another.   Until Eugene's men should have reached
their distant stations, Marlborough's army did nothing
more than lay bridges of pontoon planks and faggots across
the marshes of the Nebel.   Religious service was held at
the head of each regiment in the diverse tongues and according to the diverse rites of the races drawn together in the
common cause of resistance to the hegemony of the Grand
Monarch.*   The recent victory at the Schellenberg and
the complete confidence felt by all in Marlborough and

* The very great majority of the victors of Blenheim were Protestants of one
kind or another.   Even Eugene's infantry were Prussians and Danes.

Eugene, gave to that motley host a unity and a spirit which was to prove superior on that day to the tradition of the hitherto unconquered army of Louis, already conscious of weakness and division among its leaders.

During the period of waiting, the band music of the rival armies was clearly heard on both sides of the Nebel, but it was silenced at frequent intervals by the voice of the cannon.   The French had over ninety, the Allies over fifty guns ;   but Colonel Blood's gunners were marksmen, and Marlborough placed each of his batteries in person, waiting to watch the range and effect of the first shots. When all was done—

His Grace rode along the lines to observe the posture and coun-tenances of his men, and found them and the officers of all nations of the Allies very cheerful and impatient of coming to a closer engage-ment with the enemy.   And as he was passing in front of the first line a large cannon ball from one of the enemy's batteries grazed upon a ploughed land, close by his horse's side, and almost covered him with dust.   He never halted his pace for this, but moved on, and finding everything in order, sat down at length to refresh himself till Prince Eugene was ready.

The morning hours slipped by, and still with impassive countenance he watched the men he treasured fall under the cannon shots.   Messenger after messenger galloped off to hasten Eugene, struggling through marsh and woodland far away.   But till his colleague was ready to attack, the Duke would not give the word.   What were his thoughts as he lunched among his staff in the open field, perhaps for the last time ?   He well knew it was the day that either made him or undid him quite :   his fortunes could not survive defeat.   And with his own ambitions, the liberties of England and of Europe had come to the last hazard, to be decided, not in any famous city or crowded meeting-place of men, but here in a naked plain of reaped stubble, between villages and farms of names unknown—that tallest spire was called Blindheim, the guides said—places where unlettered peasants had for ages tilled the soil and for ages more would till it, caring nothing what the great world in its madness had come there to do that day—save only that their poor houses and barns would assuredly be burned.

Yet in this uncouth, rustic spot, the texture of Eighteenth Century civilization and thought was to take its colour for good or ill.   Hasten, Eugene !   Flesh and blood can no longer stand still under this carnage of a cannonade, and the very gods are impatient to see the invisible event.   Here at last comes his messenger galloping from the north.   He is ready : and we are more than ready.   It is past noon, but August days are long.   Cutts, the Salamander, is to lead the British and Dutch against Blindheim.   And everywhere, along four miles of the Nebel's course, the regiments and squadrons shake themselves and move down towards the marshy edges of the brook.

The Nebel immediately in front of Blindheim—or Blenheim, as the English won the right to call it—ran between banks comparatively firm to the feet.   Cutts's brigades could wade or jump the brook without breaking their order, and march straight up in line against the approaches of the village.   Blenheim was defended that day not only by its garden hedges, but by military stockades and by barriers hastily constructed of farm carts, tables and doors.   Behind these were disposed the massed battalions and batteries of the French.

It was the story of the Schellenberg over again.   The English and Dutch fell in swathes before the grape and musketry of the defence.   But they came on, line after line. Brigadier Rowe forbade firing till they reached the defences. He struck his sword into the woodwork as the signal to fire, and French and English shot and stabbed each other through the open palisade.   Rowe himself fell mortally wounded.   His Lieutenant-Colonel and Major, endeavouring to carry him off, fell dead over his body.   The French infantry sallied out into the open.   The *gens d'armerie*, with their scarlet uniforms and magnificent horses, swept round the north-east corner of the village and the English were driven back in rout over the Nebel.   The *gens d'armes* captured one of the colours of Rowe's regiment.   But the Hessian infantry saved them from destruction, repulsed the pursuing horsemen and recovered the flag.

The charges and countercharges of horse and foot close

around Blenheim continued confusedly for some time. It ended with the English and Dutch infantry established, not in the village itself, but on its northern and eastern outskirts. Cannon were brought across the Nebel, some hedges and outbuildings commanding the debouchment of the village streets were secured, and under orders from Marlborough the direct assault was turned into a strong containing action, to prevent the emergence from the village of the massed infantry that it now contained.

As at the Schellenberg, the sustained valour of the English and Dutch attack had succeeded, not in carrying the position assailed, but in drawing thither defenders whom the enemy ought to have kept elsewhere. Lieutenant-General the Marquis de Clérambault, who commanded the defence, had been frightened into the fatal error of moving into the village itself the three infantry brigades whom Tallard had placed outside it to the west. There were now as many as twenty-seven battalions of foot and twelve squadrons of dragoons crowded into its streets and farms. If Tallard had been attending to his own army, this fatal mistake could have been prevented. In his absence his subordinates quarrelled over the course they ought to pursue ; Clérambault, nervous and excitable, had an angry altercation with Mérode-Westerloo, who wished to draw twelve battalions out of Blenheim to line the banks of the Nebel above the village. But the counsel of Clérambault prevailed.

During the remainder of the day Blenheim contained, dead and alive, about twelve thousand of the best infantry of France. It was, and still is, a large, straggling village of high-gabled farms, standing side by side in irregular streets, each in its own grounds and cattle-yards.* The Maulweyer brook flows down the middle of the principal street, on its way to the Danube, which almost abuts on the village. At the opposite end, the English held the outskirts and continued to fire with musket and cannon into

* The peasants tilling their holdings in the great plains between Blenheim, Oberglau and Lutzingen appear to have lived together in these large villages. There is a striking absence of isolated farms, like Hougoumont or La Haye Sainte at Waterloo.

the streets and farmyards, doing all the more execution because of the crowds with which Clérambault's nervousness had so unnecessarily packed the place. But the issue of the battle and the fate of the garrison of Blenheim were being decided elsewhere.

The forcing of the French centre in spite of the obstacle of the Nebel marshes, was an operation so critical that Marlborough gave it his personal attention from first to last, confiding in his trusted subordinates to conduct the assault on Blenheim without his presence. The affair in the centre required the close co-operation of cavalry and infantry, a branch of the military art which had entered a new era with the adoption of the ring bayonet.* In many different parts of the field that afternoon bodies of foot, under favourable conditions, got the better of bodies of horse, even on open ground, as they had seldom done in the days of Rupert and Cromwell. Marlborough gave the world a lesson in the new tactics that day, ' interlining ' his horse and foot. He drew up the centre of his army, preparatory to the crossing of the Nebel, in four lines ; † the front and back lines were infantry, the second and third lines were cavalry sandwiched in between.

Infantry, therefore, including Churchill's English, were the first to cross the marsh in the centre, partly wading, partly using the bridges of planks and brushwood. The French batteries played on them but could not stop their passage. Having reached firm ground on the far side, they covered the crossing of the cavalry. The French would have done well to advance before the Allied infantry were all across. But they stood watching from a distance, even when the first squadrons, in the wake of the infantry, came leading their horses by the bridle, picking their way across the improvised bridges.

At length, when perhaps half the Allies had crossed, but had not yet completed their battle ranks on the far side, the French cavalry came on, late but with fiery onset. In some

---

* See p. 223 above.

† Each ' line ' may have been two, or three, or even four deep, differing in the case of different regiments and squadrons.

places they drove the Allies back to the edge of the morass. Eye-witnesses have left accounts of many different charges and counter-charges of horse and foot in the hours of confused combat that followed. To distinguish them all is impossible. But it is to be noted that the slow but sure progress of the Allies in the centre that afternoon was due to the superior numbers and handling of their infantry. They were no longer placed in front of the cavalry as at the crossing. While the cavalry charged in front, they were drawn up in reserve, with gaps in their line so as to allow the cavalry to retreat through them for shelter, while they poured platoon volleys into the pursuing horsemen. Only well-drilled infantry could engage in such a game as that.

Besides many German regiments, British infantry under General Charles Churchill were employed in this service in the centre. After the first operation of covering the passage of the cavalry over the marsh, Churchill left Lord Orkney with a few of the island battalions to continue the support of the cavalry in the centre, while he himself, with other English foot, went to attach himself to the flank of Cutts, in the dangerous conflict swaying to and fro on the north side of Blenheim village.

The nine battalions of infantry who alone supported the French horse were young recruits, brave as young French recruits have often proved, worthy ancestors of the ' Marie Louises ' of 1813. They were hopelessly outnumbered. The Allied infantry, including Lord Orkney's British, and the batteries which the indefatigable Colonel Blood had brought over by a pontoon bridge, plied them with musketry and grape. The poor lads never moved, but were mowed down in their ranks and lay in straight lines of white-coated corpses.*

Meanwhile, the Prussian and Danish infantry under Eugene, splendid troops under a splendid leader, though poorly supported by the Imperialist cavalry, were pressing Marsin's French and Bavarians in the plain between

---

* Apparently they fought not in line but in square, presumably for fear of cavalry ; Orkney speaks of them as ' in battalion quarre (*carré*) in the best order I ever saw, till they were cut to pieces almost in rank and file.' *E.H.R.*, Ap., 1904.

Oberglau and Lutzingen, and through the skirts of the pine forests to the extreme north. Eugene's was, in fact, a containing action, gallantly performed at great cost of life ; it was essential to Marlborough's victory elsewhere, but had little likelihood of local success.

Late in the afternoon the crisis of the still uncertain day drew near. The French and Irish infantry massed in Oberglau made a sortie in force on to the flank and rear of the Allied centre. During the dozen years since Sarsfield and the first exiles had left Limerick, the regiments of Irish in the European armies of Louis had won themselves a reputation for disciplined valour that had atoned for the rout of the undrilled hordes at the Boyne. They now made from Oberglau a charge into Marlborough's flank, which almost severed the connection between his army and that of Eugene. Several German battalions were routed. The scales of the battle trembled and seemed to turn. But Marlborough himself was there. He brought up more German infantry and Danish horse, thrust the assailants back into Oberglau and planted cannon and musketry to command the exits from the village. No further sortie was made.

At last the hour of decision had come. The confused fighting in the centre all that afternoon had brought the Allied line forward some little distance from the Nebel.* The French infantry there had been reduced to a handful of boys who knew nothing of battles except how to die at their post. The French squadrons were fighting as separate units rather than as a single force ; after many a gallant charge they were becoming tired, and the flame of their first confidence had burnt out. Tallard had joined them at last, but he was not the man to put spirit or order into their ranks.

Such was the condition of the centre when, about five o'clock, Marlborough marshalled the English and Allied cavalry in one magnificent line for the decisive charge. His orders were that they should advance at a smart trot

---

* To talk of a ' hill ' in the French centre, as several of the narratives do, is liable to mislead readers who have not seen the ground for themselves. The slope up from the Nebel is very gradual indeed. The general aspect is a vast level plain.

that would enable them to keep their ranks thigh to thigh, but a trot that was to get faster as they approached the enemy with drawn swords and no firearms in hand. The French, instead of charging in the same style, halted to 'present their fusils.' Their disunited and disheartened squadrons were engulfed and borne along in the trot, that soon broke into a gallop for dear life on one side, for hot revenge on the other. In the heave of that resistless wave, the thinned ranks of the infantry recruits vanished, like a child's castle on the sands melting in the wash of waters.

Far to north, on the hills above Lutzingen, along the battle-stained edge of the fir forest, Prussian, Dane and Austrian, French and Bavarian, in the intervals of their charges and counter-charges, stood straining their eyes southward over the battlefield, which they alone of the combatants could see in its entirety. Four miles away their vision was bounded by the pillar of battle-smoke which concealed the spire of Blenheim. At the supreme moment of the day, those eager spectators on the hillside had seen the two waves of opposing cavalry approach, meet and mingle into one long, locked line of combat ; then, in an ecstasy of suspense, they had watched it heave, bend, break, and scatter to the west. The remoter distances of the plain soon appeared to be sprinkled with innumerable moving spots, all making, like insects in desperate haste, towards the brushwood line of the Danube or the tall, sentinel Schloss of Höchstädt. In those few minutes the watchers on the hills had seen the turn of the tide in Europe, the ebb of the highwater mark of King Louis's effort for universal monarchy.

All effective resistance in the centre was at an end. Some squadrons attempted to rally behind the tents of the abandoned camp, only to be swept away once more as the chase rolled on towards the marshes of the Danube and the Pulverbach. Across the latter there were roads of escape at Diesenhofen and at Höchstädt ; but only strong swimmers could hope to win across the Danube. Towards its banks, on either side of Sonderheim, was shepherded the largest throng of fugitives. One of these unhappy folk, Count Mérode-Westerloo, survived to tell the tale : the horse he rode seemed to him to be borne along in the press with its feet off the ground, till the quivering mass of terror-stricken creatures was pitched over the edge, ' two pikes high,' into the marsh below.   The drop, down which horses and men were hurled to destruction, is still clearly visible, dividing the level of the great plain from the level of the Danube marshes.*

But one poor gentleman remained on the bank above. Marshal Tallard had tried in vain to get orders sent through to the infantry in Blenheim to retreat.   Of the messengers who attempted to steer their way back athwart the rout

> no more was told
> Than of leaf on Danube rolled.

At length the Marshal saw it as his own duty to extricate his infantry or share their fate.   He had just started on his way back to Blenheim on this manful errand when, close to Sonderheim, he was surrounded by Hessian cavalry, who recognized him by the Order of the Saint-Esprit on his coat and carried him to the presence of the victor.

Marlborough we may imagine at this time sitting his horse somewhere in the middle of the great plain, a good two miles west of Blenheim, sending orders to check the pursuit on the edge of Pulverbach marshes, and endeavouring to draw his centre together in time to impede the retreat of Marsin and the Elector.   But that retreat was carried out in excellent order from Oberglau and Lutzingen to Mörslingen.   The armies of Eugene and Marlborough were too much exhausted to make another serious effort against unbroken troops.   The Prince and the Duke both declared that they had scarcely a battalion or a squadron that had not

---

* But the Danube marshes, like those of the Nebel, have since been drained and cultivated, and the Danube canalised.   This crowning disaster was celebrated in poems, one of which, as Macaulay wrote, ' has been rescued from oblivion by the exquisite absurdity of three lines ' :

> Think of two thousand gentlemen at least,
> And each man mounted on his capering beast ;
> Into the Danube they were pushed by shoals.

charged four or five times.   So Marsin and the Elector
took their men off westward in safety into the gathering
dusk.   They were much less than half the enemy's total
force, and of the larger army of Tallard little indeed
would be left, if the infantry in Blenheim failed to escape.

In victory, as on all other occasions of life, Marlborough
was the Prince of courtesy, for which he won a name from
the polite and sensitive nation whom he defeated.   His
coach and six had followed up along the high road across the
Nebel and there, with many compliments, the unfortunate
Marshal was accommodated, till, a few days later, his own
coach was fetched back from the retreating army under a
flag of truce.   In haste, with a stump of pencil on the back
of ' a bill of tavern expences ' spread out upon his saddle, the
Duke wrote the most celebrated of his letters to Sarah, of
which the precise text ran as follows : *

Aug. 13, 1704.
I have not time to say more, but to beg you will give my duty to
the Queen, and let her know Her Army has had a Glorious Victory
Monsr. Tallard and two other Generals are in my coach and I am
following the rest : the bearer my Aide de Camp Coll. Parke will
give Her and account of what has pass'd.   I shall doe it in a day or
two by another more att large.

MARLBOROUGH.

When he wrote these words, it is probable that Marlborough did not know that the infantry in Blenheim had
surrendered, but felt certain that they could not escape.
Late in the evening, ' about nine at night,' he sent a message
to the English officers investing the village that they should
keep close guard during the hours of darkness and he would
bring the rest of the army in the morning to force the
position.   But in fact the catastrophe had already been
hastened without his intervention, and the doings of the
great day made complete.†

The moment the French line had given way in the
centre, Lord Orkney, with admirable promptitude, had
wheeled his English and Scots off to the left to join their

* It is reproduced in facsimile in *Coxe*, i, p. 306.
† *E.H.R.* Ap., 1904, p. 310 note, Abercromby's statement.

comrades under Churchill and Cutts.   He and Ingoldsby
extended Churchill's line of investment beyond the Maulweyer brook, down to the marshes of the great river.   The
circle of troops round Blenheim was thus made complete
except for the short distance where the Danube acted as
a no less effectual barrier.*   General Clérambault realized
too late the consequences of his folly in bringing all the
infantry into the village.   He had not the courage to face
the position he had created, but galloped out like a madman
and leaped his horse into the river, whether to escape by
swimming or by suicide is not clear.   He perished in the
Danube.

The Brigadiers, whom he had left without a word of
orders or explanation, proved to be men as incompetent as
himself.   Deserted by some and cut off from all their
commanding officers, they should have taken counsel
together to unite their brigades and force their way out by
a concerted movement.   They might have succeeded, at
least in part, and could certainly have sold their lives dear.
The moral effect of Blenheim on the French army and on
European opinion would in that case have been very
different from what it was.   The British officers who had
surrounded them regarded such an attempt as by no means
certain to fail, especially if made after nightfall ; and they
were the more anxious to obtain a surrender while the
evening was still grey.

On such occasions a little bluff may be useful, especially
in dealing with junior officers overwhelmed with the weight
of unexpected responsibilities.   The game was excellently
played by two canny Scots, George Hamilton, first Earl
of Orkney, and his aide-de-camp, Sir James Abercromby.
The contrast between Marlborough and Tallard that day is
hardly greater than the contrast between the subordinate
officers by whom they were respectively served.

But the final negotiation was preceded by a renewal of
desperate attacks on the village.   On the east side, Cutts's
men came on for a fifth time, and for a fifth time were
repulsed ; but they clung to the outskirts, still keeping up

---

* See inset of Map VI., p. 375, above.   Rowe's and Ferguson's brigades were
under Cutts.

their fire.   Orkney's men from the west twice reached the
churchyard, but were twice driven back from the wall, ten
feet high, that surrounds it like a fortress.   They established
themselves within a few yards of the church, and set fire to
that side of the village, 'which incommodat' the enemy
'very much.'   The fire of the Scots Greys, who as dragoons
dismounted to aid the infantry, prevented the debouchment
of the French from the streets.

But at this stage Orkney was alarmed to see two whole
brigades mustering to attack his troops, whom he knew to
be 'very much fatigued.'   The French came on, till the
head of the column was 'within 35 yards of him,' when they
halted in apparent irresolution.*   Acting on a sudden
impulse, the Scottish lord bade his drums beat a parley, and
then and there offered them fair quarter.   The French
Brigadier to whom he spoke was Dénonville, a young man
of fashion little acquainted with war.   He consented to
capitulate on condition that no prisoners were plundered,
a condition that was religiously observed.   Ingoldsby
received the surrender of the other brigade on the same
terms.   This remarkable feat of taking the surrender, without a shot fired, of a large body of troops who had marched
out to force a passage, was in part due to the personal
superiority established by the British officers over the
French officers and men on the spot.   While Orkney was
in treaty with Dénonville, his aide-de-camp, Sir James
Abercromby, 'rode up to the Royal Regiment and pulled
the colours out of the ensign's hands, and was slightly
wounded over the arm by him.   I asked them,' Abercromby relates, 'if they did not hear what the General
offered ; but his Lordship was come up by this time,
without giving any fire, and ordered them to lay down
their arms, which they did, asking quarter.'   These two
tough Scottish aristocrats were not men to be easily gain-
said ; and they probably spoke French better than most
of their English brother-officers.   Orkney was the husband
of Elizabeth Villiers, perhaps the cleverest woman in

* A comparison of Abercromby's narrative, *E.H.R.*, Ap., 1904, p. 309 note,
with *Description of the Seats of War* (1707), p. 188, makes clear what happened at
this critical moment.

England after Duchess Sarah, and his conduct this day
showed him well worthy to be her latest lord.

The two French Brigadiers were then asked by their
captors what troops were left in the village. The reply,
that there were still twenty battalions of foot and twelve
squadrons of dragoons, ' I own struck me,' says Orkney ;
' however I made the best countenance I could, and desired
the same brigadier to return along with my aide-de-camp '
to the Marquis of Blansac—now in command of the village
since Clérambault's tragic elopement.

Inside the village the psychological drama was played
out amid the various and conflicting passions of ten thousand
men, trapped in a situation that was startlingly novel to the
proudest regiments in Europe. The French army, deprived of its proper chiefs and finding itself in the hands of
men it did not trust, showed something of the emotional
and equalitarian temper which in later ages so often raised
it above or debased it below armies more invariably submissive to discipline. Young Dénonville, anxious to have
the policy of capitulation that he had initiated for his own
troops endorsed and justified by the rest, most improperly
harangued the rank and file on the necessity of surrender,
not without visible effect on many, though the regiment of
Navarre was furious. Blansac protested, but in the end
allowed himself to be conducted out of the village by
Abercromby to the spot where Orkney waited in well-
concealed anxiety. The French General, emerging for
the first time from the battle-smoke that had wrapped the
village all day, saw the great plain under sunset swept clear
of all his friends, and heard the calm assurances of the
imposing Milord that Marlborough himself was speedily
coming with the whole Allied army—' though to tell the
truth it was a little gasconade in me,' writes Orkney, for it
must have been some time before the Duke could come in
full force. But the impression was made, and Blansac
decided to fall in with the humour of the majority of his
men, and to surrender at discretion. When Abercromby
was sent through the middle of the village and out at its
eastern barricades to request the Salamander to cease fire
because the enemy had yielded, Cutts could hardly believe

his ears, for Rowe's and Ferguson's brigades were quite incapable of making another attack.

The losses in the crowded village had been very great, but at least 9,000 unwounded soldiers, including the most famous regiments in France, laid down their arms and standards. Only the Regiment of Navarre, which was taken a thousand strong, burnt their battle-flags with tears of rage. About nine o'clock the captured army filed out of the village to an open space where they bivouacked for the night. The British soldiers were posted around with bayonets fixed till dawn, trying to keep awake in turns, for they had been afoot since one in the morning and had seen some service. ' Without vanity, I think we did our pairts,' wrote Orkney, who had been twenty hours in the saddle. ' It is,' he added, ' perhaps the greatest and completest victory that has been gained this many ages ! ' [323]

It was eight days before England had the news. It could travel no faster than Colonel Parke could ride and sail. Day after day, and night after night, he covered the leagues between, and in every town where he changed horses he told the tidings that made Germany free of Frenchmen for another epoch. At Frankfurt the well-informed British Resident, Henry Davenant, wrote to Stepney :

Yesterday Colonel Parke came here with the agreeable news of the victory we have gained over the enemies. This battle will in all appearance put an end to the war in the Empire, and give the means of assisting the Duke of Savoy who is very near his ruin. The Duke of Marlborough has beyond all dispute saved the Empire. Affairs were in no very good condition before this engagement.

And to Harley, Davenant wrote : ' The people here confess that they owe to the Duke of Marlborough and to our troops the safety of Vienna.'

Leaving the Germans rejoicing behind him, Parke reached Rotterdam, and the Dutch learnt how the regiments they had hazarded on the Danube with so many fears, had reaped there a hundred-fold of safety for Holland. Alexander Stanhope, our Representative at the Hague, had been in the lowest depression on the eve of the battle, writing that if Marlborough evacuated Bavaria, 'they would lose the benefit of all they have done hitherto,' and fearing that the Duke's rumoured intention to accept the title of Prince of the Empire from Leopold would not be 'at all for his service in England.' But after the passage of Parke, followed next day by the arrival of Colonel Panton with the Duke's letters to the States-General, Stanhope changed his tune :

We cannot speak of anything else but these glorious advantages. There has not been in our age or scarce to be found in story so complete a victory as Prince Eugene and our Duke have gained. . . . I fancy the great Monarch now in Augustus' condition after the defeat of Varus, tearing his flesh, stark mad, and roaring out, '*O, Tallard, Tallard, rendez mes bataillons.*' [324]

But it was not with the effect of the news in Germany, or in Holland, or in France that Parke was most concerned. 'What will they say in England ?' must have been his thought, every hour of his four days' gallop, and while he paced the deck of the weary ship for three days more. At length he landed. On August 10th, by the home reckoning, he traversed London on his way to Windsor, leaving the news as he passed. 'In a few minutes,' the cannon of the Tower were set firing, the bells rang in Wren's steeples, and the whole population poured out into the streets.

Parke called at the Duchess's town house, and gave her the famous note. She gave it back to him to take on to the Queen. But copies of it were struck off in the presses of London and circulated in thousands, in time for folk to read as they 'were sitting down to dinner.' That night men could talk of little else but the wonderful note, 'writ on horseback with a black leaden pencil,' and the pregnant fact of Tallard in the coach.

Aug. $\frac{10}{21}$ 1704

Only the Jacobite coffee houses were thronged at the very juncture when the news arrived ; the poor fellows moved like mere engines and vanished in a hurry. But as these disappeared the loyal, honest Englishmen repaired in crowds to the loyal coffee houses and you might read satisfaction in every face. Bohee tea, coffee, chocolate, ratafia and Nants Brandy were insipid liquors. Away they adjourned to the tavern, every bumper was crowned with the Queen's or the Duke of Marlborough's health and the loyal citizens emptied the cellars so fast I think two-thirds were foxed next morning. Never were such illuminations, ringing of bells, such demonstrations of joy since the laying of London stone.

Leaving the turbulent town behind, the Colonel galloped on for the last lap of his great ride. That evening he was ushered into the closet that overlooks the Terrace at Windsor Castle, delivered the note with Sarah's homage to the Queen, and told what he had seen of the battle. It was usual to give £500 to the bearer of victorious dispatches. But Parke's only dispatch was the Duke's note to his wife,* and this was no common victory. At his own request, Anne gave him, instead of the customary bag of guineas, her own portrait in miniature. When he came to die, he left his family the picture of himself by Sir Godfrey Kneller : the Colonel stands wearing round his neck this royal token, commemorating the ride that brought the good news from Danube to Thames.[325]

On the night after the battle, Marlborough, having given special orders for the care of the wounded, slept in a water-mill near Höchstädt, full of barrels of the enemy's powder. He did not enter the town, which was protected by walls and commanded by the tall Schloss, still occupied by 600 of the enemy. But he set guards round it for the night and it surrendered early next day.†

In the morning, after inspecting the stores in Höch-städt, and arranging for an immediate advance on the traces of the flying foe, Marlborough and Prince Eugene went to visit Marshal Tallard. Before this visit the dejection among the captured French

Aug. $\frac{3}{14}$ 1704

* Colonel Lord Tunbridge was following Parke at an interval of twenty-four hours with the real ' dispatches.' *Add. MSS.*, 9114, f. 107 ; *P.R.O., S.P.*, 84, 227, f. 27.

† See Hare in *Add. MSS.*, 9114, f. 104. There is a local tradition at Höchstädt to the effect that the English refrained from attempting to occupy the town on the evening of the battle because they saw the sun reflected on the leaden tops of the wooden crosses in the churchyard, which they mistook for the cuirasses of the French. Since the Kaspars of the neighbourhood persuaded themselves that this occurred, it is worth recording, at least as a curiosity. In the Museum in the Schloss at Höchstädt one of these crosses is exhibited (1930).

officers had been great.   The Duke's chaplain was in the room with about seventy of them :

some were blaming the conduct of their own generals, others walking with their arms folded, others laid down lamenting their hard fortune and complaining for want of refreshment, till at last, abandoning all reflections of this nature, their chief concern was for their King, abundance of these muttering and plainly saying, '*Oh, que dira le Roy !*'

But on the arrival of Marlborough and Eugene the chivalry of honourable foes charmed away for a few minutes the bitterness of defeat.

There were a great many of the French generals with the Marshal, all of which came crowding about His Grace and admired his person, as well as his tender and gracious behaviour towards them.   They had all something to say for themselves, which His Grace and Prince Eugene received with the greatest modesty and compassion.   Prince Eugene . . . frankly told how often and how bravely he was repulsed by them. . . . After staying with the Marshal above an hour, the Duke and all his company returned to our army which he now ordered to march beyond Höchstädt as far as Stenheim, whilst he rode over the field of battle from the right to the left, the dead of both armies lying stripped upon the ground.

The prisoners, all save a hundred, had been captured by Marlborough's army, but he divided them equally with Eugene, partly out of compliment to the Prince and his master, and partly for convenience, since the guarding, feeding and disposal of 11,000 men was a serious matter. The number rose in a few days to nearly 15,000, as the cavalry sent in front of the Allied advance picked up more and more, and as deserters, stragglers and rearguards gave themselves up to escape the vengeance that the German peasantry were wreaking on the invaders.   Three thousand Germans in the French service came over to enlist with the victors.[326]

Tallard was sent to England, where he lived for several years in a house placed at his disposal in Nottingham. Accustomed as Ambassador to get on well with the English, he attained a considerable local popularity, introducing the cultivation of celery, and exchanging visits with the gentry for twenty miles round.[327]

The losses of the Allies were over 12,000 killed and wounded, nearly a quarter of their total force. Of these casualties the British and Dutch bore about 2,200 each. The only other nationals to suffer as much were the Danes, who had lost 2,400. Nominally neutrals in the war with France,* the troops of the King of Denmark had fought as a 'mercenary army' in the strictest sense of the word, and had given good value for their money, both on foot under Eugene and in the centre among Marlborough's horse.[328]

The French loss cannot be so exactly estimated. A large part of it took place in the wastage of the ten days' retreat, with the angry peasants around them, the Allied hussars close on their rear, and discomfiture and panic in their own ranks. Marsin's army had come off the field unbeaten and in admirable order, but anyone who has been involved in a military disaster may have chanced to witness how the atmosphere of retreat and the contagion of a rabble of fugitives can sometimes dissolve the discipline of regiments who have not themselves been worsted in the battle. And so it proved now with Marsin's army in contact with the wreckage of Tallard's force. According to some of their own reports, the French never camped at night, nor pitched tents, but lay beside their arms in constant alarm.

In short we are in terrible consternation. We have lost our drums and standards. We have only 250 officers in all our armies who are not wounded or killed. Only 200 men left in four regiments of dragoons. The city of Ulm is so full of wounded officers they don't know how to put them apart from the common soldiers. The peasants are wild against us.

The relations of the French army with the German civilians continued to be those of mutual atrocity; Mérode-Westerloo confesses that his comrades marked the line of their flight with pillage and arson. Some of their letters intercepted by the Allies placed their total loss at 40,000, and by August 28 Marlborough mentioned the figure as

* See p. 297, above.

not improbable.   In any case, much less than half the
Grand Army that fought at Blenheim remained with the
standards ; moreover, the bulk of the Elector's own army,
which he had left scattered in Bavaria, was disbanded in
the late autumn under a treaty made by the Allies with the
Electress in Munich.   She remained in her palaces, but
Bavaria was subjected to the occupation and extortion of
the Imperialist armies.   The Elector had followed the
waning fortune of France, taking with him the 4,000
Bavarians who had escaped from the battle.   He returned
to resume his position of Vicar-General of the Netherlands.

Sept. 10 (N.S.) 1704   When Ulm had capitulated, the last enemy fortress on the Danube had fallen, and the last of
the cannon of the Grand Army, save half a dozen
field-pieces, fell into the hands of the Allies ; most
of the artillery had been taken on the field of Blenheim.[329]

The wreck of the French army never halted till it
reached Alsace, and Marlborough followed hot on its traces,
leaving Ulm blockaded behind him.   At the end of the
first week of September he crossed the Rhine near Philipps-
burg and went up against Landau.   The war in Germany
was finished.

Marlborough was loaded with compliments by the
Emperor Leopold, and at last consented to accept from him
a Princedom of the Empire, with the little Principality of
Mindelheim, south of the Danube, a territory which would
in England have been called a nobleman's estate.   It was
no longer possible for his enemies in England to make
capital out of his acceptance of an honour, which seemed
now to redound to the credit of the whole English
nation.*

But the Duke would have been even better pleased if
the Emperor had taken his constantly reiterated advice to
make terms with the Hungarian Constitutionalists and
Protestants, and so attain power to finish the Italian war
next year.   For the Duke of Savoy was still only reprieved,
not saved.   In September, Hill, the British Minister at
Turin, wrote, ' We shall go on to suffer some time longer,

---

* Mindelheim was taken from him and restored to Bavaria at the Treaty of
1714.   But the princely title and rank remains in the Marlborough family.

and live upon the merits of the battle of Hockstead.' *
Victor Amadeus, all agreed, was still ' in extremity.'   But
the Emperor would rather risk the loss of Italy than come
to any terms with the Hungarian demands.   Blenheim
only hardened his heart and he began to resent personally
the repeated attempts, made by Stepney at Vienna, to mediate
between himself and his subjects.   The Jesuits at his ear
were against compromise, and, as our Whiggish diplomats
complained, ' rode tantivy as Churchmen always do where
they have power, to destroy all they have made their
enemies.' 330

Marlborough indeed gained little at Vienna in reward
for Blenheim, except the title of Prince.   Once the Empire
was safe, the influence of Eugene waned, and the efforts of
the War Office relaxed.   The Imperialist General, Lewis of
Baden, unable to forgive Marlborough for sending him to
Ingolstadt like a fool while the battle was afighting, in
future did his best to delay military operations and successfully
spoilt Marlborough's autumn campaign on the Moselle.†

But nothing could undo the effects of Blenheim.
Italy and the Netherlands, indeed, had still to be reconquered before the war was won according to the terms so
well laid down by William in the Treaty of Grand Alliance.
Austrian lethargy and Dutch fears of battle might yet
postpone that consummation for a couple of years.   But
the chances of success had now visibly turned to the side of
the Allies, with their two great generals, and with the certain
confidence that inspired their troops whenever either of those
generals was allowed to lead them into action.   And, above
all, the hopefulness and spirit of the armies of King Louis
were fatally shaken by the circumstances of the battle of Blenheim.   ' Malbrook ' had become to them a name of terror.
Not for another four years and more, not until the new and
extravagant demands of the Allies after victory had put the
whole French nation with its back to the wall, was the
morale of the French army restored.

* For several years the English used the names Blenheim and Höchstädt
indifferently for the battle ;   gradually the name Blenheim ousted its rival in
England, though not on the Continent.

† I shall leave the Moselle affair of Sept.–Oct. 1704 till the next volume.   It is
less a continuation of the Blenheim campaign than a preparation for that of 1705.

CHAPTER XIX

Opening of the Peninsular War.   Capture of Gibraltar.   Battle of Malaga.
  Political reactions of the year's campaign.

ALMOST a month after the battle of Blenheim, when Marlborough had already crossed the Rhine, he heard by way
of England that Gibraltar had been captured.   Yet in fact
the achievement of the fleet had preceded by ten days the
victory on the Danube.

In 1704 Queen Anne launched her Pretender for the
throne of Spain, a fair reply to Louis's claimant for the throne
of Britain.   The Austrian Courtiers had been unwilling to
send abroad their Arch-Duke Charles ; they wished, as English diplomats complained, to ' Keep him like a fine thing not
to be exposed to wind and weather, which is not the way to
make him King.' [331]   But as Austria could not aid the
Spanish enterprise either with ships, with troops, or with
money, England insisted that at least the young man must
come in person, for on no other condition would Portugal
enter the war.   He was brought over to Windsor in
January, feasted there royally as King Charles III
Jan.-Feb. of Spain, and packed off to Portugal in midwinter
1704   under Rooke's escort, accompanied by an English
army.   At the end of February they reached Lisbon,
where ' Charles III ' was landed ' with about three hundred
Germans of all sorts.' [332]   The Allied force that commenced
the campaign on his behalf along the Portuguese border in
May consisted of some four thousand English, two
thousand Dutch, and twenty thousand Portuguese armed
and paid for chiefly by the Maritime Powers.*

* See pp. 300-302, above, for the Portuguese Treaty. *For this chapter see
Map of Europe at end of volume.*

Against them came the French and Spaniards, under Marlborough's nephew, the Duke of Berwick, illegitimate son of James II and Arabella Churchill. Old Sir Winston Churchill decidedly had the trick of transmitting military talent. For, next to Villars, Berwick was the best general still in the active service of France. Fortunately for the Allies, he was hampered in 1704, not only by the lethargy of all things Spanish, but by the furious quarrel raging at Madrid between the Queen's *Camarera Mayor*, the Princess des Ursins, a French-born cosmopolitan, and the French Ambassador the Cardinal d'Estrées, neither of whom could brook a rival. This feud, which absorbed the whole energies of the Court, involved not merely the personal issue, but the attempt of the Spaniards to save their country from complete political subjection to France. For the Princess des Ursins, though sent to Spain by Louis to manipulate the royal couple on his behalf, had taken up the cause of ' Spain for the Spaniards.' The Savoyard girl-Queen and her elderly *Camarera Mayor*, the bravest hearts in Spain, had manhood enough, though King Philip had none. They defied the French Ambassador and no one at Madrid could think of anything but this quarrel. Nothing was done that spring or summer to carry out the works agreed on to fortify Gibraltar, and no adequate garrison was placed there, in spite of the Governor's earnest prayers. Nor was Berwick furnished with ammunition and stores for his Portuguese campaign. Two-thirds of his cavalry horses died, because, as he himself records, the French were too proud to take the advice of the Spaniards and feed the beasts on barley since ordinary forage was wanting in that barren land.[333]

These circumstances saved the Allies from losing Lisbon in the first weeks of the Peninsular War. The campaign on the Portuguese border, begun in May, was brought to an end in July by the summer heats that made further effort intolerable to man and beast. But before nature imposed her annual truce, a number of fortresses on the Tagus had been surrendered to Berwick at the first summons, although he had no powder to bombard them. The Portuguese took particular delight in compelling the

1704

English who were in garrison with them to surrender, on one occasion wetting their powder to prevent any attempt at resistance. Two whole regiments, the Ninth and Eleventh Foot, were thus lost. Further to the north, the Portuguese veteran, Las Minas, aided by the Dutch, won some minor successes against the Spaniards.

From the first moment of their landing, the mortality had been great among the English, utterly unprovided for in that land of neglect, where the magazines were empty, the transport non-existent, the native army a mob. 'The only comfortable thing I have seen since I landed,' wrote Colonel Hamilton from Lisbon, 'was one rainy day. Several, both English and Portuguese, are every morning found dead in our streets, for murder is as frequent here and passes as unregarded as picking of pockets at Common [Covent] Garden Playhouse.' It is difficult to say whether the Spaniards or the Portuguese were the more hostile to their respective allies. The Portuguese, under the influence of the priesthood, hated the heretics perhaps rather more than the Spaniards hated the French. On one occasion a detachment of Portuguese, challenged by a Dutch sentry, and not understanding this common military usage, took him for an enemy and massacred him and his fellow-countrymen ; when they discovered their mistake, they merely stripped the dead and wounded and went callously on their way.

It would have needed a man of Marlborough's patience and power to deal with the brutal ignorance of such allies. The general in command of the English was Meinhard Schomberg, son of the noble old soldier who had been William's right-hand man in his English and Irish campaigns. But Meinhard was lazy and indifferent to the welfare of his troops. He roused himself only to quarrel violently and to no purpose with Dutch and Portuguese alike. Before the end of the summer Marlborough had him recalled and replaced by another English general of Huguenot origin, Ruvigny, Earl of Galway, who had won his laurels in the Irish wars of the last reign.

1704

The news of the 'better success' of the Allies at the Schellenberg confirmed the wavering loyalty of the Court of Lisbon ; 'otherways we had been an undone people,' wrote Colonel John Richards from the frontier-fort of Almeida,' 'but now there is life in a muscle.' Meanwhile young Paul Methuen gave spirited lectures on unpreparedness to King Peter, the best man at the Court of Portugal, who listened patiently, and endeavoured to apply what remedy he could to the incompetence of his subjects.[334]

So began that strange Peninsular War of eight years, famous for its romantic vicissitudes and tragic in its waste of English life and treasure, in return for which the only palpable gain to England, the rock of Gibraltar, was won by a by-blow of naval enterprise in the very first campaign.

Since Lisbon was this year at the disposal of the English fleet as a base, Rooke entered the Mediterranean earlier and in better humour than might have been expected from his conduct in 1702. After seeing the English Levant trading-fleet safe through the Straits, he put himself into touch with the Duke of Savoy through the port of Nice. Marlborough had planned a joint attack upon Toulon by Rooke's fleet, the Savoyard army, and the rebels of the Cevennes. But it was already evident that Victor Amadeus would have enough to do that year in maintaining himself in Turin against the French armies. The Toulon scheme was abandoned and Rooke sailed to Barcelona.

The inhabitants of the Province of Catalonia hated the Spaniards of Castile who had trodden upon their ancient liberties. The Catalans stood in the same relation to the foreign government at Madrid as the Hungarian patriots to the Emperor at Vienna. It was known that they were not unwilling to welcome ' Charles III ' as their King. Rooke therefore put ashore near Barcelona some twelve hundred English and four hundred Dutch marines, under the command of Prince George of Hesse, the able young German Prince, who had earned popularity as Governor of Catalonia in the former war against France. The conditions were curiously similar to those which led to the capture of Barcelona and the rising of Eastern Spain in 1705, but they had no such consequence in 1704. For

May
1704

there was no Englishman present capable of the dare-devil
enterprise shown by Peterborough on the later occasion.
The Governor of Barcelona, Don Francisco de Velasco, was
a Spaniard of unusual vigour and tact, who kept the dis-
affected element quiet and Philip's partisans on the alert.
After a fortnight of waiting in vain for a Catalan outbreak
or treachery within the walls of Barcelona, Prince George
and the marines came aboard again and Rooke set sail for
other shores.

Meanwhile the French Admiral Toulouse, one of
Louis XIV's illegitimate sons, was sailing for the Straits
with the Brest fleet.   Since the English had chosen the
Mediterranean as the seat of the naval war, Louis decided
to send his principal fleet and Admiral to that station.
Rooke tried hard to prevent the formidable junction of the
forces of Toulon and Brest, but the French ships, fresh
from their own harbours, were in better condition than the
English ships from Lisbon, fitted up according to Portuguese rather than English ideas of what a naval base should
be like.   Owing, therefore, to the foul bottoms of Rooke's
ships, Toulouse sailed round him, escaped his eager pursuit,
and arrived in Toulon.   Thenceforth, he was the commander of the enlarged Toulon fleet, which had become the
Grand Fleet of France.   The arrival at the Straits of another
squadron from England, under Sir Cloudesley Shovell, put
the Allied forces in these waters on a numerical equality
with that of Toulouse.   But since the French Admiral was
safe in Toulon, where he spent some time establishing himself in his new base, Rooke, who had turned back to join
Shovell in the neighbourhood of Cadiz and Gibraltar,
looked round for some new enterprise consistent with his
instructions.[335]

King Peter of Portugal and ' King Charles ' of Spain
sent word from Lisbon that they wished another attempt to
be made against Cadiz.   Methuen also believed it to be
still ungarrisoned and easy to take.   But whether easy
to take or not, it would be hard to keep, against large
French and Spanish armies that would certainly be sent
to recover it.   The fateful Council of War, held on
Rooke's flagship in the Straits, decided against another

attack on Cadiz.   The wisdom of the refusal cannot be
doubted.   The Allied ships were not on this occasion
carrying any such force as Ormonde's army
July 17
(O.S.)
1704
that had failed there two years before ; the
fleet had on board only a couple of thousand
marines.

But something else might be tried.   Cadiz was not the
only place on the coast.   As those old Admirals sat at
Council in their full-bottomed wigs on that summer day,
off Tetuan ' under the Barbary coast,' it is odds but that they
could see, through the portholes of Rooke's cabin, dim in
the northern distance, the summit of Gibraltar Rock.
There, as they well knew, was a tiny garrison, on guard along
the crumbling walls and bastions of the sea-front, like to
prove but a fragile screen against an English fleet in the
Bay ;   whereas, if the place were once taken, a few companies of resolute men like the marines could make good
the land front, fortified by nature herself in a style beyond
the art of Vauban and Cohorn.   Whole armies could not
take Gibraltar from the north, so long as the friends of the
garrison held the sea.

The cabin was hot and the Admirals were testy.   Perhaps it was fortunate that Admiral Byng, political and
personal rival of Rooke, ' thought lightly ' of the proposal.
Opposition from that quarter roused Rooke's enthusiasm
for the project.   He declared that Byng himself should
lead a squadron of twenty English and Dutch ships into
Gibraltar Bay, to bombard and capture the place.   Between
pique and jest it was settled so, and the Council broke up,
every Admiral in his own humour.   Rooke this year was
no longer the surly and lethargic invalid that he had shown
himself on the voyage of 1702.

The idea of taking Gibraltar was no sudden inspiration
of the hour.   Rooke and his advisers on the spot must have
full credit for seeing and seizing the fleeting moment of
opportunity.   But the idea was old and widely spread.
Cromwell had turned his powerful thoughts that way, and
dreamed of turning the Spanish rock into an English island
by a canal across the isthmus.   William had marked
it for England, to hold the French power by the throat.

Marlborough was heir to that policy. Godolphin had received reports on the value of Gibraltar to our Mediterranean trade and warfare.* Admiral Leake and the Prince of Hesse were in favour of the attempt. Methuen was all agog to take both it and Cadiz.

The great grey rock, sheer precipice on its long eastern side looking into the Mediterranean and on its narrow northern end overlooking Spain, slopes on its western side towards the Bay in screes broken by crags and interlaced with forest and brushwood ; at the foot, the little town is crowded in between the Bay, the mountain, and its own steeply climbing walls.

The Phoenicians, when they first sailed into history, used the Rock as a seamark, but their trading stations were on the mainland. For two thousand years the northern Pillar of Hercules was famous in the talk of seafaring folk, but was seldom trodden by the foot of man. The Roman saw no use in it. Even the Viking passed it by. Wild beasts roamed its steep jungle, and spirits were said to haunt there. Its human history begins in 711, when the Moors settled there in warlike guise and named it after their chief, 'the Rock of Tarik.' Later generations of Moors built the Citadel, much as it stood in 1704 and still stands to-day. Charles V, and the Kings of Spain who followed him for a hundred years, added to the Moorish works and extended the defences southward along the seafront. But under Charles II they fell into the general decay of all things Spanish. And no one, Moor or Christian, had yet placed batteries in the side of the Rock itself, but only at its lowest foot, no higher than the Citadel.

---

* A curious report of the relative merits of Gibraltar and Cadiz as objects of attack will be found in the Godolphin Papers (*Add. MSS.* 28058, f. 31).

'Gibraltar and Ceuta make the very mouth of the Mediterranean, the first [viz. Gibraltar] may be taken and afterwards kept easier than Cadiz, for it is but badly fortified and may quickly be made an island ; and Ceuta must soon fall for want of provisions from Spain. The Bay of Gibraltar is capable of holding as many and as big ships as that of Cadiz, and being in the very passage may much better hinder ships and galleys passing into and out of the Straits than at so great a distance as Cadiz is. . . . And the people of Spain in general will be more affected by the loss of Gibraltar than Cadiz, this [Cadiz] being envied for so many strangers [English and Dutch merchants] residing in it, and the other [Gibraltar] esteemed the key of the Kingdom.'

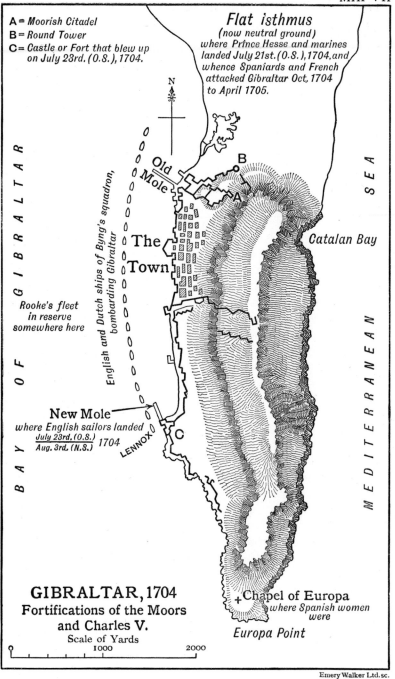

MAP VII

A = *Moorish Citadel*
B = *Round Tower*
C = *Castle or Fort that blew up on July 23rd. (O.S.), 1704.*

Flat isthmus
(now neutral ground)
where Prince Hesse and marines landed July 21st. (O.S.), 1704, and whence Spaniards and French attacked Gibraltar, Oct, 1704 to April 1705.

N

BAY OF GIBRALTAR

Old Mole

English and Dutch ships of Byng's squadron, bombarding Gibraltar

B

A

The Town

Catalan Bay

Rooke's fleet in reserve somewhere here

SEA

MEDITERRANEAN

New Mole
where English sailors landed
July 23rd, (O.S.)
Aug. 3rd, (N.S.) 1704

LENNOX

C

GIBRALTAR, 1704
Fortifications of the Moors
and Charles V.

Scale of Yards

0   1000   2000

+ Chapel of Europa
where Spanish women were

Europa Point

Emery Walker Ltd. sc.

The heights of the precipice do not come into the story of its capture : the action took place along the sea-front below.

The whole fleet stood over to Gibraltar Bay. Byng's squadron of sixteen English and six Dutch ships ranged themselves against the line of the defences from the Old to the New Mole : the Dutch were under their Vice-Admiral Van der Dussen. Eighteen hundred English marines,* under Prince George of Hesse, were landed on the low-lying isthmus that divided the Rock from the mainland, cutting off from the town all hope of reinforcement or supply. The Prince summoned the Governor in the name of King Charles III, by a trumpeter at the north gate. Don Diego de Salinas, though determined to save his honour, knew in his heart that he had no real means of resistance. Again and again he had importuned the Court for a garrison, military stores, and all the things necessary to stand a siege, and always in vain. Now the hour he had so long dreaded had struck. By his own account he had ' no more than fifty-six men of whom there were not thirty in service.' In addition to these regulars he hastily collected a few hundred civilian militia ' armed as God willed,' and ' of such bad quality that before they arrived they began to run away.' He had a hundred cannon of various ages and kinds, but few of them were in a state to be fired, and fewer still had gunners to fire them.

July 21
Aug. 1
1704

The second day passed in preliminaries. Don Diego sent back a defiant reply to the summons in the grand old Spanish style. The countryman of Don Quixote was prepared to die like a gentleman. The ships of Byng's squadron warped themselves in along the sea front as close as the depth permitted : Captain Jumper brought the *Lennox* within actual musket range of the New Mole. These operations, carried out in a dead calm, were not impeded by a few shots from the Spanish batteries. At midnight the English sailors burnt

July 22
Aug. 2

---

* The Royal Marines, in the modern acceptation of the word, viz. a military force specially maintained for use with the fleet, primarily as soldiers, had been established in the first year of Anne. The double object was to have such a force ever ready for the service of the fleet and to evade disbandment, the usual fate of the army proper owing to the jealousy of Parliament. *Corbett*, II, 475–477.

a French privateer lying off the Old Mole which had been firing at the camp of the marines.

Sunday, July 23rd, English Style, was Gibraltar's doomsday. About five o'clock on a glorious summer's morning, Byng's squadron opened fire, and continued hour after hour to pour an iron cascade on to the crumbling walls and forts. Don Diego reckoned the number of bombs and cannon balls that he received at 30,000, and although the English reckoned it at less, there is no doubt that the bombardment left the fleet short of ammunition at Malaga next month. The actual damage done was small in proportion to the expenditure of shot.

July 23 Aug. 3

Two miles from the southern gate, rose the famous shrine at Europa Point, decorated by the votive offerings of lordly Spanish Admirals who had once ruled the Mediterranean with the galley and the oar. There the women of Gibraltar knelt and clung together, safe but in terror, listening to the ceaseless thud and echo of the guns. Their menfolk could be seen by the English flying out of the town up the mountain side.

There was no wind, and the smoke of the great bombardment soon hung like a cloud, hiding from the gunners any glimpse of their work. Byng, therefore, sent orders, first that only the lower tier of guns should be fired, and then that the bombardment should cease. These messages were taken from ship to ship by Captain Edward Whitaker who was acting as Byng's aide-de-camp. When, about eleven o'clock, his boat reached the *Lennox* at the southern end of the line, he found its captain, Jumper, gazing hard through the lifting smoke at the New Mole and the fort that commanded its abutment on the land. The enemy appeared to have fled. The two captains agreed that a landing could be effected there unopposed. Whitaker hastened back to Byng, who ordered the boats of the squadron to be made ready, and sent Whitaker to ask Rooke's leave to launch the attack. It was at once granted, and a flotilla of English row-boats raced for the New Mole.

Meanwhile the panic-stricken women at Europa shrine, seeing the heretics about to land between them and their homes, began to run back towards Gibraltar. The English, able again to see what was going on ashore since the bombardment had stopped, sent a cannon-ball for warning in front of the column of women, who fled back to the shrine out of harm's way. This shot was mistaken by the eager fleet for a signal to resume fire ; the bombardment began again, and under its cover the landing party did its work.

Not a gun was fired in defence at the New Mole and its environs. The foremost sailors leapt from their boats and clambered into the breached and undefended fort.* They tumbled in, happy-go-lucky, some of them with lighted gun-matches in their hands. They had forgotten the possibility of a powder-magazine. The fort went up in the air, nearly two hundred English sailors were hurled in every direction, and several of the landing-boats sank at their moorings.

A momentary panic ensued, for the first instinct of the survivors was to suppose that the enemy had laid a trap and caused the disaster, which was really due to the carelessness of their own comrades. There was a rush for the remaining boats, but at this critical moment Captain Whitaker landed with reinforcements, rallied the fugitives, and in a few minutes two or three hundred of the ships' crews were marching behind him along the deserted ramparts of the seafront, towards Gibraltar. Arrived within half a musket shot of Charles V's southern wall of the town, Whitaker halted the sailors in a bastion on the shore, hoisted the Union Jack, and awaited what should happen next.†

Byng at once came ashore and joined Whitaker with several hundred more seamen. The town was thus invested

---

* *Marked C. in the map*, p. 409.

† The direct statement of Whitaker, confirmed by the narrative from Byng's notes, establishes the fact that the ' Union Jack,' ' our colours,' were hoisted on this first occasion. *Camden Misc.*, VIII (1883), *Haddock Corr.* p. 48 ; *Torrington*, p. 143. The English flag probably continued to be flown in parts of the fortifications during the occupation that followed, but the flag of Charles III also was flown, as the English held the town in his name till the Treaty of Utrecht. The statement of the Spanish historian Ayala that the English pulled down Charles's flag and proclaimed Queen Anne as sovereign of Gibraltar is, like some other statements of Ayala, quite untrue.

The Union Jack had been in frequent use since the Union of the Crowns of England and Scotland under James VI and I.

on the south, as well as on its stronger northern side where
the marines had all this while been keeping up a demonstration.   The fleet was bombarding from the west, and the
Old Mole had been deserted by the defenders.   Many of
the scanty civilian militia had run away up the mountain,
and there was no force left in the town capable of resisting
an assault.   To allow the place to be stormed would merely
expose the remaining inhabitants to the horrors of a sack.
Their wives at Europa Point were already prisoners in the
hands of the English, who had placed officers there to protect them from rough usage ; the desire to recover these
women was a further inducement to come to terms.   Don
Diego saw that all was lost—except his honour, ever the
dearest point to a true Spaniard.   He agreed to terms
that saved the lives and property of those committed to
his care.[336]

Under the capitulation, all the inhabitants who would
take the oath of allegiance to Charles III as King of Spain
could remain in the town, with religion and property
guaranteed.   But, except half a dozen families, they elected
to depart to the mainland, where shortly afterwards the
exiles founded the pleasant country town of San Rocque,
among the hills in sight of their ancient home.   Gibraltar
has ever since been anything but a Spanish town in its racial
character.

The voluntary departure of the inhabitants was inspired
by loyalty to Philip V as standard-bearer of Spanish
nationality against foreign and heretical invasion.   The
priests told their flocks that the French would retake
Gibraltar in a few weeks and restore the old regime.   Moreover, the Spaniards observed that, although the heretics
kept their hands off women, they did not spare churches.
The English sailors were hearty Protestants, and they
were out for loot.   At Europa shrine they first seized
all the treasures, and then knocked the head off the image,
' The Oracle of Spain,' and threw it and the Child Jesus out
of doors among the stones.   Such conduct aroused the same
anger in Spain as had been aroused among the men of
Devon a dozen years before, when the French landing-

party tore up the Bible in Teignmouth parish church.   In Gibraltar itself all the churches save one were sacked, besides private houses.   One marine was hanged for plundering, and a good many of the sailors were sent back to the ships.   But several of their officers had secured valuable loot.   There is the less wonder that, amid scenes of such disorder, the Spanish inhabitants elected to go into exile, in hopes of a speedy and triumphant return.   Rooke wrote home from Gibraltar that the Spaniards were so exasperated against the Allies that ' they use the prisoners they take as barbarously as the Moors.' *

The site of Our Lady of Europa is still to be distinguished by the remains of its Moorish flooring, and a fragment of Moorish building, with an inscription to the effect that the shrine was turned into a guard-house in 1704 and destroyed in the Siege of 1782.

Thus was Gibraltar taken, at the cost of about 200 seamen wounded and 60 killed, almost all of them in the explosion of the fort.

Methuen at once urged the necessity for a permanent English garrison.   This was in fact supplied ; the marines who had helped to take it remained to hold it, and were joined in the course of a few months by several companies of regular troops.   But the English Ministry throughout the war tried to get their Allies, the Portuguese and Dutch, to contribute to the defence.   It was perhaps fortunate that these efforts failed, and that Gibraltar, from first to last, was, in fact, held by English troops at England's cost. But it was held in King Charles's name, and in 1705 we find him writing to Queen Anne about '*Ma ville de Gibraltar.*'   If we had succeeded in placing him on the throne at Madrid, the difficulty of keeping the Rock for England would have been politically very great.[337]

Gibraltar had not been taken ' in a fit of absence of mind.'   Its importance was widely understood.   It was chiefly valued by the English public for the protection it

* *Torrington*, p. 194.   *Add. MSS.* (*St.*) 7058, f. 360.   Details of the sack can be found in the notes of Don Juan Romero, the good priest who stayed in Gibraltar and saved his church, St. Mary the Crowned, from pillage.   These notes are in the Parochial Register of the City of Gibraltar at San Rocque, where I have seen them. An extract from them made in 1908 is in the Garrison Library at Gibraltar.

was expected to afford to our trading interests in the further Mediterranean. A month after its capture, Secretary Hedges described it as—

A footing for the King of Spain in the strongest fort belonging to that country, and of great use to us for securing our trade and interrupting of the enemy's.

A few years later Addison wrote, ' The Streight's mouth is the key to the Levant.' The piratical Moors of the African shore would, it was hoped, be prevented from attacking our merchants when they saw the English power established on the Straits ; this hope was largely realised, and the Princes of Barbary became the Allies of Queen Anne.

Yet it was well known that Gibraltar had its limitations as a harbour. When the news of its capture reached London, one Member of Parliament wrote to another :

It will not protect a fleet against a superior one, but 'twill be of use and safety for single ships, or four or five men-of-war, and in that respect of great advantage to our trade.

Though sheltered from the worst of the winter winds, the Levanter, it could never afford such shelter as Lisbon, and in 1704 was in no way fitted out as a base. Before that had been done, Port Mahon had been captured, 1708 a better harbour and better situated for watching the Toulon fleet and the Mediterranean coasts. But the immense advantage expected from Gibraltar's command of the Straits proved no delusion.[338]

A little enterprise was the only quality required for the taking of Gibraltar, but to keep it heroism was needed, both by sea and by land. Within a few weeks of its capture, Toulouse came to retake it, and on that issue the one full-dress naval engagement of the war was fought off Malaga between the Allied and French Grand Fleets. And afterwards, throughout the following winter and spring, the armies of Spain and France battered in vain at the land approaches of Gibraltar, defended by a mere handful of English soldiers, sailors, and marines.*

* The story of the defence of Gibraltar, October 1704 to April 1705, must come into the next volume of this work. I end this volume with the Battle of Malaga, so nearly contemporaneous with Blenheim.

The news of the loss of Gibraltar was received with
deep humiliation at Madrid, and with anger and alarm by
the Toulon fleet, who learnt of it at Barcelona. Admiral
Toulouse immediately set out to recover the Rock, with the
chief naval armament of France—fifty French battleships,
accompanied by two dozen of oared war-galleys. In the
action that followed, the galleys proved of some service in
calm weather, in towing battleships in and out of action
when the wind was not serviceable, and in attacking or
rescuing injured vessels. The fleet of Toulouse was
approximately equal, in number of men and guns, to
Rooke's force of forty-one English and twelve Dutch battleships.* It was in better condition, coming straight from
home ports, and it was better supplied with powder and
shot, since the wasteful bombardment of Gibraltar had
reduced Rooke's store. He had left England with forty
rounds per gun, and had now only twenty-five on the
average, though half the fleet had not been engaged at
Gibraltar.

If Toulouse could drive Rooke out of the Straits, he
could, in the then condition of Gibraltar, retake it from the
sea without any difficulty at all. The battle off Malaga,
which decided this issue, took place after some curious
manoeuvring by the two fleets between the African and
Spanish coasts. Rooke, though taken by surprise, did
not wish to fight till he had re-embarked and distributed
throughout the ships half the marines garrisoning Gibraltar,
and completed the watering of his fleet then in process on the
African shore. While he was thus engaged the two fleets
unintentionally changed places, and at daybreak on
Aug. $\frac{13}{24}$ August 13th, the French were seen lying between
1704   Rooke and Gibraltar. The Allies had the advantage of the wind which was blowing from the east.

Rooke, who had no lack of moral courage or technical
ability in his plain duty as a sailor, did not hesitate for a
moment to accept battle under circumstances of disadvantage, in order to save Gibraltar. He knew that he was
somewhat short of ammunition, and wished to close with
the enemy so as to win a rapid victory. He sailed down

* Compare *Leake*, I, pp. 174–175, to note in *Corbett*, II, pp. 527–528.

with the wind, and the battle of the giants began and raged all day. The seamen of France, Holland, and England all did their duty, to mutual admiration.* The French retreated to keep their distance, and Rooke's attempt to finish the battle at once at close quarters failed. But the quarters were often uncomfortably close. By the end of the day both sides had their bellyful. In the opinion of the allied seamen, the French had shot too high, and their ships were in the worse case by nightfall. No vessels were sunk or captured in the action on either side, but few were uninjured, and many were practically out of service from shot holes and broken masts. A number of English ships had not a shot left in their lockers. The Dutch had rather less than 400 killed and wounded, the English list was 2,368. The French admitted in general terms a loss of 1,500, which the Allies considered a gross under-estimate. Besides Rooke himself, Leake, Byng, Shovell, the Dutch Callenburgh and Van Wassenaer, and the French Marquis de Villette, had all been deeply engaged, and their flagships had borne their full share of the very brunt of the conflict. Toulouse himself had been wounded and many Frenchmen of rank killed.

So the rival fleets lay all night, licking their wounds, the French galleys busy towing in their disabled ships. Next morning Toulouse still lay between the English and Aug. $\frac{14}{25}$ 1704 Gibraltar, and had now the advantage of the wind, which had shifted to the north-west. He could, therefore, renew the battle if he chose. The Allies lay there all day to leeward of him, challenging him to come on if he dared. But he had had enough ; and he did not know the secret that might yet have lost Gibraltar to England, that Rooke was anxiously distributing cannon-balls and powder through his fleet, ' so that by the best computation, when all was supplied, they made up some to eight, some to ten, and most to twelve round of shot ' per gun.

* ' Sir George Rooke says he never observed the true English spirit so apparent and prevalent in our seamen as on this occasion. Sir Clowdisley [Shovell] observes the engagement was very sharp, and he thought the like between the two fleets never had been in his time. The French, to give them their due, though forced in the van to give way, behaved remarkably well.' *Leake*, I, pp. 169–170.

Having lain a whole day challenging a renewal of the battle, Rooke and his Council decided that all required by honour had been done, that not even the French Court could say the English had been beaten (though here they under-estimated the powers of Versailles), and that it was high time to get back to Gibraltar and refit.   Orders were issued that the fleet should cut its way thither if necessary through the intervening French fleet.   Captains whose ammunition was exhausted were to sail on and *rendez-vous* at Gibraltar.   The wind had shifted back and was now blowing from the east to carry the English to the Straits.   It was an ugly situation for Rooke's half-armed fleet if Toulouse lay across their path.   But in the course of the following night he disappeared. Next morning Rooke supposed he had gone forward to the Straits ; the Allied fleet reached Gibraltar thinking that another battle might still lie before them.   But in fact the French fleet had slipped back eastward and was returning to Toulon.   From that port it never again emerged in full force.   The English Grand Fleet was never again challenged to battle.   Malaga was the Jutland of the war. Louis, under the financial strain of the land-war after Blenheim, could not afford to maintain his fleet in fighting trim.   Not only was Gibraltar saved, but the Mediterranean was abandoned to the English fleet.   Louis and his courtiers might chant *Te Deum* for the victory of Malaga, but it was the dirge of French naval power.[339]

Aug. $\frac{15}{26}$ 1704

The campaign of 1704 on the Danube and in the Straits had gone far to redress the balance of power in Europe.   It was characteristic of Englishmen, or at least of English politicians, that instead of being merely thankful, they managed, before Christmas had come, to divide themselves on party lines even in the counting of their blessings.

In the first reaction to the news of Blenheim, the Ministerial Tories had taken the lead in the national rejoicings.

I question [one of them wrote in August] whether there has been so decisive a battle since that of Pharsalia.   That at Pavia was not so extensive, Christendom not being so much concerned in the consequence of it.   On Sunday I was at Windsor, where I found my Lord Treasurer sensibly overjoyed, for this has given the balance of Europe into the Queen's hands. . . . Since the news I have not seen any creature so like a Jacobite as a Whig : their looks, their blood and their goodwill to the Government are the same.

The Tory squires ceased that autumn to complain of the Land Tax.   'Our public good news of late has caused a general rejoicing and raised our English general above all detracting tongues ; the country people say there is something for their money.' *   Ned Ward, the popular Tory poet, exploited the occasion for party purposes by contrasting the success of Marlborough as the Tory hero with William's long and fruitless campaigns :

> Long did Nassaw his Belgick valour try,
> By English arms to curb French tyranny,
> Vast sums were given, and great armies raised,
> And wonders done, that glorious Prince be praised !
> Whose matchless conduct all men must allow,
> Performed strange things, the Lord knows where or how.
>
> .   .   .   .   .   .
>
> But thou, Great Marlborough, hast in two campaigns,
> Made happy Ann's surpass all other reigns,
> And by thy conduct, at a moderate cost
> Retrieved that honour fourteen years had lost.[340]

If the Tories had united on this line and adhered to it, they could have secured for their party the credit of the victorious war, kept Marlborough for their hero, and made peace, greatly to the advantage of England and Europe, as soon as the objects set forth in the Treaty of Grand Alliance were achieved.   But there was another element in the party, the High Tories under Rochester, Seymour, and Nottingham, deeply embittered against the Godolphin Ministry by the events that had recently driven them from office.†   The Duchess wrote that, on the news of Blenheim, they spoke as if her husband ' instead of beating the French had beat the Church.'   And as the autumn went on, these voices in disparagement of Marlborough began to be more loudly heard.   Never fond of red-coats,

---

* See pp. 293-295 above.   † See pp. 274, 335–336 above.

the High Tories were tempted by Gibraltar and Malaga to
set up the deeds of Rooke and the Navy in rivalry to those
of Marlborough and the Army.   At the end of September
De Foe wrote to Harley from Bury St. Edmunds :

> The High Church Party look on Sir George Rooke as their own.
> The victory at sea they look upon as their victory over the Moderate
> Party, and his health is now drunk by those here who won't drink the
> Queen's nor your's.   I am obliged with patience to hear you damned,
> and he praised, and Her Majesty slighted and the sea victory set up
> against the land victory ;   Sir George exalted above the Duke of
> Marlborough, and what can the reason of this be but that they con-
> ceive some hopes from this that their High Church Party will revive
> under his patronage ? [341]

So far did this movement extend, that when Parliament
met in November the Commons carried a congratulatory
resolution to the Queen that mentioned, as equally important,
Blenheim and Malaga ;   Marlborough's friends thought
' that and Blenheim ought not to be mentioned on a day,'
and were better pleased with the Lords' resolution which
treated the Duke's victory as the singular event of the year.

'In the House of Commons,' wrote one observer
early in November, ' the Tories run out in commendation
of Sir George and talk of my Lord Marlborough's victory
as a small matter.'   The same division appeared even among
the clergy.   'The Houses of Convocation have divided
about their address : the higher would not name Sir George
Rooke ; the lower would.'

Thus, while the High Churchmen belittled the Duke
and declared that Rooke had done as much as he, the
Ministerialists and Whigs declared, with equal injustice,
that Rooke had no merit at all.   This bitter and absurd
quarrel sprang from and further enhanced the existing
divisions on the Occasional Conformity Bill and on the
general policy of the war.   It drove the Queen, the
Godolphin Ministry and the Whigs more than ever into
one camp, and prepared the way for the General Election
of 1705 which overthrew the High Tory power in the
House of Commons, and left Ministers definitely dependent
on Whig support.[342]

The majority of the Whigs had, indeed, hailed Marl-

borough's victories that summer with genuine delight in
their party papers, such as the *Observator* ; and the moment
they saw the line taken by the High Tories they flung themselves into the fray.   They had never had any love for
Rooke.   Marlborough now became the hero of the Whigs,
though he was never a Whig hero.   As the Venetian Ambassador reported to his government, the prestige and popularity won by the Duke and the Godolphin Ministry as a
result of Blenheim enabled them to defy their High Tory
critics, and emboldened them to seek more openly the
alliance of the Nonconformists.   'The Whigs triumph,
and assume the merit of a policy which the events of the war
have approved,' wrote Mocenigo, while the Ministerialist
Tories, who are not '*passionati*' about home affairs, agree to
take full advantage of the situation for the benefit of the
nation and the '*equilibrio*' of Europe.[343]

In this quarrel the Queen, little as she liked the Whigs,
was on the side of Marlborough.   She showered upon him
honours and rewards.   The famous Royal Manor of
Woodstock became his, and Vanbrugh was commissioned
to erect there Blenheim Palace at the Queen's expense.
In September, while the Duke was still abroad pushing his
success across the Rhine, Anne went in state to St. Paul's,
to give thanks for Blenheim.   The Strand, Fleet Street,
and Ludgate Hill were ' railed and hung with blue cloth '
on both sides of the roadway, and behind the barriers the
City Militia were drawn up.   The fronts of the houses on
the route were gay with Eastern carpets and rich tapestries.
The sidewalks, windows and roofs were thronged with
spectators, eager to see the long procession of State coaches,
Beefeaters and Horse Guards.   Inside Wren's Cathedral,
now almost finished, two battalions of Foot Guards made a
lane from the West Door to the Choir.   The invalid Queen
bore her pain bravely to go through with the ceremony.
At her hand walked the Duchess, modestly dressed in
the part of a faithful ' Abigail,' but the proudest subject in
England that day.

Nor was this the last of the Blenheim pageants.   Next
January, after the Duke's return, a grand military march,
with all London again looking on, carried ' 34 standards

and 128 colours' captured in the great battle, from the Tower to Westminster Hall.   Old men remembered seeing the flags taken at Worcester fight hung with pomp in the same Hall, to vanish at the Restoration.   They blessed God that this time the trophies had been torn from a foreign foe.

The flags thus deposited in Westminster Hall, the crowded thoroughfare of the Courts of Justice, remained throughout the reign of Anne one of the celebrated sights of London.   Political poems were written about them, in one of which ' a jolly red-coat ' points out to ' an honest tar ' that, whatever his Tory friends may tell him, the flags were all taken by the Army.[344]   The Army became, for awhile, more popular than it had ever been before.   The music of ' The Grenadiers' March ' was heard everywhere : Farquhar introduced it at the beginning and end of his ' Recruiting Officer ' :

Beat the Grenadier March—Row, row, tow !   Gentlemen, this piece of music, called an overture to a battle, was performed with wonderful success at the great operas of Vigo, Schellenberg and Blenheim.   It came off with the applause of all Europe excepting France.   The French found it a little too rough for their *delicatesse*.

The events of 1704 drew Godolphin closer than ever to Marlborough, and a little nearer to the Whigs.   In September, in discussing a matter on which he differed from the Duke, he wrote to Harley, ' I can believe in him against my own senses.'   Anxious to make the most of Blenheim —and also to curry favour with the rising power of the Whig Junto—Godolphin, who was himself a patron of jockeys rather than poets, consulted Lord Halifax, the Maecenas of the age, and at his advice sent Henry Boyle, the Chancellor of the Exchequer, to find Joseph Addison in his modest lodging and engage him to write a poem worthy of the occasion.   ' The Campaign ' duly appeared with its comparison of the Duke directing the battle to the angel guiding the storm,

' Such as of late o'er pale Britannia passed.'

The town, accustomed to a poorer style of fustian, was pleased by its dignity and sense.   Early in 1706

Addison, hitherto only a scholar and poet, became an Under-Secretary of State in the office of Sir Charles Hedges. Such, in those days, was the close connection of poetry and politics, when poetry could serve the purposes of pamphleteering.

Marlborough, for all his patience, was human, and he did not like it when so many of his old political associates disparaged his victories. He wrote that autumn to Sarah from Germany :

> I will endeavour to leave a good name behind me in countries that have hardly any blessing but that of not knowing the detested names of Whig and Tory.[345]

But for all their nonsense and faction, the English were acquiring a new conception of the place of their country in the world, as the mistress of the Mediterranean, ' the scourge of France, the arbitress of Europe,' to whom foreign Princes and peoples looked for help and justice not in vain. England was more than all she had been under Elizabeth, more than all she had been under Cromwell, for she was now a united nation with a fixed and free Constitution. Whig and Tory might bark and bicker, but they carried on the nation's work between them, because the blood-feud of sects and parties had been staunched by the compromise of the Revolution Settlement, which, by giving to England domestic peace, based more securely than on force, had opened to her the paths of greatness oversea.

APPENDICES

APPENDIX A

Marlborough's Letters to Heinsius

I do not think that any English historian or biographer has made use of Marlborough's letters to Heinsius for the years 1701–5, of which the original MSS. are in the Rijks-archief at the Hague, though Noorden had seen them. Only the later letters of this correspondence, from 1706 onwards, have been known to English historians since their publication by Vreede in 1850. The good relations of Marlborough and Heinsius were the keystone of the whole Alliance in the early and decisive years of the war, and I think it will be of interest if I print for the first time these extracts from the Duke's share in their correspondence. The first four extracts are from letters written in William's life-time. I have preserved the Duke's original spelling in this Appendix, though not in the text of the book.

Dec. $\frac{5}{16}$, 1701. Wee have here no talk but of the Elections, I hope in God thay will be such, as will doe their utmost against ffrance.

Jan. $\frac{6}{17}$, 170$\frac{1}{2}$. The Treatys [of Grand Alliance] have been this day layd before the House of Commons and I hope it will take them into considerations, soe that wee may know what to depend upon ; and I have good reason to think that every thing will goe well.

Jan. $\frac{9}{20}$, 170$\frac{1}{2}$. It is with a very hearty joy I send you the good news of the House of Commons have this day agreed to the 40000 men for the quota that England is to furnish abroad. This was unanimously agreed to, by which you may have the satisfaction of seeing that the Gentlemen of England are intirely in the interest of Holland, and as I heartily wish it may continue long, I beg if possible that care may be taken that your prints may make noe Party distinctions. [Viz. that the Dutch newspapers should not extol the Whigs over the Tories and so alienate the most important section of 'the Gentlemen of England,' some of whom would have been surprised to learn that they were 'intirely in the interest of Holland.']

Jan. $\frac{13}{24}$, 170$\frac{1}{2}$. The Parl. having agreed what the quota of England shall be, his Majy [W. III] is desirous you shou'd send mee a draught that is proper for the convention that is to settle the denombrement [number of troops agreed to be supplied by each of the Allies]. I shou'd be alsoe oblig'd if you would let mee have your thoughts as to an article the Parl. has addressed to have added to the Treaty with the Emperor and the States ; . . . we desire you shou'd ingage not to have peace till his Majy has satisfaction as to the pretended Prince of Whalles. [See p. 151 above.]

March $\frac{8}{19}$, 170$\frac{1}{2}$ [the very day on which King William died]. I have had the favour of three of yours by yesterdays post, but the great lose wee have had makes me incapable of giving any answer to them by this opertunity. Her Majy has commanded mee to give you asurances of her unalterable resolutions of remaining ferm to the interest of Holland, and the Common Cause. She is very desirous you shou'd give this asurance to the States [General] ; I am such a hurry that you will pardon my saying noe more, but be asur'd that my heart is, and alwise shall be with you. The resolutions of both Houses and the Queens speach to the Councell, mr Stanhope will give you.

The next letter shows Marlborough's endeavours to calm the anxiety of the Dutch at the substitution of so many Tory for Whig Ministers and magistrates in England in the new reign, the Tories being regarded abroad as more anti-Dutch and less zealous for ' the Common Cause.' The statement that ' there will be at least six Wiggs for one of the other Party ' is monstrously untrue, unless we suppose that Marlborough, in writing to his foreign friend, computes all who were enthusiastic for the war as ' Wiggs,' and counts only the High Tories as ' the other Party.' But even so it is a gross exaggeration.

April 21, 1702. I am soe uneasy in my own mind that I wou'd give a great deall that I had the happyness of being with you, to let you know the true thoughts of her Majy concerning the alterations she has and will make. In the mean time you will give mee leave to asure you that her Majy is fermly resolv'd not to enter into any party, but to make use of all her subjects, that is what will appear very quickly in England, her Majy being resolved very quickly to shut the dore upon any other alterations, and I may asure you that when she has done all that she intends, there will be at least six Wiggs for one of the other Party. For the good of the Common Cause I beg of you to use your endeavours that there may be noe jealousies.

The next letter is very interesting. It is on the subject of Queen Anne's attempt to have the Allied troops in the Netherlands put under her husband (Prince George of Denmark) instead of Marlborough, see p. 166, above. It will be seen from this letter how very delicate and even dangerous a position was that in which Marlborough was placed in the matter, and how carefully he had to walk among so many enemies at home and abroad. Christian

Plessen was a Danish statesman, specially attached to Prince George in England.

Aug. 21, 1702. I am told that you have had the same information I have received, that Mons. Plessen is persuaded that it is my fault that the Prince of Denmark has not the command of your troops ; he is going for England and I suppose will passe by the Hague. I take him to be an honest man, but he is impossed upon by Lord Rochester's means, who wou'd be glade to have him come into England with this opinion ; if you see Plessen you must not lett him know that I, or you, know anything of this, but as occation offers I am sure you will doe mee the friendly part of letting him see the great desire I had to have it done ; and if there be any hopes that it will be done this winter, I think you shou'd lett him see it, for he has power with the Prince, and that will keep them [Anne and her husband] in good humour.

May 29, 1703. I have received a second letter from Ld Nottingham, not doubting but we may spare the 12000 men [from the Netherlands for Spain]. If wee should doe it, we shall be necessitated to put ourselves upon the defensive. But you will be sensible that this must not be my opinion to his Lordship, but I must form my answer agreable to what you shall say. [This follows on a similar letter of May 26 on the same subject.]

It will be seen from these last two letters that, in the interest of the Common Cause, Marlborough had secret understandings with Heinsius against the moves and policy of his High Tory colleagues in the Cabinet.

In the following letters we read Marlborough's bitter complaints to Heinsius of the restrictions put on his action by the Dutch Generals (not Deputies) in the field in 1703. In 1702 he had been much more reticent on this subject. In 1703 he was in a position to speak out to Heinsius and even to threaten resignation.

June 22, 1703. I think the Common Interest dose requier that noe more time shou'd be lost, but that wee either attack Antwerp or Ostend ; or else put ourselves upon the defensive, and send the rest to Germany, for two months, which may save the whole in Germany, and be here again time enough to take Huy, Limbourg and make themselves masters of the Mosel to Treves. This letter is whatt will let you see my thoughts as to the operations of this Campagne, which I think will be the last I shall be able to serve you in, and I beg you to believe that if I had been born at Amsterdam I could not be more desirous for the prosperity of Holland then I am, being truly convinc'd that when you are unfortunate, England must be undone.

July 31, 1703. It is impossible the warr can goe on with success att this rate, if measurs must be taken between two armys, and the quarrels and animositys of private pepel shall make a delay, which hinders the whole, it is my opinion impossible to avoyde in length of time some great misfortune, which gives mee soe much trouble, that I know not if I shall be able to outlive

this campagne, but I am shure I have not coridge to make another. . . .
I own to you that I have the spleen to a very great degree.

Aug. 26, 1703. Vall Notre Dame. My opinion is for attacking the
Lyns, as well as those Generals which have signed the paper [see p. 316,
above]. . . . All that they [the Dutch Generals] say is to incline us to act
defensively, which I take to be destruction. I can't forbear telling you that
all the disafected pepel in England will take occasion to make use of the
arguments given by your generals to convince our Parliament men that the
warr ought to be made in other places and not in this country.

Sep. 3, 1703. Val nostre Dame. If I might have millions given mee
to serve another yeare and be oblig'd to doe nothing but by the unanimous
consent of the Generals, I would much sooner dye. . . . I hope they will
approve of the one expedient I can think of, which is my being att the head
of the troupes payde by England, and they joyne any such of theirs to mee
as they shall Judge for the good of the service. Att the sam time I shall be
very desirous to have as many Deputys in the Army with mee as they please,
for I shall never have a thought but what I shou'd be glad thay shou'd judge
off.

Sep. 10, 1703. St. Tron. I doe call God to witness that after I had
seen the Lyns upon Wensday and Thursday, I was conferm'd in my opinion
that wee shou'd have forced them with the lose of very few men.

The remaining letters here printed are concerned with the pro-
jects for saving the Empire and their result in the Danube campaign.

May 24. 1703. [Copy in Marlborough's handwriting of 'my letter
to Mr. Secretary Hedges,' which he encloses to Heinsius.]
The Emperor is oblig'd by the Great Alliance to have 90000 men and
the contingent troops of the Empir shou'd be 120.000, of which I am very
very sure that since the first 15 battalions marched from hence to the upper
Rhyn, which was in Feb. last, there had not marched of the contingent
troops of the Empir 10000 men, but they all hope by staying att home to
draw mony from England and Holland. If there can't be a method found
to oblige the Emperor and Empir to defend themselves, I am afraid the
consequence at last must prove fatall to England and Holland. I can't but
observe one thing that the Marishall Villiers has not 26000 men with him
besides the troops at Baviar, and the Marishall de Tallard does not pretend
to more than 18; by which you may see how little the Empire dose for
themselves.

March $\frac{7}{18}$, 170$\frac{3}{4}$. The intelligence from all parts of the Empire agree
that if England and Holland doe not assist the Empire by sending an army
early to the Moselle, the whole Empire must be undone. I should be glad
you would lett mee know what measures you have taken concerning this,
and what Coehorn says as to the siege of Thionville, for I find by P. Eugen's
paper that he thinks that siege necessary [viz. for success on the Moselle.
Nothing is said about the Danube].

Then comes the news of the death of Cohorn, the great military engineer, Vauban's rival, and on March $\frac{14}{25}$ Marlborough writes of it, referring to his failure in the field in the campaign of 1703 :

Had he dyed one yeare sooner, any Nation might have been proud of such a subject.

March 24, 170$\frac{3}{4}$. You will see by the enclos'd Memoriall of Count Wratislagh to her Majesty what aprehensions thay have in Germany ; our Councell here are very much inclin'd to the helping of Germany, in order to the reducing of the Elector of Bavaria, which we think here is soe necessary, that all things must goe wrong, if that Elector be not brought to reason. All that I have been able to prevaile on Her Majty and Her Councell is to come to no resolution on this matter, but that I shou'd att my arrivall att the Hague setle this business with the States General. . . . The Count Wratislagh comes along with mee, his zeal for his Master's service, as well as his own natural heat will make him presse this matter very much.

May 21, 1704. Camp of Kulsecken. [Since Villeroi is marching away from the Netherlands after Marlborough] it wou'd be very much for the good of your service to draw into the army a good part of your troupes in your garrisons, by which means you might send us soe many troupes as might make mee succeed against the Elector of Bavaria ; and Mons. Auverkerk be able to undertake what ever you shou'd think best in Flanders.

May 25. Coblence. I am come here with the horse and shall passe the Mosel and the Rhyne tomorrow, and the Meine the 28th or 29th att furthest, for I shall make all the diligence I can to joyne the troupes about Philipsbourg. I am sure when you reflect on the great number, as well as the goodness of the troupes the Marshall de Villeroy has taken with him, you will be in no doubt of the King of ffrance doing all that is in his power to reduce the Emperor, and that I hope you will lett us have all the assistance you can. I doe not say this because I am her, but I protest before God if I were in flanders I shou'd be of the same opinion, for shou'd the Emperor be oblig'd to make an ill peace, England and Holland must pay for itt. On the other hand if wee can be putt in a condition of being able to reduce the Elector of Bavaria, ffrance must submit to such termes as wou'd be for the good of the Common Cause.

May 30. Mayence. I believe I shall not see Prince Lewis till I gett to the Danube.

June 15. Ebersbach. I send you enclos'd what I have received from the Gentleman imploy'd by the King of Prussia [to treat with the Elector of Bavaria]. If the Elector shou'd in earnest have a mind to treat, itt will be when we shall gett nearer to him.

June 19. Gros. Seissen. I very much fear he [Villeroy] may make the P. Eugene very uneasy on the Rhine, but it is his opinion as well as mine that whatever happens on the Rhine, that must not devert us from doing all wee can to ruin the Elector, for on that depends the good or bad success of the Common Cause. . . . I beg you will take care that I receive noe orders from the States that may put mee out of a condition of reducing the Elector, for that wou'd be of all mischiefs the greatest.

Jully 16. [Gives news of temporary break down of the negotiations with the Elector of Bavaria owing to the rumour of Tallard's advance.]

Thus you see that matter is at an end for the present. . . . This Treaty has not made us loose any time, for we have been attacking the town of Rain, which has this day capitulated. And as we are advancing into the heart of Bavaria to destroy the country and oblige the Elector on way or other to a complyance.

Jully 20. Aicha. We shal march tomorrow and post ourselves [at Friedburg] soe that the Elector will be able to draw very little subsistence for his army from his own country, which we flater ourselves will make them very uneasy.

Jully 31. Friberg. Mons. de Tallard is advancing and may be with the Elector in three or four days. If we have a fair opertunity you may be sure we shall not decline ingaging them, our troupes being full of corage and desiring nothing more.

Aug. 10. When P. Eugene and I are joyned our army will consist of 160 squadrons and 65 battalions. P. Lewis has with him for the siege [of Ingoldstadt] 31 squadrons and 24 battalions. The ffrench make their boast of having a great superiority, but I am very confident they will not venture a battaile, but if wee find a fair occasion wee shal be glad to venture itt, being persuaded that the ill condition of affaires in most partes requiers itt.

[Aug. 13. Battle of Blenheim.]

Aug. 17. I had nether time nor health to write to you when I sent my aid de camp to the Estates with the account of our late victory, which appeares every day greater, for I believe att this time the number of Prisoners are above 11000. And for the honour of the troupes sent by England and Holland it is they that have done the whole business, for I can assure you that the Imperial troups have not 100 prisoners.

Aug. 25. Sefelingen [near Ulm]. It is impossible to say enough of the bravery of all the officers and soldiers, for as the enemy was stronger than wee, the greatest part of ours were obliged to charge four or five times a peece. But that which I bless God for every day is the unity and friendship in which we live, for to this minute I have not seen any discontent in any one officer, nor any one officer asked me what I intend to doe, but have all obey'd with cheerfulness.

Aug. 28. Sefelingen. By the letters we have intercepted of the enemy's, going to Paris from their camp, they all own to have lost above 40,000 men, which probably will oblige them to make detachments both from Italie and fflanders.

APPENDIX B

Principal Officers of State in the first years of the Godolphin Ministry

	1702	1703	1704
Lord Treasurer . . .	Sidney, Lord Godolphin		
Lord President of the Council .	Thos. Herbert, Earl of Pembroke		
Lord Privy Seal . . .	John Sheffield, Duke of Buckingham		
Chancellor of the Exchequer .	Hon. Henry Boyle		
Lord Keeper of the Great Seal . (No Lord Chancellor these years)	Sir Nathan Wright		
Secretary of State (Northern Department)	Sir Charles Hedges		Succeeded May 1704, by (Speaker) Robert Harley
Secretary of State (Southern Department)	Daniel Finch, Earl of Nottingham		Succeeded May 1704, by Sir Charles Hedges
Lord Lieutenant of Ireland . .	Lawrence Hyde, Earl of Rochester	Succeeded by James Butler, Duke of Ormonde, in Feb. 1703	

[P.T.O.

432

APPENDIX B—*continued.*

PRINCIPAL OFFICERS OF STATE IN THE FIRST YEARS OF THE GODOLPHIN MINISTRY

	1702	1703	1704
Lord High Admiral . . .	Prince George of Denmark, Prince Consort		
Secretary of War .	William Blathwayt		Succeeded by Henry St. John, May 1704
Master-General of the Ordnance .	Duke of Marlborough		
Comptroller of the Household .	Sir Edward Seymour		Succeeded by Thomas Mansell, May 1704
Lord Chamberlain . .	Edward Villiers, Earl of Jersey		Succeeded by Earl of Kent, May 1704

In this whole list there is not a single Whig, with the possible exception of the Earl of Kent, a person of slight ability and importance.

APPENDIX C

War Then and Now

War was a very different thing in Queen Anne's reign from what it is to-day. In the year 1704 the British Army and Navy decided the fate of Europe. The British killed outright in the four great actions of the year were computed as follows :

Gibraltar	60
Malaga	695
Schellenberg	452
Blenheim	672
	1879

1879 (say 2000 as some estimates are a little higher).

We have no figures of those who died later of wounds, of disease, of hardship, or were killed in smaller actions. But I think 5000 would amply cover the total of loss of life to Britain due to her participation in that decisive year of the war. Between 1914 and 1918 the average loss of life in war to Great Britain per year was about 200,000. The population of the island had risen about seven times, and the cost of war in youthful life about forty times.

It is true that in the later years of Queen Anne's war the number of deaths was sometimes larger, because the number of British soldiers had then been doubled and the proportion of them employed under unhealthy conditions in Spain increased. But even at Malplaquet, where the slaughter shocked opinion at home and hastened the advent of peace, the total number of British killed was about 600, though the Dutch lost perhaps four times as many.

ABBREVIATIONS USED IN THE NOTES

Abbey = Chas. Abbey. *The English Church and its Bishops* 1700–1800 (1887).
Add. MSS. = British Museum, *Additional MSS.* Some of the principal collections are thus alluded to :

    Coxe = Archdeacon Coxe's transcripts from the Marlborough (Blenheim) and Godolphin papers.
    E.   = Ellis Papers.
    H.F. = Hatton Finch Papers (Nottingham).
    L'H. = L'Hermitage (the Dutch agent).
    Mc. = Sir James McKintosh's transcripts.
    St.   = Stepney.

Ashton = J. Ashton. *Social Life in the Reign of Queen Anne*, 1882.
Atkinson = C. T. Atkinson. *Marlborough*, 1921. (*Heroes of Nations Series*.)
Augustan = *Social and Political Ideas of some English Thinkers of the Augustan Age*, ed. by Prof. Hearnshaw, 1928.
Baudrillart = A. Baudrillart, *Phil. V et la Cour de France.*
Bod. MSS. = Manuscripts in the Bodleian, Oxford.
Burchett = Josiah Burchett. *Transactions at Sea*, 1720.
Burnet = Bishop Burnet's *History of his own Time*, ed. 1823.
Calamy = J. T. Rutt's *Life of Edmund Calamy*, 1830.
Conduct = *Account of the Conduct of the Duchess of Marlborough* (by herself), 1742.
Colonie = de la Colonie. *Chronicles of an old Campaigner* 1692–1717 (1904).
Corbett = Julian Corbett. *England in the Mediterranean*, ed. 1917.
C.S.P. = *Calendar State Papers—Dom.* = Domestic ; *Am.* = *America and W. Indies* ; Tr. = Treasury, 1702–1707.
Coxe = Archdeacon Coxe. *Memoirs of Marlborough* (page references are to the ed. of 1818).
Cunningham = W. Cunningham. *Growth of English Industry and Commerce*, ed. 1903.
Davenant = Charles Davenant's Collected *Works*, 1771.
Defoe = Defoe's *Tour through Great Britain*, ed. 1 ; reprint by G. D. H. Cole, 1927.
De Jonge = J. C. De Jonge, *Geschiedenis van het Nederlandsche Zeewezen*, 1841, IV, ii.
Dispatches = *Marlborough' · Dispatches*, ed. Sir G. Murray, 1845.
Dowell = St. Dowell. *History of Taxation in England*, ed. 1884.
D'Urfey = D'Urfey's collection of songs. *Pills to Purge Melancholy*, 1719. (Reprinted.)
E.H.R. = *English Historical Review.*
Ec.H.R. = *Economic History Review.*
Ernle = Lord Ernle. *English Farming*, ed. 1922.
Feiling = Keith Feiling. *History of the Tory Party*, 1924.

Feldzüge = *Feldzüge des Prinzen Eugen*, Wien, 1879. Serie I, Band VI.

Fiennes = Diary of Celia Fiennes. *Through England on a Side Saddle*, 1888.

Fortescue = Sir John Fortescue. *History of the British Army*, 1899.

Hardwicke = *Hardwicke's State Papers*, 1778.

Heinsius MSS. = Letters of Marlborough to Heinsius in the Rijks-archief at the Hague (see Appendix A, above, for some excerpts).

Hervey, L.B. = *Letter-Books of John Hervey, first Earl of Bristol*, 1894.

Hervey, D. = *Diary of John Hervey, first Earl of Bristol*, 1894.

Hill = *Diplomatic Correspondence of Richard Hill*, 1845.

H.M.C. = *Historical Manuscripts Commission.* (R. 8 = *Eighth Report*, and so forth.)

H.C.J. = *House of Commons Journals.*

H.L.J. = *House of Lords Journals.*

H. of L. MSS. = *MSS. of House of Lords*, printed under authority of the *H.M.C.*

Klopp = Onno Klopp. *Fall des Hauses Stuart.*

Lady M. Montagu = *Lady Mary Wortley Montagu's Letters*, 1893.

Lambeth MSS. = MSS. in the Library of Lambeth Palace.

Lamberty = *Mémoires pour servir à l'histoire du* 18 *siècle*, de Lamberty, 1735.

Leake = *Life of Sir John Leake* (Navy Records Soc., 1920).

Lediard, N.H. = Thomas Lediard. *Naval History*, 1735.

Lediard, Marl. = Thomas Lediard. *Life of Marlborough*, 1736.

Legrelle = A. Legrelle, *La diplomatie française et la succession d'espagne.*

Macky = *A Journey through England*, by John Macky, fifth ed. 1732.

Martin = *Life of Capt. Stephen Martin* (Navy Records Soc., 1895).

Mayor = J. E. B. Mayor. *Cambridge under Queen Anne* (diaries of foreigners in England), 1911.

Millner = John Millner, *Journal of marches, etc.*, 1733.

Noailles = Duc de Noailles. *Mémoires politiques et militaires*, 1777.

Noorden = Carl von Noorden, *Europäische Geschichte*, 1870.

Ormonde = *Life of Ormonde*, 1747.

Parker = Capt. Robert Parker's *Memoirs*, 1746.

Parl. Hist. = Cobbett's *Parliamentary History*, vol. vi.

Pelet = General Pelet. *Mémoires militaires relatifs à la succession d'espagne* (The French military correspondence of the period), 1835.

Priv. Corr. = *Private Correspondence of Duchess of Marlborough*, 1838.

P.R.O. = *Public Record Office Manuscripts* (S.P. = *State Papers* ; *Tr.* = *Transcripts*).

R.H.S. = *Royal Historical Society* publications.

Rooke = *Journal of Sir George Rooke* (Navy Records Soc., 1897).

Rox = *Roxburghe Club* publications.

Salomon = F. Salomon. *Geschichte des letsten Ministeriums Königin Annas*, 1894.

Select Docs. = *Select Documents for Queen Anne's Reign*, 1702–7, ed. G. M. Trevelyan, 1929.

Spy = Ned Ward's *London Spy*, ed. 1924.

Sykes' Gibson = *Edmund Gibson, Bishop of London*, by Rev. Norman Sykes, 1926.

Taylor = C. W. Taylor. *The Wars of Marlborough*, 1921.

Tindal = Tindal's Continuation of Rapin's *History of England*, ed. 1744.

Torrington = *Memoirs relating to Lord Torrington* (Byng). *Camden Soc.*, 1889.

Turberville = A. S. Turberville. *House of Lords in Eighteenth Century*, 1927.

Wake MSS. = Archbishop Wake's Manuscripts in the Christ Church Library, Oxford.

Westerfield = R. B. Westerfield. *Middlemen in English Business, 1660–1760* (Yale, 1915).

Wilson = F. W. Wilson. *The Importance of the reign of Anne in English Church History*, 1911.

NOTES

CHAPTER I

[1] P. 3. Steele's *Guardian*, no. 9 (March 21, 1713), reminds us how often coalmines and industry were favourably regarded by the landed interest, because they increased the market and profits of neighbouring landlords and farmers.

[2] P. 4. *H.M.C. Portland*, IV, p. 272 (Oct. 8, 1705).

[3] P. 8. Evelyn. *Memoirs for my grandson*, 1704 (ed. 1926, p. 17).

[4] P. 8. W. Robinson. *History of Enfield*, 1823, I, p. 207.

[5] P. 9. *Defoe*, I, pp. 129, 140–141.

[6] P. 9. *Defoe*, I, p. 292.

[7] P. 10. R. G. Albion. *Forests and sea power*. (A valuable American contribution to British History.) ; *Ec. H. R.* Jan., 1930, pp. 269–270.

[8] P. 11. *Defoe*, I, p. 78. See also Defoe, *English Tradesman*, Pt. II, Chap. III, on the Trade in liquors.

[9] P. 11. *H.M.C. Coke* (1889), p. 164.

[10] P. 13. Sir William Ashley, *The Bread of our forefathers* (1928), *passim* specially p. 8 ; Westerfield, pp. 169–170 ; Moffit, *England on the eve of the Industrial Revolution* (1925), *passim* ; Defoe's *Tour*, *passim*, and his *English Tradesman* (ed. 1727), Pt. 2, II, pp. 30–46 ; *Ernle*, pp. 148–152 ; (*Rox.*) *Hooke's Corr.*, I., pp. xi, 426 ; *R.H.S.* 1926, *Cattle Trade* ; *P.R.O. Tr.* 14 (Venetian), 112, f. 24.

[11] P. 13 n. *H.M.C. Clements* (1913) pp. 242, 249 ; *Ernle*, pp. 148, 452 ; *Westerfield*, p. 169 ; Barrett's *Bristol*, p. 696. The degree to which England, in the early Eighteenth Century, regarded herself as a corn-exporting country, is illustrated in the lines in James Thomson's *Seasons* (*Spring*), where Britain is exhorted to rely on the export of cloth and corn to purchase the world's luxuries for herself :

> 'Nature's better blessings pour
> O'er every land ; the naked nations clothe ;
> And be th' exhaustless granary of a world.'

[12] P. 14. Webb, *Manor and Borough*, p. 128, 166, 183 ; Gonner, *Common Land and Enclosure, passim*.

[13] P. 14. Clapham, *Ec. History Modern Britain*, I, p. 22 ; Gonner, *passim*.

[14] P. 14. *Cunningham*, p. 706, note.

[15] P. 15. *H.C.J.*, XIV, p. 352.

[16] P. 15. *Defoe*, I, pp. 210, 285–286.

[17] P. 15. *E.H.R.*, Jan. 1929, pp. 40–60.

[18] P. 16 n. *Ernle*, p. 150 ; *H.M.C. Clements* (1913), p. 230.

[19] P. 17. Gregory King's calculations can be found in Chalmers' *Estimate of the comparative strength of Britain*, ed. 1804, or in slightly variant form in *Davenant*, II, p. 184, or in *Ernle*, pp. 453–454. A brief but important comment upon them by Professor Clapham should be studied in the *Cambridge Historical Journal*, Vol. I, no. I, pp. 94–95. King estimated thus : Freeholders, 180,000 ; Farmers, 150,000 ; artisans and handicraftsmen, 60,000 ; labouring people and out-servants, 364,000 ; cottagers and paupers, 400,000. These figures represent the number of 'families' to be multiplied by $3\frac{1}{2}$, 5 or 7 to obtain the number of persons.

[20] P. 18. *Cunningham*, pp. 564–565 ; *Defoe*, II, p. 602.

[21] P. 18 n. In one year the quarter sessions for Devon proclaimed that a

bailiff in husbandry should receive not more than £5 a year; a common man-servant in husbandry not more than £4 a year; women labouring at hay not more than threepence a day with food, or sixpence without—at reaping, sixpence with or a shilling without; master carpenters not more than eightpence with food, or one and fourpence without; and so forth through the whole category of labour in field and shop. A. H. A. Hamilton, *Quarter Sessions*, pp. 272–274; *H.M.C. Clements* (1913), pp. 223, 238–239; *E.H.R.*, *July* 1928, pp. 398–404.

The wages of twenty servants in a nobleman's family was reckoned at £170; that is £8 10*s*. on the average, but they had also perquisites, 'vails' (tips) and commissions. *Country Gentleman's Vademecum*, 1717; *Ashton*, I, p. 77.

Ernle, p. 440, gives the variations of wheat prices per quarter at Eton for the first fourteen years of the century. The political historian will observe that during the dangerous crisis of the war, 1702–1706, popular content was facilitated by cheap bread, and in 1709–1711 the Tory agitation for peace was aided by scarcity. In William III's reign prices of wheat had been more than twice what they were in the first half of Anne's reign.

1701	34/5	1708	37/11
1702	26/11	1709	71/11
1703	33/–	1710	71/6
1704	42/7	1711	49/6
1705	27/6	1712	42/5
1706	23/8	1713	46/9
1707	26/1	1714	46/1

These prices answer approximately to those given in Fleetwood's *Chronicon Preciosum*, ed. 1707, p. 128.

[22] P. 19. *Economic Journal*, May 1927, pp. 214–228 : Mrs. George's article.

[23] P. 19 n. Defoe, *Giving Alms no Charity*, 1704; *Duty of a Husbandman* (anon.) 1703, p. 36.

[24] P. 21. Miss Leonard justly remarks : 'Many are affected by the Poor Law who never receive relief; it takes away some of the horror of failure from all who may if unfortunate need help of the kind, and so renders the struggle for existence less brutal to the whole labouring class. In the Seventeenth Century this assistance to the poor helped to make England a peaceful community, and it has probably had the same effect ever since' (*English Poor Relief*, pp. 302–303); Webb, *English Poor Law* (1927), especially Chap. V on the Law of Settlement; *Wealth of Nations*, Book I, end of Chap. X; Lecky, *England*, II, pp. 203–209; *Lady M. Montagu*, I, pp. 394–395; Cunningham, pp. 567–577; *H. of L. MSS.*, 1704–1706, pp. xiv–xvi; Knowles and Boyle, *Vestiges of Old Newcastle*, pp. 154–155.

[25] P. 22. *H.M.C. Coke* (1889), p. 94, Aug. 1710.

[26] P. 23. *Stats. of Realm*, 22–23, C. II, XXV, 4 *W. and M. XXIII*; *Spectator*, no. 122.

[27] P. 24. *Stats. of Realm*, 4 *W. and M. XXIII*; *Freeholder*, nos. 22, 44; *Spectator*, nos. 116, 122; Blome's *Gentleman's Recreation*, first published in 1685, was reissued by subscription in 1710 but with few alterations. References to grouse shooting are frequent in the correspondence of the time : 'in moor game time I will go to the mountains' (*H.M.C. Clements*, p. 229, ann. 1704).

[28] P. 25. Mr. Collingwood, the historian of the Lake District, has called attention to 'the old farm-houses, dating everywhere from the Restoration to Queen Anne, and their solid oak furniture, inscribed very rarely with a year before 1660. Earlier stone buildings and oak fittings were not of the statesmen (free-holders), but of the gentry, or—earlier still—ecclesiastical. But now almost every-one lived in a new world of comfort and well being.' W. G. Collingwood, *Lake District History* (1925), pp. 1, 140.

[29] P. 25. *Fiennes*, pp. 159–164 ; *Calamy*, II, p. 220–221. *Defoe*, II, p. 679. *Macky* (II, p. 167) passes ' in a day or two through the little county of Westmorland where there is nothing remarkable ' and never turns aside to Lakeland. Robinson, Rector of Ousby in Cumberland, published in 1709 a *Natural History of Westmorland and Cumberland* of a hundred pages, chiefly about the minerals. It contains this one sentence about the scenery, worth reading as perhaps the earliest extant note of appreciation of the beauties of Lakeland : ' These lofty mountains contribute to the entertainment of our visive faculty, with most curious and delightful landskips.' But casual visitors saw nothing to admire.

[30] P. 26. Gibson's *Camden* (1695), p. 874. *Newcastle Courant*, 1711–1712. According to Miss *Fiennes* (p. 176) Newcastle ' most resembles London of any place in England,' and *Macky* (II, p. 241) calls it ' next to Bristol the greatest trading town in England.' North's *Life of Guildford* gives an interesting account of Newcastle and the Tyne valley at the end of Charles II's reign ; by 1702 the region was still more civilized and wealthy.

[31] P. 27. *Mayor*, pp. 135, 360–361 ; *The Lover*, no. 10, for Addison on china; *Art of Painting and an Essay towards an English School*, 1706.

[32] P. 27. Sir Reginald Blomfield, *History of Renaissance Architecture in England* ; James Gibbs, *Rules of Architecture* (reprinted 1924, with introduction by Barman, see pp. xxii–xxiv).

CHAPTER II

[33] P. 28. *Freeholder*, no. 44 (date 1715).

[34] P. 29. *Tatler*, no. 182.

[35] P. 30. *Lady Montagu*, I, p. 150 (1710).

[36] P. 30. *Bodleian MSS. Ballard*, 47.

[37] P. 31. The volumes of the *Historical MSS. Commission* are too numerous to cite in this connection. Those of Coke and Molesworth (Clements) will serve as typical examples, together with the *Letter Books of John Hervey* (1894). These and other family papers induce me to think that the incomes ascribed by King to the titled persons and larger gentry in 1688 were either under-estimated or had greatly increased by Queen Anne's time. Macaulay, in his third chapter of his *History*, drew a scarcely exaggerated picture of the small rustic squire's lack of culture. But he forgot to make clear what great varieties of wealth and culture existed among the class of country gentlemen. In Anne's reign there was more wealth and more culture than in 1685.

[38] P. 31. *H.M.C. Kenyon*, p. 449 ; Percy Thornton, *Harrow School*, pp. 101–104 ; *H.M.C. Rutland*, II (1889) p. 186 ; *Egerton MSS. B.M.* 1695.

[39] P. 32. *H.M.C. Clements*, pp. xix, 221, 224, 232, 235, 243, 248, 268. See p. 229, above, on Jack Molesworth's pay.

[40] P. 34. *H.M.C. Chequers* (1900), p. 96.

[41] P. 34. *H.M.C. Dropmore* (1892), I, p. 13.

[42] P. 35. Locke, *On Education* ; Swift, *Modern Education* ; *Burnet*, VI, p. 195 (648) ; *H.M.C. Wood*, p. 83 ; in *Spectator*, no. 168, Steele writes of schools : ' Many a hand have I seen whipped till it was covered with blood, perhaps for smiling or writing an O for an A. Many a brave and noble spirit has been there broken. Others have run from thence and were never heard of afterwards.' Yet such treatment cannot have been universal : Henri Misson considered children to be more kindly treated in England than France, *Voyage en Angleterre* (1698), p. 228.

[43] P. 36. *Athenian Oracle* (1710), IV, p. 327 ; *Lady M. Montagu*, II, pp. 3–4 ; Farquhar, *Recruiting Officer*, I, 2. Addison and Swift, *passim*.

[44] P. 37.   *H.M.C. Clements*, p. 246 ; *R.H.S.* (1917) *Guise*, pp. 150–151 ; *H.M.C. Coke*, p. 178 ; Coxe's *Walpole*, II. pp. 7–8 ; *Turberville*, p. 7.

[45] P. 37.   Secretan's *Nelson*, p. 197 ; *Postman*, Jan. 1, 1704, and Jan. 2, 1705, advertisements of political packs ; Hine's *Hitchin*, II, p. 253.

[46] P. 39.   *Hearne's Collections*, I, p. 324 ; Swift, *On Himself*, 1713 ; *Fiennes*, pp. 9, 218 ; *Life of Nash* (1762), p. 25 ; H. Misson, *Voyage en Ang.*, pp. 390–392 ; *Ashton*, I, pp. 206–213.

[47] P. 39.   See p. 214, above, on Queen Anne's visit to Bath in 1702, and its effects on the city.   Nash began his long domination of Bath about 1704.   He was 'by profession a gambler' though a most honourable one.   Nash's *Life*, pp. 21, 38–41, 51 ; Wood's *Bath, passim* ; *Macky*, II, pp. 137–140 ; *Fiennes*, pp. 12–15.

[48] P. 40.   Dec. 17, 1702.   *H.M.C. Beaufort*, p. 96.   Actually 'Beau Feilding' survived his wound.   Duels at this period were sometimes fought with pistol as well as sword—*H.M.C. Clements*, p. 251 ; *Mayor*, p. 370 ; *Guardian*, nos. 143, 145 ; *Life of Wharton*, p. 35 ; *Ashton*, II, pp. 185–196 ; Centlivre, *Beau's Duel*, II, 1 ; *Perplexed Lovers*, V ; *State Trials*, William III and Anne, *passim*.

[49] P. 41.   *D'Urfey*, I, p. 268 ; IV, p. 55 ; Defoe, *Compleat Gentleman* (ed. 1890), pp. 65, 248 ; *Freeholder*, no. 22 ; *Spectator*, no. 116 ; *Edinburgh Rev.*, Oct. 1927 ; *Gentleman's Recreation*, 1710 ; *Verney Letters 18th Cent.* (1930), I, *passim*.

[50] P. 41.   Sorbières, *Voyage to England*, translation of, 1709, p. 9 ; *H.M.C. Portland*, VI, p. 76 ; *D'Urfey*, II, p. 172.

[51] P. 42.   *Macky*, I, pp. 164, 167 ; *Mayor*, p. 355 ; *Add. MSS.* 28080, f. 74.

[52] P. 42.   *H.M.C. Coke*, p. 7 ; *Mayor*, pp. 316, 322, 363–364, 409 ; *Hill*, I, p. 381.

[53] P. 42.   Alexander Hamilton.   *New Account of the East Indies* (1727), II, pp. 271–273.

CHAPTER III

[54] P. 46.   *Tatler*, no. 255 ; *Spectator*, no. 106 ; *Ashton*, II, pp. 121–125; *Diary of Rev. T. Brockbank* (*Chetham Soc.* 1930).

[55] P. 46.   See a very remarkable letter of Archbishop Tenison to Queen Anne, Jan. 1713, expostulating with her for issuing a warrant of dispensation for holding two such livings more than than thirty miles apart, which Tenison declares had never once been done since 1676.   William and Mary, adds the Whig Primate to the Tory Queen, thought 'the distance of six miles much more expedient than that of thirty,' *Lambeth MSS.* 1133, ff. 31–39.   Actually Spratt, the High Church but time-serving Bishop of Rochester and Dean of Westminster, who first sat on James II's High Commission and then took the oaths to William, did very well for his son in the way of plurality without breaking the canonical rule.   The young gentleman took orders in 1704, was made by his father's interest Prebendary and Archdeacon of Rochester that same year, vicar of Boxley, Kent, in 1705, Rector of Stone, Kent, 1707, Prebendary of Winchester, 1712, Prebendary of Westminster, 1713.   Prebendaries not having cure of souls did not fall under the thirty mile rule.   He retained all these till his death in 1720.   Pearce's *Sons of the Clergy*, 1928, p. 188.   See also Richard Newton's *Pluralities Indefensible* for the practice in this matter in the early Eighteenth Century.

[56] P. 47.   *Bod. MSS., Ballard*, 4, f. 65 ; *Diary of Francis Evans, Sec. of Bishop Lloyd*, 1699–1706, pp. viii, xix, 24–25, 94–96 ; *Wake MSS., Epist.* 3, for the Lincolnshire list.

[57] P. 47.   *Wake MSS., Epist.* 5, Mr. Pujolas, 1709.

[58] P. 48. *Lambeth MSS.* 1120 ; *H. of L. MSS.* 1702–1704, pp. 558–559 ; Burton, *Queen Anne,* I, pp. 52–55 ; *Address to Persons of Quality,* Robert Nelson, 1715, Appendix 7 ; Foxcroft's *Burnet,* pp. 344–345, 408 ; Overton, *English Church, 1660–1714,* pp. 69, 229–230 ; *Life of Sharp,* 1825, I, pp. 338–339 ; *Burnet,* V, pp. 117–122 (369–371).

[59] P. 49. *Bod. MSS., Rawlinson, D.* 834, *Parochial Libraries.* Robert Nelson was on the committee and Henry Newman Secretary of the Society for the Propagation of the Gospel.

[60] P. 52. *Character of a Low Churchman,* 1702, p. 26.

[61] P. 52. J. Wickham Legge, *English Church Life,* pp. 30–37 ; *Wake MSS., Misc.* 5 and 11 ; *Lambeth MSS.* 1115.

[62] P. 54. *Vindication of the Clergy,* by a Divine of the Church of England, 1709, p. 4 ; *Burnet,* IV, p. 377 (211) ; *Abbey,* Chap. I ; Leslie Stephen, *English Thought in the Eighteenth Century* ; *D'Urfey,* VI, p. 214 ; Bass Mullinger, *Cambridge in the Seventeenth Century* ; Atterbury, *Letters,* II, pp. 30–31, III, pp. 314–318 ; *Bod. MSS., Ballard,* 9, f. 75 ; *Account of the Growth of Deism in England,* 1709 ; Hickeringill's *Priestcraft,* 1705, and the ensuing controversy ; *Priestianity,* 1720 ; works of Toland, Collins, Shaftesbury and pamphlets in answer ; Swift, *Argument against abolishing Christianity in England* ; William Nelson, *Rights of the Clergy,* 1712, introduction.

[63] P. 57. *Wake MSS., Misc.* 5 and 11 ; *Lambeth MSS.* 1115 ; *Memoirs of the Family of Cavendish,* Archdeacon Kennett, 1708, p. 29 ; *Defoe,* II, p. 465 ; *H. of L. MSS.* (1704–1706), pp. xxvii, 413–423 ; *Bod. MSS., Rawlinson, D.* 387 ; Estcourt, *English Catholic Nonjurors of 1715* from P.R.O. documents ; *H.M.C.* (1906) *Stonyhurst,* pp. 177–182 ; *Sykes' Gibson,* pp. 292–297 ; *B. M. Lansdowne MSS.* No. 825, ff. 180–181. In spite of the Protestant talk of the number of Roman Catholics in London, the actual returns of avowed Roman Catholics show a negligible quantity—in Middlesex and outer London a few more. They may not be complete.

[64] P. 58. Hine, *History of Hitchin,* II, pp. 32–34, for case of Skingle ; *Davenant,* IV, p. 411 ; *Wake MSS., Misc.,* 5 and 11, and *Lambeth MSS.* 1115, show how much stronger Dissenters, especially Quakers, were in Bucks than in Lincs or Kent.

[65] P. 58. The Chapelries were thus divided, 26 Presbyterian, 23 Baptist, 12 Independent, 14 Quaker, 13 French Protestant, *H.C.J.,* April 6, 1711.

[66] P. 59. E.g. *A Letter from some aged Nonconformist Ministers,* 1702, and Nonconformist sermons, *passim* ; *cf.* to Sacheverell's sermons and pamphlets, and Leslie's *Rehearsal* for difference in tone of controversy.

[67] P. 59. *Thoresby's Diary, passim,* and II, pp. 255–257 ; *Wake MSS., Misc.,* 5.

[68] P. 60. Stephen, *Criminal Law,* I, pp. 378–383, 399–400, 415–417, 427, II, pp. 430–436 ; *State Trials,* XIV, pp. 639–654 ; *Case of the Hertfordshire Witches considered,* dedicated to Sir John Powell ; Lecky, *England,* I, p. 333. In Addison's *Drummer,* V, the coachman asks : ' Sir, I would know whether the poor beast is bewitched by Goody Crouch, or Goody Flye ? ' ' Neither,' answers Sir George.

[69] P. 60. Addison, *Drummer,* I ; Bass Mullinger, *History of St. John's,* pp. 210–213 ; *Spectator,* no. 110.

[70] P. 61. Swift, *Baucis and Philemon* ; Wordsworth, *Prelude,* Book V.

[71] P. 63. Swift, *Examiner,* no. 44 (no. 43 in the reprint).

[72] P. 63. *Bod. MSS., Ballard,* 12, f. 52.

[73] P. 63. There is a copy, with no printer's name, in the Library of Trinity College, Cambridge, I, 1, 27 (13). On the *Nonjurors,* see the well-known work of T. Lathbury, 1845 ; *Augustan,* Ch. V ; Secretan's *Nelson* ; Hearne's

Collections ; *Aylesbury (Rox.)*, II, p. 531 ; J. Wickham Legge, *English Church Life*, pp. 16–20 ; *Bod. MSS., Rawlinson*, D. 845–848, Letters 91–92, 98 ; *Bod. MSS., Ballard*, 12 ; L. M. Hawkins, *Allegiance in Church and State* (1928). Leslie's works are best studied for the Nonjurors position in Anne's reign.

[74] P. 65. An early version of the *Vicar of Bray* will be found in Ned Ward's *Poems*, 1706, called *The religious Turncoat or the Trimming Parson*.

[75] P. 66. *Davenant*, IV, p. 396.

[76] P. 67. Overton, *English Church*, pp. 212–213 ; Josiah Woodward, *Rise and Progress of the Religious Societies* ; Secretan's *Nelson*, pp. 90–150 ; *Edinburgh Review*, Oct. 1927, on *Humanitarian London, 1688 to 1750*.

[77] P. 67. *Wake MSS., Misc.*, 5 and 11, and *Lambeth MSS.* 1115, replies from parsons in Lincs, Bucks, Kent and Sussex, to the questions ' Is there any public school in your parish ? ' and ' Has any Charity School lately been set up in your parish ? ' In the rural parishes the replies are negative in the great majority of cases.

[78] P. 68. *Bod. Rawlinson MSS.*, D. 839, papers of Henry Newman, Secretary of the Society for the Propagation of the Gospel, contains much information on Charity Schools, *circa* 1708. *Address to Persons of Quality*, Robert Nelson, 1715, Appendix no. 12 ; *Wilson*, pp. 47–48 ; Overton, *Life in English Church*, pp. 224–228 ; Secretan's *Nelson*, pp. 118–134 ; *Strype's Stow's London*, 1720, Bk. V, pp. 47–48 ; *Present State of Great Britain*, 1708, pp. 672–684, List of Charity Schools. On Dissenters' Schools see *Calamy*, I, pp. 132–136, II, pp. 10–13, 282–294. I am indebted to Miss Jones of Girton for ideas and information about the Charity Schools. She pointed out to me the importance of the controversy on the subject in Mandeville's *Fable of the Bees, e.g.* 6th ed. 1732, pp. 314–318 of Volume I.

[79] P. 69. *Mayor*, p. 353 ; *Persuasive to the Serious Observance of the Lord's Day*, 1712 ; *Burnet*, V, p. 18 (318), Onslow's note on Holt's views ; Overton, *English Church*, pp. 213–215 ; *Life of Sharp*, I, pp. 170–189 ; Defoe's *Reformation of Manners, a Satyr*, 1702 ; Webb, *Manor and Borough*, pp. 312–315, for the Mayor of Deal ; Secretan's *Nelson*, 96–103 ; Sacheverell's *Character of a Low Churchman*, 1702, p. 17 ; *Bod. MSS., Rawlinson*, D. 1396–1399, for records of prosecutions in Anne's reign ; the commonest seem to have been for Sunday trading.

CHAPTER IV

[80] P. 72. Defoe, *Giving Alms no Charity*, and *Tour*, I, p. 43, II, p. 435.

[81] P. 73. *Calamy*, II, pp. 119–141.

[82] P. 74. Mrs. George, *London Life, passim* ; *Edinburgh Review*, Oct. 1927.

[83] P. 74. *H.M.C. Downshire* (1924), pp. 903–904.

[84] P. 74. *Spy*, pp. 108–109.

[85] P. 77. *Mayor*, p. 324 (F. Burman's Diary) ; *Add. MSS.* 17677 YY. (L'H.), f. 266, Nov. 6–17, 1702.

[86] P. 78. *Strype's Stow's London* (1720), Book I, pp. 65–119 ; *Macky*, I, pp. 274–283 ; *P.R.O., Barbary States* (S.P.), 71.

[87] P. 79. *Strype's Stow's London* (1720), Book I, p. 42 and *passim* ; Webb, *Manor and Borough*, pp. 212–227, 569–692.

[88] P. 80. *Defoe*, I, pp. 6, 157, 160–165, 382–385.

[89] P. 81. *Strype's Stow's London, passim* and maps ; Sir W. Foster, *John Company*, Chap. VIII ; *Defoe*, I, p. 350.

[90] P. 81. Loftie, *London*, I, pp. 8–12 and maps ; *Strype's Stow's London* and maps ; Gibson's *Camden*, p. 335.

[91] P. 82. *Mayor*, pp. 362, 414 ; *Letters of Shaftesbury to Molesworth*, p. 6, letter of Oct. 12, 1708.

92 P. 84. Wright and Fayle's *History of Lloyd's*, 1928 ; *Spy, passim* ; *Tatler*, nos. 1 and 268 ; *Spectator*, no. 46 ; *Macky*, I, p. 195 ; Sorbières' *England* (trans. of 1709), p. 54 ; *Ashton*, I, pp. 214–236, II. pp. 262–268 ; Swift, *Modern Education* ; *Flying Post*, May 12, 1702, advertisement of the Windsor Coffee House.

93 P. 84. *Macky*, I, p. 193.

94 P. 84. *Colley Cibber's Life* (1740), p. 190.

95 P. 85. *Colley Cibber's Life*, pp. 76–77, 83–87 ; *Spectator*, no. 45 ; *H.M.C. Egmont*, II, p. 240 ; *Tatler*, nos. 1, 71, 167.

96 P. 85. E.g. *The Evil and danger of Stage plays, in almost 2000 instances taken from the plays of the last two years*. Rev. Arthur Bedford, 1706, and later editions ; Secretan's *Nelson*, pp. 107, 110 ; *D'Urfey*, II, p. 45.

97 P. 86. *Colley Cibber's Life*, p. 225.

98 P. 86. *E.g.* the famous passage in Swift's *Modern Education* ; Ned Ward's *Mars strip't of his armour*, 1709. See also *An Apology for the Army*, 1715, on Tory attacks on the Army.

99 P. 87. *Mayor*, p. 373 (1712).

100 P. 87. *Macky*, I, pp. 193–194 ; *Mayor*, pp. 133, 350 ; *Lady M. Montagu*, I, p. 151 ; *Spectator*, no. 278 ; *Wentworth Papers*, p. 66 ; Tickell's Prologue to Addison's *Rosamund* ; Dr. Johnson in his life of Gay says, 'We owe to Gay the Ballad Opera' ; see also his life of Hughes, on the Italian Opera.

101 P. 88. *H.M.C. Coke* (1889), p. 178.

102 P. 89. *H. of C.J.*, XIV, p. 338.

103 P. 90. Fox Bourne, *English Newspapers*, I, pp. 81–84. There is a good collection of Queen Anne newspapers in the British Museum.

104 P. 91. *State of Great Britain*, 1708 (a sort of 'Whitaker'), pp. 713–714 ; Moffit, *Eng. on eve of Ind. Rev.*, pp. 243–244 ; *Defoe*, I, pp. 343–344.

105 P. 92. H. G. Graham, *Social Life of Scotland, Eighteenth Century*, I, p. 46–48 ; *Mayor*, p. 115 ; *Westerfield*, p. 282 ; Capt. Alexander Smith, *Complete History of the Highwaymen* ; *H.M.C. Clements*, p. 234–235.

106 P. 93. *Mayor*, pp. 348, 409 ; *Thoresby's Diary*, II, p. 17 ; Webb, *King's Highway*, pp. 6, 65–67 ; Defoe, *Tour*, I, p. 129 ; *H.M.C. Portland*, VI, p. 76 ; Campbell's *Chancellors, Cowper*, IV, p. 267.

107 P. 93. Webb, *King's Highway*, Chaps. I, III, V, VII.

108 P. 94. Webb, *King's Highway*, p. 66 ; *Defoe*, II, p. 615, *Eng. Tradesman*, Pt. 2, II, pp. 27–30 ; *Dowell*, IV, pp. 413–414 ; *Strype's Stow's London*, II, Bk. V, p. 293 ; *Stats. of Realm* (1702), VIII, pp. 178–180 ; *H. of L. MSS.* (1702–1704), pp. xxxiii–iv, 225–240.

109 P. 95. A contemporary account of the explosion, or 'dreadful earthquake,' at Chester-le-Street, by the Rev. Mr. Salter, Minister of the Gospel in those parts, will be found in the B.M., bound up with other 'Popular Histories,' 1076, l, 22 ; L. W. Moffit, *Eve of Ind. Rev.*, pp. 161–166, 239–242 ; *R.H.S.*, 1925, Miss Moller on *Seventeenth Century coalmining* ; *Defoe*, II, p. 683, and his *Tradesman* (1727), Pt. 2, II, p. 29, 70 ; *Fiennes, passim* ; *Northumberland Table, Bk. I*, p. 341 ; *Coal Industry in the Eighteenth Century*, Ashton and Sykes, pp. 1–7 and *passim* ; *Dartmouth MSS.*, at Patshull, Letter of Nottingham to Lord Dartmouth, Sept. 6, 1707.

110 P. 96. *Defoe*, I, pp. 266–267, II, p. 602.

111 P. 96. *Defoe*, I, pp. xiv–xvi, 600–615 ; *Westerfield*, pp. 274–276, 287–288.

112 P. 97. Macpherson, *Annals of Commerce* (1805), II, p. 707 ; *Defoe*, I, p. 123 ; *H. of L. MSS.* (1702–1704), 72, 333 ; (1706–1708), xxiv–v ; *Ec.H.R.* Jan. 1928, p. 275 ; *C.S.P. Dom.* 1702, p. 520 ; Miss Murray's *Commercial Relations, Engl. and Ireland*, pp. 58–61 ; R. H. Murray, *Rev. Ireland*, pp. 401–403.

[113] P. 97. *H. of L. MSS.* (1702–1704), p. 70 ; Defoe, *Eng. Tradesman*, 1727, Pt. 2, II, pp. 51, 65–69 ; *Ec.H.R.* Jan. 1928, p. 262.

[114] P. 98. *H. of L. MSS.* (1702–1704), p. 73 ; *Hue and cry after East-India goods*, 1701 ; Khan, *East India Trade in Seventeenth Century*, 1923 ; *Davenant*, I, pp. 85–123.

[115] P. 100. Webb, *Manor and Borough*, pp. 266–267, 384–385.

[116] P. 101. *Stats. of Realm* (1702), pp. 52–53.

[117] P. 102. *H.M.C. Eliot Hodgkin* (1897), pp. 341–344 ; *H.M.C. Coke*, p. 162 ; Alexander Smith, *History of Highwaymen*, ed. 1926, introd., pp. v–xv ; *Spy*, pp. 136–138.

CHAPTER V

[118] P. 117. There is some difference as to the seriousness of her resistance between A. W. Ward (*Electress Sophia*), pp. 305–324, and *Klopp*, VIII, pp. 554–570, IX, pp. 144–153. See also *Hardwicke*, II, pp. 442–443 ; Kemble, *State Papers*, pp. 43–44, 243–249.

[119] P. 118. Clarke's *Life of James II* (1816), II, pp. 559–560 ; *Lamberty*, I, p. 121 ; *Klopp*, VIII, p. 559 ; Macpherson's *Original Papers*, II, p. 223, the Pretender's letter of May 1711 to Queen Anne refers to such a promise made by her to their father at some time not specified

[120] P. 118. *H.M.C. Downshire* (1924), I, p. 805.

CHAPTER VI

[121] P. 123. Defoe, *English Tradesman*, 1727, Pt. 2, II, pp. 65–66 ; *Ec.H.R.*, Jan. 1928, pp. 262.

[122] P. 130. *Corbett*, II, pp. 298–299, 419–423, 460–474, 494–495 ; *Legrelle*, II, pp. 288, 312, 319, 322–328. For the whole affair of the succession from 1697–1701 compare the documents in Legrelle to those in Hippeau, *Avènement des Bourbons au trone d'espagne*, 1875.

[123] P. 136. *P.R.O. Tr.*, 3 (France), 186, ff. 270–280 ; 187, ff. 301–329 ; 188, ff. 370–385.

[124] P. 137. *Legrelle*, IV, pp. 341–351, a most enlightening correspondence. See also *Klopp*, IX, pp. 403–404 ; *Noailles*, II, pp. 148–157 ; *Baudrillart*, I, pp. 90, 119–120.

[125] P. 138. *P.R.O.* (S.P.), 87, 4, ff. 196, *Dutch Mémoire of* 1712.

[126] P. 139. *H.M.C. Downshire* (1924), p. 824 (March 1704) ; Lavisse, *Hist. de France*, VIII, p. 84. That work and *Legrelle* and *Baudrillart* should be studied for Louis's conduct in 1700–1702.

[127] P. 140. *P.R.O. Spain* (S.P.), 94, 75, Aglionby's and Schonenberg's letters. On Aglionby, see G. N. Clark in *Notes and Queries*, 12th Series, IX, pp. 141–143.

[128] P. 141. *P.R.O. Spain* (S.P.), 94, 75, Aglionby to Vernon, Ap. 6, 1701.

[129] P. 141. Davenant, III, p. 345 ; *Essay upon the Balance of Power*, 1701, p. 76 ; *True Picture of a Modern Whig*, 1701. For the close relationship of Poussin and Davenant, see Poussin's letters of Aug. 11 and Sept. 8, 1701, in *P.R.O. Transcripts*, 3 (France), 189, ff. 500, 519. Poussin proposed to bribe Davenant, but whether Davenant actually took any money does not appear. See also *Salomon*, p. 50, note 3.

[130] P. 142. *P.R.O. Tr.*, 3 (France), 188, f. 424, May 23, 1701. See *Feiling*, Chap. XII, on all these events, and Defoe, *Kentish Petition*.

CHAPTER VII

[131] P. 146. Bolingbroke, *On the Study and Use of History*, Letter VIII.

[132] P. 147. Geikie (R.), *Barrier Treaty*, MS. in King's College, Cambridge.

[133] P. 148. *Coxe*, I, Chap. IX, pp. 97-98 ; also *Add. MSS.* (Mc.) 34518, ff. 140-141, M. to Hedges and to Godolphin, Oct. 3-14, 1701.

[134] P. 148. *Coxe*, I, Chap. IX, pp. 92-94 ; *Diplomatic Instructions Sweden* (*R.H.S.*, 1922), I, pp. 22-23.

[135] P. 150. *B.M. Add. MSS.* 20241, ff. 18-19, 20242, f. 23, *Gualterio Papers* ; F. W. Head, *The Fallen Stuarts*, pp. 95, 128-131, 335-340.

[136] P. 150. Acton, *Lectures on Modern History*, pp. 256-257.

[137] P. 150. *B.M. Add. MSS.* 36621, *Mémoire de Mons. de Bonrepaux*.

[138] P. 151. For the origin of the ' Seymour Clause ' of the Grand Alliance, see *H.C.J.* and *Add. MSS.* (*L'H.*) 17677, xx, p. 170. For the clause itself, see *Klopp*, IX, p. 500, though the date given there is a year too late, see Pribram, *Osterreichische Staatsverträge, England*, I, p. 226. Stepney writes from Vienna on April 28, 1702, that the Austrian Court, in spite of its Catholicism, makes no difficulty about adding the clause (*P.R.O.* (S.P.) 80, 18).

[139] P. 153. *Klopp*, IX, p. 334 ; *Ec.H.R.* Jan. 1928, p. 268 ; *Hardwicke*, II, p. 450.

[140] P. 153. Just before his enforced departure from England, Poussin reported (Oct. 3, 1701) the state of parties. The Whigs and Tories ' partagent et agitent aujourdhui presque toute l'Angleterre.' Both are now for war ; the Whigs 'n'y entre que par passion et par les vues particulières ' ; the Tories ' par politique et en quelque sorte malgré eux mêmes.' The French agent Vaudoncourt, after Poussin's departure, writes on Dec. 27 that if the Tories have the majority they will be constrained to make war, because the people are absolutely for war ; but they will try to make it as auxiliary only to Holland, not sending any large English force to the continent, but giving subsidies to Austria and Holland, *P.R.O. Tr.* (*France*), 189, ff. 537, 545. In the same week L'Hermitage reported to Holland that the Whigs are for raising English troops and the Tories for giving subsidies to raise foreign troops (*B.M. Add. MSS.* 17677, xx, f. 147).

[141] P. 153. *Hardwicke*, II, pp. 443-463.

[142] P. 154. *H.M.C. Downshire* (1924), I, Pt. 2, p. 811.

[143] P. 156. *Pelet*, I, pp. 47-154 ; *Klopp*, IX, pp. 393-411.

[144] P. 156. *Add. MSS.* (E.) 28910, f. 253, f. 291 ; *Coxe*, Chap. IX, p. 104 ; *Heinsius MSS.*, Marlborough's letters of Jan., see Appendix A above.

[145] P. 157. See p. 86 above, on the Whig playwrights, *e.g.* the first scene of Farquhar's *Trip to the Jubilee* and his *Recruiting Officer* ; *Luttrell's Diary*, Feb. 26 and Feb. 28, 1701-1702.

[146] P. 158. *Add. MSS.* (*L'H.*) 17677 xx, ff. 162, 165, 177, 235-237, 242 ; *Feiling*, pp. 356-357.

[147] P. 158. *Add. MSS.* (*L'H.*) 17677, xx, ff. 224-227 ; *H.C.J.*, Feb. 26 ; *Luttrell's Diary*, Feb. 26.

[148] P. 159. *Add. MSS.* (H.F.) 29588, ff. 16-17, 22 ; *H.M.C. Coke* (1889), p. 2.

[149] P. 160. *Feiling*, pp. 356-358 ; *Burnet*, IV, pp. 535-540 (298) ; *H.M.C. Coke*, p. 2 ; *Stats. of Realm*, VIII, pp. 218-220 ; *Case of the Abjuration Oath endeavoured to be cleared*, 1702 ; Lecky, *Ireland*, I, p. 158 ; Swift, *Examiner*, Nos. 40 and 44 (39 and 43 in the reprint).

[150] P. 161. *Add. MSS.* (H.F.) 29588, f. 16.

[151] P. 161. For some of the expectations on William's death, see *Add. MSS.* 32258 (*Deciphers*, April 4, 1702) ; *Add. MSS.* 36621.

CHAPTER VIII

[152] P. 163. *Heinsius MSS.*, Marlborough's letter of March $\frac{8}{19}$, see Appendix A, above ; *Coxe*, Chap. X, i, p. 109. (Sunderland's letter is not printed in later editions of Coxe.)

[153] P. 164. *Add. MSS. (L'H.)* 17677, xx, ff. 65–69, 249–254 ; *H.M.C., R.* 2, p. 242.

[154] P. 164. *Add. MSS. (L'H.)* 17677, xx, f. 153.

[155] P. 165. *Legrelle*, IV, pp. 259–263. On internal Dutch parties and the war, see Professor Geyl's *Nederland's Staatkunde in de Spaansche Successieoorlog*, Amsterdam, 1929, pp. 6–8 ; for Marlborough's relations to Buys see *Dispatches*, I, pp. 216, 602.

[156] P. 166. Heinsius to Bentinck, March 13–24, 17–28, *Correspondentie van W. III en van Bentinck*, Japikse, 1927, Deel I, pp. 524–525 ; *P.R.O.* 84, 224 (Holland), ff. 3–9, 14, Stanhope to Vernon ; *Coxe*, Chaps. X–XI ; *Klopp*, X, pp. 32, 72 ; *Heinsius MSS.*, see Marlborough's letters in Appendix A, above.

[157] P. 167. *Add. MSS.* 9090, f. 107, Vernon to Shrewsbury, June 9, 1701.

[158] P. 168. *Mayor*, p. 372 ; *Priv. Corr.* II, pp. 66, 120 ; *Rox., Sir J. Clerk*, p. 72.

[159] P. 168. *Conduct*, p. 20 ; *H.M.C., R.* 8, p. 52.

[160] P. 168. *Add. MSS. (L'H.)* 17677, xx, f. 262. Swift (*Journal*, July 31, 1711) writes : 'The queen . . . hunts in a chaise with one horse, which she drives herself, and drives furiously, like Jehu, and a mighty hunter like Nimrod. Dingley has heard of Nimrod, but not Stella, for it is in the Bible.' This bears out L'Hermitage, since ' furiously ' is clearly humorous.

[161] P. 169. *Rox., Sir J. Clerk*, pp. 62, 72.

[162] P. 169. *Surtees Soc.* No. 54, *de la Prynne's Diary*, p. 49 ; *Mayor*, p. 368.

[163] P. 170. *Add. MSS. (H.F.)* 29548, several notes of Anne to Nottingham of 1702 and 1703.

[164] P. 171. *H.M.C. Downshire*, I, II, p. 828.

[165] P. 172. *E.H.R.*, Ap. 1930, Mr. Sykes' article. For Ken's pension, see *C.S.P.Tr.*, pp. xii and 422.

[166] P. 173. *Coxe*, Chap. X, note 1 ; *H.M.C., R.* 8, p. 52.

[167] P. 173. *P.R.O. Transcripts*, 3 (*France*), 190, ff. 56–57, Vaudoncourt's cypher letter to Torcy, May 1702.

[168] P. 174. *Hooke's Correspondence (Rox.)*, I, pp. 13–15.

[169] P. 174. *P.R.O. Transcripts*, 3 (*France*), 190, ff. 73–79.

[170] P. 175. *H.M.C., R.* 8, p. 52 ; Nichols' *Lit. Anecdotes*, II, pp. 499–502. Boswell's *Johnson*, *sub.* 1712.

[171] P. 176. *Coxe*, Chap. LI, Aug. 30–Sept. 10, 1706.

[172] P. 176. *H.M.C., R.* 8, p. 42, July 3, 1708.

[173] P. 180. *John and Sarah Marlborough*, Stuart Reid, p. 110. This book contains a few quotations from the Blenheim papers that are not in *Coxe* or the Coxe transcripts in the B.M. But many of the passages referred to in the volume as *Blenheim Papers* can also be found in Coxe.

[174] P. 185. *Add. MSS. (Coxe)* 28070, ff. 2–3b.

CHAPTER IX

[175] P. 190. *Last Will of the Impostor George Fox*, Francis Bugg, Feb. 170$\frac{2}{3}$; *H.M.C. Portland IV*, 188, May 17 and 190, May 31, 1705 ; *Bod. MSS. Willis*, 54, 56, poll books of Bucks and Sussex, 1713, where the Quakers can be distinguished

by their making ' affirmation ' instead of taking the loyal oath required of other voters.   At the end of Mrs. Centlivre's *Gotham Election*, the Whig mob carries about a Pope and wooden shoes, and the Tory mob ' a tub with a woman preacher in it.'   For a specimen of the bitter attacks on Quakerism early in Anne's reign, see George Keith's pamphlets.

[176] P. 192.   *Memorial of the Church of England*, 1705, p. 15.

[177] P. 193.   *Turberville*, p. 45 ; *H. of L. MSS.* (1702–1704), pp. 200–201 ; *Parl. Hist.*, VI, p. 1003 ; *H.L.J.*, Feb. 22, 1710–1711.

[178] P. 197.   *Add. MSS.* (H.F.) 29584, pp. 95, 109–110.

[179] P. 198.   *Shaftesbury's Letters to Molesworth* (1721), p. 44, letter of November 1, 1709 ; on Wharton see also *Burnet*, V, p. 116 (369), Onslow's note, and p. 328 (431), Dartmouth's note.

[180] P. 202.   *H.M.C. Downshire*, I, II, pp. 838–839 ; Elliot's *Godolphin*, p. 248 ; *H.M.C. Buccleugh*, II (1903), *Shrewsbury's Diary*, pp. 763–768, 791–792 ; *Burnet*, V, pp. 437–439 and notes (546) ; *Add. MSS.* (*Coxe*) 9090 *passim*, especially ff. 171–172 for Shrewsbury's correspondence with Vernon and Godolphin from Rome ; *Macky's* (?) *Characters*, Rox. (1895), pp. 37–39.

[181] P. 203.   *H. of C.J.* ; *H.M.C.*, R. 8, p. 53, on Somerset's advice to Queen Anne ; *Add. MSS.* (*L'H.*) 17677, xx, ff. 258–259, 266 ; *Burnet*, V. p. 13 (315).

[182] P. 204.   *Add. MSS.* (*L'H.*) 17677, xx, f. 287 ; *Tindal*, III, p. 544 ; Barrett's *Bristol*, p. 696 ; *H.M.C. Bagot*, R. 10. Pt. IV, p. 337 ; Strickland's *Queens*, VIII, pp. 145–157.

[183] P. 204.   Boyer's *Anne*, p. 14 ; *Tindal*, III, p. 545 ; *Add. MSS.* (*L'H.*) 17677, xx, ff. 292, 295, 299.

[184] P. 205.   *Coxe*, Chap. XVIII, i, pp. 204–205, June 10, 1703.

[185] P. 206.   *H.C.J.* ; *Add. MSS.* (*L'H.*) 17677, xx, ff. 299–300 ; Boyer's *Anne*, pp. 14–15.   The actual proposal was ' that no person be an officer in England or Ireland, in Her Majesty's new-raised forces, but such as were born in England, Scotland or Ireland, or the dominions thereto belonging, or of English parents, unless they were before on half pay.'

[186] P. 208.   *H. of L. MSS.*, VI (1704–1706), pp. xvii–xviii, note ; Leadam, *Pol. Hist.* IX, p. 35 ; *H.M.C. Portland*, IV., pp. 122, 269 ; *Feiling*, pp. 362, 367 ; *H.M.C. Coke* (1889), p. 15 ; *E.H.R.* Apr. 1900, p. 243.

[187] P. 208.   Lord Weymouth to Nottingham, June 5, 1702, *Add. MSS.* 29588, f. 47.

[188] P. 209.   *Add. MSS.* 29568, ff. 67, 114.

[189] P. 209.   *H.M.C. Coke*, p. 13.

[190] P. 209.   See *Hervey, D.*, 24, 35, 37, for the Corporation of Bury St. Edmunds and Hervey.

[191] P. 210.   *Camden Soc.* 1875, *Prideaux's Letters*, p. 200.

[192] P. 210.   *English advice to the freeholders of England*, 1714, p. 4.

[193] P. 211.   *B.M. Add. MSS.* (H.F.) 29579, letter of Sir C. Lyttelton, July 15, 1702.

[194] P. 211.   *H.M.C. Chequers Court* (1900), p. 78 ; *Add. MSS.* (*Coxe*) 9092, ff. 2–3.

[195] P. 211.   *Guise Memoirs* (R.H.S.), p. 144 ; *Burnet*, V, pp. 47–48 and note (335) ; *H.C.J.* XIV, pp. 5–6, 37–38.   Sir Simon Harcourt was unseated on petition in Jan. 1709, in the Whig Parliament.

[196] P. 211.   *H.M.C. Somerset* (1898), p. 194 ; *Guise Memoirs*, R.H.S., pp. 145–146, for the tricks by the Gloucester Tories that year.   For more electioneering methods, see *B.M. Lansdowne MSS.*, 547, 548, election petitions, Anne.

[197] P. 212.   *Defoe's Review*, June 8, 1708.

[198] P. 212.   *Defoe*, I, p. 73 ; *Macky*, I, p. 135, 278–280 ; *Somers Tracts* (1814), XII, pp. 399–416.

[199] P. 213.   Campbell's *Chancellors*, IV, pp. 347–348.

[200] P. 213.   *H.M.C. Portland*, IV, p. 291.   This was in 1706 ; in the Parliament of 1702–5, the number of Whigs would have been less and the Tories more.

[201] P. 213.   *B.M. Stowe MSS.*, 354, f. 161b.

[202] P. 214.   See p. 39 above, for Bath ; Boyer's *Anne*, p. 33 ; *Queen's Famous Progress* (old tract), 1702 ; *Add. MSS.* 28095, f. 32 ; R. Warner's *Bath* (1801), pp. 209, 224.

CHAPTER X

[203] P. 215.   *Shaftesbury's letters to Molesworth* (ed. 1721), p. xxiii.

[204] P. 216.   *Fortescue*, I, pp. 554–556 ; *H. of C.J.*, Jan. 28, 1711–12.

[205] P. 217.   Only the three regiments of Guards and the Royal Scots had more than one battalion each, in Anne's reign.   *Fortescue*, I, p. 555.

[206] P. 218.   *Fortescue*, I, pp. 556, 567 ; *H.M.C. Wood* (1913), p. 87 ; *Aylesbury's Memoirs*, II, p. 523 ; *Mars stript of his armour*, 1709, by Ned Ward.

[207] P. 220.   *D'Urfey*, V, pp. 319–321 ; *Luttrell's Diary*, May 30 and Nov. 9, 1704, for the Ely incident ; *Beaux's Stratagem*, Act III, sc. 3 ; Burton, *Reign of Anne*, I, pp. 197–205 ; *Stats. of Realm*, Vol. VIII ; *Memoirs of Peter Drake* (1755) ; *H.M.C. Coke*, p. 70 ; *H.M.C., R. 8, Chester MSS.*, p. 394, Jan. 25, 1707 ; *Tindal*, III, p. 644 ; Hamilton, *Quarter Sessions under Anne*, pp. 275–276 ; *H.M.C. Portland*, IV, pp. 279, 289, 295, 316, 335 ; *Fortescue*, I, Chap. XI *passim*, above all.

[208] P. 221.   *Add. MSS. (E.)* 28948, f. 1, for a Militia summons, *temp.* Queen Anne ; Evelyn, *Memoirs for my grandson*, 1704 (Nonesuch Press, 1926), pp. 23–24.

[209] P. 222.   Kane, General R., *Campaigns and Discipline, etc.* (1745), p. 110 ; Firth, *Cromwell's Army*, Chap. V.

[210] P. 223.   *Parker*, p. 105.

[211] P. 224.   *Fortescue*, I, pp. 584–585 ; *Parker*, p. 139.

[212] P. 226.   *Add. MSS. (L'H.)* 17677, xx, f. 291 ; *Lamberty*, II, p. 495 ; *Add. MSS. (H.F.)* 29588, f. 51 ; *Heinsius MSS.*, Marlborough's letter, Ap. 27, 1702.

[213] P. 227.   *Fortescue*, I, p. 586 ; an account of British Court Martial proceedings abroad under Marlborough in 1708 will be found in *Journal of the Soc. for Army Historical Research*, IV (1925), pp. 161–168.   Careful attention seems to have been given to the cases and to the character of the prisoners as reported.

[214] P. 228.   John Deane, *Journal of Campaign in Flanders*, pp. 4–6 ; *Fortescue*, I, pp. 559–562.   *H.M.C. Somerset* (1898), p. 114.

[215] P. 229.   *P.R.O. (S.P.)* 84 (*Holland*) 224, ff. 200, 233 ; (*Barbary States*), 71, 27, ff. 139, 175 ; 90, 2 (*Prussia*), Raby, June 9, 1703 ; (*Spain*) 94, 75, Aglionby *passim* ; *H. of C.J.*, XIV, p. 365, and *D.N.B.* for Michelborne ; *C.S.P. Tr.*, pp. 140–141 for Browning's widow, and p. x on Debts of Crown generally.

[216] P. 229.   *H.M.C. Clements* (1913), pp. xix, 257.   For Godolphin's support of the army under Marlborough's command, see *Apology for the Army*, 1715, by An Officer, p. 36 : ' The late war in Flanders was also by the admirable management of my Lord Godolphin so well supported that the forces there could scarce complain of any wants or hardships.'

[217] P. 231.   Hamley, *Operations of War*, ed. 1907, pp. 38–39 ; conversation with Sir George Aston.   For the exchange of prisoners see *Lamberty*, II, pp. 412–413, and *C.S.P. Dom.*, *passim*.

CHAPTER XI

[218] P. 234. *Klopp*, IX, pp. 376–377.

[219] P. 235. For the vain hopes built by Louis on the Wolfenbüttel diversion in North Germany, see *Add. MSS.* 32306, ff. 51–60.

[220] P. 235. *Add. MSS.* (H.F.) 29588, ff. 155–158 ; 34518 (*Mc.*), ff. 142–144 ; *P.R.O.* (S.P.) 80, 18, Stepney from Vienna, June 24, 1702.

[221] P. 238. *Coxe*, XIII, i. p. 147 ; *Burnet* V, p. 31 (326).

[222] P. 238. *Pelet*, I, pp. 24–25 ; Mons. de Puysegur's letter shows the French clearly understood this when they decided to march to Kaiserswerth and Bonn in 1701.

[223] P. 240. *Parker*, p. 69 ; Berwick *Mémoires* (1778), I, pp. 121–122. For this campaign compare *Pelet*, Coxe's *Marlborough*, Marlborough's *Dispatches*, Taylor, *Wars of Marlborough*, and Fortescue, *Br. Army*.

[224] P. 240. *Add. MSS.* (St.) 7063, ff. 15–16.

[225] P. 242. *Parker*, p. 73 ; *H.M.C. Coke* (1889), p. 16.

[226] P. 243. *Coxe*, Chap. XIII.

[227] P. 244. Max Emanuel's letters on the subject will be found in *Klopp*, X, pp. 127–130.

[228] P. 245. *Pelet* II, pp. 368–442 ; *Colonie*, pp. 95–112 ; *Add. MSS.* (St.) 7064, f. 102.

CHAPTER XII

[229] P. 246. See p. 140, above, Aglionby's letter ; *Add. MSS.* (E.), 28910 f. 328, and *P.R.O.* (S.P.) 93, 3, Jan. 17 and Aug. 8, 1702, for French in Naples, 1702 ; *Mémoires de Forbin* and *Add. MSS.* 16458, f. 40, and *P.R.O.* (S.P.) 100, 29, Ap. 23, 1703, for the incident at Malamocco ; *P.R.O. Tr.* 3, *France*, 189, f. 535, for English despair of their Levant trade.

[230] P. 247. *P.R.O.* (S.P.) 87, 4, f. 194–196, the Dutch Apology, 1712.

[231] P. 249. *Add. MSS.* 28079, ff. 162–165, proposals *temp.* Anne for a register to be made of 100,000 seamen who are to be called up at stated periods for short service ; never carried out. See also *Burchett*, 10th and 11th pages of the Preface.

[232] P. 253. Benbow's despatches, the Report of the Court Martial and other relative documents will be found in *C.S.P. Am.*, 1702, pp. viii–xiii, 673–678, 744, ditto 1702–1703, pp. 82–87. See also *State Trials*, XIV, pp. 538–546 ; *Burchett*, pp. 590–598 ; *Lediard, N.H.*, II, pp. 741–744 ; Boyer's *Anne*, pp. 48–51 ; O. Troude, *Batailles navales de la France*, I, pp. 243–245.

The personal reminiscences about Benbow in Campbell's *Lives of the Admirals* cannot be trusted far, for they were largely derived from Calton, who palmed off on Campbell the spurious letter attributed to Du Casse. Laughton in his article on Benbow in the *D.N.B.* rightly warns us against Campbell, yet quotes Campbell as his only authority for the statement that Benbow had used the gentlemen captains ' a little briskly ' at Jamaica, whence Laughton accuses Benbow of ' goading them to crime.' I do not deny the possibility of all this, but I do not think it rests on any positive evidence. Laughton in the same article says Kirby was one of the officers ' of good repute and good service.' But his own account (see Kirby, *D.N.B.*) of Kirby's previous conduct on board the *Southampton* seems to me to render this also doubtful.

[233] P. 254. *C.S.P. Am.* 1708–1709, pp. xi, 38–40, 56, 95 ; *Burchett*, pp. 706–707 ; *Lediard, N.H.*, II, pp. 835–838 ; see also *H. of L. MSS.* (1704–1706), p. viii, and note for the misconduct of the *Elizabeth* in action.

[234] P. 254. *P.R.O. Tr.* 14 *Ven.* 112, f. 21 ; *Corbett*, II, p. 479.

[235] P. 255. *H.C.J.* XI, p. 578.

[236] P. 256.   *Martin*, pp. xxix–xxxii.

[237] P. 256.   *Ec.H.R.*, Jan. 1928, pp. 265–267.

[238] P. 256.   *C.S.P. Am.* 1702, p. 744 ; 1708–1709, pp. xi, 202, 270 ; 1710–1711, pp. xx–xxi, 32 ; G. N. Clark, *Dutch Alliance, etc.*, pp. 48–49.

[239] P. 257.   *C.S.P. Am.* 1710–1711, pp. 68, 126.

[240] P. 257.   *Ec.H.R.*, Jan. 1928, pp. 262–264 ; *Hill*, I, p. 252 ; *Mémoires* of *Forbin* and *Duguay-Trouin*, *passim* ; *H. of L. MSS.* 1704–1706, pp. 14–26 ; 1702–1704, pp. 227–239.

[241] P. 258.   *Burchett*, p. 636 ; *Add. MSS.* 17677 *WWW*, ff. 679–688.

[242] P. 258.   *Ec.H.R.*, Jan. 1928, p. 264 ; Chalmer's *Estimate* (1782), table opposite p. 37, reprinted in *Cunningham*, II, p. 932.

[243] P. 258.   *H. of L. MSS.* 1702–1704, pp. 67–69, 333, and *ditto* 1706–1708, pp. 263–264 ; *Burchett*, pp. 631–634 ; *C.S.P. Am.* 1702–1703, pp. viii, 668 ; *Defoe*, I, pp. 212, 215, 227 ; Wyatt Tilby, *British North America*, pp. 265–270 ; *Leake*, I, pp. 90–104.

[244] P. 260.   *Corbett*, Chaps. XXVIII–XXXIII *passim* ; Adm. Richmond, *National Policy and Naval Strength*, pp. 36–43 ; *Enquiry into Naval Miscarriages*, 1707 (printed in *Harleian Misc.*, Vol. XI) ; Swift, *Conduct of the Allies*.   For Rochester's views, see his Introduction to *Clarendon's History*, ed. 1702 ; Bolingbroke in his *Study and Use of History* takes retrospectively a middle view, approving the land operations of Marlborough, but urging that the systematic waylaying of the Spanish treasure ships would have brought Louis to his knees.   For designs on Spanish America see *Add. MSS.* 28079, ff. 39–50.

[245] P. 261.   *Corbett*, II, pp. 464–474.

[246] P. 262.   *Torrington*, pp. 81–87.

[247] P. 262.   *Corbett*, II, pp. 467–468 ; *Add. MSS. (Coxe)* 28058, f. 31 ; *P.R.O. (S.P.)*, 94, 75, Schonenberg's letter, Sept. 21, 1701.

[248] P. 262.   *Corbett*, II, pp. 470–471 ; *P.R.O. (S.P.)* 104, 202, ff. 183–186, Wratislaw's proposals ; *P.R.O. (S.P.)* 80, 19, Stepney's letter of Sept. 9, 1702.

[249] P. 263.   *Rooke*, p. 243.

[250] P. 263.   *Burchett*, p. 622.

[251] P. 265.   *Coxe*, Ch. XIII i. p. 148.

[252] P. 266.   *C.S.P. Dom.* 1702–1703, pp. 301–303 ; see *Ec.H.R.*, Jan. 1928, p. 262, on English and Dutch traders at Cadiz.

[253] P. 266.   *Rooke*, pp. 212–213 ; *Ormonde*, pp. 265–266 ; *Add. MSS. (E.)* 28926, ff. 151–152*b*.

[254] P. 267.   For the Cadiz operations see *Corbett*, II, pp. 480–487 ; *Rooke*, *passim* ; *Martin*, pp. 48–56 ; *Ormonde*, pp. 239–266 ; *Spain under Charles II*, 1840, pp. 162–169 (Stanhope's letters from before Cadiz) ; *De Jonge*, pp. 211–219 ; *Dangeau*, *Journal* (ed. 1857), IX, pp. 11, 358 ; *Add. MSS. (E.)* 28926, ff. 140–152 ; *H. of L. MSS.* 1702–1704, pp. xxviii, 101–124 ; *Burchett*, pp. 619–628 ; *Tindal*, III, p. 569 ; Laughton, *Howard to Nelson*, pp. 127–158.   It is best to pay no attention to *Burnet* on sea affairs ; he had no knowledge of the sea and was prejudiced against Rooke.

[255] P. 268.   *Rooke*, pp. 227–231 ; *Add. MSS. (E.)* 28926, ff. 158, 160 ; *Corbett*, II, pp. 487–490 ; *Lediard, N.H.*, II, p. 753 note ; *Tindal*, III, p. 570 ; *Burchett*, pp. 625–626 ; *Noailles*, II, pp. 321–326 ; *Add. MSS. (L'H.)* 17677 *YY*, f. 261 ; *Add. MSS. (H.F.)* 29590, ff. 130, 135, 137, 151 ; *Lamberty*, II, pp. 252–253.

[256] P. 272.   *Add. MSS. (St.)* 7068, f. 215 ; *Add. MSS.* 29588, ff. 330–331.

[257] P. 272.   *Add. MSS. (H.F.)* 29568, f. 101, Verney's letter, Nov. 10, 1702.

[258] P. 272.   For the affair at Vigo see *Corbett*, II, pp. 490–492 ; *Rooke*, pp. 230–234 ; *Martin*, pp. 56–59 ; *Burchett*, pp. 626–628 ; *Lediard, N.H.*, II, pp. 754–757 ;

Tindal, III. pp. 570–571 ; *Torrington*, pp. 91–94 ; *Add. MSS.* (E.) 28926, ff. 156–164, official accounts of the action by Ormonde and his secretary and by Hopsonn for Rooke ; *H. of L. MSS.* 1702–1704, p. 124 ; *Lamberty*, II, pp. 252–255 ; *Ormonde*, pp. 273–282 ; *Add. MSS.* 16459, f. 151, report in Italian by the Spanish Commandant of Vigo ; O. Troude, *Batailles navales de la France*, I, pp. 241–243 ; *De Jonge*, pp. 219–231.

CHAPTER XIII

[259] P. 273. *Add. MSS.* (L'H.) 17677 *YY*, f. 270 ; *H.M.C. Beaufort*, p. 95 ; *Luttrell's Diary*, V, p. 235.

[260] P. 275. *Fortescue*, I, pp. 408–409, sums up the Ranelagh case well. See *Parl. Hist.* and *H. of L. MSS.* 1702–1704, for the documents produced in these cases.

[261] P. 277. *Hervey, L.B.* I, pp. 179–181 ; *Conduct*, p. 127 ; *Burnet*, V, p. 66 (344–345) ; *Add. MSS.* (*Coxe*) 9121, f. 12, where Sarah declares that Lord Hervey was 'the only Peer I was ever concerned in '—viz. in procuring his elevation. She says she asked for his peerage because she had promised Sir Thomas Felton to do so as soon as the Queen came to the throne.

[262] P. 280. The pamphlet *Account of the Proceedings* printed and published by order of the Lords, Feb. 24, 1702 ; *Burnet*, V, pp. 49–54 (336–338) ; he is wrong in saying the Bill proposed to extend its action beyond the persons affected by the old Test Act, as the text of the Bill shows ; *Feiling*, pp. 368–369 ; *Turberville*, pp. 51–54 ; *Calamy*, I, pp. 465–474 ; *Abbey*, I, pp. 17–23.

The literature on the subject is immense. A good sample of the Tory case for the Bill by a moderate man is *The Case fairly stated*, 1702, while *Moderation a Virtue*, 1703, justifies the practice of occasional conformity. The political and electoral objects of the bill and of the later Schism Act are frankly confessed by Bolingbroke in the early pages of his *Letter to Sir William Windham*.

[263] P. 283. *H.M.C. Portland*, IV, p. 61 ; *Add. MSS.* (H.F.) 29589, f. 400 ; *E.H.R.*, Apr. 1900, pp. 238–241 ; Essay on Defoe by John Forster ; *Augustan*, pp. 157–170.

[264] P. 287. T. Lathbury, *History of Convocation* (1853) ; Canon Beeching, *Atterbury* (1909), Chaps. III, IV ; *Burnet, sub. loc.* ; *Add. MSS.* (H.F.) 29584, f. 101, for Nottingham's attempted mediation ; *Sykes' Gibson*, Chap. II ; *Abbey*, I, pp. 13–14 ; *Wilson*, pp. 58–66. The pamphlets on all sides of this question are very numerous.

[265] P. 288. *Add. MSS.* (H.F.) 29589, f. 107 ; 28895, f. 316 ; *Salomon*, p. 352.

[266] P. 289. *H.M.C. Portland*, IV, p. 75. In 1713 Bolingbroke wrote to Oxford : 'Let the forms of business be regularly carried on in the Cabinet, and the secret of it in your own closet,' *H.M.C. Portland*, V, p. 311.

CHAPTER XIV

[267] P. 292. *Dowell*, II, pp. 71, 402–403.

[268] P. 293. Acts *Annae Reginae* for each year, for text of the Property (or Land) Tax Acts. *Dowell*, II, pp. 50–53, 70–84 ; T. Cunningham, *History of Taxes* (1778), pp. 98–108 ; *Davenant*, I, pp. 1–81, *Ways and Means* : on p. 60 Davenant says, ' Probably there is nothing but excises that will truly and equally rate all sort of wealth and substance.'

[269] P. 295. For Corn prices 1701–1714, see note 21 above. *H.M.C. Coke*, pp. 38, 52, 67 ; *H.M.C. Portland*, IV, pp. 58, 110, 113 ; *Hervey, L.B.*, I, pp. 195, 345 ; *Aylesbury* (Rox.) II, p. 647 ; *Add. MSS.* (H.F.) 29576, f. 111, Nov. 12, 1702, C. Hatton to Visc. Hatton.

[270] P. 298. Mr. G. N. Clark is the authority on this subject, see his articles in *Ec.H.R.*, Jan. 1928, and in *Br. Year Book of Internat. Law*, 1928, reprinted by Oxford Univ. Press. For Anglo-Irish trade with France see *H. of L. MSS.* 1704–1706, p. 111, and *C.S.P. Dom.* 1703–1704, p. 561 ; for Spanish American trade see *ditto*, p. 200, and *C.S.P. Am.* 1708–1709, pp. xiii, xxxvi, 56, 62, 69, 428, and *Add. MSS.* 17677 *WWW*, ff. 486–488. For Dutch trade with France and English complaints, see *H.C.J.*, XIV, p. 105 ; *Add. MSS.* 17677 *YY*, f. 34 ; *Add. MSS.* (H.F.) 29568, f. 111 and 29588, f. 330 ; *P.R.O.* (S.P.) *Holland*, 84, 227, ff. 11–12 ; 224, ff. 139, 298, 368 ; 226, ff. 156–160, 421–424. The three-power Treaty of Apr. 1703 is in *P.R.O.* (S.P.) 108, 340.

[271] P. 300. *P.R.O.* (S.P.) 89, 18 (*Portugal*), ff. 66, 72, 210 ; *Add. MSS.* (St.) 7058, ff. 211–212, 359.

[272] P. 301. *The British Merchant* (ed. 1721), III, pp. 81–92 ; *Letter to a West Country Clothier* (1713), pp. 9–10 ; *Dowell*, II, pp. 72, 283, IV, p. 168 ; *Cunningham*, pp. 459–463 ; W. J. Ashley, *Surveys* (1900), pp. 268–303, *Tory Free Trade*.

[273] P. 303. *Corbett, passim*, on value of Lisbon harbour. For the treaty, see *H.C.J.*, XIV, pp. 224–226 ; *C.S.P. Dom.*, 1702–1703, pp. 246, 670–671, 697–699 ; *Add. MSS.* (St.) 7058, ff. 20, 207, 211–212, 359 ; *Add. MSS.* (H.F.) 29595, f. 242 ; *P.R.O.* (S.P.) 104, 204, f. 111 ; *P.R.O.* (S.P.) 87, 4, ff. 204–205.

[274] P. 304. For Hungary, see *P.R.O.* (S.P.) 104, 202, ff. 134, 258, 260 ; *Add. MSS.* (St.) 7058, ff. 99, 339, 341 ; (H.F.) 29593, March 16, 1704 ; *Legrelle*, IV, pp. 305–334. Nottingham's activities in foreign affairs will be evident to anyone studying the *Stepney, Coxe* and *Hatton Finch* papers in the *B.M.* We see him throughout 1703 working in apparent harmony with Godolphin about Portugal, Savoy, Bavaria and Hungary. He seems to have been trusted and liked by our envoys abroad, e.g. *Hill*, I, p. 381. For his preference of the Spanish to the Netherlands war see Appendix A above, Marlborough's letter to Heinsius of May 29, 1703.

[275] P. 307. *Corbett*, II, pp. 501–513 ; *Leake*, I, pp. 118–126 ; *Coxe*, Chap. XIX, pp. 212–214 (Coxe is wrong in saying Hill arrived at Turin in Aug. 1703 ; he was kept at the Hague till December). *Hill*, I, pp. 357, 378 and *passim* ; *St. Simon* (ed. 1884), III, pp. 6–7, 19, 458, IV, pp. 8–10 ; *Tessé, Lettres* (1888), pp. xi–xii ; *Add. MSS.* (H.F.) 29595, f. 230 ; 29588, ff. 424–427 ; (St.) 7058, ff. 231, 351 ; 7073, f. 164. Carutti, *Storia di Vitt. Am. II*, pp. 214–247.

[276] P. 307. *Lamberty*, II, pp. 574–575 ; *Corbett*, II, pp. 499–502, 507, 510 ; *C.S.P. Dom.* 1702–3, p. 698 ; *Lavisse, France*, VIII, pp. 378–383 ; *Legrelle, Revolte des Camisards* ; *Hill, passim* ; *Kemble, State Papers*, pp. 384–432 ; *Quarterly Rev.*, Apr. 1928 ; *Add. MSS.* (H.F.) 29587, f. 91 ; 29588, f. 399.

[277] P. 309. *Lediard, N.H.*, II, pp. 779–780 note ; P. Chamberlen, *Queen Anne*, 1738, pp. 126–127 ; *Martin*, pp. 72–73 ; *Leake*, I, pp. 126–130 ; *Defoe*, I, pp. 121–122, 228 ; *Burnet*, V, pp. 81–82 (353) ; *P.R.O.* (S.P.) 84 (*Holland*), 226, f. 156 ; Dangeau, *Journal*, Dec. 29–30 ; Burton, *Queen Anne*, I, pp. 104–105.

[278] P. 311. *H.M.C. Rutland*, II (1889) p. 177 ; W. Richards, *Hist. of Lynn* (1812), pp. 874–875 ; Bowles' *Ken*, II, pp. 240–243 ; Defoe, *The Storm* (ed. 1704), pp. 82, 141, 175–177 ; Barrett's *Bristol*, p. 696 ; Evelyn, *Diary*, Nov. 26–27, and *Sylva* (ed. 1786), II, p. 329 ; Secretan's *Nelson*, p. 107 ; Chamberlen, *Queen Anne*, p. 127 ; Strickland, *Queens of England*, VIII, p. 188.

CHAPTER XV

279 P. 314. *Coxe*, Chap. XV ; Coxe's *Memoirs of Lord Walpole* (1802), p. 4.

280 P. 316. *Fortescue, Coxe, Taylor, Atkinson, Dispatches sub. loc. H.M.C. Chequers Court*, pp. 119–121 ; *Parker*, pp. 76–79 ; *Pelet*, III, pp. 1–146. For Aug. 24, see *Dispatches*, I, pp. 165–168, 173, and *Add. MSS.* 29547, f. 41, and 22196, ff. 3–4 for Cadogan's letter on it. Maps of the affair of Maastricht and the battle of Ekeren will be found in *Tindal*, III, pp. 620–621. Appendix A, above, for Marlborough's letters to Heinsius.

281 P. 317. *Heinsius MSS.*, Marlborough's letters of June–Sept. 1703, see Appendix A, above. *Dispatches*, I, p. 157.

282 P. 317. *Villars, Mémoires, sub. ann.* 1703. For the courtiers' dislike of Villars, see his own *Mémoires* and the prejudices of *St. Simon*, e.g. vol. III, Chap. XXII.

283 P. 318. *Stowe MSS.*, B.M., 222, f. 216.

284 P. 318. *Add. MSS.* (*St.*) 7064, ff. 96–102, 129–132, 137 ; *P.R.O.* (*S.P.*) 81, 168 ff. 18, 193–196, 285, 425–426 ; *Add. MSS.* 16459, f. 105.

285 P. 318. *Colonie*, pp. 107, 112, 173–174 ; *Add. MSS.* (*St.*) 7064, f. 132 ; Villars, *Mémoires* for 1703.

286 P. 319. *Pelet*, II, p. 429 ; Villars, *Mémoires* for 1703.

287 P. 320. *Pelet*, III, pp. 624–625, Villars' letter to the King, June 17, which bears out his subsequent statements in his *Mémoires*, and confutes St. Simon's gossip on the subject.

288 P. 321. *Pelet*, III, pp. 234–264, 642–656, 828–832 ; Pelet's *Atlas* volume gives the movements of each army each day. Villars, *Mémoires* for 1704 ; *Colonie*, pp. 140–149.

289 P. 321. *P.R.O.* (*Hanover*), S.P. 81, 160. Poley's letter of Dec. $\frac{17}{28}$, 1703.

CHAPTER XVI

290 P. 329. *Swift's Correspondence* (Elrington Ball), I, pp. 38, 44, Dec. 16, 1703, and Feb. 3, 170$\frac{3}{4}$ to Tisdall.

291 P. 330. *Add. MSS.* (H.F.) 29589, f. 121 ; *Coxe*, Chap. XVIII–XIX, i, pp. 203–207, 216–220 ; *Add. MSS.* (*St.*) 7063, f. 38 ; *Heinsius MSS.*, Marlborough's letter of May 29, 1703, on Nottingham, see Appendix A, above.

292 P. 331. *Add. MSS.* (H.F.) 29568, f. 151 ; *H.L.J.*, Vol. XVI, pp. 331, 348 ; *Coxe*, Chap. XIX ; p. 220 ; *Burnet*, V, pp. 104–106 (363) ; *Davenant*, IV, pp. 274–439, V, 1–69, especially IV, p. 415 ; *The True Tom Double*, 1704 (High Tory answer to Davenant) ; *Poems on Affairs of State* (ed. 1707), IV, pp. 121–122 ; *Turberville*, pp. 55–56 ; *Tindal*, III, p. 628 ; R. S. Forsythe, *A Noble Rake* on Mohun's career.

293 P. 332. *Coxe*, Chap. XX, i. pp. 227–229 ; *Feiling*, p. 373 ; *Burnet*, V, pp. 117–120 (369–371).

294 P. 333. *Klopp*, XI, pp. 92–97 ; *Feldzüge*, pp. 50–54 ; *Add. MSS.* (*Coxe*) 9114 (*Hare's Journal*), pp. 6–12 ; *Coxe*, Chap. XX, i, pp. 224–226. (I think Coxe is wrong in supposing Marlborough already regarded the Moselle plan as a blind. Hare's Journal, written afterwards with Marlborough's sanction, bears out the opposite view of Klopp based on Wratislaw's correspondence.)

295 P. 334. *Klopp*, XI, pp. 97–110 ; *Feldzüge*, pp. 54–58.

296 P. 335. *Klopp*, XI, pp. 99–104 ; *Heinsius MSS.*, see Marlborough's letter of

March 24, 1704, Appendix A, above; *Lediard, Marl.* I, pp. 285–287, gives Wratislaw's Memorial and the Queen's answer, though otherwise misinformed.

[297] P. 337. *H.M.C. Bagot* (R. 10, Pt. IV), p. 337 ; *Noorden*, I, pp. 509–510.

[298] P. 339. *E.H.R.*, Apr. 1900 and Jan. 1907 ; *H.M.C. Portland*, IV, pp. 221–222, 269–272 and *passim* ; *Augustan*, pp. 157–170 ; *The Review* and *The Rehearsal* and the *Observator*.

[299] P. 340. *Feiling*, pp. 383–388 ; *Noorden*, I, p. 507 ; Bolingbroke, *On the Study and Use of History*.

CHAPTER XVII

[300] P. 343. *Heinsius MSS.*, Marlborough's letter of May 24, 1703, see Appendix A, above ; Heinsius' letter to Portland, Nov. 1703, printed on p. 435 of Pt. II (1928), Japikse's *Correspondentie van William III en van Bentinck* (Nijhoff).

[301] P. 347. *Coxe*, Chap. XXI ; *Klopp*, XI, p. 109.

[302] P. 347. *Add. MSS.* 9114, ff. 28, 34–35 ; *Select Docs.*, p. 97 ; *Heinsius MSS.*, Marlborough's letter of June 2, 1704.

[303] P. 348. *Dispatches*, I, pp. 259, 279, 297 ; *Add. MSS.* 9114, f. 32*b* ; *Heinsius MSS.*, Marlborough's letters of May 21, 25, 30, 1704, see Appendix A, above ; *Lediard, Marl.*, I, p. 303.

[304] P. 350. *Pelet*, IV, pp. 440–445, 465–505 ; *Add. MSS.* 9114, ff. 24–25, 28*b*, 31*b* ; *Add. MSS.* (St.) 7063, f. 50 ; *Dispatches*, I, pp. 274–279, 286–287 ; *Select Docs.*, pp. 97, 100 ; *Colonie*, pp. 166–171.

[305] P. 351. *Select Docs.*, pp. 98–101, 112–113, 142 ; *Coxe*, Chap. XXI, i, pp. 242–245 ; *Millner*, p. 83 ; *H.M.C. Coke*, p. 36.

[306] P. 352. *Add. MSS.* 9094, f. 5 ; *Select Docs.*, pp. 101, 160.

[307] P. 353. *Select Docs.*, pp. 101, 160.

[308] P. 353. *Add. MSS.* 9114, f. 38*b*.

[309] P. 354. *Select Docs.*, p. 102 ; *Coxe*, Chap. XXII, i, p. 256 ; *Add. MSS.*, 9114, ff. 40–41 ; *Lediard, Marl.*, I, pp. 315–316.

[310] P. 354. *Lediard, Marl.*, I, p. 319 ; *H.M.C. Downshire*, I, Pt. ii (1924), p. 831 ; *Burnet*, V, p. 150 note ; *H.M.C. Coke*, pp. 37–38.

[311] P. 355. *Colonie*, pp. 164–165, 173–174 ; *Mérode-Westerloo, Mémoires* (1840), p. 287.

[312] P. 356. *Add. MSS.* 9114, f. 37*b.*, 41–42 ; *Heinsius MSS.*, Marlborough's letters of June 11, 15, 19, 25.

[313] P. 364. The best authority for the battle of Schellenberg on the English side is Hare's account, written under Marlborough's eye (*Add. MSS.* 9114, ff. 43–55), most of which is reprinted in *Dispatches* (*q.v.* also for the Duke's own letters on the action). For the Bavarian side, D'Arco's exculpatory narrative (reprinted in *Journal of the Campaign in Germany*, 1704, pp. 23–25) has value, but understates the total number of the defending army and the disasters of the rout. On these and other points the best authority on the Franco-Bavarian side is *Colonie*, who took a leading part in the action, and *Mémoires du Marquis de Maffei*, 1741, pp. 29–46. See also *Millner*, pp. 94–100 ; *H.M.C. Rutland*, p. 181 ; *Pelet*, IV, pp. 531–532, for Tallard's letter ; *Mémoires de Feuquière*, 1741, IV, pp. 80–82 ; *Heinsius MSS.*, Marlborough's letters of July 3 and 4. The excellent modern narratives of Coxe, Frank Taylor, and Fortescue should be carefully studied. For the Scots Greys and their horses, see R. Cannon's *Historical Record* of the regiment, 1837, pp. 37–43. There are numerous contemporary prints of the battle in the Donauwörth museum, particularly representing the flight and pursuit.

[314] P. 366. *Coxe*, Chaps. XXIII–V, XXX, i, pp. 268–271, 341 (p. 268, line 22, *home* should be *Rome*) ; *H.M.C. Shrewsbury* (1903), II, p. 782 ; *Hervey, L. B.*, I, pp. 206–209 ; see pp. 404–405, above, for the effect of the news of the Schellenberg in Portugal ; *Add. MSS.* 34518, f. 52*b.*, Marlborough to Duchess, July 30, 1704, on *Observator* ; *Observator, passim*, especially July 1–5, Aug. 12–16, 16–19.

[315] P. 366. *Coxe*, Chaps. XXIII–XXIV, i, pp. 268, 273–274.

[316] P. 367. *Coxe*, I, pp. 272–273 ; *Add. MSS.* 9114, f. 65.

[317] P. 367. *Coxe*, I, pp. 275–276 ; *Colonie*, pp. 198–203 ; *Dispatches*, I, pp. 380–381 ; *Cambridge Univ. Lib. MSS.*, letter of Sam Noyes from Friedberg, July 19, 'Ammunition is hard to be got amongst the Germans, besides their gunners have really no skill,' hence the difficulties before Rain.

[318] P. 369. *Heinsius MSS.*, Marlborough's letter of July 16 ; *Dispatches*, I, pp. 352 note, 358, 378–379 ; *Add. MSS.* 34518, f. 52*b*, a fuller version of Marlborough's letter to the Duchess than *Coxe*, I, pp. 277–278 ; *Add. MSS.* 9114, ff. 65–66 ; *Colonie*, p. 207. See also the defence of the burning of Bavaria in Frank Taylor's *Marlborough.*

[319] P. 370. *Colonie*, pp. 209–224 ; *Pelet*, IV, pp. 563–564, printed in *Select Docs.*, p. 119.

[320] P. 370. *Mérode-Westerloo, Mémoires*, 1840, I, p. 287.

[321] P. 371. *Heinsius MSS.*, Marlborough's letter of July 31 ; *H.M.C. Bath*, III (*Prior Papers*), 1908, p. 433.

[322] P. 373. *Coxe*, Chap. XXV ; *Dispatches*, I, pp. 384–389, 394–395 ; *Add. MSS.*, 9114, ff. 73–83 ; *Heinsius MSS.*, Marlborough's letters of August ; *P.R.O.* (S.P.) 81, 88, Davenant's letter from Frankfort on Aug. 17 on dangers to Southern Germany from Villeroi before Blenheim ; *Add. MSS.* 28056, ff. 114–116, for the desperate condition in Italy before Blenheim ; *Mémoires de Feuquière*, 1741, III, pp. 268–270, on inability of the Allies to remain in Bavaria if a battle had been avoided. For Prince Eugene's movements and opinions in the week before Blenheim, see *Feldzüge*, pp. 465–477.

CHAPTER XVIII

[323] P. 395. Besides guidance from *Fortescue, Atkinson* and *Taylor*, personal examination of the battlefield, and prints and relics in the local museums at Donauwörth and the Schloss at Höchstädt, my account of Blenheim has been composed out of the following authorities, some of which I have reprinted in *Select Docs.*:

For the French Army: The letters of Tallard and other French officers in *Pelet*, IV, pp. 566–588, 917–918 ; letters of Marsin and other French officers in *Lediard, Marl.*, I, pp. 409–410, 424–437 ; *Mérode-Westerloo, Mémoires*, 1840, I, pp. 298–319 ; *de Feuquière, Mémoires*, 1741, III, pp. 266–287 ; *Maffei, Marquis de, Mémoires*, 1741, pp. 46–58 ; *Dangeau, Journal*, Aug. 29, 1704. (See my reprints of *Pelet* in *Select Docs.*, pp. 118–133.)

For Eugene's Army: *Feldzüge*, pp. 478–531, 859–863 ; *Add. MSS.* 16466, ff. 223–240, narrative (in Italian) by an officer of Eugene's army.

For Marlborough's Army and the battle in general: *Coxe*, Chap. XXVI ; *Add. MSS.* 9114, ff. 82–83, 89*b* top, 103*b*–106*b*, for parts of Hare's Journal not printed in *Dispatches* ; *Dispatches*, I, pp. 390–409 ; *Add. MSS.* (*E.*) 28918, ff. 287–288, Cardonnel's narrative (printed in *Select Docs.*, pp. 107–111) ; *Parker*, pp. 87–95 ; *Millner*, pp. 113–129 ; *Lediard, Marl.*, I, pp. 362–437 ; *Add. MSS.* 16466, ff. 215, 219–222, letters of officers in Dutch service to the States-General on the battle ;

H.M.C. Coke, p. 40 ; *Pelet*, IV, pp. 598–601, allied narratives; *Tindal*, III, pp. 656–661 ; Boyer, *Queen Anne*, 1735, pp. 149–153.

For the taking of Blenheim village in particular : *E.H.R.*, Apr. 1904, Orkney's and Abercromby's letters ; *Select Docs.*, pp. 109–110 ; *H.M.C. Athole* (1891), p. 62, another letter by Orkney ; *Description of all the Seats of War*, 1707, pp. 188–190, a narrative clearly based on information from Orkney or Abercromby ; *St. Simon*, IV, pp. 125–130, for Court gossip on Dénonville and Blansac's conduct ; *Ailesbury, Mem.* (Rox.), II, p. 571 bottom.

For some of our subsidies to the foreign troops who fought at Blenheim, see *Add. MSS.* 17711, ff., 7–8.

[324] P. 396. *P.R.O.* (S.P.) 81, 88, and *Add. MSS.* (St.) 7066, f. 15, for Davenant's letters of Aug. $\frac{6}{17}$. In one he says Parkes passed Frankfurt ' yesterday ' ; in the other ' the day before yesterday.' I think the earlier date is right as Stanhope speaks of him as passing through Holland Aug. $\frac{6}{17}$. For Stanhope's letters, see *Add. MSS.* (St.), 7069, f. 170 and 172, and *P.R.O.* (S.P.) 84, 227, f. 27.

[325] P. 397. *H.M.C. Coke*, p. 39 ; Aug. 16, 1704 ; *L'Hermitage, Add. MSS.*, 17677 ZZ, f. 380 ; *Observator*, Aug. 16, 1704 ; *Luttrell's Diary*, Aug. 10 ; *Coxe*, Chap. XXVI and XXX, i, pp. 305–306, 337–338 ; *P.R.O. Ven. Transcripts*, 46, Mocenigo's letter from Windsor, Aug. $\frac{11}{22}$, 1704.

[326] P. 398. Hare's Journal, *Add. MSS.* 9114, ff. 104–107, 110 ; *Add. MSS.* 16466, ff. 242–243, French officers' letters ; *Coxe*, Chap. XXVII, i, p. 313 ; Ap. A, below, Marl.'s letter to Heinsius of Aug. 17 ; *H.M.C. Coke*, p. 42 ; *Add. MSS.* (St.) 7558, f. 26 ; *Hervey, L. B.*, I, pp. 211–212 ; *P.R.O.* (S.P.) 105, 73, f. 117.

[327] P. 399. *Count Tallard's exile in Nottingham*, A. Stapleton ; *Add. MSS.* (L'H.) 17677 *AAA*, f. 20.

[328] P. 399. Lists of casualties in *P.R.O.* (S.P.) 87, 2 ; *Feldzüge*, pp. 522, 863 ; *Millner*, p. 128.

[329] P. 400. *Mérode-Westerloo, Mémoires*, I, p. 325 ; *H.M.C. Coke*, p. 42, Ap. A, below, Marl.'s letter of Aug. 28 ; *Add. MSS.* 16466, ff. 242–243, 287 ; *MSS.*, 9114, f. 110 ; *Millner*, pp. 124–127, 136 ; *Feldzüge*, pp. 868–876, 902–905 ; *Maffei, Mémoires*, pp. 95–101.

[330] P. 401. *Add. MSS.* (St.) 7069, Stanhope to Stepney, Aug. 29, 1704 ; 7058, ff. 28, 35, 99, 360b, and 7059, f. 31 ; *Add. MSS.* (Coxe) 28056, ff. 152.

CHAPTER XIX.

[331] P. 402. *Add. MSS.* (St.) 7067, f. 15 (Stanhope to Stepney).

[332] P. 402. *H.M.C. Rutland*, II (1889), pp. 178–179 ; *H.M.C. Lonsdale*, p. 117 ; *Burchett*, pp. 662–666.

[333] P. 403. Berwick's *Mémoires* (ed. 1778), I, pp. 162–164 ; *Stowe MSS.* (B.M.), 468, ff. 73–75. On the Princesse des Ursins affair, two good modern books have recently been added to the vast literature on the subject—by Madame Taillandier and Miss Maud Cruttwell respectively.

[334] P. 405. *Stowe MSS.* (B.M.), 468, f. 73–75 (Richards' letters) ; Burton, *Reign of Queen Anne*, II, pp. 73–74, 88–100 (Methuen's letters) ; Berwick's *Mémoires*, I, pp. 162–164 ; *H.M.C. Chequers Court* (1900), p. 181 ; *Galway's Conduct in Spain*, 1711, pp. 1–3 ; *Fortescue*, I, pp. 447–448.

[335] P. 406. *Corbett*, II, pp. 503–506 ; *Hill*, I, pp. 345–355 ; *Leake*, I, pp. 139–150 ; *Burchett*, pp. 666–676 ; *H. of L. MSS.* (1704–1706), pp. viii–x, 150–153 ; *Add. MSS.* (H.F.) 29589, f. 408 ; *De Jonge*, pp. 293–294.

[336] P. 413. The Spanish Governor's report is printed in C. F. Duro, *Armada*

Español, VI, p. 63 ; Monti, *Historia de Gibraltar*, pp. 85–87 ; Lopez de Ayala, *Hist. de Gibraltar* ; *Noailles*, III, pp. 225–226 ; *Corbett*, II, pp. 517–523 ; *Burchett*, pp. 677–678 ; *Leake*, I, pp. 152–156 ; *Camden Misc.* VIII (1883), *Haddock Corr.*, pp. 46–48 ; *Torrington*, pp. 136–146, 185–195 ; *H. of L. MSS.*, 1704–1706, pp. 167–171 ; *Lediard, N.H.*, II, p. 789 ; *De Jonge*, pp. 296–301.

The Spanish estimate of 30,000 shot cast in the town and its defences is probably not above double the reality. *Lediard, N.H.*, II, p. 789, says : ' 15,000 shot being made in five or six hours' time.' If there were 500 cannon playing on Gibraltar from the 22 ships, that would mean an average of 30 rounds per gun, not an extravagant estimate for six hours. We know the fleet left England with an average of 40 rounds per gun, and had an average of 25 rounds after the Gibraltar bombardment. See *Journal United Service Inst.*, Feb.–Nov. 1923, p. 373. Not much had been used at Barcelona, so Byng's squadron, only a portion of the whole fleet, must have used a great deal at Gibraltar. I therefore think Lediard's 15,000 probably right and the estimate in *Torrington*, p. 145, of ' 14,00 shot ' as the total is, I expect, a copyist's error for 14,000.

[337] P. 414. *P.R.O. (Port.)* S.P. 89, 18, f. 144 ; *Add. MSS. (St.)* 7058, f. 360 ; *H.M.C. Bath* (1904), I, p. 80 ; *H.M.C. R.*, 9, p. 467, Oct. 23, 1705.

[338] P. 415. *Add. MSS. (St.)* 7058, f. 360 ; Addison, *Present State of the War* (*Works*, ed. 1736, III, p. 245) ; *H.M.C. Coke*, p. 42 ; *H.M.C. Dartmouth*, p. 297 ; *P.R.O. (S.P.) Barbary States*, 71, *passim*.

[339] P. 418. L. G. Carr Laughton's article on Malaga in *Journal of United Service Inst.*, Feb.–Nov. 1923, pp. 367–390 ; *Corbett*, II, pp. 524–535 ; *Torrington*, pp. 146–164 ; *Burchett*, pp. 678–680 ; *Leake*, I, pp. 156–184 ; *Martin*, pp. 76–80 ; *Tindal*, III, 665–666 note (Shovell's Letter) ; *London Gazette*, Sept. 18, 1704 ; for Toulouse's account of the action see *H.M.C. Portland*, VIII, pp. 143–147 ; Mommerqué's *Mémoires du Marquis de Villette*, 1844, pp. 154–158, 349–353 ; O. Troude, *Batailles navales de la France*, I, pp. 249–255 ; *De Jonge*, pp. 304–325 ; *St. Simon*, IV, chap. VIII, for the story told at Versailles.

[340] P. 419. *H.M.C. Coke*, p. 41 ; *H.M.C. Portland*, IV, pp. 110, 113 ; *Ward's Poems* (ed. 1706), pp. 244–245.

[341] P. 420. *Conduct*, p. 146 ; *H.M.C. Portland*, IV, p. 137.

[342] P. 420. *Carstares' Letters*, 1774, p. 730 ; *H.C.J.*, Oct. 25, 1704 ; *H.C.L.*, ditto ; Leadam, *Pol. Hist. England*, vol. ix, p. 65 ; *Add. MSS.* 22267, f. 123, Whig poem on Malaga ; for the historical aftermath of this quarrel, see Burnet's absurd depreciation of the value of Gibraltar and of Rooke's merit in the matter, and the equally absurd over-praising of the feat of its capture by Ralph (*Burnet*, V, pp. 153–155 and note).

[343] P. 421. *P.R.O. Ven. Transcripts*, 112, ff. 14–15.

[344] P. 422. *Strype's Stow's London* (1720), Bk. III, pp. 172 ; Bk. VI, p. 49 ; *Poems on Affairs of State*, 1707, iv, pp. 113–114 ; *Add. MSS. (L'H.)* 17677 AAA, f. 40.

[345] P. 423. *H.M.C. Bath*, I (1904), pp. 62–63 ; *Coxe*, Chap. XXX, i, p. 343.

INDEX

Printed in England at THE BALLANTYNE PRESS
SPOTTISWOODE, BALLANTYNE & CO. LTD.
Colchester, London & Eton

MAP VIII

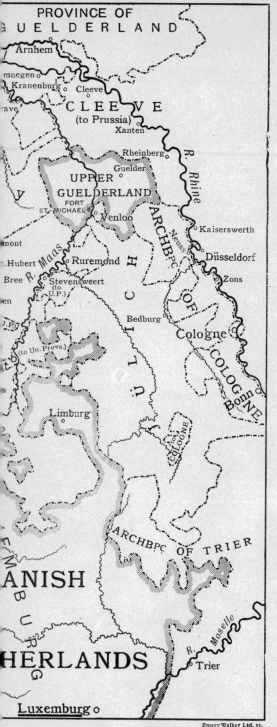

PROVINCE OF
GUELDERLAND

Arnhem

mnegen
Kranenburg
Cleeve

rave
CLEEVE
(to Prussia)
Xanten

Rheinberg

Guelder

UPPER
GUELDERLAND
FORT
ST. MICHAEL
Venloo

R. Rhine

Kaiserswerth

Neuss

Düsseldorf

mont
ARCHBP.C.
.Hubert
Bree
R. Maas
Ruremond
Zons

Stevensweert
(to
U.P.)

en
Bedburg

U.P.
J
Ü
(to Un. Provs.)
L
I
C
H

Cologne

OF

COLOGNE

Bonn

Limburg

(to
COLOGNE)

ARCHBP.C. OF TRIER

ANISH

E
M
B
U
R
G

Moselle

HERLANDS

R.
Trier

Luxemburg

Emery Walker Ltd. sc.